THE **POLITICS**
OF THE **TEXTBOOK**

THE POLITICS

OF THE
TEXTBOOK

EDITED BY

Michael W. Apple

AND

Linda K.
Christian-Smith

New York •
London

Published in 1991 by

Routledge
An imprint of Routledge, Chapman and Hall, Inc.
29 West 35 Street
New York, NY 10001

Published in Great Britain by

Routledge
11 New Fetter Lane
London EC4P 4EE

Library of Congress Cataloging-in-Publication Data

The Politics of the textbook / edited by Michael W. Apple and Linda K.
  Christian-Smith.
      p.   cm.
  Includes bibliographical references (p.   ) and index.
  ISBN 0-415-90222-3.   ISBN 0-415-90223-1 (pbk.)
    1. Textbooks—United States—History. 2. Textbooks—Political
aspects. 3. Textbook bias. 4. Education—United States—Curricula.
5. Education—United States—Philosophy. I. Apple, Michael W.
II. Christian-Smith, Linda K.
LB3047.P65 1991
371.3′2′0973—dc20   90-38277

British Library cataloguing in publication data also available

Contents

Acknowledgments

All edited books are by their very nature collective enterprises. We cannot thank all of the individuals who have assisted us in thinking through the content of this book. Some, however, need to be given special note. Among them are Rima Apple, Peter Apple, Diane Falkner, and Kenneth Smith.

Maureen MacGrogan and the editorial and production staff at Routledge once again proved why they are rightly considered such a talented and committed group of people to work with.

1

The Politics of the Textbook

Michael W. Apple and Linda K. Christian-Smith

Whose Knowledge Is of Most Worth?

Reality doesn't stalk around with a label. What something is, what it does, one's evaluation of it, all this is not naturally preordained. It is socially constructed. This is the case even when we talk about the institutions that organize a good deal of our lives. Take schools, for example. For some groups of people, schooling is seen as a vast engine of democracy—opening horizons, ensuring mobility, and so on. For others, the reality of schooling is strikingly different. It is seen as a form of social control or, perhaps, as the embodiment of cultural dangers, institutions whose curricula and teaching practices threaten the moral universe of the students who attend them.

While not all of us may agree with this diagnosis of what schools do, this latter position contains a very important insight. It recognizes that behind Spencer's famous question about "What knowledge is of most worth?" there lies another even more contentious question, "*Whose* knowledge is of most worth?"

During the past two decades, a good deal of progress has been made on answering the question of whose knowledge becomes socially legitimate in schools.[1] While much still remains to be understood, we are now much closer to having an adequate understanding of the relationship between school knowledge and the larger society than before. Yet little attention has actually been paid to that one artifact that plays such a major role in defining whose culture is taught—*the textbook*. Of course, there have been literally thousands of studies of textbooks over the years.[2] But until relatively recently, by and large, most of these remained unconcerned with the politics of culture. All too many researchers could still be characterized by the phrase coined years ago by C. Wright Mills, "abstract empiricists." These "hunters and gatherers of social numbers" remain unconnected to the relations of inequality that surround them.[3]

This is a distinct problem since texts are not simply "delivery systems" of "facts." They are at once the results of political, economic, and cultural

1

activities, battles, and compromises. They are conceived, designed, and authored by real people with real interests. They are published within the political and economic constraints of markets, resources, and power.[4] And what texts mean and how they are used are fought over by communities with distinctly different commitments and by teachers and students as well.

As one of us has argued in a series of volumes, it is naive to think of the school curriculum as neutral knowledge.[5] Rather, what counts as legitimate knowledge is the result of complex power relations and struggles among identifiable class, race, gender/sex, and religious groups. Thus, education and power are terms of an indissoluble couplet. It is at times of social upheaval that this relationship between education and power becomes most visible. Such a relationship was and continues to be made manifest in the struggles by women, people of color, and others to have their history and knowledge included in the curriculum. Driven by an economic crisis and a crisis in ideology and authority relations, it has become even more visible in the past decade or so in the resurgent conservative attacks on schooling. "Authoritarian populism" is in the air, and the New Right has been more than a little successful in bringing its own power to bear on the goals, content, and process of schooling.[6]

The movement to the right has not stopped outside the schoolroom door. Current plans for the centralization of authority over teaching and curriculum, often cleverly disguised as "democratic" reforms, are hardly off the drawing board before new management proposals or privatization initiatives are introduced. In the United States, evidence for such offensives abounds with the introduction of mandatory competency testing for students and teachers, the calls for a return to a (romanticized) common curriculum, the reduction of educational goals to those primarily of business and industry, the proposals for voucher or "choice" plans, the pressure to legislate morality and values from the right, and the introduction of state-mandated content on "free enterprise" and the like. Similar tendencies are more than a little evident in Britain and in some cases are even more advanced.

All of this has brought about countervailing movements in the schools. The slower but still interesting growth of more democratically run schools— the growth of practices and policies that give community groups and teachers considerably more authority in text selection and curriculum determination, in teaching strategy, in the use of funds, in administration, and in developing more flexible and less authoritarian evaluation schemes—is providing some cause for optimism in the midst of the conservative restoration.[7]

Even with these positive signs, however, it is clear that the New Right has been able to rearticulate traditional political and cultural themes. In so doing, it has often effectively mobilized a mass base of adherents. Among its most powerful causes and effects has been the growing feeling of disaffection about public schooling among conservative groups. Large numbers of parents and other people no longer trust either the institutions or the teachers and administrators in them to make "correct" decisions about what should be taught and how to teach it. The rapid growth of evangelical schooling, of censorship, and of textbook controversies, and the emerging tendency of many parents to teach their children at home rather than send them to state-supported schools are clear indications of this loss of legitimacy.[8]

The ideology that stands behind this is often very complex. It combines a commitment to both the "traditional family" and clear gender roles with the commitment to "traditional values" and literal religiosity. Often packed into this is also a defense of capitalist economics, patriotism, the "Western tradition," anti-communism, and a deep mistrust of the "welfare state."[9] When this ideology is applied to schooling, the result can be as simple as dissatisfaction with an occasional book or assignment. On the other hand, the result can be a major conflict that threatens to go well beyond the boundaries of our usual debates about schooling.

Few places in the United States are more well-known in this latter context than Kanawha County, West Virginia. In the mid-1970s it became the scene of one of the most explosive controversies over what schools should teach, who should decide, and what beliefs should guide our educational programs. What began as a protest by a small group of conservative parents, religious leaders, and business people over the content and design of the textbooks approved for use in local schools soon spread to include school boycotts, violence, and a wrenching split within the community that in many ways has yet to heal.

There were a number of important contributing factors that heightened tensions in West Virginia. Schools in rural areas had been recently consolidated. Class relations and relations between the country and the city were becoming increasingly tense. The lack of participation by rural parents (or many parents at all, for that matter) in text selection or in educational decision making in general had also led to increasing alienation. Furthermore, the cultural history of the region, with its fierce independence, fundamentalist religious traditions, and history of economic depression, helped create the conditions for serous unrest. Finally, Kanawha County became a cause célèbre for national right-wing groups who offered moral, legal, and organizational support to the conservative activists there.[10]

It is important to realize, then, that the controversies over "official knowledge" that usually center around what is included and excluded in textbooks really signify more profound political, economic, and cultural relations and histories. Conflicts over texts are often proxies for wider questions of power relations. They involve what people hold most dear. And, as in the case of Kawawha County, they can quickly escalate into conflicts over these deeper issues.

Yet textbooks are surely important in and of themselves. They signify—through their content *and* form—particular constructions of reality, particular ways of selecting and organizing that vast universe of possible knowledge.

They embody what Raymond Williams called the *selective tradition*—someone's selection, someone's vision of legitimate knowledge and culture, one that in the process of enfranchising one group's cultural capital disenfranchises another's.[11]

Texts are really messages to and about the future. As part of a curriculum, they participate in no less than the organized knowledge system of society. They participate in creating what a society has recognized as legitimate and truthful. They help set the canons of truthfulness and, as such, also help re-create a major reference point for what knowledge, culture, belief, and morality really *are*.[12]

Yet such a statement—even with its recognition that texts participate in constructing ideologies and ontologies—is misleading in many important ways. For it is not a "society" that has created such texts, but specific groups of people. "We" haven't built such curriculum artifacts, if "we" means simply that there is universal agreement among all of us and this is what gets to be official knowledge. In fact, the very use of the pronoun "we" simplifies matters all too much.

As Fred Inglis so cogently argues, the pronoun "we"

> smooths over the deep corrugations and ruptures caused precisely by struggle over how that authoritative and editorial "we" is going to be used. The [text], it is not melodramatic to declare, really is the battleground for an intellectual civil war, and the battle for cultural authority is a wayward, intermittently fierce, always protracted and fervent one.[13]

Let us give one example. In the 1930s conservative groups in the United States mounted a campaign against one of the more progressive textbook series in use in schools, *Man and His Changing World* by Harold Rugg and his colleagues. This textbook became the subject of a concerted attack by the National Association of Manufacturers, the American Legion, the Advertising Federation of American, and other "neutral" groups. They charged that Rugg's books were socialist, anti-American, anti-business, and so forth. The conservative campaign was more than a little successful in forcing school districts to withdraw Rugg's series from classrooms and libraries. So successful were they that sales fell from nearly 300,000 copies in 1938 to only approximately 20,000 in 1944.[14]

We, of course, may have reservations about such texts today, not least of which would be the sexist title. But one thing that the Rugg case makes clear is that the *politics* of the textbook is not by any means something new. Current issues surrounding texts—their ideology, their very status as central definers of what we should teach, even their very effectiveness and their design—echo the past moments of these concerns that have had such a long history in so many countries.

Few aspects of schooling currently have been subject to more intense scrutiny and criticism than the textbook. Perhaps one of the most graphic descriptions is provided by A. Graham Down of the Council for Basic Education:

> Textbooks, for better or worse, dominate what students learn. They set the curriculum, and often the facts learned, in most subjects. For many students, textbooks are their first and sometimes only early exposure to books and to reading. The public regards textbooks as authoritative, accurate, and necessary. And teachers rely on them to organize lessons and structure subject matter. But the current system of textbook adoption has filled our schools with Trojan horses—glossily covered blocks of paper whose words emerge to deaden the minds of our nation's youth, and make them enemies of learning.[15]

This statement is made just as powerfully by Harriet Tyson-Bernstein, the author of a recent study of what she has called "America's textbook fiasco":

> Imagine a public policy system that is perfectly designed to produce textbooks that confuse, mislead, and profoundly bore students, while at the same time making all of the adults involved in the process look good, not only in their own eyes, but in the eyes of others. Although there are some good textbooks on the market, publishers and editors are virtually compelled by public policies and practices to create textbooks that confuse students with non sequiturs, that mislead them with misinformation, and that profoundly bore them with pointlessly arid writing.[16]

Regulation or Liberation and the Text

In order to understand these criticisms and to understand both some of the reasons why texts look the way they do and why they contain the perspectives of some groups and not those of others, we also need to realize that the world of the book has not been cut off from the world of commerce. Books are not only cultural artifacts. They are economic commodities as well. Even though texts may be vehicles of ideas, they still have to be "peddled on a market."[17] This market, however—especially in the national and international world of textbook publishing—is politically volatile, as the Kanawha County experience so clearly documented.

Texts are caught up in a complicated set of political and economic dynamics. Text publishing often is highly competitive. In the United States, where text production is a commercial enterprise situated within the vicissitudes of a capitalist market, decisions about the "bottom line" determine what books are published and for how long. Yet this situation is not just controlled by the "invisible hand" of the market. It is also largely determined by the highly visible "political" hand of state textbook-adoption policies.[18]

Nearly half of the states—most of them in the southern tier and the "sun belt"—have state textbook-adoption committees that by and large choose what texts will be purchased by the schools in that state. The economics of profit and loss of this situation makes it imperative that publishers devote nearly all of their efforts to guaranteeing a place on these lists of approved texts. Because of this, the texts made available to the entire nation, and the knowledge considered legitimate in them, are determined by what will sell in Texas, California, Florida, and so forth. There can be no doubt that the political and ideological controversies over content in these states, controversies that were often very similar to those that surfaced in Kanawha County, have had a very real impact on what and whose knowledge is made available. It is also clear that Kanawha County was affected by and had an impact on these larger battles over legitimate knowledge.

Economic and political realities structure text publishing not only internally, however. On an international level, the major text-publishing conglomerates control the market of much of the material not only in the capitalist centers, but in many other nations as well. Cultural domination is a fact of life for millions of students throughout the world, in part because of the economic control of communication and publishing by multinational firms, in part because of the ideologies and systems of political and cultural control of new elites within former colonial countries.[19] All of this, too, has led to complicated relations and struggles over official knowledge and the text between "center" and "periphery" and within these areas as well.

We want to stress that all of this is not simply—as in the case of newly emerging nations, Kanawa County, or the Rugg textbooks—of historical interest. The controversies over the form and content of the textbook have not diminished. In fact, they have become even more heated in the United States in particular. The changing ideological climate has had a major impact on debates over what should be taught in schools and on how it should be taught and evaluated. There is considerable pressure to raise the standards of texts, to make them more "difficult," to standardize their content, to make certain that the texts place more stress on "American" themes of patriotism, free enterprise, and the "Western tradition," and to link their content to state and nationwide tests of educational achievement.

These kinds of pressures are felt not only in the United States. The text has become the center of ideological and educational conflict in a number of other countries as well. In Japan, for instance, the government approval of a right-wing history textbook that retold the story of the brutal Japanese invasion and occupation of China and Korea in a more positive light has stimulated widespread international antagonism and has led to considerable controversy in Japan as well.

Along these same lines, at the very time that the textbook has become a source of contention for conservative movements, it has stood at the center of controversy for not being progressive enough. Class, gender/sex, and race bias has been widespread in the materials. All too often, "legitimate" knowledge does not include the historical experiences and cultural expressions of labor, women, people of color, and others who have been denied power.[20]

All of these controversies are not "simply" about the content of the books students find—or don't find—in their schools, although obviously they are about that as well. The issues involve profoundly different definitions of the common good,[21] different views about our society and where it should be heading, about cultural visions, and about our children's future. To quote Inglis again, the entire curriculum, in which the text plays so large a part, is "both the text and context in which production and values intersect; it is the twistpoint of imagination and power."[22] In the context of the politics of the textbook, it is the issue of power that should concern us the most.

The concept of power merely connotes the capacity to act and to do so effectively. However, in the ways we use the idea of power in our daily discourse, "the word comes on strongly and menacingly, and its presence is duly fearful."[23] This "dark side" of power is, of course, complemented by a more positive vision. Here, power is seen as connected to a people acting democratically and collectively, in the open, for the best ideals.[24] It is this dual concept of power that concerns us here, both at the level of theory (how we think about the relationship between legitimate knowledge and power) and practice (how texts actually embody this relationship). Both the positive and the negative senses of power are essential for us to understand these relationships. Taken together, they signify that arguments about textbooks are really a form of *cultural politics*. They involve the very nature of the connections between cultural visions and differential power.

This, of course, is not new to anyone who has been interested in the history of the relationship among books, literacy, and popular movements. Books—and one's ability to read them—have themselves been inherently caught up in cultural politics. Take the case of Voltaire, that leader of the Enlightenment who so wanted to become a member of the nobility. For him, the Enlightenment should begin with the "grands." Only when it had captured the hearts and minds of society's commanding heights could it concern itself with the masses below. But for Voltaire and many of his followers, one warning should be taken very seriously. One should take care to prevent the masses from learning to read.[25]

For others, teaching "the masses" to read could have a more "beneficial" effect. It enables a "civilizing" process, in which dominated groups would be made more moral, more obedient, more influenced by "real culture."[26] And for still others, such literacy could bring social transformation in its wake. It could lead to a "critical literacy," one that would be part of larger movements for a more democratic culture, economy, and polity.[27] The dual sense of the power of the text emerges clearly here.

Thus, activities that we now ask students to engage in every day, activities as "simple" and basic as reading and writing, can be at one and the same time forms of regulation and exploitation *and* potential modes of resistance, celebration, and solidarity. Here, we are reminded of Caliban's cry, "You taught me language; and my profit on't is, I know how to curse."[28]

This contradictory sense of the politics of the book is made clearer if we go into the classrooms of the past. For example, texts have often been related to forms of bureaucratic regulation of the lives of both teachers and students. Thus, one teacher in Boston in 1899 relates a story of what happened in her first year of teaching during an observation by the school principal. As the teacher rather proudly watched one of her children read aloud an assigned lesson from the text, the principal was less than pleased with the performance of the teacher or her pupil. In the words of the teacher:

> The proper way to read in the public school in 1899 was to say, "page 35, chapter 4" and holding the book in the right hand, with the toes pointing at an angle of forty-five degrees, the head held straight and high, the eyes looking directly ahead, the pupil would lift up his voice and struggle in loud, unnatural tones. Now, I had attended to the position of the toes, the right arm, and the nose, but had failed to enforce the mentioning of page and chapter.[29]

Here, the text participates in both bodily and ideological regulation. The textbook in this instance is part of a system of enforcing a sense of duty, morality, and cultural correctness. Yet, historically, teachers struggled both *for* and *against* the standardized text. Faced with large classes, difficult working conditions, insufficient training, and—even more important—little time to prepare lessons for the vast array of subjects and students they were responsible for, teachers often looked upon texts not necessarily as impositions but as essential tools. For young women elementary-school teachers, the text helped to prevent exploitation.[30] It solved a multitude of practical problems. It led not only to de-skilling, but time to become more skilled as a teacher as well.[31] Thus, there were demands for standardized texts by teachers even in the face of what happened to that teacher in Boston and to so many others.

This struggle over texts was linked to broader concerns about who should control the curriculum in schools. Teachers, especially those most politically active, constantly sought to have a say in what they taught. This was seen as part of a larger fight for democratic rights. Margaret Haley, for instance, one of the leaders of the first teachers union in the United States, saw a great need for teachers to work against the tendency of making the teacher "a mere factory hand, whose duty it is to carry out mechanically and unquestioningly the ideas and orders of those clothed with authority of position."[32] Teachers had to fight against the de-skilling or, as she called it, "factoryizing" methods of control sponsored by administrative and industrial leaders. One of the reasons she was so strongly in favor of teachers' councils as mechanisms of control of schools was that this would considerably reduce the immense power over teaching and texts that administrators then possessed. Quoting John Dewey with approval, Haley wrote:

> If there is a single public-school system in the United States where there is official and constitutional provision made for submitting questions of methods, of discipline and teaching, and the questions of curriculum, textbooks, etc. to the discussion of those actually engaged in the work of teaching, that fact has escaped my notice.[33]

In this instance, teacher control over the choice of textbooks and how they were to be used was part of a more extensive movement to enhance the democratic rights of teachers on the job. Without such teacher control, teachers would be the equivalent of factory workers whose every move was determined by management.

These points about the contradictory relationships that teachers have had with texts and the way such books de-power and em-power at different moments (and perhaps at the same time) document something of importance. It is too easy to see a cultural practice or a book as totally carrying its politics around with it, "as if written on its brow for ever and a day." Rather, its political functioning "depends on the network of social and ideological relations" in which it participates.[34] Textbook writing, reading, and use can be retrogressive or progressive (and sometimes some combination of both) depending on the social context. Textbooks can be fought because they are part of a system of moral regulation. They can be championed both as providing essential assistance in the labor of teaching and as part of a larger strategy of democratization.

What textbooks do, the social roles they play for different groups, is then *very complicated.* This has important implications not only for the politics of how and by whom textbooks are used, but for the politics of the internal qualities, the content and organization, of the text. Just as crucially, it also has an immense bearing on how people actually read and interpret the text. It is to these issues that we now wish to turn.

The Politics of Cultural Incorporation

We cannot assume that because so much of education has been linked to processes of class, gender/sex, and race stratification,[35] all of the knowledge chosen to be included in texts simply represents relations of, say, cultural domination or only includes the knowledge of dominant groups. This point requires that we speak theoretically and politically here, for all too many critical analyses of school knowledge—of what is included and excluded in the overt and hidden curricula of the school—take the easy way out. Reductive analysis comes cheap. Reality, however, is complex. Let us look at this in more detail.

Each of us has argued in considerable detail elsewhere that the selection and organization of knowledge for schools is an ideological process, one that serves the interests of particular classes and social groups.[36] However, as we just noted, this does not mean that the entire corpus of school knowledge is "a mirror reflection of ruling class ideas, imposed in an unmediated and coercive manner." Instead, "the processes of cultural incorporation are dynamic, reflecting both continuities and contradictions of that dominant culture and the continual remaking and relegitimation of that culture's plausibility system."[37] Curricula are not imposed in countries like the United States. Rather, they are the products of often intense conflicts, negotiations, and attempts at rebuilding hegemonic control by actually incorporating the knowledge and perspectives of the less powerful under the umbrella of the discourse of dominant groups.

This is clear in the case of the textbook. As disenfranchised groups have fought to have their knowledge take center stage in the debates over cultural legitimacy, one trend has dominated in text production. In essence, very little tends to be dropped from textbooks. Major ideological frameworks do not get markedly changed. Textbook publishers are under considerable and constant pressure to include *more* in their books. Progressive *items* are perhaps mentioned, then, but not developed in depth.[38] Dominance is partly maintained here through compromise and the process of "mentioning."

Tony Bennett's discussion of the process by which dominant cultures actually become dominant is worth quoting at length here:

> Dominant culture gains a purchase not in being imposed, as an alien external force, on to the cultures of subordinate groups, but by reaching into these cultures, reshaping them, hooking them and, with them, the people whose consciousness and experience is defined in their terms, into an association with the values and ideologies of the ruling groups in society. Such processes neither erase the cultures of subordinate groups, nor do they rob "the people" of their "true culture": what they do do is shuffle those cultures on to an ideological and cultural terrain in which they can be disconnected from whatever radical impulses which may (but need not) have fuelled them and be connected to more conservative or, often, downright reactionary cultural and ideological tendencies.[39]

In some cases, "mentioning" may operate in exactly this way, integrating selective elements into the dominant tradition by bringing them into close association with the values of powerful groups. There will be times, however, when such a strategy will not be successful. Oppositional cultures may at times use elements of the dominant culture against such groups. Bennett goes on, describing how oppositional cultures operate, as well:

> Similarly, resistance to the dominant culture does not take the form of launching against it a ready-formed, constantly simmering oppositional culture—always there, but in need of being turned up from time to time. Oppositional cultural values are formed and take shape only in the context of their struggle with the dominant culture, a struggle which may borrow some of its resources from that culture and which must

concede some ground to it if it is to be able to connect with it—and thereby with those whose consciousness and experience is partly shaped by it—in order, by turning it back upon itself, to peel it away, to create a space within and against it in which contradictory values can echo, reverberate and be heard.[40]

Some texts may, in fact, have such progressive "echoes" within them. These are victories in the politics of official knowledge, not only defeats.

Sometimes, of course, not only do people succeed in creating some space where such contradictory values can indeed "echo, reverberate and be heard," but also transform the entire social space. They create entirely new kinds of governments, new possibilities for democratic political, economic, and cultural arrangements. In these situations, the role of education takes on even more importance, since new knowledge, new ethics, and a new reality seek to replace the old. This is one of the reasons that those of us committed to cultures that are more participatory and democratic, both inside and outside schools, must give serious attention to changes in official knowledge in those nations that have sought to overthrow their colonial or elitist heritage. Here, the politics of the text takes on special importance, because the textbook often represents an overt attempt to help create a new cultural reality.

New social contexts, new processes of text creation, a new cultural politics, the transformation of authority relations, and new ways of reading texts—all of this can evolve and help usher in a positive rather than a negative sense of the power of the text. Less regulatory and more emancipatory relations of texts to real people can begin to evolve, a possibility made real in many of the programs of critical literacy that have had such a positive impact in nations throughout the world. Here people help create their own "texts," ones that signify their emerging power in the control of their own destinies.

However, we should not be overly romantic here. Such transformations of cultural authority and mechanisms of control and incorporation will not be easy.

For example, the ideas and values of a people are certainly not directly prescribed by the conceptions of the world of dominant groups, and it is just as certain that there are many instances in which people will be successful in creating realistic and workable alternatives to the culture and texts in dominance. Yet we do need to acknowledge that the social distribution of what is considered legitimate knowledge *is* skewed in many nations. The social institutions directly concerned with the "transmission" of this knowledge, such as schools and the media, *are* grounded in and structured by the class, gender, and race inequalities that organize the society in which people live. The area of symbolic production is not divorced from the unequal relations of power that structure other spheres.[41]

Speaking only of class relations—but much the same could be said about race and gender—Stuart Hall, one of the most insightful analysts of cultural politics, puts it this way:

Ruling or dominant conceptions of the world do not directly prescribe the mental content of the illusions that supposedly fill the heads of dominated classes. But the circle of dominant ideas *does* accumulate the symbolic power to map or classify the world for others; its classifications do acquire not only the constraining power of dominance over other modes of thought but also the initial authority of habit and instinct. It becomes the horizon of the taken-for-granted: what the world is and how it works, for all practical purposes. Ruling ideas may dominate other conceptions of the social world by setting the limit on what will appear as rational, reasonable, credible, indeed sayable or thinkable within the given vocabularies of motive and action available to us. Their dominance lies precisely in the power they have to contain within their limits, to frame within their circumference of thought, the reasoning and calculation of other social groups.[42]

In the United States, there has been a movement of exactly this kind. Dominant groups—really a coalition of economic modernizers, what has been called the "old humanists," and neoconservative intellectuals—have attempted to create an ideological consensus around the return to traditional knowledge: the "great books" and "great ideas" of the "Western tradition" will preserve democracy. By returning to the common culture that has made this nation great schools will increase student achievement and discipline, increase our international competitiveness, and ultimately reduce unemployment and poverty.

Mirrored in the problematic educational and cultural visions of volumes such as Allan Bloom's *The Closing of the American Mind* and E. D. Hirsch's *Cultural Literacy*,[43] this position is probably best represented in quotations from former secretary of education William Bennett. In his view, we are finally emerging out of a crisis in which "we neglected and denied much of the best in American education." For a period, "we simply stopped doing the right things [and] allowed an assault on intellectual and moral standards." This assault on the current state of education has led schools to fall away from "the principles of our tradition."[44]

Yet, for Bennett, "the people" have now risen up. "The 1980's gave birth to a grass roots movement for educational reform that has generated a renewed commitment to excellence, character, and fundamentals." Because of this, "we have reason for optimism."[45] Why? Because

the national debate on education is now focused on truly important matters: mastering the basics; . . . insisting on high standards and expectations; ensuring discipline in the classroom; conveying a grasp of our moral and political principles; and nurturing the character of our young.[46]

Notice the use of "we," "the people," here. Notice as well the assumed consensus on "basics" and "fundamentals" and the romanticization of the past both in schools and the larger society. The use of these terms, the attempt to bring people in under the ideological umbrella of the conservative restoration, is rhetorically very clever. As many people in the United States, Britain, and elsewhere—where rightist governments have been very active in transforming what education is about—have begun to realize, however, this ideological incorporation is having no small measure of success at the level of policy, at the level of whose knowledge and values are to be taught.[47]

If this movement has its way, the texts made available and the knowledge included in them will surely represent a major loss for many of the groups who have had successes in bringing their knowledge and culture more directly into the body of legitimate content in schools. Just as surely, the ideologies that will dominate the official knowledge will represent a considerably more elitist orientation than what we have now.

And yet, perhaps surely is not the correct word here. The situation is actually more complex than this, something we have learned from many of the newer methods of interpreting how social messages are actually "found" in texts.

Allan Luke has dealt with such issues very persuasively, and it would be best to quote him at length here:

> A major pitfall of research in the sociology of curriculum has been its willingness to accept text form as a mere adjunct means for the delivery of ideological content: the former described in terms of dominant metaphors, images, or key ideas; the latter described in terms of the sum total of values, beliefs, and ideas which might be seen to constitute a false consciousness. For much content analysis presumes that text mirrors or reflects a particular ideological position, which in turn can be connected to specific class interests. . . . It is predicated on the possibility of a one-to-one identification of school knowledge with textually represented ideas of the dominant classes. Even those critics who have recognized that the ideology encoded in curricular texts may reflect the internally contradictory character of a dominant culture have tended to neglect the need for a more complex model of text analysis, one that does not suppose that texts are simply readable, literal representations of "someone else's" version of social reality, objective knowledge and human relations. For texts do not always mean or communicate what they say.[48]

These are important points for they imply that we need more sophisticated and nuanced models of textual analysis. While we should certainly *not* be at all sanguine about the effects of the conservative restoration on texts and the curriculum, if texts do not simply represent dominant beliefs in some straightforward way, and if dominant cultures contain contradictions, fissures, and even elements of the culture of popular groups, then our readings of what knowledge is "in" texts cannot be done by the application of a simple formula.

We can claim, for instance, that the meaning of a text is not necessarily intrinsic to it. As poststructuralist theories would have it, meaning is "the product of a system of differences into which the text is articulated." Thus, there is not "one text," but many. Any text is open to multiple readings. This puts into doubt any claim that one can determine the meanings and politics of a text "by a straightforward encounter with the text itself." It also raises serious questions about whether one can fully understand the text by mechanically applying any interpretive procedure. Meanings, then, can be—and are—multiple and contradictory, and we must always be willing to "read" our own readings of a text, to interpret our own interpretations of what it means.[49] Answering the question of "whose knowledge" is in a text is not at all simple, it seems, although clearly the Right would very much like to reduce the range of meanings one might find.

This is true of our own interpretations of what is in textbooks. But it is just as true for the students who sit in schools and at home and read (or in many cases do not read) their texts. We want to stress this point not only at the level of theory and politics, as we have emphasized here, but also at the level of practice.

We cannot assume that what is "in" the text is actually taught. Nor can we assume that what is taught is actually learned. Teachers have a long history of mediating and transforming text material when they employ it in classrooms. Students bring their own classed, raced, gendered, and sexual biographies with them as well. They, too, selectively accept, reinterpret, and reject what counts as legitimate knowledge. As critical ethnographies of schools have shown, students (and teachers) are not empty vessels into which knowledge is poured. Rather than participants in what Freire has called "banking" education[50] students are active constructors of the meanings of the education they encounter.[51]

We can talk about three ways in which people can potentially respond to a text: dominated, negotiated,and oppositional. In the dominated reading of a text, one accepts the messages at face value. In a negotiated response, the reader may dispute a particular claim, but accept the overall tendencies or interpretations of a text. Finally, an oppositional response rejects these dominant tendencies and interpretations. The reader "repositions" herself or himself in relation to the text and takes on the position of the oppressed.[52] These are, of course, no more than ideal types, and many responses will be a contradictary combination of all three. But the point is not only that texts themselves have contradictory elements, but also that audiences *construct* their own responses to texts. They do not passively receive texts, but actually read them based on their own class, race, gender/sex, and religious experiences.

An immense amount of work needs to be done on student acceptance, interpretation, reinterpretation, and partial and/or total rejection of texts. While there is a tradition of such research,much of it quite good, most of this in education is done in an overly psychologized manner. It is more concerned with questions of learning and achievement than it is with the equally as important and prior issues of whose knowledge it is that students are learning, negotiating, or opposing and what the socio-cultural roots and effects are of such processes. Yet we simply cannot fully understand the power of texts, what they do ideologically and politically (or educationally, for that matter), unless we take very seriously the way students actually read them—not only as individuals but also as members of social groups with their own particular cultures and histories.[53] For every textbook, then, there are multiple texts—contradictions within it, multiple readings of it, and different uses to which it will be put. Texts—be they the standardized grade-level-specific books so beloved by school systems or the novels, trade books, and alternative materials that teachers use either to supplement these books or simply to replace them—are part of a complex story of cultural politics. They can signify authority (not always legitimate) or freedom.

To recognize this, then, is also to recognize that our task as critically and democratically minded educators is itself a political one. We must acknowledge and understand the tremendous capacity of dominant institutions to regenerate themselves "not only in their material foundations and structures but in the hearts and minds of people." Yet, at the very same time, we need never to lose sight of the power of popular organizations—of real people—to struggle, resist, and transform them.[54] Cultural authority, that which counts as legitimate knowledge, the norms and values represented in the officially sponsored curriculum of the school—all of these serve as important arenas in which the positive and negative relations of power surrounding the text will work themselves out. And all of them involve the hopes and dreams of real people in real institutions, in real relations of inequality.

From all that we have said here, it should be clear that we oppose the idea that there can be one textual authority, one definitive set of "facts" divorced from their context of power relations. A "common culture" can never be an extension to everyone of what a minority means and believe. Rather, and crucially, it requires not the stipulation and incorporation within textbooks of lists and concepts that make us all "culturally literate," *but the creation of the conditions necessary for all people to participate in the creation and recreation of meanings and values.* It requires a democratic process in which all people— not simply those who see themselves as the intellectual guardians of the "Western tradition"—can be involved in the deliberation of what is important.[55] It should go without saying that this necessitates the removal of the very real material obstacles—unequal power, wealth, time for reflection—that stand in the way of such participation.[56]

The very idea that there is one set of values that must guide the "selective tradition" can be a great danger, especially in contexts of differential power. Take, as one example, a famous line that was inscribed on an equally famous public building. It read: "There is one road to freedom. Its milestones are obedience, diligence, honesty, order, cleanliness, temperance, truth, sacrifice, and love of country." Many people may perhaps agree with much of the sentiment represented by these words, and it may be of some interest to them that the building on which they appeared was in the administration block of the concentration camp at Dachau.[57]

Multiple Perspectives on the Text

Each of the chapters that follow takes up important elements of this discussion of the politics of the textbook. Some are concerned with the political and economic realities of text publishing. Others delve into the cultural and ideological content and form of texts of various kinds, paying attention to the politics of cultural authority and the selective tradition, and to how texts are actually read. Still others focus not only on the national but also on the international context. Our aim in this volume has not been to give the final word on any of the debates about the politics of the text. Indeed, no one book could, or should, do such a thing. Rather, we have sought to open up discussions that need to take place, to extend previous analyses and to illuminate some of the hidden realities behind the dominance of the textbook. We are concerned as well that a sense of the very possibility of a different politics of official knowledge is enhanced. Because of this, the book closes with an example of a more liberating cultural politics that sought to democratize cultural authority and the text in practice.

Some of the chapters that follow will raise very practical pedagogical and curricular problems. Others will cause us to pay greater attention to the power of political, economic, and ideological dynamics than we may have in the past. A number of the chapters ask us to become considerably more sophisticated theoretically in our analyses of the relationship between culture and power in texts themselves. Taken together, the chapters included here provide us with a much clearer picture of the politics of knowledge, how texts work, and why the look the way they do.

In Chapter 2, setting the stage for many of the chapters that follow, Michael Apple investigates how the selective tradition is produced by the complex political and economic circumstances surrounding the world of textbook publishing. He traces part of the history of these conditions and then goes inside the publishing industry to show how internal and external pressures and "rational" decisions cause textbooks to look the way they do. In the process, he asks us to go beyond the overly reductive analyses that have often dominated our investigations of the relationship between power and culture.

In Chapter 3, Linda Christian-Smith examines the growing technologization of publishing. She illuminates the effects of the computerization of the entire book production process on the people who actually work on producing the book itself. Of particular importance is her analysis of the impact of such changes on women workers. Her discussion should make us much less sanguine about the "benefits" of the new technology in textbook publishing.

The politics of the textbook is directly related to the role of government agencies in producing, selecting, and legitimating the books that dominate the curriculum. In Chapter 4, Dan Marshall goes behind the scenes in Texas, one of the states that—because of its policy of state-wide approval—plays a profound role in determining the form and content of the texts that are sold in the entire nation. He looks in particular at how members of the textbook-adoption committee function and how pressure groups work in influencing government and publishers' decisions.

Christine Sleeter and Carl Grant, in Chapter 5, take us inside the major textbooks now being used in many classrooms throughout the United States. They engage in a detailed content analysis of recent texts in social studies, reading and language arts, science, and mathematics. Not content to stress one relation of power in the knowledge the texts present, they analyze the ways race, class, gender, and disability are treated. Their conclusions are truly disturbing in many ways.

For many people in the United States, the basal reader was the first and most important textbook of their daily lives in schools. Among the most influential of these texts were the famous (or infamous, depending on your point of view) "Dick and Jane readers." Entire generations of students were faced with the definitions of reading and literacy embodied in these books. It is not widely known that there was a separate version of these texts for Catholic schools. In Chapter 6, Allan Luke engages in a disciplined and insightful historical and semiotic reading of the Catholic Dick-and-Jane readers—of their visions of authority, community, gender, race, and social conflict. He provides an important model of textual analysis that goes beyond our traditional forms.

There has not been sufficient attention paid to the creation of oppositional knowledge and voices. Kenneth Teitelbaum, in Chapter 7, brings some of this to life for us. Even when the dominant ideological tendencies in the content of schooling did not allow for adequate representation of working people and the vast majority of the American people, this did not mean that progressive educators and community members stood by and accepted this situation. One important example of such "counter-hegemonic" practices was the formation of "Socialist Sunday Schools" in many cities in the United States. Teitelbaum provides a unique picture of the material that was developed to teach students in these schools about alternative forms of economic, political, and cultural life. While the material itself was often contradictory, it serves as a crucial reminder of past struggles to alter the politics of official knowledge.

Often we assume that the standardized textbook is the only or the primary means of establishing legitimate knowledge in the classroom. Yet many teachers, distressed by the treatment or invisibility of oppressed groups in the texts, bring in other voices to counter the utter lack of serious attention to, say, the vibrant cultures of people of color. In Chapter 8, Joel Taxel focuses on the work of Mildred Taylor, a novelist who writes about the African American experience for young readers. For Taxel, progressive educators can overcome

the selective tradition by uncovering the voices of opposition in children's literature that have been too often silenced in the past, and by guaranteeing their
availability to our students.

Not all such trade books are oppositional, to say the least. One of the
fastest growing segments of book publishing has been romance novels. Not only
are millions of these sold worldwide to adult readers. Millions more are published for the teenage market. Such adolescent romance novels are aimed especially at young women. These books have not remained outside the classroom
door. Many teachers are using them as what are called H/Ls—high interest, low
ability—for their students who are not doing well in reading. The ideological
orientation of such books is often less than liberating in terms of gender, race,
and class relations. Yet young women read such novels in contradictory ways,
with contradictory effects. Linda Christian-Smith, in Chapter 9, discusses adolescent romance novels and provides us with a rich picture of the construction
of textual meaning by their teenage readers. Gender, class, and race contradictions will be very evident.

The texts about which we should be concerned are not only those found
in schools. We need to pay considerable attention to those ''texts,'' widely
sponsored, reviewed, and read, that try to convince ''the public'' that the wrong
knowledge is now being taught in our educational institutions. The conservative
restoration is now very advanced in many nations. Part of its politics is cultural
and ideological. Not only does it want to transform what education is for, it
wants to dramatically alter what counts as legitimate knowledge in the process.
In Chapter 10, Stanley Aronowitz and Henry Giroux engage in a detailed critical
deconstruction of the arguments put forward by Allan Bloom and E. D. Hirsch
as to what we should teach. Many people have been strongly influenced by
positions taken by Bloom and by Hirsch, and pressure is being placed on education at all levels to have texts that are ''culturally literate'' and embody the
''wisdom'' of the ''Western tradition.'' The arguments of Aronowitz and Giroux will assist all of us in countering these tendencies.

In Chapter 11, Philip Altbach directs our attention to the international
dimensions of publishing in general and to textbook publishing in particular.
He pays a good deal of attention, and justifiably so, to the role of multinational
publishers in maintaining first-world dominance and in making it increasingly
more difficult for cultural independence and autonomy to develop in ''peripheral'' nations. He also enables us to see the possibilities and dangers that may
arise in this situation over time.

When social movements transform a repressive situation, ushering in new
and more democratic governments, education itself is subject to major transformations as well. In Chapter 12, Didacus Jules, the former permanent secretary
for education in the Bishop government in Grenada, describes the critical shifts
in the process and politics of text production and content after the initial success
of the democratic movement there. We have much to learn from the progressive

tendencies such attempts involve. Yet we also need to remember the fragility of such democratic movements in the context of international economic, political, and cultural dominance. After all, the United States sought to ensure that the Grenadian experiment in democracy was short-lived. Jules's discussion does suggest the very possibility of difference, however—surely an important hope in the current context.

The chapters we have described are themselves "texts" that are open to multiple readings, to multiple interpretations and responses. Because of this, and because all of the authors included here are committed to a more democratic politics of knowledge, we urge you to write to us with comments, disagreements, questions, or even affirmations about what you have read in this volume. Only in this way will we too learn about how the cultural politics of books actually works.

Notes

1. See, for example, Michael W. Apple and Lois Weis, eds., *Ideology and Practice in Schooling* (Philadelphia: Temple University Press, 1983).

2. For a current representative sample of the varied kinds of studies being done on the textbook, see Arthur Woodward, David L. Elliot, and Kathleen Carter Nagel, eds., *Textbooks in School and Society* (New York: Garland, 1988).

3. Fred Inglis, *Popular Culture and Political Power* (New York: St. Martin's Press, 1988), p. 9.

4. Allan Luke, *Literacy, Textbooks and Ideology* (Philadelphia: Falmer Press, 1988), pp. 27–29.

5. Michael W. Apple, *Ideology and Curriculum,* 2d ed. (New York: Routledge, 1990); idem, *Education and Power* (New York: Routledge, 1985); and idem, *Teachers and Texts: A Political Economy of Class and Gender Relations in Education* (New York: Routledge, 1986).

6. Michael W. Apple, "Redefining Equality: Authoritarian Populism and the Conservative Restoration," *Teachers College Record* 90 (Winter 1988): 167–84.

7. Ann Bastian, Norm Fruchter, Marilyn Gittell, Colin Greer, and Kenneth Haskins, *Choosing Equality: The Case for Democratic Schooling* (Philadelphia: Temple University Press, 1986).

8. See, for example, Susan Rose, *Keeping Them Out of the Hands of Satan* (New York: Routledge, 1988).

9. Allen Hunter, *Children in the Service of Conservation* (Madison, Wis.: University of Wisconsin Institute for Legal Studies, 1988).

10. James Moffett, *Storm in the Mountains* (Carbondale, Ill., Southern Illinois University Press, 1988).

11. Raymond Williams, *The Long Revolution* (London: Chatto and Windus, 1961). See also Apple, *Ideology and Curriculum.*

12. Fred Inglis, *The Management of Ignorance: A Political Theory of The Curriculum* (New York: Basil Blackwell, 1985), pp. 22–23.

13. Ibid., p. 23.

14. Miriam Schipper, "Textbook Controversy: Past and Present," *New York University Education*

Quarterly 14 (Spring/Summer 1983): 31–36. The continuing controversy over *Our Bodies, Our Selves* in schools documents the immense power of gender in struggles over texts as well. Class is not the only dynamic that operates here. We need to stress the historical and current importance of race and gender in conflicts over official knowledge.

15. A. Graham Down, "Preface" to Harriet Tyson-Bernstein, *A Conspiracy of Good Intentions: America's Textbook Fiasco* (Washington, D.C.: The Council for Basic Education, 1988), p. viii.

16. Harriet Tyson-Bernstein, *A Conspiracy of Good Intentions,* p. 3.

17. Robert Darnton, *The Literary Underground of the Old Regime* (Cambridge, Mass.: Harvard University Press, 1982), p. 199.

18. For a history of the social roots of such adoption policies, see Michael W. Apple, "Regulating the Text: The Socio/Historical Roots of State Control." *Educational Policy* 3 (June 1989): 107–23.

19. The issues surrounding cultural imperialism and colonialism are nicely laid out in Philip Altbach and Gail Kelly, eds., *Education and the Colonial Experience* (New York: Transaction Books, 1984). For an excellent discussion of international relations over texts and knowledge, see Philip Altbach, *The Knowledge Context* (Albany, N.Y.: State University of New York Press, 1988).

20. For some of the most elegant discussion of how we need to think about these "cultural silences," see Leslie Roman and Linda Christian-Smith with Elizabeth Ellsworth, eds., *Becoming Feminine: The Politics of Popular Culture* (Philadelphia: Falmer Press, 1988).

21. Marcus Raskin, *The Common Good* (New York: Routledge, 1986).

22. Inglis, *The Management of Ignorance,* p. 142.

23. Inglis, *Popular Culture and Political Power,* p. 4.

24. Ibid.

25. Darnton, *The Literary Underground of the Old Regime,* p. 13.

26. Janet Batsleer, Tony Davies, Rebecca O'Rourke, and Chris Weedon, *Rewriting English: Cultural Politics of Gender and Class* (New York: Methuen, 1985).

27. Colin Lankshear with Moira Lawler, *Literacy, Schooling and Revolution* (Philadelphia: Falmer Press, 1987).

28. Batsleer, Davies, O'Rourke, and Weedon, *Rewriting English,* p. 5.

29. James W. Fraser, "Agents of Democracy: Urban Elementary School Teachers and the Conditions of Teaching," in *American Teachers: Histories of a Profession at Work,* ed. Donald Warren (New York: Macmillan, 1989), p. 128.

30. Apple, *Teachers and Texts.*

31. For further discussion of deskilling and reskilling, see Apple, *Education and Power.*

32. Margaret Haley, quoted in Fraser, "Agents of Democracy," p. 128.

33. Haley, quoted in ibid., p. 138.

34. Tony Bennett, "Introduction: Popular Culture and 'the Turn to Gramsci,' " in *Popular Culture and Social Relations,* ed. Tony Bennett, Colin Mercer and Janet Woollacott (Philadelphia: Open University Press, 1986), p. xvi.

35. The literature here is voluminous. For a more extended treatment see Apple, *Education and Power;* and Cameron McCarthy and Michael W. Apple, "Race, Class and Gender in American Educational Research," *Class, Race and Gender in American Education,* ed. Lois Weis (Albany, N.Y.: State University of New York Press, 1989).

36. See Apple, *Ideology and Curriculum,* and Linda Christian-Smith, *Becoming a Woman Through Romance* (New York: Routledge, 1990).

37. Luke, *Literacy, Textbooks and Ideology,* p. 24.

38. Tyson-Bernstein, *A Conspiracy of Good Intentions,* p. 18.

39. Tony Bennett, "The Politics of the 'Popular' and Popular Culture," in Bennett, Mercer and Woolacott, eds., *Popular Culture and Social Relations,* p. 19.

40. Ibid.

41. Stuart Hall, "The Toad in the Garden: Thatcherism Among the Theorists," in *Marxism and the Interpretation of Culture,* ed. Cary Nelson and Lawrence Grossberg (Urbana, Ill.: University of Illinois Press, 1988), p. 44.

42. Ibid.

43. Allan Bloom, *The Closing of the American Mind* (New York: Simon and Schuster, 1987), and E. D. Hirsch, Jr., *Cultural Literacy* (New York: Houghton-Mifflin, 1986).

44. William Bennett, *Our Children and Our Country* (New York: Simon and Schuster, 1988), p. 9.

45. Ibid., p. 10.

46. Ibid.

47. Apple, "Redefining Equality."

48. Luke, *Literacy, Textbooks and Ideology,* pp. 29–30.

49. Lawrence Grossberg and Cary Nelson, "Introduction: The Territory of Marxism," in Nelson and Grossberg, eds., *Marxism and the Interpretation of Culture,* p. 8.

50. Paulo Freire, *Pedagogy of the Oppressed* (New York: Herder and Herder, 1973).

51. See, for example, Paul Willis, *Learning to Labor* (New York: Columbia University Press, 1981); Angela McRobbie, "Working-Class Girls and the Culture of Femininity," in *Women Take Issue,* ed. Women's Studies Group (London: Hutchinson, 1978), pp. 96–108; Robert Everhart, *Reading, Writing and Resistance* (Boston: Routledge and Kegan Paul, 1983); Lois Weis, *Between Two Worlds* (Boston: Routledge and Kegan Paul, 1985); and Bonnie Trudell, *Constructing the Sexuality Curriculum-in-Use* (unpublished doctoral thesis, University of Wisconsin-Madison, 1988). The list could, and should, be continued.

52. Tania Modleski, "Introduction," in *Studies in Entertainment* (Bloomington, Ind., Indiana University Press, 1986), p. xi.

53. See Elizabeth Ellsworth, "Illicit Pleasures: Feminist Spectators and *Personal Best,*" in Roman and Christian-Smith with Ellsworth, *Becoming Feminine,* pp. 102–19; Elizabeth Ellsworth, "Why Doesn't This Feel Empowering?" *Harvard Educational Review* 59 (August 1989): 297–324; and Christian-Smith, *Becoming a Woman through Romance.*

54. Batsleer, Davies, O'Rourke, and Weedon, *Rewriting English,* p. 5.

55. This is discussed in more detail in the new preface to the second edition of Apple, *Ideology and Curriculum.*

56. Raymond Williams, *Resources of Hope* (New York: Verso, 1989), pp. 37–38.

57. David Horne, *The Public Culture* (Dover, N.H.: Pluto Press, 1986), p. 76.

2

The Culture and
Commerce of the Textbook

Michael W. Apple

I.

We can talk about culture in two ways, as a lived process, as what Raymond Williams has called a whole way of life, or as a commodity.[1] In the first, we focus on culture as a constitutive social process through which we live our daily lives. In the second, we emphasize the products of culture, the very thingness of the commodities we produce and consume. This distinction can, of course, be maintained only on an analytic level, because most of what seem to us to be things—like lightbulbs, cars, records, and, in the case of this essay, books—are really part of a larger social process. As Marx, for example, spent years trying to demonstrate, every product is an expression of embodied human labor. Goods and services are relations among people, relations of exploitation often, but human relations nevertheless. Turning on a light when you walk into a room is not only using an object, it is also to be involved in an anonymous social relationship with the miner who worked to dig the coal burned to produce the electricity.

This dual nature of culture poses a dilemma for those individuals who are interested in understanding the dynamics of popular and elite culture in our society. It makes studying the dominant cultural products—from films, to books, to television, to music—decidedly slippery, for there are sets of relations behind each of these "things." And these in turn are situated within the larger web of the social and market relations of capitalism.

Although there is a danger of falling into economic reductionism, it is essential that we look more closely at this political economy of culture. How do the dynamics of class, gender, and race "determine" cultural production? How is the organization and distribution of culture "mediated" by economic

This chapter is an updated version of one that appeared under the same name as Chapter 4 in my *Teachers and Texts: A Political Economy of Class and Gender Relations in Education* (New York: Routledge, 1988).

and social structures?[2] What is the relationship between a cultural product—say, a film or a book—and the social relations of its production, accessibility, and consumption? These are not easy questions to deal with, in at least two ways. First, the very terms of these questions and the concepts we use to ask them are notoriously difficult to unpack. That is, words such as determine, mediate, social relations of production, and so on—and the conceptual apparatus that lies behind them—are not at all settled. There is as much contention over their use currently as there has ever been.[3] Thus, it is hard to grapple with the issue of the determination of culture without at the same time being very self-conscious of the tools one is employing to do it.

Second—and closely related to the first, perhaps because of the theoretical controversies surrounding the topic—there have been fewer detailed and large-scale empirical investigations of these relations recently than is necessary. While we may have interesting ideological or economic analyses of a television show, film, or book,[4] there are really only a few well-designed empirical studies that examine the economics and social relations involved in films and books in general. Because of this, it is hard to get a global picture.

This hiatus is a problem in sociological analysis in general, and yet it is even more problematic in the field of education. Even though the overt aim of our institutions of schooling has more than a little to do with cultural products and processes, with cultural transmission, only in the last decade or so have the politics and economics of the culture *actually* transmitted in schools been taken up as a serious research problem. It was almost as if Durkheim and Weber, to say nothing of Marx, had never existed. In the area that has come to be called the sociology of the curriculum, however, steps have been taken to deal with this issue in some very interesting ways. A good deal of progress has in fact been made in understanding whose knowledge is taught and produced in our schools.[5]

While not the only topics with which we should be concerned, it is clear that major curriculum issues have to do with content and organization. What should be taught? In what way? Answering these is difficult. The first, for example, involves some very knotty epistemological issues—e.g., what should be granted the status of knowledge?—and is a politically loaded question as well. To borrow the language of Pierre Bourdieu and Basil Bernstein, the "cultural capital" of dominant classes and class segments has been considered the most legitimate knowledge.[6] This knowledge, and one's "ability" to deal with it, has served as one mechanism in a complex process in which the economic and cultural reproduction of class, gender, and race relations is accomplished. Therefore, the choice of particular content and of particular ways of approaching it in schools is related both to existing relations of domination and to struggles to alter these relations. Not to recognize this is to ignore a wealth of evidence—in the United States, England, Australia, France, Sweden, Germany, and elsewhere—that links school knowledge, both commodified and lived, to class, gender, and race dynamics outside as well as inside our institutions of education.[7]

The recognition of the political nature of the curriculum, by itself, does not solve all of our problems. The statement that school knowledge has some (admittedly complex) connections to the larger political economy merely restates the issue. It does not in itself answer how these connections operate. Although the ties that link curricula to the inequalities and social struggles of our social formation are very complicated, research occasionally becomes available that helps to illuminate this nexus, even when it is not aimed, overtly, at an educational audience. I want to draw on this research to help us begin to uncover some of the connections between curriculum and the larger political economy. The most interesting of this research deals with the culture and commerce of publishing. It wants to examine the relationship between the ways in which publishing operates, internally—its social relations and composition—and the cultural and economic market within which it is situated. What do the social and economic relations within the publishing industry have to do with schools, with the politics of knowledge-distribution in education? Perhaps this can be made clearer if we stop and think about the following question.

How is this "legitimate" knowledge made available in schools? By and large it is through something to which we have paid much too little attention— the textbook. Whether we like it or not, the curriculum in most American schools is not defined by courses of study or suggested programs, but by one particular artifact, the standardized, grade-level–specific text in mathematics, reading, social studies, science (when it is even taught), and so on. The impact of this on the social relations of the classroom is also immense. It is estimated, for example, that seventy-five percent of the time elementary and secondary students are in classrooms and ninety percent of their time on homework is spent with text materials.[8] Yet, even given the ubiquitous character of the textbook, it is one of the things we know least about. While the text dominates curricula at the elementary, secondary, and even college levels, very little critical attention has been paid to the ideological, political, and economic sources of its production, distribution, and reception.[9]

In order to make sense out of this, we need to place the production of curricular materials such as texts back into the larger process of the production of cultural commodities—such as books—in general. There are approximately forty thousand books published each year in the United States.[10] Obviously, these are quite varied, and only a small portion of them are textbooks. Yet, even with this variation, there are certain constants that act on publishers.

We can identify four "major structural conditions" that by and large determine the shape of publishing currently in the United States. As Coser, Kadushin, and Powell state:

(1) The industry sells its products—like any commodity—in a market, but a market

that, in contrast to that for many other products, is fickle and often uncertain. (2) The industry is decentralized among a number of sectors whose operations bear little resemblance to each other. (3) These operations are characterized by a mixture of modern mass-production methods and craft-like procedures. (4) The industry remains perilously poised between the requirements and restraints of commerce and the responsibilities and obligations that it must bear as a prime guardian of the symbolic culture of the nation. Although the tensions between the claims of commerce and culture seem to us always to have been with book publishing, they have become more acute and salient in the last twenty years.[11]

These conditions are not new phenomena by any means. From the time printing began as an industry, books were pieces of merchandise. They were, of course, often produced for scholarly or humanistic purposes, but before anything else their prime function was to earn their producers a living. Book production, hence, has historically rested on a foundation where from the outset it was necessary to "find enough capital to start work and then to print only those titles which would satisfy a clientele, and that at a price which would withstand competition." Similar to the marketing of other products, then, finance and costing took an immensely important place in the decisions of publishers and booksellers.[12] Febvre and Martin, in their analysis of the history of book printing in Europe, argue this point exceptionally clearly:

> One fact must not be lost sight of: the printer and the bookseller worked above all and from the beginning for profit. The story of the first joint enterprise, Fust and Schoeffer, proves that. Like their modern counterparts, 15th-century publishers only financed the kind of book they felt would sell enough copies to show a profit in a reasonable time. We should not therefore be surprised to find that the immediate effect of printing was merely to further increase the circulation of those works which had already enjoyed success in manuscript, and often to consign other less popular texts to oblivion. By multiplying books by the hundred and then thousand [compared to, say, the laborious copying of manuscripts], the press achieved both increased volume and at the same time more rigorous selection.[13]

Drawing upon Pierre Bourdieu's work, we can make a distinction between two types of "capital"—*symbolic* and *financial*. This enables us to distinguish among the many kinds of publishers one might find. In essence, these two kinds of capital are found in different kinds of markets. Those firms that are more commercial, that are oriented to rapid turnover, quick obsolescence, and to the minimization of risks, are following a strategy for the accumulation of financial capital. Such a strategy has a strikingly different perspective on time, as well. It has a short time-perspective, one that focuses on the current interests of a particular group of readers. In contradistinction to those publishers whose market embodies the interests of finance capital, those firms whose goal is to maximize the accumulation of symbolic capital operate in such a way that their time-perspective is longer. Immediate profit is less important. Higher risks may be taken, and experimental content and form will find greater acceptance. These publishers are not uninterested in the "logic of profitability," but long-term accumulation is more important. One example is provided by Beckett's *Waiting for Godot,* which sold only ten thousand copies in the first five years after its publication in 1952, yet then went on to sell sixty thousand copies as its rate of sales increased yearly by twenty percent.[14]

The conceptual distinction based on varying kinds of capital does not totally cover the differences among publishers in the kinds of books they publish, however. Coser, Kadushin, and Powell, for example, further classify publishers according to the ways in which editors themselves carry out their work. In so doing, they distinguish among trade publishers, text publishers, and finally the various scholarly-monograph or university presses. Each of these labels not only refers to editorial policy, but also speaks to a wide array of differences concerning the kind of technology employed by the press, the bureaucratic and organizational structures that coordinate and control the day-to-day work of the company, and the different risks and monetary and marketing policies of each. Each label also refers to important differences in relations with authors, in scheduling, and ultimately in defining what counts as "success."[15] Behind the commodity, the book, stands indeed a whole set of human relations.

These structural differences in organization, technology, and economic and social relations structure the practices of the people involved in producing books. This includes editors, authors, agents, and, to a lesser extent, sales and marketing personnel. Digging deeper into them also enables us to understand better the political economy of culture. By integrating analyses of internal deci-sion-making processes and external market relations within publishing we can gain a good deal of insight into how particular aspects of popular and elite culture are presented in published form.

Let us set the stage for our further discussion historically. From the period just after the Civil War to the first decade of the twentieth century, fiction led in the sheer quantity of titles that were published. We can see this if we take one year as an example. In 1886 *Publishers Weekly* took the nearly 5,000 books published in the U.S. and broke them down into various categories. Those ten categories with the most volumes were: fiction (1,080), law (469), juvenile (458), literary history and miscellaneous (388), theology (377), education and language (275), poetry and drama (220), history (182), medical science (177), and social and political science (174).[16] These data do not account for the many informal political booklets and pamphlets that were published. But who the readership actually was, what the rates of literacy were between particular classes and genders, and what the economic conditions of publishing and pur-chasing were—all of this had an impact on what was published.

These figures have tended to change markedly over the years. Yet it is not just the type of book published that is of import historically or currently. Form and content have been subject to the influences of the larger society as well. To take one example, market constraints have often had a profound impact on what gets published and even on what authors will write. Again, certain aspects of fiction-writing and -publishing offer an interesting case in point. Wendy Griswold's analysis of the manner in which different market positions occupied by various authors and publishers had an impact documents this nicely.

In the nineteenth century, topics treated by European writers had a distinct market advantage in the United States, due to the oddities of our copyright laws. As Griswold states:

> During most of the 19th century, American copyright laws protected citizens or permanent residents of the United States but not foreign authors. The result was that British and other foreign works could be reprinted and sold in the United States without royalties being paid to their authors, while Americans did receive royalty payments. Many interests in the United States benefited from this literary piracy and lobbied to maintain the status quo. (Actually piracy is something of a misnomer, for the practice was perfectly legal.) The nascent printing industry was kept busy. Publishers made huge profits from reprinting foreign books. Readers had available the best foreign literature at low prices; for example, in 1843 *A Christmas Carol* sold for ¢.06 in the United States and the equivalent of $2.50 in England.[17]

Clearly, such a situation could lead to some rather difficult circumstances for authors. American publishers had little inducement to publish "original native works" because a copyright had to be paid to their authors. The American author was largely left, then, unable to earn his or her living as a fiction writer because he or she was excluded from the fiction market. This also had an impact on the very content of writing as well. Discouraged from dealing with subjects already treated in the cheaper editions of European works, American authors often had to stake out a different terrain, areas that were unusual but would still have enough market appeal to convince publishers to publish them.[18]

These influences did not constitute a new phenomenon. In fact, the growth of particular genres and styles of books themselves has been linked closely to similar social forces operating earlier. As Ian Watt and Raymond Williams have argued, the rise of something as common today as the novel is related to changes in political economies and class structures and to the growth of ideologies of individualism, among other things.[19] In the eighteenth century in Europe, for instance, "the rapid expansion of a new audience for literature, the literate middle class, especially the leisured middle class women," also led to novels focusing on "love and marriage, economic individualism, the complexities of modern life, and the possibility of personal morality in a corrupting world." The economic conditions of publishing also changed a good deal. A decline in patronage was accompanied by the growth of the bookseller who combined publishing, printing, and selling. Authors were often paid by the page. The speed of writing and amount of pages written was of no small value, as one might imagine.[20]

These small examples give a sense of the historical complexity of the influences on publishing and on its content, readership, and economic realities. Book publishing today lives in the shadow of this past and the social, ideological, and economic conditions that continued their development out of it. This is particularly the case in understanding the commercial and cultural structures involved in the publication of textbooks for schools. An excellent case in point is the production of texts for tertiary level courses. As we shall see, the "culture and commerce" of college-text and other text production can provide some important insights into how the process of cultural commodification works.

II.

While we may think of book publishing as a relatively large industry, by current standards it is actually rather small compared with other industries. The *entire* book-publishing industry, with its 65,000 or so employees, would rank nearly forty to fifty positions below a single one of the highest grossing and largest employing American companies. While its total sales in 1980 were approximately six billion dollars and this does in fact sound impressive, in many ways its market is much less certain and is subject to greater economic, political, and ideological contingencies than other, larger companies.

Six billion dollars, however, is still definitely not a pittance. Book publishing *is* an industry, one divided up into a variety of markets. Of the total, $1.2 billion was accounted for by reference books, encyclopedias, and professional books; $1.5 billion came from the elementary, secondary, and college-text market; $1 billion was taken in from book clubs and direct mail sales; books intended for the general public—what are called trade books—had a sales level of $1 billion; and, finally, nearly $660 million was accounted for by mass-market paperbacks. With its $1.5 billion sales, it is obvious that the textbook market is no small segment of the industry as a whole.[21]

The increasing concentration of power in text publishing has been marked. There has been more and more competition recently, but this has occurred among a smaller number of larger firms. The competition has also reduced the propensity to take risks. Instead, many publishers now prefer to expend most of their efforts on a smaller selection of "carefully chosen 'products.' "[22]

Perhaps the simplest way to illuminate part of this dynamic is to quote from a major figure in publishing, who, after thirty-five years of involvement in the industry; reflected on the question, "How competitive is book publishing?" His answer, succinct and speaking paragraphs was only one word—"Very."[23]

A picture of the nature of the concentration within text publishing can be gained from a few facts. Seventy-five percent of the total sales of college text-books was controlled by the ten largest text publishers, with 90% accounted for by the top twenty. Prentice-Hall, McGraw-Hill, the CBS Publishing Group, and Scott, Foresman—the top four—accounted for 40% of the market.[24] In what is called the "elhi" (elementary and high school) market, the figures are also very revealing. It is estimated that the four largest textbook publishers of these materials account for 32% of the market. The eight largest firms control 53%. And the twenty largest control over 75% of sales.[25] This is no small amount, to be sure. Yet concentration does not tell the entire story. Internal factors—who works in these firms, what their backgrounds and characteristics are, and what their working conditions happen to be—also play a significant part.

What kind of people make the decisions about college and other texts? Even though many people find their way into publishing in general by accident, as it were, this is even more the case for editors who work in firms that deal with, say, college texts. "Most of them entered publishing simply because they were looking for some sort of a job, and publishing presented itself."[26] But these people are not all equal. Important divisions exist within the houses themselves.

In fact, one thing that recent research makes strikingly clear is the strength of sex-typing in the division of labor in publishing. Women are often found in subsidiary rights and publicity departments. They are often copy editors. While they outnumber men in employment within publishing as a whole, this does not mean that they are a powerful overt force. Rather, they largely tend to be hired as "secretaries, assistants, publicists, advertising managers, and occupants of other low- and mid-level positions." Even though there have been a number of women who have moved into important editorial positions in the past few years, by and large women are still not as evident in positions that actually "exercise control over the goals and policy of publishing." In essence, there is something of a dual labor market in publishing. The lower-paying, replaceable jobs, ones with less possibility for advancement, form the "female enclaves."[27]

What does this mean for this particular discussion? Nearly seventy-five percent of the editors in college-text publishing either began their careers as sales personnel or held sales or marketing positions before being promoted to editor.[28] As there are many fewer women than men who travel around selling college or other level texts or holding positions of authority within sales departments that could lead to upward mobility, this will have an interesting effect on the people who become editors and on the content of editorial decisions as well.

These facts have important implications. Most editorial decisions dealing with which texts are to be published—that is, concerning that which within particular disciplines is to count as legitimate content which students are to receive as "official knowledge"—are made by individuals who have specific characteristics. The vast majority of these editors will be male, thereby reproducing patriarchal relations within the firm itself. Second, their general background will complement the existing market structure that dominates text production. Financial capital, short-term perspectives, and high profit margins will be seen as major goals.[29] A substantial cultural or educational vision and the concerns associated with strategies based on symbolic capital will necessarily take a back seat, where they come into play at all.

Coser, Kadushin, and Powell recognize the influence of profit, the power of what they call commerce, in text production. As they note about college-text publishing, the major emphasis is on the production of books for introductory-level courses that have high student enrollments. A good deal of attention is paid to the design of the book itself and to marketing strategies that will cause it to be used in these courses.[30] Yet, unlike most other kinds of publishing, text publishers define their markets not in terms of the actual reader of the book but in terms of the teacher or professor.[31] The purchaser, the student, has little power in this equation, except where his or her views may influence a professor's decision.

Based on the sense of sales potential and on their "regular polling of their markets," a large percentage of college-text editors actively search for books. Contacts are made, suggestions given. In essence, it would not be wrong to say that text editors create their own books.[32] This process is probably cheaper in the long run.

In the United States, it is estimated that the production costs of an introductory text for a college-level course is usually between $100,000 and $250,000. Given the fact that text publishers produce a relatively small number of books compared with large publishers of, say, fiction, there is considerable pressure on the editorial staff and others to guarantee that such books sell.[33] For the "elhi" market, the sheer amount of money and risks involved are made visible by the fact that, nearly a decade ago, for every $500,000 invested by a publisher in a text, it had to sell 100,000 copies just to break even.[34] Publishers of basal reading textbooks may perhaps play for the highest stakes here, as their start-up costs range from $10 million to $40 million. Such high costs give current basal publishers a virtual monopoly over the market.[35]

These conditions have an impact on the social relations within the firm besides that of the patriarchal structure noted earlier. Staff meetings, meetings with other editors, meetings with marketing and production staff to coordinate the production of a text, and so on—these kinds of activities tend to dominate the life of the text editor. As Coser and his coauthors so nicely phrase it, "text editors practically live in meetings."[36] Hence, text publishing will be much more bureaucratic and will have decision-making structures that are more formalized. This is partly due to the fact that textbook production is largely a routine process. Formats do not markedly differ from discipline to discipline. And, as I mentioned, the focus is primarily on producing a limited number of *large sellers* at a comparatively high price compared to fiction. Lastly, the emphasis is often on marketing a text with a standard content, a text that—with revisions and a little bit of luck—will be used for years to come.[37]

All of these elements are heightened even more in another aspect of text publishing that contributes to bureaucratization and standardization, the orchestrated production of "managed" texts. These volumes are usually written by professional writers, with some "guidance" from graduate students and academics, although such volumes often bear the name of a well-known professor. Closely coordinated are text and graphics, language and reading levels, and the main text and an instructor's manual. In many ways, these are books without formal authors. Ghostwritten under conditions of stringent cost controls, geared to what will sell, not necessarily to what is most important to know, managed texts have been finding a place in many college classrooms. While the dreams of some publishers that such texts will solve their financial problems have not been totally realized, the managed text is a significant phenomenon and deserves a good deal of critical attention not only at the college level but also in elementary and secondary schools, since the managed text is not at all absent in these areas, to say the least.[38]

Even with the difficulty some managed texts have had in making the anticipated high profits, there will probably be more centralized control over writing and over the entire process of publishing material for classroom use. The effect, according to Coser, Kadushin, and Powell, will be "an even greater homogenization of texts at a college level,"[39] something we can expect at the elementary and high school level as well.[40] In fact, even after reviewing different sets of basal series extensively for many weeks, teachers and administrators often find it very difficult to tell one set from another, because of the similarity of organization and content.[41]

These points demonstrate some of the important aspects of day-to-day life within publishing. With all the meetings, the planning, growing sampling of markets, the competition, and so forth, one would expect that this would have a profound impact on the content of volumes. This is the case, but perhaps not quite in the way one might think. We need to be very careful here about assuming that there is simple and overt censorship of material. The process is much more complicated than that. Even though existing research does not go into detail about such things within the college-text industry specifically, one can infer what happens from its discussion of censorship in the larger industry.

In the increasingly conglomerate-owned publishing field at large, censorship and ideological control as we commonly think of them are less of a problem than might be anticipated. It is not ideological uniformity or some political agenda that accounts for many of the ideas that are ultimately made or not made available to the larger public. Rather, it is the infamous "bottom line" that counts. As Coser, Kadushin, and Powell state: "Ultimately . . . if there is any censorship, it concerns profitability. Books that are not profitable, no matter what their subject, are not viewed favorably."[42]

This is not an inconsequential concern. In the publishing industry as a whole, only three out of every ten books are marginally profitable; only thirty percent manage to break even. The rest lose money.[43] Further, it has become clear that sales of textbooks in particular have actually been decreasing. If we take as a baseline the years of 1968 to, say, 1976, costs had risen considerably, but sales at a college level had fallen 10%. The same is true for the "elhi" text market; coupled with rising costs was a drop in sales of 11.2%[44] (this may have changed for the better given recent sales figures). If we speak specifically of basal textbooks, beyond the leading five basal publishers, which control over eighty percent of the market,[45] ten publishers compete for the remaining $8 million.[46] With start-up costs so high and with revision costs estimated at between $5 million to $8 million,[47] issues of profit are in fact part of a national set of choices within corporate logic.

If this is the case for publishing in general, and probably—in large part—for college-text production, is this case generalizable to those standardized secondary and, especially, elementary textbooks I pointed to earlier? Are market, profit, and internal relations more important than ideological concerns? Here we must answer: Only in part.

The economics and politics of elementary- and secondary-school text production are somewhat more complicated. While there is no official federal government sponsorship of specific curriculum content in the United States (as there is in those countries where ministries of education mandate a standard course of study), the structures of a national curriculum are produced by the marketplace and by state intervention in other ways. Perhaps the most important aspect of this is to be found in the various models of state adoption now extant.

As many know from personal experience, in quite a few states—most often in the southern tier around to the western sun-belt—textbooks for use in the major subject areas must be approved by state agencies or committees, or they are reviewed and a limited number are selected as recommended for use in schools. If local school districts select material from such an approved list, they are often reimbursed for a significant portion of the purchase cost. Because of this, even where texts are not mandated, there is a good deal to be gained by local schools in a time of economic crisis if they do in fact ultimately choose an approved volume. The cost savings here, obviously, are not inconsequential.

Yet it is not only here that the economics of cultural distribution operates. Publishers themselves, simply because of good business practice, must by necessity aim their text-publishing practices towards those states with such state adoption policies. The simple fact of getting one's volume on such a list can mean all the difference in a text's profitability. Thus, for instance, sales to California and Texas can account for over twenty percent of the total sales of any particular book—a considerable percentage in the highly competitive world of elementary- and secondary-school book publishing and selling. Due to this, the writing, editing, promotion, and general orientation and strategy of such production is quite often aimed toward guaranteeing a place on the list of state-approved material. Since this is the case, the political and ideological climate of these primarily southern states often determines the content and form of the purchased curriculum throughout the rest of the nation. And since a textbook series often takes years to both write and produce and, as I noted earlier, can be very costly when production costs are totaled, "publishers want [the] assurance of knowing that their school book series will sell before they commit large budgets to these undertakings."[48]

Yet even here the situation is complicated considerably, especially by the fact that agencies of the state apparatus are important sites of ideological struggle. These very conflicts may make it very difficult for publishers to determine a simple reading of the needs of "financial capital." Often, for instance, given the uncertainty of a market, publishers may be loath to make decisions based on the political controversies or "needs" of any one state, especially in highly charged curriculum areas. A good example is provided by the California "creationism versus evolutionism" controversy, where a group of "scientific creationists" supported by the political and ideological Right, sought to make all social studies and science texts give equal weight to creationist and evolutionary theories.

Even when California's board of education, after much agonizing and debate, recommended "editorial qualifications" that were supposed to meet the objections of creationist critics of the textbooks, the framework for text adoption was still very unclear and subject to many different interpretations. Did it require or merely allow discussion of creation theory? Was a series of editorial changes that qualified the discussions of evolution in the existing texts all that was required? Given this ambiguity and the volatility of the issue in which the "winning position" was unclear, publishers "resisted undertaking the more substantial effort of incorporating new information into their materials."[49] In the words of one observer: "Faced with an unclear directive, and one that might be reversed at any moment, publishers were reluctant to invest in change. They eventually yielded to the minor editorial adjustments adopted by the board, but staunchly resisted the requirement that they discuss creation in their social science texts."[50] Both economic and ideological forces enter here in important ways, both between the firms and their markets and undoubtedly within the firms themselves.

Notice what this means if we are to fully understand how specific cultural goods are produced and distributed for our public schools. We would need to unpack the logic of a fairly complicated set of interrelationships. How does the political economy of publishing itself generate particular economic and ideological needs? How and why do publishers respond to the needs of the "public?" Who determines what this "public" is?[51] How do the internal politics of state adoption policies work? What are the processes of selecting people and interests to sit on such committees? How are texts sold at a local level? What is the actual process of text production from the commissioning of a project to revisions and editing to promotion and sales? How and for what reasons are decisions on this made? Only by going into considerable detail with each of these questions can we begin to see how a particular groups' cultural capital is commodified and made available (or not made available) in schools throughout the country.[52]

My discussion of the issues of state adoption policies and my raising of the questions above are not meant to imply that all of the material found in our public schools will be simply a reflection of existing cultural and economic inequalities. After all, if texts were totally reliable defenders of the existing ideological, political, and economic order, they would not be such a contentious area currently. Industry and conservative groups have made an issue of what knowledge is now taught in schools precisely because there *are* progressive elements within curricula and texts.[53] This is partly due to the fact that the authorship of such material is often done by a particular segment of the new middle class, with its own largely liberal ideological interests, its own contradictory consciousness, its own elements of what Gramsci might call good and bad sense, ones that will not be identical to those embodied in profit maximization or ideological uniformity. To speak theoretically, there will be relatively autonomous interests in specific cultural values within the groups of authors and editors who work for publishers. These values may be a bit more progressive than one might anticipate from the market structure of text production. This will surely work against total standardization and censorship.[54]

These kinds of issues—concerning who writes and edits texts, whether they are totally controlled by the complicated market relations and state policies surrounding text publishing, and what the contradictory forces are at work—all clearly need further elaboration. My basic aim has been to demonstrate how recent research on the ways in which culture is commodified can serve as a platform for thinking about some of our own dilemmas as teachers and researchers in education who are concerned with the dynamics of cultural capital.

III.

So far, I have employed some of the research on book publishing to help understand an issue that is of great import to educators—how and by whom the texts that dominate the curriculum come to be the way they are. As I mentioned at the very outset of this chapter, however, we need to see such analyses as a serious contribution to a larger theoretical debate about cultural processes and products as well. In this concluding section, let me try to make this part of my argument about the political economy of culture clear.

External economic and political pressures are not somewhere "out there" in some vague abstraction called the economy. As recent commentators have persuasively argued, in our society hegemonic forms are not often imposed from outside by a small group of corporate owners who sit around each day plotting how to "do in" workers, women, and people of color. Some of this plotting may go on, of course. But just as significant are the routine bases of our daily decisions, in our homes, stores, offices, and factories. To speak somewhat technically, dominant relations are reconstituted on an ongoing basis by the actions we take and the decisions we make in on our own local and small areas of life. Rather than an economy being out there, it is right here. We rebuild it routinely in our social interaction. Rather than ideological domination and the relations of cultural capital being something that is imposed on us from above, we reintegrate them within our everyday discourse merely by following our commonsense needs and desires as we go about making a living, finding sustenance and entertainment, and so on.[55]

These abstract arguments are important to the points I want to make. For while a serious theoretical structure is either absent or hidden within the data presented by the research I have drawn upon, a good deal of this research does document some of the claims made in these abstract arguments. As Coser, Kadushin, and Powell put it in their discussion of why particular decisions are made,

> For the most part, what directly affects an editor's daily routine is not corporate ownership or being one division of a large multi-divisional publishing house. Instead, on a day-to-day basis, editorial behavior is most strongly influenced by the editorial policies of the house and the relationship among departments and personnel *within* the publishing house or division.[56]

This position may not seem overly consequential, yet its theoretic import is great. Encapsulated within a changing set of market relations that set limits on what is considered rational behavior on the part of its participants, editors and other employees have "relative autonomy." They are partly free to pursue the internal needs of their craft and to follow the logic of the internal demands within the publishing house itself. The past histories of gender, class, and race relations, and the actual "local" political economy of publishing, set the boundaries within which these decisions are made and in large part determine who will make the decisions. To return to my earlier point about text editors usually having their roots in the sales department, we can see that the internal labor market in text publishing, the ladder upon which career mobility depends, means that in these firms, sales will be in the forefront ideologically and economically. "Finance capital" dominates, not only because the economy out there mandates it, but because of the historical connections among mobility patterns within firms, because of rational decision making based on external competition, political dynamics, and internal information, and thus because of the kinds of discourse that tend to dominate the meetings and conversations among all the people involved within the organizational structure of the text publisher.[57] This kind of analysis makes it more complicated, of course. But surely it is more elegant and more grounded in reality than some of the more mechanistic theories about the economic control of culture, theories that have been a bit too readily accepted. This analysis manages to preserve the efficacy of the economy while granting some autonomy to the internal bureaucratic and biographical structure of individual publishers, and at the same time recognizes the political economy of gendered labor that exists as well.

Many areas remain that I have not focused upon here, of course. Among the most important of these is the alteration in the very technology of publishing. Just as the development and use of print "made possible the growth of literary learning and journals" and thereby helped to create the conditions for individual writers and artists to emerge out of the more collective conditions of production that dominated guilds and workshops,[58] so too would one expect that the changes in the technology of text production and the altered social and authorial relations that are evolving from them will have a serious impact on books. At the very least, given the sexual division of labor in publishing, new technologies can have a large bearing on the de-skilling and re-skilling of those "female enclaves" I mentioned earlier.[59]

Further, even though I have directed my attention primarily to the "culture and commerce" surrounding the production of one particular cultural commodity—the standarized text used for tertiary- and elhi-level courses—it still remains an open question as to exactly how the economic and ideological elements I have outlined work through some of the largest of all text markets, those for the elementary and secondary schools. However, in order to go significantly further we clearly need a more adequate theory of the relationship between the political and economic (to say nothing of the cultural) spheres in education. Thus, the state's position as a site for class, race, and gender conflicts, how these struggles are "resolved" within the state apparatus, how publishers respond to these conflicts and resolutions, and ultimately what impact these resolutions or accords have on the questions surrounding officially sponsored texts and knowledge—all of these need considerably more deliberation.[60] The recent work of Carnoy and Dale on the interrelations between education and the state, and Offe's analyses of the state's role in negative selection, may provide important avenues of investigation here.[61]

This points to a significant empirical agenda, as well. What is required now is a long-term *and* theoretically and politically grounded ethnographic investigation to follow a curriculum artifact such as a textbook from its writing to its selling (and then to its use). Not only would this be a major contribution to our understanding of the relationship among culture, politics, and economy, it is also absolutely essential if we are to act in ways that alter the kinds of knowledge considered legitimate for transmission in our schools.[62] As long as the text dominates curricula, to ignore it as simply not worthy of serious attention and serious struggle is to live in a world divorced from reality.

Notes

1. Raymond Williams, *Marxism and Literature* (New York: Oxford University Press, 1977), p. 19. See also, Michael W. Apple and Lois Weis, eds., *Ideology and Practice in Schooling* (Philadelphia: Temple University Press, 1983), especially chap. 1.

2. Janet Wolff, *The Social Production of Art* (London: Macmillan, 1981), p. 47.

3. I have described this in more detail in Michael W. Apple, ed., *Cultural and Economic Reproduction in Education: Essays on Class, Ideology and the State* (Boston: Routledge and Kegan Paul, 1982). For further analysis of this, see Williams, *Marxism and Literature;* Colin Sumner, *Reading Ideologies* (New York: Macmillan, 1979); G. A. Cohen, *Karl Marx's Theory of History: A Defense* (Princeton, N.J.: Princeton University Press, 1978); and Paul Hirst, *On Law and Ideology* (London: Macmillan, 1979).

4. See Todd Gitlin, "Television's Screens: Hegemony in Transition," in Apple, ed., *Cultural and Economic Reproduction in Education.* The British journal *Screen* has been in the forefront of such analyses. See also, Will Wright, *Sixguns and Society* (Berkeley, Calif.: University of California Press, 1975). An even greater number of investigations of literature exist, of course. For representative approaches, see Terry Eagleton, *Marxism and Literary Criticism* (Berkeley, Calif.: University of California Press, 1976).

5. Michael W. Apple, *Ideology and Curriculum,* 2d ed. (Boston: Routledge and Kegan Paul, 1990). It is important to realize, however, that educational institutions are *not* merely engaged in transmission or distribution. They are also primary sites for the *production* of technical/administrative knowledge. The contradiction between distribution and production is one of the constitutive tensions educational institutions try to solve, usually unsuccessfully. For arguments about the school's role in the production of cultural capital, see Michael W. Apple, *Education and Power,* revised ARK Edition (Boston: Routledge and Kegan Paul, 1985), especially chap. 2.

6. Pierre Bourdieu and Jean-Claude Passeron, *Reproduction in Education, Society and Culture* (Beverly Hills, Calif.: Sage, 1977), and Basil Bernstein, *Class, Codes and Control,* vol. 3 (Boston: Routledge and Kegan Paul, 1977).

7. For an analysis of recent theoretical and empirical work on the connections between education and cultural, economic, and political power, see Apple, *Education and Power.*

8. Paul Goldstein, *Changing the American Schoolbook* (Lexington, Mass.: D. C. Heath, 1978), p. 1. On which subjects are taught the most, see John I. Goodland, *A Place Called School* (New York: McGraw-Hill, 1983).

9. I do not want to ignore the importance of the massive number of textbook analyses that concern themselves with, say, racism and sexism. Although significant, these are usually limited to the question of balance in content, not the relationship between economic and cultural power. Some of the best analyses of the content and form of educational materials can be found in Apple and Weis, eds., *Ideology and Practice in Schooling.* See also Sherry Keith, "Politics of Textbook Selection," Institute for Research on Educational Finance and Governance, Stanford University, April 1981. Among the best recent critical studies of textbooks are Allan Luke, *Literacy, Textbooks and Ideology* (Philadelphia: Falmer Press, 1988), and Patrick Shannon, *Broken Promises: Reading Instruction in Twentieth Century America* (Granby, Mass.: Bergin and Garvey, 1989).

10. Lewis Coser, Charles Kadushin, and Walter Powell, *Books: The Culture and Commerce of Publishing* (New York: Basic Books, 1982), p. 3.

11. Ibid., p. 7.

12. Lucien Febvre and Henri-Jean Martin, *The Coming of the Book* (London: New Left Books, 1976), p. 109. As Febvre and Martin make clear, however, in the fifteen and sixteenth centuries printers and publishers also acted as "the protectors of literary men," published daring books, and frequently sheltered authors accused of heresy. See p. 150.

13. Ibid.

14. Ibid., p. 44.

15. Ibid., p. 54.

16. Wendy Griswold, "American Character and the American Novel: An Expansion of Reflection Theory in the Sociology of Literature," *American Journal of Sociology* 86 (January 1981): 742.

17. Ibid., p. 748.

18. Ibid., pp. 748–49.

19. See Ian Watt, *The Rise of the Novel* (Berkeley, Calif.: University of California Press, 1974), and Raymond Williams, *The Long Revolution* (London: Chatto and Windus, 1961).

20. Griswold, "American Character and the American Novel," p. 743.

21. Leonard Shatzkin, *In Cold Type* (Boston: Houghton and Mifflin, 1982), pp. 1–2. For estimated figures for the years after 1980, see John P. Dessauer, *Book Industry Trends, 1982* (New York: Book Industry Study Group, Inc., 1982).

22. Coser, Kadushin and Powell, *Books,* p. 273. While I shall be focusing on text production here, we should not assume that texts are the only books used in elementary, secondary, and college markets. The expanding market of other material can have a strong influence in publishing decisions. In fact, some mass-market paperbacks are clearly prepared with both school and college sales in the forefront of their decisions. Thus, it is not unusual for publishers to produce a volume with very different covers depending on the audience for which it is aimed. See Benjamin M. Compaine, *The Book Industry in Transition: An Economic Study of Book Distribution and Marketing* (White Plains, N.Y.: Knowledge Industry Publications, 1978), p. 95.

23. Shatzkin, *In Cold Type,* p. 63.

24. Coser, Kadushin, and Powell, *Books,* p. 273.

25. Goldstein, *Changing The American Schoolbook,* p. 61.

26. Coser, Kadushin, and Powell, *Books,* p. 100.

27. Ibid., pp. 154–55.

28. Ibid., p. 101.

29. Coser, Kadushin, and Powell, however, do report that most editors, no matter what kind of house they work for, tend to be overwhelmingly liberal. Ibid., p. 113.

30. Ibid., p. 30.

31. Ibid., p. 56.

32. Ibid., p. 135.

33. Ibid., pp. 56–57.

34. Goldstein, *Changing The American Schoolbook,* p. 56.

35. Kenneth Goodman et al., *Report Card on Basal Readers* (Katonah, N.Y.: Richard C. Owen, 1988), pp. 45–50.

36. Coser, Kadushin, and Powell, *Books,* p. 123.

37. Ibid., p. 190.

38. Keith, "Politics of Textbook Selection," p. 12.

39. Coser, Kadushin, and Powell, *Books,* p. 366.

40. I have discussed this at greater length in Michael W. Apple, "Curriculum in the Year 2000: Tensions and Possibilities," *Phi Delta Kappan* 64 (January 1983): 321–26.

41. Roger Farr, Michael Tully, and Deborah Powell, "The Evaluation and Selection of Basal Readers," *Elementary School Journal* 87 (January 1987): 267–81.

42. Coser, Kadushin, and Powell, *Books,* p. 181.

43. Compaine, *The Book Industry in Transition,* p. 20.

44. Ibid., pp. 33–34.

45. Goodman et al., *Report Card on Basal Readers.*

46. R. Auckerman, *The Basal Reading Approach to Reading* (New York: John Wiley, 1987).

47. James Squire, "A Response to the *Report Card on Basal Readers,*" paper presented at the Annual Meeting of the National Council of Teachers of English, Los Angeles, California, November 1987.

48. Keith, "Politics of Textbook Selection," p. 8.

49. Goldstein, *Changing the American Schoolbook,* p. 47.

50. Ibid., pp. 48–49.

51. For an interesting discussion of how economic needs help determine what counts as the public for which a specific cultural product is intended, see the treatment of changes in the radio sponsorship of country music in Richard A. Peterson, "The Production of Cultural Change: The Case of Contemporary Country Music," *Social Research* 45 (Summer 1978): 292–314. See also Paul Di Maggio and Michael Unseem, "The Arts in Class Reproduction," in Apple, ed., *Cultural and Economic Reproduction in Education,* pp. 181–201.

52. I have discussed the relationship between the commodification process and the dynamics of cultural capital at greater length in Apple, *Education and Power.*

53. Ibid., especially chap. 5.

54. A related argument is made in Douglas Kellner, "Network Television and American Society," *Theory and Society* 10 (January 1981): 31–62. See also Philip Wexler, "Structure, Text and Subject: A Critical Sociology of School Knowledge," in Apple, ed., *Cultural and Economic Reproduction in Education,* pp. 275–303.

55. This is discussed in greater detail in Apple, ed., *Cultural and Economic Reproduction in Education.*

56. Coser, Kadushin, and Powell, *Books,* p. 185.

57. Wexler's argument that texts need to be seen as the result of a long process of transformative activity is clearly related here. In essence, what I have been attempting to demonstrate is part of the structure in which such transformations occur and which makes some more likely to occur than others. See Wexler, "Structure, Text and Subject," and Philip Wexler, *Social Analysis and Education* (New York: Routledge, 1987).

58. Wolff, *The Social Production of Art,* p. 36.

59. The relationship among de-skilling, re-skilling, and the sexual division of labor is treated in more depth in Michael W. Apple, *Teachers and Texts* (New York: Routledge, 1988). See also David Gordon, Richard Edwards, and Michael Reich, *Segmented Work, Divided Workers: The Historical Transformation of Labor in the United States* (New York: Cambridge University Press, 1982).

60. See. for example, Apple, *Education and Power;* Roger Dale, Geoff Esland, Ross Furguson, and Madeleine MacDonald, eds., *Education and the State,* vol. 1 (Barcombe, England: The Falmer Press, 1981); Michael W. Apple, "Common Curriculum and State Control," *Discourse* 2, no. 4 (1982): 1–10; and Michael W. Apple, "Social Crisis and Curriculum Accords," *Educational Theory* 38 (Spring 1988): 191–201.

61. I am indebted to Dan Liston for documenting the possible power of Offe's work. See Daniel Liston, *Capitalist Schools* (New York: Routledge, 1989); Martin Carnoy, "Education, Economy and the State," in Apple, ed., *Cultural and Economic Reproduction in Education,* pp. 79–126; Roger Dale, "Education and The Capitalist State: Contributions and Contradictions," in Apple, ed., *Cultural and Economic Reproduction in Education,* pp. 127–161; and Roger Dale, *The State and Education Policy* (Bristol, Pa.: The Open University Press, 1989).

62. I do not want to imply that what is "transmitted" in schools is necessarily what is in the text. Nor do I want at all to claim that what is taught is wholly "taken in" by students. For analyses of teacher and student rejection, mediation, or transformation of the form and/or content of curriculum, see Paul Willis, *Learning to Labour* (Westmead, England: Saxon House, 1977); Robert Everhart, *Reading, Writing and Resistance* (Boston: Routledge and Kegan Paul, 1983); Michael W. Apple, *Teachers and Texts;* and the chapters by Linda McNeil, Andrew Gitlin, and Lois Weis, in Apple and Weis, eds., *Ideology and Practice in Schooling.*

3

Texts and High Tech:
Computers, Gender, and Book Publishing

Linda K. Christian-Smith

When one speaks of books, that which is often conjured up are images of
sheathes of paper bound between somber or very colorful covers, and the antici-
pation of a good read. While books have this physical and emotional dimension,
they also have an economic aspect as commodities produced to make a profit.[1]
Books can also be thought of as the point of convergence of sets of processes
and relationships that are known as book publishing. Like any other segment
of commodity production, publishing has its own means of producing its product, books, as well as its own patterns of interaction between the people making
books and the larger society in which publishing takes place[2] In this volume,
Apple notes that a sexual division of labor characterizes publishing, and that
women are most often found in clerical and lower editorial eschelons. Although
some women may have positions involving more editorial control, their responsibilities rarely extend to formulating policy or long-range planning. There are
still other ways in which publishing is politically important.

From its earliest beginnings, book publishing has constantly sought to
improve and control the processes of printing books through the use of technology. This quest for better technology has taken on an urgency in light of the
recent acquisition of publishing houses by multinational conglomerates whose
interests center on profit making. According to Shatzkin and Whiteside,[3] publishing is now changing from a labor-intensive to a capital-intensive industry.
The latest chapter in the technological history of publishing is currently being
written by the computer. There exist today totally computer-integrated publishing systems. This is significantly altering not only how books are published,
but also the nature and conditions of work in publishing today.[4]

This chapter is concerned with the impact of computerization on one aspect
of commercial book publishing—transforming a manuscript into its published
form. To understand the implications of computer-aided publishing it is necessary to look at the social, economic, and technological aspects of publishing.
Accordingly, I situate publishing within the larger economic context, then
sketch the technological history of publishing and describe the electronic publi-

cation of books. I analyze how the labor process associated with publishing is being changed through computerization. Next, I focus on the impact of the new technology on women workers. I then present evidence of women workers' resistance to computerization and provide some concluding remarks.

Who Owns Whom: Corporate
Ownership of Publishing

Publishing has always been both a cultural activity and a business. A frequent image of book publishing is the publisher or editor who lovingly supervises a manuscript's journey to becoming a book. This image must be expanded to include the fact that editors in this traditional sense are being steadily replaced by professional managers having technological, business, or legal backgrounds.[5] These developments have occurred in the wake of the "merger mania" of the 1970s and 1980s, a mania that has concentrated ownership of the "culture industry" (music, film, television and book publishing) in the hands of a few multinational corporations, thus creating media conglomerates.[6] However, the trend toward multinational ownership of book publishing actually began in the 1960s with the merger of Alfred Knopf and Random House, and, later that of Random House and RCA. Through these mergers the interests of electronic companies were joined with book publishing.

In 1959 the privately owned Random House went public with a stock issue in order to secure the company's holdings for family survivors in the event of the death of partners Bennett Cerf and Donald Klopfer.[7] Random House merged with Knopf in 1961, and by the mid 1960s various large electronics companies had also become interested in the publishing business. These interests were stimulated by the existence of enormous federal funds available to schools for program development. The electronics companies saw tremendous profit in the merging of book production with their plans for computerized teaching machines in the schools. The major publishers held the key because they controlled the access to books whose content could be transformed into the software run by the computers.[8] The publishers also had highly developed systems of distribution and easy access to schools.

In the late 1960s Random House was approached by RCA because of its lucrative line of juvenile books and strategic position within the elementary and high school (elhi) market. According to Cerf, the May 1966 merger with RCA was the result of "our conviction that publishing and electronics are natural partners."[9] Following this merger, many other family-owned publishing houses became segments of electronics-communications corporations. CBS acquired Holt, Rinehart & Winston, and Praeger. Xerox, which had also entered the computer industry, bought the large textbook publisher Ginn. Following suit, other electronics firms bought Van Nostrand, Reinhold, American Book Company, and McCormick-Mathers. ITT purchased Bobbs-Merrill and Howard

Sams.[10] However, RCA's and Xerox's visions of an electronic schoolhouse would not be realized in the climate of the Vietnam War, and with the dwindling federal funding of education. Such mergers, however, have left their indelible mark upon today's publishing industry.

Recent mergers have these characteristics. The communications-electronics complex now controls much of the culture industry through ownership.[11] For example, Gulf + Western not only owns Paramount pictures and Desilu Productions, but is the world's largest publisher by virtue of its acquisition of Prentice-Hall and Simon and Schuster.[12] Electronics-based parent companies have brought big-business mentalities to publishing. According to Ron Busch, of Pocket Books, "With all the conglomerate money in publishing today, it's like playing monopoly."[13] Busch's observation characterizes not only the big money in publishing, but also the prevailing entrepreneural mentality. The bottom line, five-year plans, and market research now characterize book publishing.

Corporate ownership has also brought to publishing the techniques of production, marketing, and distribution commonly used in industrial production and offices. Communications-electronics corporations are heavily computerized. Many have long used central computerized inventory, accounting, ordering and automated parts of their production process. The latter is evident in the film, television, and music industries which have developed computer-driven videotape machinery in television studios, computer imaging for film production, and electronically synthesized music.[14] Electronic corporations have long regarded offices as the central market for their products. The commercial publishing office represents a largely undeveloped market for electronic products and office systems, which Card[15] estimated to have a three billion dollar potential. In purchasing publishing houses, parent corporations have also acquired a new market for their products.

Book publishing can then be regarded as the point of convergence of these tendencies within the communications-electronics industry. However, according to Wallace and Kalleberg[16] there are also tensions within these developments emanating from the publishing industry itself, which, historically, has not accepted new technologies without resistance.[17]

Technology and Publishing

Apple (in this volume) relates that from the very earliest days of publishing books were merchandise designed to help someone earn a living. Gutenberg's invention, five hundred years ago, of a moveable type that could be used many times before having to be recast in molten lead paved the way for the quest for new technologies to produce finer-quality books more quickly and more economically.[18] Gutenberg's "hot type" process prevailed until well into the nineteenth century.[19] It was quite common for a single craftsperson to perform most of the tasks of book production, such as setting and editing the type by hand, engraving plates, preparing the galleys (the metal trays into which type is placed), running the press, and printing the pages. This print process was slow and very labor-intensive. Much of this changed with the introduction of the linotype machine by the Mergenthaler Company in 1886. The linotype was one of the more frequently used varieties of typecasters. This technology transformed typesetting from hand work to an automated series of processes that would produce type in a continuous line in a galley tray ready to be handset. In the late 1950s both the linotype machine and its operator disappeared from the composing room with the appearance of teletypesetting (TTS) machines and the introduction of phototypesetters in the newspaper industry. Teletypsetting involves making a perforated tape for wire transmission between various offices. Through the use of a basic typewriter keyboard, the process of typesetting was even further simplified.

In the 1960s the computer was introduced into the newspaper composing room bringing an end to the hot-metal-type processes that had dominated printing for five hundred years.[20] Typists using special electronic typewriters equipped with perforators could impress characters on computer tape. The computer could then process the data, store it, or transfer it to high-speed typesetting machines that converted the tape into film ready for printing. Because this process uses photographic film rather than cast-metal type, it has become known as "cold type." When linked to phototypsetting equipment, computer software could arrange text into columns precisely as they would appear in the newspaper. Cold-type processes automated the remaining craft elements of printing and obliterated the traditional craft of typesetting.[21] Other technological developments impacted on copy writing and the editorial aspects of newspaper production as well. Word processing equipment made it possible for reporters to write and edit their stories on video display terminals.[22] The final version could then be stored on tape or diskette, thus eliminating the need for copy typists. With automatic page- format available on the screen, computers also eliminated the traditional skilled work of "makeup"—the laying out of articles, headlines, and advertisements by hand before typecasting in metal.

These technologies have resulted in almost totally computer-intergrated commercial newspaper publishing and have paved the way for electronic book publishing as well. These developments, coupled with the immense financial resources of parent corporations, are making the automation of almost every aspect of book publishing a reality.

Texts and High Tech

Although large commercial publishers have been using computers in the newspaper industry for at least fifteen years, it has only been with the development of the minicomputer and complex software that computer-integrated book publishing has been possible.[23] According to Frank[24] electronic publishing is seen by upper-level management as a means to reduce overall costs, publish books faster, and gain an advantage in a very competitive industry. Today's publishers are using computers to aid in the handling of day-to-day business and as tools for manuscript development and production. Electronic publishing in the form of integrated text-management systems combines state-of-the-art computer technology with book-editing, production, and design software aids to automate book publishing from editing through the makeup of finished pages.

The most sophisticated integrated text-management systems feature one or several central minicomputers or small mainframes that are connected to several "intelligent terminals," where the editing is done. Electronic book publishing can start with writers who have written their manuscripts on computer, and who transmit them electronically over the phone lines or send diskettes or magnetic tape through the mail. However, unless the writer and the publisher possess the same word-processing software and computer, the electronic manuscript must be converted into an acceptable form through costly processes. To date, the conversion aspect of electronic publishing is still being developed.[25] More commonly, a manuscript arrives typewritten or as a printout. A device such as Compugraphics's MCS TextSaver can be used to "read" a typewritten page electronically in any of the eight most common printer/typewriter print styles, and to transfer it electronically to a computer for storage.[26]

At that point the file (text) can be retrieved for editing. Computers have transformed the work of editing as well. The Penta System has a full-feature editor's work-station, where editors can edit on the screen or on paper and then transmit the file to the composing room. There the printing codes are inserted and a computerized makeup terminal produces copy ready to be typeset.[27] Another system, ViewTech, takes this one step further by permitting users to create, display. and edit pages with both text and graphics in typeset form on the screen with its special "What-You-See-Is-What-You-Get" (WYSIWYG) feature.[28] The WYSIWYG feature permits the entering of all the necessary information at one time: photos and artwork using optical character recognition equipment, and the text from magnetic tape or disk. Once all these elements are entered, the computer can automatically arrange the page using batch processing, or the elements can be arranged by hand using interactive page processing.[29] The actual printing of the book can be accomplished by electronic link to the new high-speed laser printers and their laser-based imaging systems which function like very sophisticated photocopiers. One such system, Tegra's Genesis, produces typographic-quality images and high-resolution graphics.[30] Computerized inventory, accounting, and ordering systems complete the high-tech book publishing process.

The cost of acquiring such technology is not inexpensive; it currently requires the kinds of financial resources provided by the wealthy corporations that back publishing. The cost of text-management systems can be anywhere from $25,000 to $100,00 depending on the degree of integration of electronic publishing desired.[31] Typesetting systems have a $30,000 to $100,000 price-tag. However, an incentive does exist for publishers to automate; savings of up to $200.00 per page can be realized through these systems. A Booz, Allen, and Hamilton study of companies contemplating electronic publishing[32] calculates that the net savings after expenses based on three hundred workers would be anywhere from $2,000 to $5,800 per person per year.

Commercial publishers are automated to varying degrees. McGraw Hill has developed equipment that allows the publisher to accept manuscripts written on computer diskettes from fifty different computers. The remainder of the production process is fully automated. Springhouse was the first publisher to pilot the Penta System and is close to total automation.[33] Sybex, a heavily automated book publisher, will replace standard techniques of illustration with computer-graphics systems. At Osborne a Ward's catalogue was produced by "burning" printing plates from disk, thereby eliminating half the production costs.[34]

Thus far I have described computerization in book publishing. This discussion has raised several important questions about work in electronic publishing houses: How has computerization changed the labor process of publishing? What kinds of changes in relations have occurred between people working in publishing? What has been the impact of technology on women workers? What does publishing have in common with office work? The following several sections will address these questions.

Labor Process, Publishing, and Gender

While it is true that computer technology can speed the publication of books and is an important factor in paring down production costs, it has had contradictory consequences for those who work in publishing, in particular for women. Computerization has resulted in the standardization and routinization of many aspects of book production and has de-skilled many workers. Technical control of work processes is increasing as well. These factors have transformed commercial book production from a highly skilled craft, put the terminal in control, and sharpened the parallels between book publishing and clerical work. These developments have a special meaning for women workers because they tend to outnumber men two to one in publishing,[35] and have the jobs most affected by new technologies.

According to Edwards,[36] technical control "involves designing machinery and planning the flow of work to minimize the problem of transforming labor power into labor as well as to maximize the purely physically based possibilities for achieving efficiencies." Edwards further argues that although mechanization often paves the way for technical control, technical control tends to be the outcome of machine design and not merely that of the presence of machinery. Technical control is also an important element in making an industry more profitable. Computerization is accomplishing the latter goal in the book-publishing industry through the way it has restructured work, eliminated jobs, speeded up production, and provided the means for increased control over workers.[37]

Technical control of the book-production process has been gradual. Predecessors can be seen in the old teletypesetting machines, which had the capability of accurately counting and recording the number of lines of tape produced as well as speeding up the production process.[38] Today's computerization has made possible a tighter control over work. Some of the integrated text-management systems can link almost every machine in the publishing house to the main computer. Most systems have a file structure that not only provides the status of a project but also can record the dates, times, and kinds of work on a project. Through software and machines, management can monitor almost every aspect of book production.

I have previously discussed how printing became highly mechanized and standardized. In a similar manner, manuscript preparation and layout stages are standardized through text-management systems.[39] Formerly, personnel working with manuscripts were called copy editors or layout designers. The change in their work is reflected in the fact that today they are designated "operators" of machines.[40] While most of these text management systems have an interactive component in which "operators" are involved in the details of each page's layout, most systems can function with little human interaction. The computer can arrange the page automatically using batch page processing. A distinctive feature of many text management systems is that they are "user friendly," and thus take little time and training to learn.[41]

One aspect of electronic publishing that has not totally automated is "format codes," which determine how the information will look once the computer has located it and it appears on the screen. Codes for carriage returns, centering lines, and underlining words, are automatically inserted into most word-processing programs. Different software use different codes for different operations. There is a movement afoot in the American Association of Publishers (AAP) to create a standard set of "generic" codes that could be embedded in all software, codes that everyone associated with publishing would use.[42] Furthermore, the New Technology Committee of the AAP is working toward industry-wide standards and author guidelines for handling manuscripts in electronic format.[43] These developments could further standardize the work of individual workers and routinize even more the organization of the book-production process.

Braverman[44] argues that one of the goals of the introduction of new technology has been the de-skilling of workers. De-skilling involves the separation of thinking through the task from executing it. De-skilling occurs through the automation, routinization, and simplification of work tasks.[45] While Braverman's de-skilling thesis illuminates important aspects of technology in the workplace, it must be expanded to account for worker resistance and gender differences in de-skilling.[46] During the Industrial Revolution in England, the Luddites violently opposed the replacement of workers by machines,[47] and currently United States Postal Workers are resisting the introduction of increasingly automated letter-sorting equipment. The study of office work in England by Crompton and Jones[48] demonstrated that men are often rapidly promoted out of routine automated work, whereas women tend to remain in these kinds of jobs. The new technologies are having a similar de-skilling effect in book publishing.

Computer-integrated publishing systems have reassembled the many separate components of various publishing tasks into a few jobs that are now largely automated. Workers can be quickly trained to use Optical Recognition Scanning equipment to avoid retyping manuscripts. Copy editors need not have traditional literary skills to do their work as computers are equipped with dictionaries, thesauruses, spelling checkers, and style and syntax sheets. After learning to use a text-management system, editors, with their specialty skills, are taken over by software. Once a system like ViewTech is learned, illustrations, designs, and "paste-up pages" can be created on-screen, processes that formerly required the attention of professional illustrators and graphic artists. ViewTech thus removes the need for the special expertise of design and production teams.[49] Software having WYSIWYG capabilities has eliminated much of the traditional work of the printing department in the production of galley proofs. New laser printers have the capacity to render the printing press obsolete, to step up the automation of printing and change the work of printers.[50]

These technological changes in the labor process of publishing is having a profound effect on both women and men. Men, who have traditionally dominated the printing aspects of publishing, have seen their jobs gradually deskilled.[51] It may be argued that traditional male editors have also experienced deskilling as well. However, the situation of women is especially acute, given their historic concentration in clerical work, and their attempts to escape what is stereotypically considered to be women's work.

When discussing the things that condition women's work, both economic and social factors emerge. In the United States women are still largely defined as wives and mothers, despite the changes in many aspects of their lives.[52] Relations between the sexes remain patriarchal and involve the dominance of men and the subordination of women. These patterns of interaction are in part anchored in an economic system characterized by maximizing profit through holding down wages and tightly controlling all aspects of work. Equally important is the differential treatment of women workers because of their perceived centrality to family life.[53] The publishing industry has been historically characterized by the paternalistic relations of male managers to female employees. While women factory workers have experienced increasing technical control of their work through automation,[54] such control is a relatively new development for women office workers.[55]

Since the nineteenth century, women have been involved in publishing through their work in independent family-owned concerns. Their traditional work has been "behind-the-scenes" infrastructure work. Women are the secretaries, proofreaders, editorial assistants, and copy editors; they work in inventory, ordering and distribution departments.[56] The work of copy and manuscript editors has traditionally offered some women entree into important editorial positions. Although women have made their greatest inroads into decision-making positions in the juvenile, trade, and mass market divisions, the top jobs are still often beyond their reach.[57]

To understand the full impact of technology on women workers in publishing, it is necessary to examine first technology and clerical work. According to Machung,[58] much of the skill involved in clerical work—such as composing, editing, and typing documents—has been obliterated by the introduction of word processors. The word processor has automated and standardized document production by building into machines standardized formats that are activated by using up a series of codes. The recent development of "boilerplates," standard models of the documents commonly used in the business world, has made the preparation of routine letters and forms merely a matter of inserting particular details. Word processors themselves have become so simplified that they require someone only with minimal typing skills and require approximately a day to learn.[59] This technology has brought women clerical workers under increasingly technical forms of control and has massively de-skilled secretarial work.[60]

Computerized text-management systems have contributed to the de-skilling of editorial work. One woman can control a computer that combines into a single task a number of editorial procedures formerly done by several people. This reintegrated work has not upgraded her skills as a majority of the new text management systems can run automatically just as well as interactively. In view of the strong tendencies toward routinization and standardization in the new publishing software, women's jobs are becoming more routine, more repetitious, and less skilled. What I have just described as women's work in publishing is equally descriptive of women's clerical work in electronic offices.[61] As editorial work becomes more and more automated, it is taking on the characteristics of the word-processing aspects of clerical work. I have described the general de-skilling of clerical work in the wake of computerization. As editing becomes redefined as word processing, women's work is de-skilled. This, combined with multinational ownership patterns—which place technologically and business-oriented people, usually males, in high-level positions—is causing the sexual stratification traditional in publishing to congeal.

Militancy at the Terminal

It would be a large mistake to think that women and men in publishing are accepting these changed work relations and conglomerate ownership. The workplace has always been the site of both formal and informal resistance. The response of male printers to new technologies has been one of massive resistance backed up by the force of a strong tradition of unionization.[62] In 1978 Houghton Mifflin authors and personnel mounted a strong resistance to a corporate take-over by Western Pacific Railroad. Their concerns had to do with fears over what this company might do to established procedures for publishing.[63] A glimpse of women's resistance to increased technical control may be seen in observations and comments of women working in the textbook department of a computerized publishing house.[64] Several women recounted how they took a long time to learn text-management systems, thus forestalling their full involvement with computerization. These women have accidentally spilled soda on the terminal, slowing down work on a manuscript; they have "fooled" the automatic key-stroke counter by holding down certain keys on the keyboard in order to relax or talk for a moment. Other women had linked up with "9 to 5," a national association for clerical workers, and had become involved in state-wide move-ments to force the enactment of legislation mandating regular breaks for video display terminal operators, better work stations, etc.[65] Some women related to me how former coworkers gained enough work experience to move to "better" jobs in less technologized, smaller publishing firms. Pat summed up the feelings of many women.

> I didn't come to work here at Parson's just to press keys. I feel just like a secretary. Get me, there's nothing wrong with being a secretary, but I was an English major in college, you know. I had these fantasies of being a big editor or someone who worked really close with authors.

Even though the women acknowledged that the new text-management systems were making it harder to resist strict control over their work, their growing resistance was becoming more organized, and held the potential of challenging patterns of work and control in their publishing house.

High Tech and the Politics of the Textbook

Whenever we pick up a book, we are holding the physical embodiment of sets of social, economic, and political relations that comprise the work of pub-lishing. We are also confronted with the fact that neither a book nor its knowl-edge is neutral or interest-free. The set of relations between the people working in publishing and the book production technology endow the textbook with economic and social meanings from the outset. Hence, whenever we read a book we are interacting with the corporate world and its values.

Thus far, I have shown how book publishing has become both an increas-ingly capital intensive and technologized industry. This is in part due to the competitive nature of the industry[66], and recent changes in ownership patterns. There now is a sharper edge to this competition due to a more pronounced emphasis on the "bottom line" in the wake of "merger mania." Insiders in publishing[67] consistently worry that the intense focus on profitability is constituting a subtle form of "censorship" through the narrowing of books published in favor of profitable ones.[68] This emphasis on the mercantile aspects of books clearly links with the computerization of the publishing industry.

The new technologies have been a factor in the de-skilling of workers, especially women, and have set in motion much militancy at the terminal. The class and gender conflicts underpinning book publishing and ownership indicate that knowledge production is a very political process. The work-related and ideological resistance of workers in this industry have their corollary in the struggles of those involved in textbook selection as discussed by Marshall in this volume. Altbach's essay presents compelling evidence for the cultural and economic hegemony that large textbook publishers exert internationally through their profit mentality. The knowledge contained in these books is shaped within the context of the increasingly profit-driven industry. That the development and publishing of the Marryshow Readers in Grenada described here by Jules is totally outside corporate publishing is not mere concidence. These books contain an implicit understanding of the way that the process of publishing imbues texts with social and economic relations that are problematic for women and men seeking to reconstruct their society.

Summary

In this chapter I have discussed the impact that technology in the form of computerization is having on the book production and how it has altered the nature of work for women and men. Microelectronically based text-management systems have evolved out of the interests of large communications conglomerates that now control substantial segments of commercial publishing. Computerization enables such publishers to cut production costs, speed up production, exert more control over workers, and, in the end, realize increased profits. Publishing, through its computerization, represents a profitable new market for microelectronics. While this new technology has de-skilled work in publishing in general, this has been especially the case in the editorial departments, which are predominantly female. Women's work in publishing is taking on more and more the characteristics of clerical work, which has also undergone massive de-skilling. I have focused on the forms of control in publishing, forms that have traditionally been highly patriarchal. I do not envision the newer technical forms of control as superseding more traditional ones. Rather, technical control continues the gradual subordination of women workers to capitalist forms. The very currency of these developments lends a certain caution to any firm predictions, although the tendencies I have discussed do characterize work in commercial book publishing.

Some have embraced computer-aided publishing as the harbinger of progress and efficiency for the publishing industry.[69] Although the text-management systems and their hardware can eliminate some of the labor-intensiveness of book production and can perhaps bring books to readers more quickly, these systems promise to make more routine and tedious the varieties of work that women perform.[70] Cerf's enthusiasm for the natural partnership between publishing and electronics must be modified in view of the dark side of technology I have described.

Notes

1. See Linda K. Christian-Smith, "Gender, Popular Culture and Curriculum," *Curriculum Inquiry* 17 (1987):365–406; and Michael W. Apple, "The Culture and Commerce of the Textbook," *Journal of Curriculum Studies* 17 (1985): 147–162.

2. For further discussion, see Louis Coser, Charles Kadushin, and Walter Powell, *Books: The Culture and Commerce of Publishing* (New York: Basic Books, 1982), and Leonard Shatzkin, *In Cold Type* (New York: Houghton Mifflin, 1982).

3. Shatzkin, *In Cold Type,* and Thomas Whiteside, *The Blockbuster Complex* (Middletown, Conn.: Wesleyan University Press, 1981).

4. These points are discussed in greater detail in Heidi Hartmann, Robert E. Kraut, and Louise Tilly, *Computer Chips and Paper Clips,* vol. 1 (Washington, DC.: National Academy Press, 1986).

5. Linda K. Christian, "The English Curriculum and Current Trends in Publishing," *English Journal* 75 (1984): 55–57; and Coser, Kadushin, and Powell, *Books.*

6. John P. Dessauer, *Book Publishing: What It Is, What It Does* (New York: R. R. Bowker, 1974).

7. See Whiteside, *The Blockbuster Complex.*

8. Ibid., p. 8.

9. Ibid.

10. Dessauer, *Book Publishing.*

11. Other media concentrations include Music Corporation of America's takeover of Putnam, Filmway's acquisition of Grosset and Dunlap, and Hearst's purchase of William Morrow. For additional discussion, see Coser, Kadushin, and Powell, *Books,* and Whiteside, *The Blockbuster Complex.*

12. Gulf + Western has historically been instrumental in persuading banks to finance the growth of conglomerates. Gulf + Western's holdings include parts manufacturing, life insurance, foundry, textiles, sugar, tobacco, and financial services as well as a larger communications block through its purchase of Paramount Pictures and Desilu Production. For an elaboration of this, see John F. Winslow, *Conglomerates Unlimited* (Bloomington: Ind.: Indiana University Press, 1973): and Madalynne Reuter and John Mutter, "Snyder Heads Gulf + Western Publishing Group, Romanos is President of S & S Trade," *Publishers Weekly,* 227 March 22, 1985, pp. 12–13.

13. Whiteside, *The Blockbuster Complex,* p. 91.

14. See Russell W, Rumberger, "The Potential Impace of Technology on the Skill Requirements of Future Jobs in the United States," in Gerald Burke and Russell W. Rumberger, eds., *The*

Future Impact of Technology on Work and Education (London: The Falmer Press, 1987), pp. 74–95.

15. David Card, "Creating Order Out of Chaos: Computer-Aided Publishing," *Electronic Business,* 12 June 1, 1986, pp. 26–27.

16. Michael Wallace and Arne L. Kalleberg, "Industrial Transformation and the Decline of Craft: The Decomposition of Skill in the Printing Industry, 1931–1978," *American Sociological Review,* 47 (1982): 307–24.

17. Andrew Zimbalist, *Case Studies in the Labor Process* (New York: Monthly Review Press, 1979).

18. Coser, Kadushin, and Powell, *Books.*

19. Zimbalist, *Case Studies.*

20. Joe Freda, "Role of Laser Printers in the In-Plant Operation," *Graphics Arts Monthly* 58 (September 1986): 68, 70.

21. Stephen Roth, *The Computer Edge: Microcomputer Trends* (New York: R. R. Bowker, 1985).

22. Zimbalist, *Case Studies.*

23. Roth, *The Computer Edge.*

24. Jerome Frank, "Toward the Total Publishing System," *Publishers Weekly,* December 7, 1984, pp. 32–40.

25. Roth, *The Computer Edge.*

26. Jerome Frank, "Electronic Publishing Captures All Eyes," *Publishers Weekly,* November 2, 1984, pp. 44–53.

27. See Frank, "Toward the Total Publishing System," and David F. Salsbury, "Will Computers Squeeze Out Books by 1990?" *Christian Science Monitor,* 76 December 5, 1983, p. 51.

28. Frank, "Electronic Publishing Captures All Eyes."

29. Lloyd H. Sappington, "Market Trend Impacts," *Graphic Arts Monthly* 58 (October 1986): 40, 42, 44, and 46.

30. Freda, "Role of Laser Printers."

31. Card, "Creating Order Out of Chaos," and John Sargent, "What's Going on Here? An In-house Market Update," *American Printer* 197 (May, 1986): 59, and 62–64.

32. Discussed in Frank, "Toward the Total Publishing System," p. 37 and passim.

33. Ibid.

34. Salsbury, "Will Computers Squeeze Out Books?"

35. Coser, Kadushin, and Powell, *Books,* p. 148.

36. Richard Edwards, *Contested Terrain: The Transformation of the Workplace in the Twentieth Century* (New York: Basic Books, 1979), p. 112.

37. That such investments are paying off is evidenced by the fact that publishing in 1985 showed a high operating profit for Gulf + Western. For a more detailed discussion, see James C. Hyatt, "G & W Earnings, on Operations Increase 5.3%," *The Wall Street Journal* March 7, 1985, p. 16.

38. Zimbalist, *Case Studies,* p. 107.

39. Frank, "Toward the Total Publishing System."

40. Frank, "Electronic Publishing Captures All Eyes."

41. *Ibid.*

42. Roth, *The Computer Edge*.

43. *Bowker Annual* (New York: R.R. Bowker, 1985).

44. Harry Braverman, *Labor and Monopoly Capital.* (New York: Monthly Review Press, 1974).

45. For elaboration, see Rosemary Crompton and Gareth Jones, *White-Collar Proletariat* (Philadelphia: Temple University Press, 1984); Edwards, *Contested Terrain;* Whiteside, *The Blockbuster Complex;* and Zimbalist, *Case Studies*.

46. This is further discussed in Veronica Beechy, "The Sexual Division of Labor and the Labor Process," in Stephen Wood ed., *The Degradation of Work?* (London: Hutchinson, 1982), pp . 54–73; Peter Cressey and John MacInnes, "Voting for Ford: Industrial Democracy and the Control of Labor," *Capital & Class* 11 (1980): 5–33; Crompton and Jones, *White-Collar Proletariat,* and Tony Elger, "Valorization and Deskilling: A Critique of Baverman," *Capital & Class* 7 (1979): 58–99.

47. Eugene Provenzo, *Beyond the Gutenberg Galaxy* (New York: Teachers College Press, 1986).

48. Crompton and Jones, *White-Collar Proletariat*.

49. Frank, "Electronic Publishing Captures All Eyes."

50. Ibid.

51. Zimbalist, *Case Studies*.

52. See Jill Lewis, "The Debate on Sex and Class," *New Left Review* 149 (1985): 108–20; and Lydia Sargent, *Women and Revolution* (Boston: South End Press, 1981).

53. It is beyond the scope of this chapter to consider the impact of family on women's work. For a discussion, see Anna Pollert, *Girls, Wives, Factory Lives.* (London: Macmillan, 1979); and Christine Griffin, *Typical Girls?* (London: Routledge and Kegan Paul, 1985).

54. More details may be found in Louise Lamphere, "'Maguiladoras': The View From the Inside," in Karen B. Sacks and Dorothy Remy, eds., *My Troubles Are Going to Have Trouble With Me* (New Brunswick, N.J.: Rutgers University Press, 1984), 228–63; and Pollert, *Girls, Wives, Factory Lives*.

55. See Jane Barker and Hazel Dowling, "Word Processing and the Transformation of Patriarchal Relations of Control in the Office," *Capital & Class* 10 (1980): 64–99; and Anne Machung, "Word Processing: Forward for Business, Backward for Women," in Sacks and Remy eds., *My Troubles Are Going to Have Trouble With Me,* pp. 125–138.

56. Coser, Kadushin, and Powell, *Books*.

57. Whiteside, *The Blockbuster Complex*.

58. Machung, "Word Processing."

59. Barker and Dowling, "Word Processing and the Transformation of the Patriarchal Relations of Control."

60. *Ibid.,* p. 97.

61. Machung, "Word Processing," p. 133.

62. Wallace and Kalleberg, "Industrial Transformation and the Decline of Craft" and Zimbalist, *Case Studies*.

63. Whiteside, *The Blockbuster Complex,* p. 125.

64. This publishing house, originally a small independent firm, was recently acquired by a large conglomerate. Because I was denied permission to conduct a full-scale investigation of the impact of computerization in this publishing house, I was confined to informal research. Several of the women with whom I spoke had been with the firm before the merger, thus possessing a "before" and "after" perspective.

65. For a thorough discussion of the health hazards for women working in highly computerized industries, see Wendy Chavkin, *Double Exposure* (New York: Monthly Review Press, 1984).

66. Shatzkin, *In Cold Type,* p. 63.

67. Whiteside, *The Blockbuster Complex,* p. 91.

68. My research into the political economy of teen romance fiction provides evidence for the link between this sector of book publishing and the often conservative gender perspectives of romance fiction publishers. For a more detailed discussion, see Linda K. Christian-Smith, *Becoming a Woman Through Romance* (New York: Routledge, Chapman and Hall, 1990).

69. Provenzo, in *Beyond the Gutenberg Galaxy,* draws an analogy between electronic publishing and early author/printers, like William Caxton. who crafted books by handling the entire process from writing through typesetting. Today such a possibility is limited to small publishing houses, which for the most part have not had the financial resources to exclusively computerize. The current control of commercial publishing, marketing and distribution by large corporations make the twentieth-century equivalent of Provenzo's author/publisher a rarity.

70. For further discussion of technology and women's work, see Eli Ginzberg, "Technology, Women, and Work: Policy Perspective," in Heidi Hartmann, ed., *Computer Chips and Paper Clips: Technology and Women's Employment* (Washington, D.C.: National Academy Press, 1987), pp. 3–22.

4

With a Little Help from Some Friends: Publishers, Protesters, and Texas Textbook Decisions

J. Dan Marshall

The best textbook adoption system remains unclear, but one thing is certain: Educational policymakers should pay more attention to this critical issue.

> —M. Kirst, "Choosing Textbooks"

This chapter describes state-level textbook selection and adoption as a systemic attempt to arrive at textbook decisions through a process that reflects and balances the values of neutral competence, executive leadership, and representativeness. The inclusion in this process of textbook publishers and protesters, whose intent is to influence these decisions directly, makes this balancing act even more important for educators to understand. Data from a study of the Texas textbook selection and adoption processes suggest that achieving such a balance is unlikely and largely illusory.

The Concept of Influence

Accepting influence as a major factor in the Texas textbook operation creates the need to borrow from allocative theory and use its assumption

> that education policymaking is a competitive process, the essence of which resides in the interplay of influence. The explanation for policy decisions, from this perspective, comes from revealing the patterns of accommodation among competing actors, actors who differ greatly in resources, intention, and skill. These patterns are organized through a governmental structure and are channeled and constrained by other systemic features as well.[1]

Influence while conceptually complex, has been defined in a commonsense fashion by Robert Dahl as follows: "Suppose there are only two people in a system, A and B. A influences B to the extent that he [*sic*] changes B's actions or predispositions in some way."[2] And although the concept of influence is closely related to concepts of power and control, careful distinctions are to be noted. Power, from this theoretical vantage point, is a bureaucratic design component of the overall system. In the case of Texas textbook decisions,

---

Epigraph taken from M. Kirst, "Choosing Textbooks," *American Educator* 8 (1984): 23.

professional educators make initial decisions, the Commissioner of Education and his staff have the power to alter or overturn those decisions, and the State Board of Education holds the power to alter or overturn those of the Commissioner. Control, here, is seen as the way in which decisions are constrained by the rules and guidelines of the system itself. Mann describes control as "a determinate, or at least a dominant influence. There is an idea of sufficient command in controlling."[3] As designed, the Texas system apparently allows no overt way for publishers or protesters to exert power or control over textbook selection and adoption decisions (although it has been argued that, in Texas, both groups might be seen as having some degree of control over textbook content).[4]

It is imperative to note, however, that the use of allocation theory as a lens for interpreting such phenomena as those that follow leaves much to be desired. This viewpoint is largely restricted to what is readily apparent and can, at best, only begin to "unpack the logic of a fairly complicated set of interrelationships"[5] such as those existing within a state-level textbook selection and adoption system like the one in Texas. More recent theoretical and empirical work continues to silence doubt about questions of economic, political, social, and ideological power and control relative to school texts.[6] The emphasis sought in this chapter (as well as in the original study), however, is one of participant understanding—that is, the extent to which it can be empirically illustrated that those who take part in the process of acquiring Texas textbooks recognize influence.[7] It was assumed at the outset that these participants could recognize and would acknowledge overt attempts to influence this carefully organized political game, which is authoritatively designed to allocate values (textbooks).[8]

The Game and Its Players

Within the United States, some twenty-two states select and adopt textbooks for use in their schools.[9] Although these legislated practices may not be particularly efficacious vis-à-vis their apparent intents,[10] the results of such decisions—particularly the decisions made in California, Florida, and Texas—have wide-ranging effects on the textbooks used in classrooms throughout the country.[11] This realization alone invites inquiry into the quiet forces at work within state-level textbook selection and adoption practices.[12]

Texas deserves special attention because of the large quantity of books it adopts annually and its unique payment system.[13] The educational governance structure of Texas, like most states, consists of a State Department of Education (in Texas, this is the Texas Education Agency—TEA), a Chief State School Officer (in Texas, the Commissioner of Education), and an elected or appointed State Board of Education. This structure permits a variety of tasks, most of which are routine and regulatory in nature. Selecting textbooks in Texas is one such task.

The basic legislation undergirding the Texas textbook selection and adoption system was overhauled at mid-century[14] and undergoes internal tinkering and refinement annually. Basically, the system consists of three decision making stages.

Stage One: Review and Selection
by the State Textbook Committee

A group of fifteen active Texas educators, the majority of whom must be classroom teachers, receives a one-time appointment to the State Textbook Committee (STC). This committee is charged with reviewing all books submitted by publishers in each of the subject areas under consideration. Given the large number of subject areas (approximately one-sixth of all subjects taught in Texas elementary and secondary schools receive new books each year) and dozens of books in each, STC members enlist the aid of advisory groups with competence in each subject area.

Committee members and their advisory groups spend an entire summer meeting with publishers and reviewing and evaluating books. In September (usually), members of the STC meet in the state capitol for a formal hearing, at which citizens and textbook representatives protest and defend the books. Following this hearing, STC members select the best books (a maximum of five) in each of the subject areas under consideration. These lists are then formally recommended to the Commissioner of Education.

Stage Two: Review by Texas
Education Agency Personnel

Books recommended by the State Textbook Committee are carefully screened during the fall months by state-level curriculum experts at the Texas Education Agency (TEA) as well as by the state's Commissioner of Education. Publishers whose books are recommended by the STC may be asked to make certain content corrections, additions, and/or deletions. The Commissioner may remove as many as three books from any list of five, but he cannot add books. When these reviews are completed and his decisions (if any) to delete books made, the Commissioner formally presents his lists of books to the State Board of Education for adoption at its November meeting.

Stage Three: Review and Adoption
by the State Board of Education

Books recommended by the Commissioner of Education are reviewed and discussed by the State Board of Education (SBOE) membership. A round of public hearings is scheduled for this group as well. This body may ask for

---

State-level Texas Textbook Decision Making Stages
Stage 3: Representativeness

State Board of Education (SBOE) members considers all TEA-forwarded texts. This body may request changes in or delete texts before finally voting to adopt state-approved texts.

Stage 2: Executive Leadership
Texas Education Association (TEA) specialists and the Commissioner of Education review all STC-selected texts. This group may request changes in or delete texts before finally sending lists of approved books to the State Board.

Stage 1: Neutral Competence
State Textbook Committee (STC) members (and their advisory groups) review all books submitted for adoption. This group selects up to five texts in each of the multiple adoption categories and sends its lists of selections to the Agency.

Figure 4.1

content changes and may also decide to remove books from any list, as long as at least two remain in each subject area. Members of the SBOE cannot add books to any list. Following their deliberations, members vote to adopt each book on each subject area list. From these final SBOE adoption lists, districts and schools throughout Texas select texts.

This multistage decision-making system (see Figure 4.1) epitomizes the state's attempt to balance three important and sometimes conflicting values: neutral competence (provided by professional educators during the initial stage); executive leadership (provided by the Commissioner of Education and his staff during the second stage); and representativeness (provided by the elected State Board of Education members during the final stage).[15] The system's bureaucratic design also acts as a series of "checks and balances" with regard to the flow of decision-making power. In the first stage, practitioners bear the heaviest work load, sifting through large numbers of textbooks in search of the best "tools" for their trade. Their decisions are then subject to approval by the Commissioner of Education, whose concerns include those of cost and uniformity of materials (based upon guidelines, called "Proclamations," developed by the TEA experts and adopted by the SBOE). But even the Commissioner is subject to the higher authority of the State Board of Education, which acts on behalf of the public-at-large. Ideally, such a system brings together information from all who might have an "interest" in textbook decisions.[16]

In addition to those empowered to make textbook decisions at each of the above stages, two groups of non–decision-makers also participate. The first group consists of textbook publishers.[17] In essence, publishers are selling materials to practitioners during stage one, repairing materials for the state education specialists during stage two, and representing (and occasionally defending) materials to the board members during stage three.

The second group consists of concerned citizens, called "petitioners" by the system. This contingent emerged full-blown in the late 1950s in Texas, and, by 1961, citizen involvement had developed into a pair of formal hearings—first before the STC and the Commissioner, and then before the SBOE.[18] Until 1982, only those wishing to criticize textbooks could act as petitioners (favorable comments, often in the form of protest rebuttals, were restricted to publishers or their representatives); thus, most who know this system refer to the members of this group textbook "protesters." This chapter, based upon data from three adoption years, looks at the relationships between those who made decisions within this system and the textbook publishers and protesters who wished to influence those decisions.[19]

Patterns of Influence
State Textbook Committee Members'
Textbook Decisions (Stage 1)

No strong patterns exist in the data of textbook committee members regarding publisher influence. As a whole, about half the members recognized that their decisions had been influenced by textbook publishers; the other half recognized no such influence.

Virtually all STC members agreed that publishers emphasized the way content was organized and presented in their text(s), the ways in which their text(s) adhered to the state's guidelines or proclamations, and strength of the text(s) as a teaching tool. These happen to be the same three aspects which State Textbook Committee members identified as important to their own textbook evaluation processes. Thus, publishers spoke to aspects of their text(s) that teachers judged most important.

In Texas, the amount and nature of contact between publishing representatives and STC members and advisors is strictly monitored and recorded. Contact, by telephone, by letter, or in person can take place in a public or private setting and be with an individual or a group. Members were asked to identify which publisher contacts seemed most influential. The majority of textbook committee members who acknowledged having been influenced by publishers indicated that this influence usually occurred at the publishers' "Round Robin" presentations. Whether made in school cafeterias or fine restaurants, these presentations were like polished theater. Not only did the committee members hear about textbook X, but they heard about it within a comparative context that highlighted the weaknesses of the competing texts. As one publisher explained:

> The one thing you better do [in order to have a chance at making the list]: you better know your product [and] you better know your competitor's product. You better evaluate how you beat your competitor and then whenever you start to emphasize something say, "Well, I wish you would look at page so-and-so because this is the way we present The Articles of Confederation. . . . We've got three more pages of coverage of Teddy Roosevelt running up San Juan Hill than the competitors do." Those kinds of things. You pick out whatever you think is going to be a definitive plus and you *use* that!

This recognition of the selective and comparative information publishers provided to STC members and advisors was noted and discussed by publishers and STC members alike.

The data plainly indicate that most STC members and advisors actually conducted two types of textbook evaluations—the first to determine the "good" books from the large number of those submitted for selection, and a second evaluation to determine comparatively the best of those good books. Publishers' efforts to play their books off the others that were being considered thus served to "guide" the STC members' winnowing process described above. In fact, publishers' contacts often defined which aspects of the "good" books needed careful attention. Decisions regarding the ranking of best books by committee members were often based on these very specific textbook aspects:

STC Member 1: There were things that I might have missed if they [publishers] had not pointed them out. And this is generally true of all of them. I mean, I looked over the books, but perhaps not as carefully as I would have if no one had. . . . [pause] You know, whenever they explained it. . . . [pause] It did help to have them there. Of course they *all* had representatives.

STC Member 2: . . . . Sometimes [publishers] were able to bring out some points about their programs that perhaps we hadn't caught.

Publisher: What I think [STC members] mean [when they recognize publisher influence] is that, by repeated presentation, either in conference or in general meetings, features of the books that they may not otherwise have seen were presented to them. . . .

Interviewer: So it's really just a matter of receiving information. . . .

Publisher: Well, I think that's what the committee members are talking about, yes. . . . It's information and it's a biased presentation, I suppose, of the information.

Other forms of publisher influence were apparent but not prevalent among the data. Mention was made by publishers and STC members both, for example, of how some administrators or curriculum supervisors in certain districts were "sold" on publisher X's materials (or publisher X's company, or publisher X's field representative) before the campaign began. Whatever the reason for this "preselection," publishers and some STC members realized that publishers' influential efforts in any textbook selection campaign were not limited to STC members and their advisors!

While half the educators who selected Texas texts recognized the influence that publishers had on their decisions, most claimed that textbook protesters were far less influential. In the cases where respondents did admit such influence, they had difficulty describing how that influence affected their decisions. This nebulous awareness of protester influence is represented in the following comments:

STC Member 1: [The testimony of the protesters at our hearing] probably caused me to look at. . . . Yes, [the testimony] did influence me somewhat. [Pause] I mean, it caused me to take another look at how I was voting, but I don't know that it changed my vote. I don't believe it did completely.

STC Member 2: By that stage of the game [the STC hearing], we had done *so* much work, *so* much evaluation, that our minds were pretty well made up as to what our top choices were going to be and what we found objectionable or what we really liked about particular textbooks. . . . I was open-minded to what [the protesters] had to say [but] ultimately, it did not affect my voting choices in the end.

Unlike the publishers, whose contacts with members of the STC were invited, frequent, and person-to-person, protesters did not take part in the STC members' summer-long deliberations. The only recognized avenues open for protesters to influence the decisions of STC members were through written reports (called Bills of Particular) and testimony before the STC at the public hearing preceding its final vote. When asked to identify the primary source of protester influence, the comparatively few STC respondents who recognized such influence identified both the written and oral protests as influential. One STC member noted:

When we got the first batch [of the thirteen volume set of Bills of Particular and publishers' responses] we were all interested to see if what we'd heard [during the hearings] and what we'd read were the same thing. And it seemed to be. After that, you didn't pay any attention to [the printed materials]. Why go through that stuff? You've heard it once.

Two possible explanations are offered for differences in the nature and extent of protester influence over the period of time studied. Some of this difference may be due to the fact that in the earliest case studied, the printed Bills of Particular were made available to the STC members at least one week before they attended the textbook hearing. Members from the later cases studied, on the other hand, did not receive those materials until the day their hearings began. Second, the length of this initial public hearing grew from a single day to a full five days during the period from which the cases were selected. The number of protesters as well as the volume of Bills of Particular and their responses also increased significantly. Greater numbers of protesters criticizing a single text or series over several days may have been an important factor in the more recent STC members' identification of the textbook hearings as the primary source of protester influence.

Asked to identify the focus or major concern of those who protested textbooks, most textbook committee members cited "personal bias." Examination of the Bills of Particular and of interviews with protesters from each case studied clearly indicates that protesters were seldom concerned with how textbook content was organized and presented but, instead, with which content was and was not included in books. These data may also help to explain why protesters had so little influence on members of the STC—who were primarily concerned with selecting teaching tools. Educators who interpret protesters' concerns to be largely unrelated to questions of pedagogical importance are not likely to be influenced by those protesters.

Records from those years studied show that in each case, heavily protested books were selected during this initial stage as frequently as lightly protested ones were not. When seen in combination with participant data, it seems that protesters had little effect on the textbook decisions of State Textbook Committee members.

Texas Education Agency Personnel (Stage 2)

The findings related to publisher influence on textbook decisions made during the second stage of the Texas state-level system are far more speculative than those related to publisher influence on the State Textbook Committee. In order to understand this influence, we must first consider the relationship between publishers and TEA personnel.

Agency staff, who are responsible for drafting textbook Proclamations and reviewing books selected by the STC, knew members of the textbook publishing industry both as salespersons and as pedagogically well-informed cohorts. Edgerton refers to publishers as the "first cousins" of professional educators,[20] and these data support the correctness of his metaphor. Most major publishing houses maintain a close relationship with the Texas Education Agency—one that serves the dual purposes of keeping the publishers attuned to the directions in which Proclamation guidelines are likely to change while maintaining a professional and personal bond between themselves and Agency staff. As one publisher explained:

Publisher: If publishers didn't have someone who was in that Agency on a bi-monthly or a bi-weekly basis trying to determine their thinking of what those people expected in books, you couldn't play the game. You couldn't bid because your book wouldn't meet the [Proclamation].

Interviewer: So one of the things that that did, then, was complicate the jobs of people like you. It gave you another territory that you had to pay attention to.

Respondent: That's right! And that was, in the long run, a very important territory. . . . I became acquaintances, friends, and sometimes offered advice as to what was going into those books. And this advice might have been influenced by what we had in our books.

Publishers who "worked" the TEA were valued for their knowledge of national educational trends as well as for their understanding of the textbook industry. Moreover publishers continued to keep a finger on the pulse of Texas schooling with their frequent travels throughout the state. Their relationship with those at the TEA, thus, was one of mutual benefit and professional trust. One former Commissioner explained how important the trust factor was in these relationships: "[Texas Education Agency personnel] were public people. . . . They had various contacts with publishers. We discouraged any socialization, although there was some. . . . You just had to depend on the fact that these people are supposed to be professional folks. . . ."

Agency staff, not always able to speak with teachers and supervisors throughout the state, used textbook publishers to learn such information as what materials worked best in which districts, and which subject specialists needed what resources. Publishers belonged to many of the same professional educational associations as Agency curriculum specialists. Both groups, presumably, were working to provide Texas schools with the best possible textbooks. Agency staff and publishers were, as the following TEA staffer noted, colleagues in the textbook endeavor:

What we try and do in the proclamation here, is reflect what teachers say they need in their instructional program, because we view ourselves as working arm-in-arm with the public school and the publishers to bring about better instructional materials that teachers need.

Beyond their professional relationships, many personal relationships were struck and maintained between publishers and Agency personnel. Each of the Commissioners interviewed claimed personal friends within the elhi (elementary and high school) textbook industry, and several of the publishers interviewed mentioned their personal friendships with staff and former Commissioners. "I enjoy the publishers," one former Commissioner noted. "I think they really wanted to satisfy the Texas market. . . . I found [them] to be honest and above-board. . . . All in all, they're a fine group of men and women."

Personal and professional relationships notwithstanding, there was no evidence among the data to suggest that such connections resulted in specific textbook decisions being rendered "as a favor to a friend." Instead, the findings suggest that the mutual need, respect, and trust between publishers and those at the TEA gave publishers *influence potential*. This influence potential was most obvious in the drafting of Proclamations and was likely to come into play during staff reviews of specific textbook protests. As for required content changes resulting from Agency reviews, some purely speculative evidence from respondents indicates that TEA staff seldom called for anything beyond "cut and paste" changes in textbooks because of their awareness of the exorbitant cost, in time and dollars, to publishers. In short, the relationship publishers cultivated and sustained with the Commissioner of Education and Texas Education Agency personnel provided them with what Dahl calls "indirect influence," which, even for publishers, is quite difficult to "see" and assess.[21]

Those responsible for textbook decisions at this second stage were far more aware, on the other hand, of the very real and concrete influence brought by textbook protesters to this set of deliberations. Interviewees from the Texas Education Agency acknowledged that protesters regularly forced them to pay close attention to the wording of subsequent Proclamations. Comparing the Proclamations from each case, it is evident that these documents became successively more lengthy and specific. This sort of influence is acknowledged, below, from the perspectives of both the state's professionals who draft the Proclamations and the political members who must formally adopt them each year:

TEA Member: I remember the first year [sex bias was an area of protester concern], we thought well, why haven't we been looking at the girls? Why did someone have to tell us to start looking at the way little girls are treated in stories . . . ?

SBOE Member: I think the Proclamations were colored by the protesters. If you had a whole siege of protesters in one year on one particular subject, . . . the Proclamations, the next [time they were prepared], in order to not have so many of the protests, were colored in the direction of eliminating that—being more specific about that [area of protest].

Protester influence on the Proclamation wording is of major importance when we consider that "adherence to the Proclamation" was the sole criterion for textbook evaluation used by Agency personnel and the only basis they had for recommending changes in textbooks or deciding to eliminate them from the list. This meant that TEA staff were required to make "judgment calls" concerning whether or not content issues (e.g., ethnic stereotyping) identified by protesters at previous adoption hearings were important enough to be included in the new Proclamation. When these issues do find their way into Proclamations, they become what Aarons refers to as "templates for publishers and authors." Such Texas templates include: " 'Textbooks shall not contain material which serves to undermine authority,' or 'Textbook content shall not encourage life styles deviating from generally accepted standards of society.' "[24]

In short, while many of the Proclamation's "templates" may indeed be traced to previously voiced protester concerns, protesters immediately have the ability to "guide" those at the TEA in their textbook reviews. Indeed, recent Proclamations state that protester allegations will be given careful consideration during Agency textbook reviews. If, for example, a book selected by the STC had fifty pictures, of which five were criticized, protesters would know that at the next decision-making stage, TEA personnel would pass judgment on the appropriateness of at least those five pictures. This is not to suggest that the other forty-five pictures would not be perused by TEA staff, but to say that only those five pictures receiving protests *required* judgment calls.

Those at the TEA acknowledge an ever-present awareness of pressure from protesters yet seldom perceive their decisions as resulting from protester influence. If the record of changes required by the Commissioner can be seen as a valid empirical indicator of protester influence on TEA textbook decision outcomes, protester influence was minimal in the three cases studied. A very small percentage of Agency-requested content changes (e.g., replacing pictures or stories) was traceable to protesters' specific Bills of Particular. This suggests both that Agency staff conducted quite thorough textbook reviews apart from the protesters' "guidance" and that protesters were not particularly efficacious vis-à-vis their attempts to have Agency personnel call for changes in textbook content.

State Board of Education Members' Textbook Decisions (Stage 3)

Most board members recognized *no* publisher influence in their textbook decisions made during the final stage of the Texas process. Several reasons for this strong pattern of response can be offered. First, board members were conscious of the influence potential of publishers and made it a point not to allow themselves to be swayed by persons who made their living convincing others of their products' goodness. As one board member testified:

We had no contact with them at all. In fact, I'll tell you what: I really don't think the publishers made any effort to [influence us] for several reasons. I think it would have backfired if they had. There are a lot of people on the board who felt like the publishers had had their say when they wrote the books and submitted them for adoption. They'd had their turn. . . . to do their thing.

None of the publishers or SBOE members who were interviewed mentioned the existence of personal or collegial relationships between the two groups, although there was no dislike or distrust mentioned either. "[None of them] made faces at me or were rude or anything like that," one board member recounted, "but there was [pause] nothing out of the way at all [regarding the purpose of their friendship]." Apparently, the conflict of interest fears of board members were strong enough to prevent most publishers from establishing the sort of personal influence potential with SBOE members that they enjoyed with Texas Education Agency personnel.

Another finding that may help to explain further the absence of publisher influence on SBOE members had to do with the way in which publishers typically presented themselves at the board's textbook hearing. Receiving pages and pages of written protest and rebuttal plus verbatim transcriptions of the earlier hearing and then listening to hours and hours of testimony became standard operating procedure before SBOE textbook decisions. As one board member groused, "We had to listen to [it all]." Most board members paid close attention to oral testimony relating to heavily protested books but little attention to the printed Bills of Particular, publishers' written responses, or transcriptions of earlier testimony.

However, publishers seldom spoke in defense of their textbooks at this second hearing before the board. Thus, most board members did not have the benefit of hearing the publishers' side of the story:

SBOE Member: Now, when we'd get in a board meeting and get ready to adopt a book and the petitioners made their oral reports, we would always ask the textbook publisher for a reply. And almost invariably they'd say, "We stand on our written reply" and they'd leave it at that. They didn't answer orally. . . . Well, we had copies of those written replies, but gee, volumes to read. And I'll be frank with you: I never read them word for word.

Interviewer: So you think the fact that publishers didn't bother to speak might have hurt them in the long run?

SBOE Member: Well, I don't know whether it hurt or not.

Interviewer: Well, . . . if you didn't read their responses, then you didn't know how they were answering those criticisms.

SBOE Member: That's right. That's right. . . . I don't know why [they didn't speak].

Finally, perhaps the simplest analysis of why publishers had so little apparent influence on members of the State Board of Education can be understood best by the comments of two board members:

SBOE Member 1:   Frankly, hell, they were salesmen.

SBOE Member 2:   They were trying to sell books! I didn't think they were too interested in the quality of the book [either].

Protesters, on the other hand, had far more success influencing members of the State Board of Education. A majority of SBOE members from both the earlier and later cases studied recognized some protester influence on their choices of certain textbooks. This finding fits the pattern that emerged regarding board members' textbook evaluations. Those protesters who were active at the initial textbook hearing and who carried their protests to the board's hearing had the strongest chance of drawing attention to their concerns about certain books. The record shows that the "certain books" board members were referring to were, for the most part, texts in what are commonly considered to be the basic subjects (e.g., reading, social studies, and science) and that would inevitably "come up as very controversial," as one SBOE member put it. Another board member recalled that "the ones I read were history books, civics books, government books, because I *knew* what we were going to get from the protesters because we'd heard it all before. And *I* wanted to know whether it said what they said it said."

According to the SBOE members, protester influence resulted largely from their testimony at the board's textbook hearing. In each of the cases studied, textbook actions called for by the State Board of Education (e.g., content changes or removal of books from a list) were traced to specific issues raised by protesters. Reason exists to refrain from alleging a direct cause-and-effect relationship, however, for these boards consisted of a majority of conservative-thinking individuals who may have called for similar changes and removals without the protesters' activities. However, the data indicate that most board members may have looked only at heavily protested books. Below are several representative responses in this regard:

SBOE Member 1:   And of course, really, we had so many things to do that I did not read each book. If there was an objection or a criticism of textbooks, yes. Otherwise, no.

Interviewer: The people you asked to look at [the books] really only looked at the ones that were under criticism . . . ?

SBOE Member 1:   I would think for the most part, yes.

SBOE Member 2:   I didn't examine all the books, no. . . . I did examine the parts,
though, that were challenged. All of them.

It seems highly unlikely that board members would independently discover
textbook "problems" without the benefit of information from protesters. The
obvious exception would be cases in which the Proclamations specifically called
for content that SBOE members could not find in a textbook or deemed insufficiently represented there.

Furthermore, protesters enjoyed personal avenues of influence with SBOE
members beyond the textbook-related calendar of events. Some protesters regularly contacted board members regarding textbooks recommended for adoption.
Several veteran publishers discussed how Mel and Norma Gabler (veteran protesters in the Texas procedure), at least, had managed over the years to become
quite influential through their personal relationships with a number of board
members. One SBOE member acknowledged the Gablers' work toward this
end: "We received letters, primarily from the protesters who came [to the
hearing], on a regular basis. Some of them, particularly the Gablers' would
call around and talk to everybody trying to influence their vote." One former
Commissioner also indicated that members of the board were influenced in this
manner:

[Board members] don't have *time* to read all those materials and study them. And
here comes a protester that they *like,* and they have *confidence* in, and she says, or
he says to the board member, "You know what's in that book? Thus-and-so." [pause]
He [the board member] gets right on it. . . . An ordinary citizen, a protester, can
[contact a board member] all she wants to. Or he. And they *do!* They *definitely* do!
They've influenced board members, yes. No question about that.

Protesters, it appears in sum, have little apparent effect on the textbook
decisions made by members of the STC. Members of the TEA tend to pay close
attention to specific protests but do not appear to make many immediate decisions in the protesters' favor. Protesters appear to have their "best shot" at the
decisions arrived at by those who serve on the SBOE.

Data related to publishers' efforts toward influencing these textbook decisions create a converse pattern. Educators who serve on the State Textbook
Committee recognized ways in which their textbook decisions were influenced
by publishers; members of the State Board of Education consciously yet politely
ignored the publishers altogether. Publishers' complex relationships with those
at the Texas Education Agency make the participants' identification of publisher
influence on TEA textbook decisions impossible to read empirically from this
study's data.

The Great Balancing Act in Perspective
Seeking Neutral Competence

These influence patterns are both interesting and disquieting in relation to the state's attempt to maintain a balanced system of neutral competence, executive leadership, and representativeness. The Texas State Textbook Committee is designed to represent a collection of the state's best educators. However, years of classroom and administrative experience do not necessarily equate with competence when these people, and the hundreds of others they select as aides, are asked to perform a task for which none has experience, most have no preparation, and for which they receive few resources. Competent educators are not necessarily competent textbook evaluators.

To say that members of the State Textbook Committee had a difficult task is a laughable understatement. Most STC members concentrated on the collection of books offered in their own subject area and left the evaluation of texts in other subject areas to their advisors. On the whole, STC members seldom met with these advisors and, in a number of cases, had never even met the advisors (who were recommended by district curriculum supervisors or superintendents). When it was time for the STC member to travel to the state capitol for the public hearing and textbook balloting, he or she gathered the prioritized lists of his or her advisors and left ready for the task at hand.

The cumulative data indicate that STC members and their advisors took their jobs quite seriously and did, indeed, spend most of their summer evaluating texts. STC members and their advisors seldom made use of local or district curriculum guidelines and reported using the state's textbook guidelines (Proclamations) primarily for the purpose of shortening the original number of books before beginning their more careful analyses. Typically, STC members employed some form of "check list"—either provided by the TEA or a district curriculum coordinator or created by themselves with the help of their advisors—when evaluating the mountain of texts available . In most cases, these checklists were generic enough so as to be used with texts in all subject areas.

Mixed throughout this period, too, were many contacts from members of the publishing industry. Although each STC member was only required to permit each publisher one "Round Robin" session, the records show certain committee members with more than a dozen contacts from a *single* publishing concern. As was noted earlier, much of the energy publishers expended throughout this process was an attempt to guide these decision-makers toward one book/series and away from others.

Textbook evaluators with no previous experience, insufficient training, and only general notions about what makes one text better than another are prime candidates for the entertaining and thoroughly informative sessions conducted by publishers, many of whom are former teachers and all of whom "speak the same language" as teachers.[23] Publishers' use of selective information as a political resource "simplifies the teacher's . . . examination of a textbook by pointing out the features that [the publishers] consider unique."[24] Textbooks, under these circumstances, are as likely to be sold as selected.[25]

And while publishers enjoyed prolonged and polished contact time with STC members, protesters had contact with them (never with their advisors) only at the public hearing. Protesters, unlike publishers, were unlikely or unwilling to empathize with teachers' needs. Instead, they carped about flaws in the same books that publishers had highlighted as strong. Protesters were frequently perceived by these educators as ideologues whose presentations were cast in a "with us or against us" vein. Not so with publishers, whose successes (and salaries) depended on pleasing the greatest number of potential customers. Furthermore, few STC members were likely to change decisions that were arrived at by so many people working over so long a period of time. The point, simply, is that the two groups of non–decision-makers were not only perceived differently by those sitting on the STC, but had different types of access and quite different approaches to these decision-makers as well. Who can be surprised, then, that protesters had the least influence upon this group while publishers had the most?

In light of this analysis, the degree of neutrality with which members of the State Textbook Committee undertake their task is highly questionable given the inclusion of publishers throughout most of the textbook evaluation period (not to mention educators' experiential predispositions toward certain texts and publishing companies or any number of additional factors). And one must accept on faith the working assumption that members selected for this committee and their advisors can—under these circumstances—recognize the few best textbooks to be made available to diverse schools throughout their state from among such a large pool of contenders in so many different subject areas.[26] These two facts alone—the invitation of publisher influence (recognized or not by participants) and the enormity of the task at hand—would seem at least to dilute the value of "neutral competence" sought during the first decision-making stage.

When this situation is viewed critically, its neutrality tends to evaporate. To begin, these educators must operate from guidelines that are themselves political documents. Furthermore, their understandings of the nature and value of textbooks results from years of work by the elhi publishing industry to create and refine the value of school texts both here and abroad.[27]

Achieving Executive Leadership

The system may, however, be closer to realizing the value of executive leadership within its second stage than it is to achieving neutral competence in its first. The Commissioner and his staff at the TEA fall somewhere between the other two decision-making groups with respect to the influence they recognize from publishers and protesters. TEA staff admittedly worked to fashion Proclamation guidelines that specifically addressed issues raised by protesters during previous adoptions, and they looked closely at books selected by the STC which had received protester complaints. Nevertheless, Agency personnel were quick to recognize ideologically oriented protests and attempted to keep their judgments pedagogically based.

The Commissioner is appointed by the State Board and hires those who work under him at the Agency. This situation places curriculum and subject-matter experts at the Agency in the difficult position of having to use their professional judgments within a largely political environment. In other words, while those at the TEA might know what they want for the schools, they must also acknowledge what will be acceptable to the state board membership. The data reveal that they did their best to filter the people's voice (represented by protester concerns) through a pedagogical lense.

Agency reviewers worked closely with publishers, and this relationship, too, has an impact on the writing of the textbook Proclamations.[28] Textbook reviews conducted during this second stage were not designed to judge the quality or wisdom of decisions made previously by STC members: all books selected were seen, by TEA personnel, as equally good. Moreover, with few exceptions, Agency staff took for granted that all books succeeded in meeting the guidelines they had established beforehand. (After all, the publishers knew precisely what the state was looking for in textbooks.) TEA personnel expected that publishers would be more than willing to make any adjustments deemed necessary at this second stage of the process, assuming these adjustments were not major ones. Both the TEA staff and the Commissioner desired a full list of five texts in each subject area; having to remove books for any reason reduced the variety of materials that would eventually be available in Texas schools. In this relationship, the TEA needs the publishers as much as the publishers need the TEA.[29] By and large, the Commissioner and his staff continually balanced their allegiances to educators, elected officials, publishers, and protesters. In doing so, they appear to represent, more or less successfully, the value of executive leadership as they arrive at their own textbook decisions.

Reiterating Representativeness

The State Board of Education, elected by the public, epitomizes the value of representativeness. Its members bring a new perspective on textbooks into the process—that of citizens who finance the schools and literally buy the books to be used by their children. This perspective helps to explain why members of the SBOE were more likely to recognize protester influence on their textbook decisions than members of the other decision-making groups: the presence of protesters is a reiteration of the value of representativeness within the system.

Additionally, board members (who formally approve the textbook Proclamations) were veterans in this process. This combination of limited focus and previous experience worked to guide their attention in directions similar to those of most protesters. Members of the Texas SBOE seldom took the time to review textbooks (although some had educators within their home districts look through certain books) or to read volumes of print information related to the specific protests and rebuttals. On the other hand, all claimed to have made it their business to look at controversial books and passages (as defined by protesters). In most cases, board members knew protesters from previous appearances before the board as well as personal contacts.[30] Few publishers bothered to defend verbally their wares before the SBOE; publishers' responses were available in writing, and none wished to chance alienating this body. Protesters were constituents; the publishers were salespersons.

Members of the SBOE respected and valued the earlier textbook decisions arrived at by both the STC and TEA; nevertheless, they represented a distinctly different vantage point within the process and saw their oversight power as "lay experts" to be valuable in its own right. Understandably, then, protesters—who were themselves concerned largely politically conservative citizens—had a comparatively better chance to influence SBOE members' textbook decisions than did publishers.[31] Seen in this light, protester input at this decision stage was actually an elaboration of the "representativeness" value epitomized by the actions of this third decision-making group.

Redirections

This analysis begs several questions. Is the process of state-level textbook selection and adoption defensible? Apple has pointed out that state-level textbook selection and adoption systems such as the one described above are historically rooted in concerns about "incompetent" teachers, "unethical" publishers, and a variety of wider social movements and conflicts.[32] Today, Tulley concludes, twenty-two states continue to control the selection and adoption of textbooks through state-level processes on the grounds that such systems (1) control textbook costs, (2) ensure some degree of curriculum uniformity, and (3) ensure the selection of quality textbooks.[33] The wisdom of such systems and the extent to which each of these arguments is viable is a matter of continued question and debate.[34] Most fundamentally, perhaps, is Aarons's contention that state-level textbook selection and adoption is antithetical to First Amendment principles because it is "so categorically restrictive of teacher professionalism and so distant from the possibilities of negotiated or mediated settlements of value conflicts possible on the school level."[35] The presentation and discussion of the data in this chapter seriously question the efficacy of such systems.

But if such systems must continue, might there not be some adjustments made to promote better the values of neutral competence, executive leadership, and representativeness? Alone, the invited presence of both protesters and textbook publishers within these systems raises serious questions, especially with respect to the neutral competence of decisions arrived at by the Texas State Textbook Committee. And what end is ultimately served by having protester input throughout the process if, in fact, the SBOE is itself the embodiment of citizen representation?

Further questions emerge relative to the distinctions between power and control. Within the system studied through the lens of allocation theory, power is a bureaucratically designed component: i.e., each decision-making group is vested with the power to arrive at a set of conclusions subject to the oversight power of the group proceeding it. Control is likened to the idea of a conscience, dominant influence or recognized, sufficient command. From this perspective, one might feel the need to look more deeply at the activities of protesters and publishers in order to determine whether or not either group enjoyed such power or control. Perhaps publishers do exhibit this sort of power over the decisions of those at the Texas Education Agency? Or perhaps protesters do project this sort of control over decisions made by members of the State Board of Education? Additional studies that employ more sophisticated theoretical lenses are also needed to get beneath the recognizable understandings of those who take part in these processes. To what extent, for example, do the relationships among the Commissioner of Education (appointed by the SBOE), specialists at the TEA (selected by the Commissioner), and STC members (selected by those at the TEA) influence Texas textbook decisions? And how and to what extent do publishers influence the content of the state textbook Proclamations? Before policy recommendations can be drawn from these data, questions relating to these matters as well as to the conceptual distinctions among influence, power, and control must be addressed.

Additional questions are prompted by the central role that the textbook guidelines or Proclamations play in this procedure. With the exception of the State Textbook Committee members, all other key participants, including protesters and publishers, had a role to play in their content and wording. Not surprisingly, each group used these guidelines to its own advantage during the process. Perhaps questions such as ''What is the nature and extent of influence on textbook guidelines?'' and ''How are these guidelines, in turn, understood and used by textbook decision makers?'' should be central to further studies.

In light of the importance textbooks have always played in this country's schooling enterprise we are rather late in discovering our professional ignorance of the phenomena surrounding textbook selection and adoption. And although much new work is beginning to shape a better understanding, we have a long way to go before educators, as a whole, will ever begin to understand and appreciate the importance of this knowledge. In the end, we may never catch up to those who have always understood its value: textbook protesters and publishers!

Notes

1. T. L. Mazzoni and R. F. Campbell, "Influentials in State Policymaking for the Public Schools," *Educational Administrative Quarterly* 12 (1976): 4.

2. R. A. Dahl, *Modern Political Analysis,* 3d ed. (Englewood Cliffs, N.J.: Prentice-Hall, 1976), p. 29. Dahl notes that although "influence-terms" such as power, authority, control, persuasion, might, force, and coercion have been central to political analysis throughout history, most theorists (beginning with Aristotle) have assumed that they needed no great elaboration, "because their meaning would be understood by men of common sense" (pp. 25–26).

3. D. Mann, "Participation, Representation, and Control," in J. D. Scribner, ed., *The Seventy-Sixth Year book of the National Society for the Study of Education, Part II: The Politics of Education* (Chicago: University of Chicago Press, 1977), p. 68.

4. See, for example, W. A. Moyer, "How Texas Rewrote Your Textbooks," *The Science Teacher* 52 (January 1985).

5. M. W. Apple, *Teachers and Texts* (London: Routledge and Kegan Paul, 1986), p. 100.

6. See, for example, S. deCastell, A. Luke, and C. Luke, eds., *Language, Authority and Criticism* (London: Falmer, 1989).

7. Survey and interview data were collected from members of the State Textbook Committees and State Boards of Education, Texas Education Agency officials, textbook publishers, and protesters who participated in three different state-level textbook selection and adoption cycles. For a detailed explanation of how and why participants were selected and the nature of the data collected, see J. D. Marshall, *The Politics of Curriculum Decisions Manifested Through the Selection and Adoption of Textbooks for Texas* (doctoral dissertation, University of Texas at Austin, 1985). ED 270 900.

8. J. D. Scribner and R. M. Englert, "The Politics of Education: An Introduction," in Scribner, ed., *The Seventy-Sixth Year book,* pp. 1–29.

9. D. M. Whorton, "Textbook Selection," in S. E. Goodman, ed., *Handbook on Contemporary Education* (New York: R. R. Bowker, 1976), pp. 410–14.

10. M. A. Tulley, "A Descriptive Study of the Intents of State-Level Textbook Adoption Processes," *Educational Evaluation and Policy Analysis* 7 (Fall 1985): 289–308.

11. See, for example, B. Crane, "The 'California Effect' on Textbook Adoptions," *Educational Leadership* 3 (1975): 283–85; and Moyer, "How Texas Rewrote Your Textbooks," pp. 22–27.

12. For a policy-oriented view of such quiet forces, see S. Keith, *Politics of Textbook Selection* (Research Report No. 81-AT, Stanford, Calif.: Stanford University School of Education, Institute for Research on School Finance and Governance, 1981). Examples of research studies include M. C. Courtland, R. Farr, P. Harris, J. Tarr, and L. Treece. *A Case Study of the Indiana State Reading Textbook Adoption Process* (Bloomington, Ind.: Center for Reading and Language Studies), and Marshall, *The Politics of Curriculum Decisions.*

13. M. W. Kirst, *Who Controls Our Schools?* (New York: W. H. Freeman, 1984), p. 15.

14. See M. E. Patrick, *The Selection and Adoption of Textbooks: Texas—A Case Study* (doctoral dissertation, Stanford University, 1949).

15. For a discussion of the attempt to balance such values, see H. Kaufman, *Politics and Policies in State and Local Governments* (Englewood Cliffs, N. J.: Prentice-Hall, 1963). For a discussion of the conflicts inherent in such decisions, see M. W. Kirst and D. F. Walker, "An

Analysis of Curriculum Policy-Making,'' *Review of Educational Research* 41 (1971): 479–509.

16. T. van Geel, *Authority to Control the School Program* (Lexington, Mass.: D. C. Heath, 1976).

17. The term ''publishers'' as used within this chapter refers to members of the elementary and high school (elhi) textbook publishing industry. The term is used to denote *anyone participating in the Texas textbook process who has a vested financial interest in any of the books considered for selection and adoption.* This includes publishing executives, editors, authors, regional managers, field representatives, and consultants. Those familiar with the industry know that the differences among these positions are so great that the definition has little value beyond that of categorization. Since this categorization is not deceptive with respect to influence patterns, and since it allowed informants to remain anonymous, its vagueness was accepted for the purposes of this investigation.

18. In two lengthy interviews with the author on July 26 and August 1, 1984, former Texas Commissioner of Education J. W. Edgar, who served throughout the years in which these citizens began to emerge, described the ways in which their participation within the selection and adoption system evolved from its legislative beginnings in 1950 to the point at which it ''settled down'' around 1961.

19. This chapter has been developed from the author's dissertation study. See Marshall, *The Politics of Curriculum Decisions.*

20. See R. B. Edgerton, ''Odyssey of a Book: How a Social Studies Textbook Comes Into Being,'' *Social Education* 33 (1969): 279–86.

21. Dahl, *Modern Political Analysis.*

22. S. Aarons, ''Lessons in Law and Conscience: Legal Aspects of Textbooks Adoption and Censorship,'' in S. deCastell, A. Luke, and C. Luke, eds., *Language, Authority and Criticism,* p. 213.

23. See, for example, A. L. Hall-Quest, *The Textbook: How to Use and Judge It* (New York: Macmillan, 1918); Edgerton, ''Odyssey''; and J. P. Dessauer, *Book Publishing* (New York: R. R. Bowker, 1974).

24. E. Brown, ''The Role of the Textbook Salesman,'' Phi Delta Kappan 36 (1952): 276. See also G. E. Sroufe, ''Evaluation and Politics,'' in Scribner, ed., *The Seventy-Sixth Year book.*

25. W. B. Spalding, ''The Selection and Distribution of Printed materials,'' in Lee J. Cronbach, ed., *Text Materials in Modern Education* (Urbana, Ill.: University of Illinois Press, 1955).

26. This point is developed more fully in J. D. Marshall, ''Better Textbooks, Better Criteria: The Role of Research in Directing Efforts for Reform,'' paper presented at the annual meeting of the American Educational Research Association, Washington, D. C. April 1987. ED 285 25.

27. R. Lorimer and P. Keeney, ''Defining the Curriculum: The Role of the Multinational Textbook in Canada,'' in S. deCastell, A. Luke, and C. Luke, eds., *Language, Authority and Criticism,* pp. 170–83.

28. See M. Brammer, ''Textbook Publishing,'' in C. B. Grannis, ed., *What Happens in Book Publishing,* 2d ed. (New York: Columbia University Press, 1967).

29. See, for example, Edgerton, ''Odyssey,'' and Cronbach ed., *Text Materials.*

30. See R. Ciolli, ''The Politics of Textbooks,'' *A.P.F. Reporter* 7 (1984): 3–7.

31. See W. E. Maxwell and E. Crain, *Texas Politics Today* (St. Paul, Minn.: West, 1978).

32. M. W. Apple, Regulating the Text: The Socio-Historical Roots of State Control,'' *Educational Policy* 3 (June 1989): 107–23.

33. Tulley, ''A Descriptive Study,'' p. 306.

34. See, for example, R. Farr, M. A. Tulley, and L. Rayford, "Selecting Basal Readers: A Comparison of School Districts in Adoption and Nonadoption States," *Journal of Research and Development in Education* 20 (Summer 1987): 59–72; and Y. Currey, "The Politics of Textbook Adoption," *PS* 21 (Winter 1988): 25–30.

35. Aarons, "Lessons in Law," p. 214.

5

Race, Class, Gender, and Disability in Current Textbooks

Christine E. Sleeter and Carl A. Grant

The publication of *A Nation at Risk*[1] escalated the continuing debate over curriculum in schools (elementary through college) to a greater intensity, and focused more attention on both the skills and the content of curriculum. It recommended, for example, that graduation requirements in English, social studies, mathematics, science, and computer science be increased. Many of the educational reform reports[2] that responded to *A Nation at Risk* argued for eliminating nonessentials in the curriculum without really defining what makes a body of knowledge nonessential, and raising standards in traditional academic subject areas.[3] However, they did not specify what content should be taught in the traditional academic subjects.

Subsequent responses did. Allan Bloom, in his number one bestseller *The Closing of The American Mind,* explains "How Higher Education has Failed Democracy and Impoverished the Souls of Today's Students," and argues for a college curriculum based on the Great Books of the Western tradition and guided by the fundamental work of Western philosophy, especially ancient Greek philosophy. Bloom notes:

> Men may live more truly and fully in reading Plato and Shakespeare than at any other time, because then they are participating in essential being and are forgetting their accidental lives. The fact that this kind of humanity exists, and that we can somehow still touch it with the tips of our outstretched fingers, makes our imperfect humanity, which we can no longer bear, tolerable. The books in their objective beauty are still there, and we must help protect and cultivate the delicate tendrils reaching out toward them through the unfriendly soil of students' souls.[4]

E. D. Hirsch, in another national bestseller, *Cultural Literacy,* asks, "Why have our schools failed to fulfill their fundamental acculturative responsibility? In view of the immense importance of cultural literacy for speaking, listening, reading, and writing, why has the need for a definite, shared body of information been so rarely mentioned in discussions of education?"[5] Hirsch answers these questions, and then recommends a list of facts literate Americans should know. It contains geographical names, historical events, famous people, patriotic lore, and scientific terms. Secretary of Education William Bennett, in an address at Harvard University during the fall of 1986, argued for a greater focus on Western civilization in the college curriculum. For example, the secretary advocated more inclusion of great works of Western art and literature and of the major achievements of the scientific disciplines.[6]

All of these responses ignored or gave only passing attention to the inequality based on race, sex, disability, and social class that continues to exist in the schools' curriculum. In fact, Bloom , makes a point of saying his curriculum is especially for "young persons who populate the twenty or thirty best universities."[7] These students, with some exceptions are white and middle class.[8] Thus, we have demands for a curriculum with more skills training, basics, and Western classical thought, demands that ignore or give only cursory attention to equity issues.

What these reports represent is part of an ongoing struggle to define the content of the curriculum. Debates about curriculum content can be understood broadly as struggles for power to define the symbolic representation of the world and of society, that will be transmitted to the young, for the purpose of either gaining or holding onto power. Symbolic representations are important, and relate to power, for several reasons. First, symbolic representations in books and other media often are used to confer legitimacy on the dominant status of particular social groups. Usually controlled and produced by dominant groups, materials and other media confirm the status of those groups whose culture and accomplishments are deemed important enough to write about.[9]

Second, symbolic representations in the curriculum render socially constructed relations as natural; subjective interpretations of reality and value judgments are projected as fact. Writing about cinema, Nichols put this very well:

> To serve ideology, representations must be made to appear to be other than what they are. Above all, they must appear to lack these very contradictions that informed their production. They must appear as signs of eternal values—harmony, wholeness, radiance, a natural and ideal world spun from the representations of an existing social order.[10]

Curricular materials project images of society, as well as of other aspects of culture such as what constitutes good literature, legitimate political activity, and so forth. The fact that one can debate the validity of such images, and that such images often uphold socially constructed unequal relationships, is hidden. Socially created versions of socially created human activity are projected as truth, as natural. Cherryholmes writes, "Textbooks implicitly present meanings as fixed in structures, and sentences on pages, pictures, charts, and graphs do nothing to dispel this appearance of stability."[11]

Third, the curriculum screens in and out certain ideas and realms of knowledge. Students are given selective access to ideas and information. This predisposes them to think and act in certain ways, and not to consider other possibilities, questions, or actions. Anyon, for example, points out that the history books she analyzed made scant reference to the working class and provided virtually no terminology or conceptual frameworks for thinking about various kinds of workers as belonging to a common social class, having common interests. As a result, she argues: "Without such a label, workers are not easily called to mind as a group, and the objective fact of the working class has no subjective reality. In this way the textbooks predispose workers and others against actions on behalf of the interests that working people have in common."[12]

Curriculum always represents somebody's version of what constitutes important knowledge and a legitimate worldview. In writing textbooks, for example, and debating what should go into them, scholars select from a wide spectrum of knowledge and versions of reality. But texts that get written considerably narrow teachers' and students' access to knowledge. Cherryholmes describes this narrowing process: "Scholars . . . often have a variety of definitions from which to choose in writing textbooks; teachers have fewer from which to choose, but often have more than one; and students usually, more so at lower levels, are given the opportunity to learn only one."[13]

In this way, curriculum usually serves as a means of social control. It legitimates existing social relations and the status of those who dominate, and it does so in a way that implies that there are no alternative versions of the world, and that the interpretation being taught in school is, indeed, undisputed fact. Knowledge helps shape power and social activity (or lack of it). As Anyon says, "The conceptual legitimacy conferred by school knowledge on powerful social groups is metabolized into power that is real when members of society in their everyday decisions support—or fail to challenge—prevailing hierarchies."[14]

The major conveyor of the curriculum—the textbook—has played a paramount role in Western education for over the past five hundred years. Cronbach recognizes its important role when he argues, "Only the teacher—and perhaps a blackboard and writing materials—are found as universally as the *textbook* in our classrooms."[15] Apple more recently underscored the central importance of the textbook when he observed that, "it is the textbook which establishes so much of the material conditions for teaching and learning in classrooms in many countries throughout the world, and it is the textbook that often defines what is elite and legitimate culture to pass on."[16] Furthermore, McMurray and Cronbach state: "The text is a device for helping the child fit into his [her] culture, but culture need not be passed on unedited, good and bad aspects alike. In fact, the nature of the text itself, as we shall see, demands that its maker be highly selective in the materials he [she] presents."[17]

Until recently, textbooks and other curricular materials were blatantly dominated by White wealthy men. As a result of social protest movements of the 1960s and 1970s, curriculum writers were forced to acknowledge voices of Americans of color and women, who demanded inclusion of their histories and works of art and literature. Banks argues that a major goal of the ethnic revival movements of the 1960s and 1970s was to change the curriculum so that it would more accurately reflect the ethnic and cultural diversity within Western societies.[18] The 1980s have witnessed a resurgence of traditional White male voices in the struggle over what knowledge should be taught, as the examples above illustrate. How have the writers and publishers of today's textbooks selected knowledge of various American racial, social class, gender, and disability groups? The chapter will examine this question.

Existing Textbook Analyses

While several analyses of racial bias in texts were done during the 1970s,[19] our knowledge of racial bias in today's texts is sketchy, and it may be tempting to assume that it has been "taken care of" by publishers. One has only to thumb through a text published during the last ten years to see people of different colors throughout. Recently published reading texts[20] and social studies text[21] have been analyzed; science texts[22] have received some attention, but math texts have not. These recent analyses tell us that texts include members of racial minority groups more often than they did in the past, but that portrayals of specific racial groups are still few, and often sketchy. Glazer and Ueda noted in 1983 that history texts provide a small amount of information that "emphasize[s] the positive features of each group, and elicits sympathy by vividly picturing the efforts of ethnic minorities to defend themselves from discrimination and to advance under inhospitable circumstances."[23] However, the history of White racism and oppression is muted, and complexities within groups or involving interaction among groups is virtually ignored. We will show the extent to which the dominance of Whites pervades the various subject areas, discuss patterns in the portrayal of various racial groups, and demonstrate the extent to which current issues of concern to various racial groups are presented.

Analyses of sex bias in recent textbooks are more numerous than analyses of racial bias. Since 1980, textbooks have been analyzed for sexism in the areas of reading,[24] social studies,[25] and science.[26] These analyses agree that females appear in texts much more than they used to. But males still usually predominate, the appearance of females in nontraditional roles is uneven, few males are in nontraditional roles, and issues involving sexism in society both today and in history are virtually ignored. While some analyses distinguish between White women and women of color,[27] others do not,[28] making it difficult to learn how texts portray women of various racial groups. This chapter will further update the portrayal of both sexes, differentiating among racial groups.

Social class and disability are absent from most textbook analyses. The most comprehensive analysis of social class issues was done by Anyon in 1979, when she examined seventeen secondary history texts. Social class is sometimes mentioned in other analyses,[29] but is otherwise overlooked. Disability is briefly mentioned in a few textbook analyses,[30] which note mainly that people with disabilities are very underrepresented in reading textbooks. These are both areas that bear investigation.

This chapter examines the treatment of various groups across four subject areas. It shows broadly how America's diversity is projected to children through the school day and their school career, and the extent to which children are challenged in any subject area to think about discrimination and oppression.

Methodology

We examined forty-seven textbooks currently used in grades 1 through 8, with copyright dates between 1980 and 1988. We analyzed textbooks in social studies, reading and language arts, science, and mathematics. We limited ourselves to these grade levels mainly to keep the project manageable.

We developed a textbook analysis instrument based on various instruments that have been developed and used elsewhere.[31] It consists of six different analyses; only those appropriate for a given text were used. The six analyses are: picture analysis, anthology analysis, "people to study" analysis, language analysis, story-line analysis, and miscellaneous.

Picture analysis involves tallying who is in each picture, categorized by sex, race (Asian American, Black American, Hispanic American, American Indian, White American, race ambiguous, and mixed race group), and disability. Pictures can be designated as individual or group pictures. In addition, racial and sex stereotypes, and the social-class background or setting, are to be noted. The anthology analysis is for analyzing each story in readers. The race, sex, and disability of the main character and supporting characters are to be tallied; and stereotypes, the social-class setting, and which groups solve the problems are to be noted. The "people to study" analysis involves tallying the race and sex of each person mentioned in the text; this is used in science, mathematics, or social studies texts. The language analysis involves examining language in the text for sexist usage, "loaded" words that contain racial or sex stereotypes, and words or phrases that obscure viewpoints or possible conflict situations.

The story-line analysis is used primarily with social studies texts. It involves analyzing which group receives the most sustained attention (whose story is being told), which group(s) resolves problems, how other groups appear, the extent to which these other groups cause or resolve problems, and who the author intends the reader to sympathize with or learn most about. Finally, other miscellaneous analyses may lend themselves to a particular book, such as analyzing race, sex, and roles of people in mathematics story problems. For each subject area, we will describe how books treat different racial groups, both sexes, the social classes, and people with disabilities.

Social Studies

We examined fourteen social studies textbooks, all of which deal with the history, life, or conditions in the United States since the early European explorers. These books were published by nine publishers.[32]

Race

Asian Americans are in less than 4% of the pictures in ten books, and in 18%, 12%, 7%, and 6% of the pictures in the other four books.[33] About 80% of the depicted Asian Americans were males. Asian Americans are depicted working—for example, on the railroad, as miners, and as laboratory technicians—or living in Hawaii and wearing traditional dress, such as kimonos. The books' story line usually includes Asian Americans only briefly, mainly as immigrants in the work force that developed the railroad, although sometimes they are also included in references to all Americans, for example in a discussion of the importance of educating all Americans.[34] The story line does not develop the reasons why Asians came to the United States during the nineteenth century, nor does it explain that Asians, much like the Pilgrims, were fleeing injustices in their countries. Furthermore, little is provided about how American business recruited Chinese immigrants to do mining, railroad construction, and agricultural work. Two short narratives about Chinese Americans provide most of one book's coverage of Asian Americans.[35] The first describes Yen Chong as a young, strong, happy Chinese railroad worker, who takes pride in working for the Central Pacific Railroad Company. In the second, Aunt Liza, a fictional character who went to Chinatown while visiting New York in 1900, says: "There is a place called Chinatown. Thousands of Chinese people live in that neighborhood. It looks like a picture book of China, but it is right here in New York City."[36] These narratives lack any real discussion about the lives of Chinese Americans and their culture, contributions, hardships, and desires to make life better for themselves and their families. Also, they do not point out that Chinese immigrants were forced by discrimination to keep to themselves and live in a separate "Chinatown."

Black Americans appear in about 11% of the pictures in eleven books, and in 23%, 18%, and 18% of the pictures in three books.[37] On the average, Black American males and females appear just about as often; however, some books may have more of one gender than the other.[38] These pictures cover the time of slavery, through the Civil Rights period, to the present day, and show Black Americans in various occupational roles.

The story line discusses Black Americans in relation to wars they fought in, the Civil Rights movement, and slavery. Some Black heroes and heroines are presented. These discussions are informative but usually do not provide a Black American perspective on events and issues, and many discussions are contextually benign. For example, one book says of Martin Luther King, Jr.: "He dreamed of a better life for all Americans. He wanted people to live together in peace. King worked hard to make his dream come true. We remember him on his birthday every year."[39] However, it neglects to discuss the oppression of Blacks that King's movement challenged. These books do not tell the reader that the Blacks' Civil Rights struggle was against Whites and laws they had passed. For example, one book does not indicate that when King said to supporters of segregation, "We will not hate you. But we will not obey your evil laws. We will soon wear you down. We will win by suffering."[40] he was talking to White segregationists. It is up to the book's fifth grade readers to conclude who the "you" is that King is referring to. However, the book is very explicit that some White people were on the side of the Black Civil Rights advocates: "Thousands of white people joined the [equal rights] movement."[41] A question to consider is: Would ten- or eleven-year-old children, not having grown up during the 1950s and 1960s, know which groups of people made up the opposing forces in the Civil Rights struggle? The books often do not explicitly provide this type of information.

Native Americans are in less than 10% of the pictures in nine textbooks. But they are in 33% of the pictures in one book,[42] and 19%, 15%, 15%, and 12% in four books.[43] About two-thirds of the Native Americans depicted are males. Most of the pictures portray Native Americans during colonial times— for example, living in teepees and hunting with bows and arrows, and resisting the westward expansion of Whites. The story line in most books places Native Americans in the early history of our country, but does not discuss their life before Columbus, or go beyond this to where they lived, how their political structure worked, how they built their homes (e.g. adobes), and how and what they hunted and gathered. Thus, Native Americans are seen mainly as historical artifacts. Only one book portrays modern reservation life somewhat insightfully.[44] Current problems and issues they face, such as disputes over fishing rights, are not treated.

Hispanic Americans are featured in 3% or less of the pictures in nine books, in 8% of the pictures in three books,[45] and in 32% and 18% of the pictures in two books.[46] Both sexes are depicted about the same number of times. These pictures generally show Hispanics of long ago, such as during the Spanish colonization, but a few more recent pictures, such as César Chavez of the United Farm Workers, also appear. In the story line, Hispanics, mainly Mexican Americans, are mentioned only briefly and incidentally, and mainly in discussions of this country's early history, the settlement of the Southwest, and the war between Mexicans and Americans. Some books focus on Spanish people as colonizers (conquerors and spreaders of Christianity). In discussions of the war with Mexico, the American view of why Americans no longer wanted to adhere to Mexican rule is stated with clarity and authority, but the Mexican view is not presented in the same manner. For example, in one book the story line runs as follows:

> In the early 1800s, much of the southwest was part of Mexico. Then, Americans began to move into the area that is now Texas. These settlers rebelled against the Mexican rule. In 1836, they declared Texas to be an independent country with its own government. In 1845, Texas joined the United States as a state. In 1848, Mexico and the United States fought a war over land in the southwest. After the United States won, Mexico was forced to sell the land that became Arizona and New Mexico to the United States.[47]

This includes neither the Mexican point of view nor an analysis of the socioeconomic and cultural forces that also encouraged the conflict. Finally, Hispanics appear in some texts in recent times as illegal aliens living in urban areas.

Over 70% of the people in pictures are White in eight books, over 60% of the people pictured are White in four books,[48] and over 40% of the people are White in two books.[49] About two-thirds of the Whites depicted are males. These pictures usually portray White males in a very positive way as explorers, soldiers, government officials, citizens, leaders, scientists, and inventors. Rarely are any Whites shown performing any negative deeds.

Regardless of time period or event, Whites, especially males, dominate the story line and are celebrated for their achievements. The language and adjectives selected to describe the actions and role of Whites during any time period is almost always glorifying and complementary, such as "conquerors" and "hero." When describing events in which the actions or the roles of Whites are known to have been brutal or unjust, the language is muted and the description sanitized in order not to be strongly critical. Observe the section on slavery from Follett:

> *Slavery.* Many Americans wanted to stop slavery. Slavery is the ownership of people by other people. In the 1700s, slavery existed in most of the colonies. By the 1840s, slavery was against the law in most northern states. It then existed mainly in the southern states. Within the southern states, slavery was most common within cotton-growing areas.
>
> Eli Whitney's cotton gin made cotton easier to clean and prepare for the textile factories. In the last chapter you read that the demand for cotton increased. The slaves who planted, harvested, and cleaned the cotton became more and more valuable to their owners. To cotton growers, slavery was a business.[50]

Furthermore, the story line allows Whites to be the center of attention by ignoring the roles or contributions of other groups of color, or placing people of color in the story line only during time periods or events of particular concern to Whites. Examples include Asian Americans working on the railroad: Black Americans in slavery and in the civil rights struggle: Hispanic Americans fighting in Texas and the Southwest: and Native Americans acting as friends of the English colonists, as the first Americans, and fighting with the White settlers.

Collectively, the picture representation of people of color is very low compared to that of Whites, less than two to one (926 Whites/458 people of color). The total number of Black Americans pictured (183) makes them a distant second, and the total number of Native Americans pictured (144) makes this group third. Asian Americans have a total of 82 pictures, which is 21 fewer than for White Americans in one book (Houghton-Mifflin, 1980). The total number of Hispanics pictured (49) is less than the number of Whites in four of the books. In fact, White males alone have 49 or more pictures in five books.

People of color collectively are not portrayed as solvers of their own problems. Blacks are the main group of color that is seen taking some responsibility for their destiny. Problems people of color face because of unfairness and the economic and political desires of White Americans are often presented in a way that helps the reader empathize with people of color, such as the Hawaiians losing their land.[51] However, the discussions of these problems are presented from a White point of view and usually do not explain in sufficient detail the harshness of White men in power and why many problems that people of color face today are the result of the racism, classism, and sexism of long ago. Situations are described in a sanitized manner, rarely giving a criticism of Whites to match the deeds they performed. These books do this by conveying brief facts about events and by suggesting that whatever took place—the good, bad, and ugly—was a part of progress. For example, one book describes the Cherokees as standing in the way of progress and therefore needing to be moved.[52] Another book mentions the brutality of slavery as a "*sad* part of American history."[53] The story line also does not include information or discussions about relationships between different groups of color. For example, did Native Americans and Black Americans have any interactions that were important to the development of the country, and were their associations related only to slavery?

Gender

Males have many more pictures than females (855/512), and there are many more pictures of White females than females of color (328/182). The majority of the books show women (mainly White) in traditional as well as nontraditional roles, but rarely is a male pictured in a nontraditional role. In the story line, "her-story" is undertold or presented as an afterthought. This is very evident, for example, in discussions of the migration of White settlers from the east coast to the west coast, where the role of women is virtually ignored. Women are contextually invisible or marginalized: their roles and contributions often are not covered in any detail in the story line. Sometimes they are given attention in a special section with a heading such as "Special People," where one woman's career and contributions are discussed, or in a special section about an event such as women's suffrage. Women are not usually discussed in sections about major decisions regarding political and economic life. This problem is compounded for American women of color, who are discussed very little in the books. For example, Sacajawea is portrayed as a friend to the White man, but Native American women who resisted White exploration and tried to prevent Whites from driving them off of the land where they were living are not mentioned. At least the authors worked hard to make certain that the language is nonsexist and came very close to succeeding, although in a few instances the reader will come across sexist language like "fireman" or "postman" instead of "fire fighter" or "mail carrier."

Disability

Pictures showing people with disabilities are virtually absent. In four books, it was not possible to identify any person with a disability.[54] In two books, the only disabled person we could identify was Franklin D. Roosevelt.[55] The largest number of times people with disabilities appear in any of the books is three, in which they are shown interacting with their nondisabled friends. [56] The story lines ignore people with disabilities, missing the opportunity to show nondisabled persons the contributions that people with disabilities have made to society, and failing to chronicle the struggles of people with disabilities for rights.

Social Class

The varying socioeconomic conditions that have always existed in this country are virtually absent from the books. The pictures show the United States as fruitful plains with corn as high as an elephant's eye, from sea to shining sea, dotted with growing and prosperous towns and cities. Only during great crises such as the Depression are Americans shown to be in want due to lack of jobs or money; some books do not show this side of America at all. The story line, one could argue, purposefully avoids this. A typical example is the story "We Move from Place To Place."[57] The following questions are provided as advance organizers: "Where are they [the people in the story] moving?" and "Why are they moving?" In the story, the mother of the central character, Carol, is thinking of moving to California: "But first she wants to look things over. She wants to see if she could get a good job. And she wants to look at houses in San Jose and find out how much they cost."[58] After this brief mention of money as a factor influencing life chances and opportunities, the story abruptly moves to Carol settling into her new community. Another story in this book, "Going with the Company," tells of a family following a company that is moving from one town to another. The family moves to obtain a promotion, an increase in salary, and a lower cost of living. These two lessons provide some of the reasons people move, but they are reasons most applicable to middle or upper-middle-class people. For example, Carol's new friend says that "All the houses are new"; the story suggests that the "well off" have worked to become even "better off" through promotion and raise in salary. Poor people or the working poor are not explicitly discussed. The closest the books come to presenting poor people is when the "common person" becomes a hero or national leader, such as Abraham Lincoln. Teachers driven by the demand to increase test scores and unknowing students could easily fail to realize that the story line is leaving out of the discussion an entire class of Americans.

Reading/Language Arts

We examined fifteen reading and language arts textbooks published by eight publishers. Eleven are readers or anthologies,[59] and four are skill books.[60] They range greatly in their treatment of diversity.

Race

The portrayal of Asian Americans ranges from complete absence[61] to 15% of the pictures and leading roles in one or two stories. Most readers have at least one Asian story, although not necessarily an Asian American story. Most have about the same number of Asian males and females. In skills books, Asian names such as Hanako and Huyen are used in sentences. Asian Americans are portrayed doing everyday things such as reading and doing artwork, and in occupations such as letter carrier, laboratory technician, teacher, and physician. They also often appear in multiracial pictures, usually not doing anything in particular.

Black Americans appear in all fifteen texts; the percentage of Black people pictured ranges from 9%[62] to 27%,[63] averaging around 16%. Several books show approximately equal numbers of Black males and females, and some show many more of one sex, but overall one sex does not predominate. Readers contain one to four stories in which the main character is Black; about half of these stories are all-Black. Blacks occasionally serve as support characters in other stories as well. Blacks appear in a variety of roles, ranging from athlete, to farmer, to business person with a briefcase. They are usually middle-class but are occasionally lower-class. The quality of their portrayal varies among books. In some books, Black people occupy nonstereotypic roles that could be filled by anyone. For example, a story in one book shows a Black boy writing letters using different creative formats; a child of any race or sex could fill this role equally well.[64] In a few books, one finds a single, stereotypic story, for example portraying Blacks as poor and rural, with no substantive counterbalancing image elsewhere.[65] Blacks in multiracial group scenes often look White, except that the artist has colored them brown. Most stories are simply not stereotypic, but not particularly set within a Black cultural context. In fact, we did not find one story that drew substantively on the Black American cultural experience.

Identifying Hispanic Americans and Native Americans in pictures is often difficult, as many books contain multiracial pictures of people with brown skin and black hair. Hispanic Americans appear in all fifteen books, ranging from no picture representation [66] to appearing in 26% of these books[67] and averaging around 5%. All the readers have at least one story with a Hispanic American main character; two have as many as five such stories, about half of which are all-Hispanic.[68] Hispanics occasionally appear in other stories. Most books show many more of one sex than the other. In all four skill books, Hispanic names such as Roberto and Mrs. Hernandez are used in sentences. Hispanics often appear in work roles such as potter, cowboy, peasant, or sailor, and they sometimes appear as immigrants. There are some authentic and nonstereotypic contemporary portrayals, however, such as a true story about a Hispanic cartoonist.[69] Two well-done stories about a Mexican American girl living in Texas, set within a contemporary Mexican American context, stress pride in Mexican heritage, although one passage differentiates between American food and Mexican food from San Antonio.[70]

Identifiable Native Americans are completely absent from five books.[71] In the other ten, the percentage of pictured people who are Native American ranges from 2% to 10%. Females tend to appear more often than males, although two books show males only[72] and three are evenly balanced. Readers contain between one and three stories in which the main character is Native American; most of these stories are all-Native, and Native American characters rarely appear in other stories. Stories are both contemporary and historical; contemporary stories show Indian children wearing jeans, for example, often living on reservations. Some stories portray specific tribes, such as Zuni, Chippewa, and Acoma; two stories portray Eskimos. The roles occupied by Native Americans are limited: potter (three stories), cowboy, shepherd, jewelry craftsperson, fisher, hunter, warrior, and athlete. Two stories depict a young male coming to grips with his heritage. Native Americans are in most stories we found in which cultural identity is explicitly discussed, and it tends to be presented as a problem to members of this group.

White Americans appear in all fifteen books. The percentage of people pictured who are White ranges from about 50%[73] to about 80%.[74] Only three books show approximately equal numbers of White males and females in pictures.[75] The rest show more males, and in four the ratio is as high as 3 to 1 male to female.[76] Readers contain between eight and twenty-one stories in which the main character is White; most of these stories are all-White. Whites also serve as support characters in other stories; one finds few stories in which Whites do not appear. Whites appear in by far the most varied roles of any racial group, and more than any other group Whites appear as famous people, at leisure, as royalty, and as upper-class people. White females tend to appear in traditional roles such as playing with dolls and cooking, but they also appear in roles such as washing a car and carrying a briefcase. White males also usually appear in traditional roles such as inventor, doctor, or construction worker; a few also appear in nontraditional sex roles. Texts tend not to portray people or situations having identifiable ethnic content, with some exceptions noted above. Most books attempt to show people doing "generic" mainstream cultural activities, speaking Standard English, and dressed and living like a "generic" American. This is probably done to avoid stereotyping. But in the process, authentic experiences that are rooted in ethnicity are shown infrequently, and positive cultural differences are rendered unimportant or nonexistent.

Gender

In four books both sexes appear in pictures in about equal numbers,[77] in one females predominate in pictures although males predominate as main characters,[78] and in the remaining ten books males predominate, ranging from 55% to 75% of the people pictured. Most people in most books appear in sex-stereotypic roles, and emotions or character traits tend to be sex-stereotypic. For example, one second-grade book has 42 stories, 22 of which have human characters; 15 of these stories depict strong sex stereotypes, with females as worriers, nurturers, concerned about their appearance, afraid and needing males to rescue them; and males appear as brave, needing to prove themselves, and desiring power.[79] Females are more likely to appear in nontraditional roles than are males: while most books show some females doing things such as participating in athletics, carrying a briefcase, or having an adventure, one must look hard to find males doing things such as taking care of children, working in the kitchen, or holding a traditionally female occupation. Even animals with a known gender tend to follow traditional gender stereotypes, and if gender is unknown, tend to be referred to as "he." Otherwise, all the books use nonsexist language.

Disability

People with identifiable disabilities appear in only seven books. In three of these books, two of which are skill books, they appear in pictures only.[80] A person with a disability is the focus of one story in three readers[81] and of two stories in one reader.[82] People with disabilities do not serve as support characters in other stories, although in one reader they occasionally appear in the background of pictures.[83] About equal numbers of both sexes appear, and they are mostly White. Altogether, a variety of disabilities appear, including, in one story, learning disabilities. So few people with disabilities are shown doing something (in pictures they tend to sit, smiling) that it is difficult to generalize about roles, except to note that in stories they are mainly coping with difficulties or being helped to learn something.

Social Class

Books show social-class diversity very little. Seven portray only middle-class people, or depict people wearing clothing, occupying houses, and using speech commonly associated with the middle class.[84] The other seven books show some identifiable social-class diversity, although the great majority of people in these books appear to be middle-class. Upper-class people most often are royalty, although some hold jobs such as physician and engineer; all are White. Lower-class people are both White and of color. Some are portrayed much like other characters but holding a low-paying job, such as short-order cook; some are portrayed sympathetically, such as wanting to make money and eventually succeeding. Some are villagers of long ago. And some lower-class people are portrayed stereotypically, foolish or uneducated. The books mainly give the impression that there is little or no social-class diversity.

Overall, these reading and language arts books depict people of various colors and both sexes, but they do very little to help young people learn about issues related to diversity, or even to learn that issues exist. They also do fairly little to help young people develop an understanding of different American cultural groups. This is epitomized by the approach that the four skills books take. The publishers of these books seem to have made an effort to distribute a variety of people and names across a variety of roles in a way that shows few patterns and that would not reflect any particular group's experiences. Even the reading books seem to avoid presenting social issues, although they present stories about interpersonal issues such as a child not fitting into a group. Books sometimes explicitly deny that inequality and injustice exist. One book, for example, is predominantly White but has a somewhat stereotypic story about Blacks and many sex stereotypes. But it also contains an article entitled "What will you be?" which shows Black and White males and females in a variety of equal roles, suggesting that anyone can be anything. Not only does this obscure the existence of discrimination, it contradicts the hidden curriculum of the rest of the book.[85]

Science

We examined ten science textbooks, published by six publishers.[86] The science books do not contain as many pictures of individual people as the other books we examined, only about ninety pictures per science book; however, the representation of groups is fairly similar.

Race

Asian Americans occupy about 5% of the pictures. Asian American males are shown in pictures a few more times than females. Asian Americans are shown mainly doing "everyday things" such as participating in a sporting event. With the exception of one book,[87] Asian Americans are rarely shown as scientists or as engaging in scientific investigation, such as using a microscope or a telescope. Only two books discuss the contributions Asians have made to science: one acknowledges the contributions of ancient Chinese astronomers,[88] and the other discusses the careers of two Asian American scientists.[89]

The percentage of pictures of Black Americans ranges from 6% to 20%, although in only two books is the percentage under 10%.[90] Pictures of Black males appear about one-third times as frequently as pictures of Black females. Most pictures show Blacks in everyday roles, as musicians, as radio repair people, and having an eye exam; but they do not show Blacks conducting scientific investigations. The exception is one book, that contains several pictures of Black American female students doing scientific experiments, and discusses the careers of two Black American female scientists.[91] The books do not address Blacks' contributions to science. Blacks do appear, however, in a discussion of sickle cell anemia.

Hispanic Americans are shown in 1% to 5% of the pictures in eight books, in 7% in one,[92] and in 12% in one.[93] Approximately the same number of Hispanic males and females are depicted. Hispanics are seen participating in everyday activities such as riding a bike, jumping rope, eating, and studying. They are not shown conducting scientific investigations or as scientists. The books do not address contributions of Hispanics to science.

Native Americans are in 1% to 5% of the pictures in eight of the books. In two books we could not identify a picture of a Native American,[94] in three more books we could not identify any Native American males,[95] and in two books we could not identify any Native American females.[96] Two pictures show a Native American male working in science, one as a geologist and the other as a guide for an expedition.[97] One book mentions how Mayan Indians observed the sky[98]; otherwise, the books do not address scientific contributions of Native Americans.

White Americans and European Whites are depicted most frequently in pictures, ranging from 55%[99] to 83%.[100] White males are seen about 40% more times than White females. Whites are shown doing scientific investigations as well as everyday things. They are also shown participating in many different branches of science such as medicine and physics. The books discuss famous White scientists and Whites' contributions to science. Whites are seen as ingenious, curious, and dedicated to solving many of life's problems through science.

Gender

The science books show more males than females (approximately 463/ 337), and more than twice as many pictures of White females as of females of color. But there is very little career or occupation role stereotyping along gender lines. Males and females (often students) are seen doing scientific things throughout the books, such as doing experiments with simple machines, testing Newton's Laws of motion, and explaining how "esters" are made. Both females and males are shown using elaborate scientific equipment, such as special computers. However, a few pictures show females doing household activities like washing and cooking, but do not show males doing household activities. Some books show pictures of famous female scientists, such as Lise Meitner, and pictures of females having a career in science, such as nuclear physics. The books do not use sexist language.

Disability

The majority of the books have at least one picture of a disabled person, although in two books we could not locate any people with disabilities.[101] These pictures do not necessarily show the disabled person doing scientific investigation, but doing everyday things such as sports.

Social Class

It was difficult to determine the socioeconomic class of the pictures. However, an educated observation would be that the majority show middle- and upper-class settings, and many of the pictures showing scientific concepts in action use middle-class and upper-class artifacts, such as boats, ballet, traditional foods, and travel. Rarely did we see a picture of a setting such as a vacant lot, or materials associated with the underclass or working class. The science laboratories and experiments conducted suggest that financial support for science equipment is not a problem. This kind of financial support for science equipment is not often seen in many schools in urban areas or in communities where the working poor reside. Brown and Haycock argue that "at every level of the education process, minority students are less likely to have access to high-quality resources—including teachers, books, and physical facilities—than other students."[102]

Mathematics

We examined eight mathematics textbooks published by five publishers,[103] and one computer textbook.[104] All have story problems and illustrations accompanying problems; several also contain photographs at the beginning or end of each chapter illustrating people in various careers.

Race

In many pictures, particularly in sketches, it is difficult to identify the race of individuals, and there is no story to help out as there is in readers. Up to 19% of the pictured people in the math texts are of ambiguous racial membership.[105] In addition, the names used in most story problems could refer to anyone, such as Ted, Sue, Dick, Tony, or Katy, although Asian and Hispanic names are also used in all the texts.

Asian Americans are shown in 1%[106] to 13%[107] of the pictures, averaging around 4%. Altogether, the books contain about the same proportion of each sex, but most have more of one sex than the other. Asian names also occasionally appear in story problems. Many Asians appear in everyday roles, such as standing, playing, driving a car, or as students. About one-third of the Asian Americans appear as well-educated middle- to upper-middle-class people holding professional positions, which frequently involve them with computers. For example, one text portrays a well-dressed female statistician in the sports department of a newspaper.[108] No Asian appears in a lower-class position.

Black Americans comprise between 14%[109] and 29%[110] of the people pictured. Three books contain equal proportions of male and female Black Americans[111]; the rest contain at least twice as many Black males as females. One generally cannot determine whether story problems refer to Blacks as traditionally Black names such as Mahalia or Willie, rarely appear, and most problems are not accompanied by pictures of people. Therefore, images of Blacks emanate mainly from pictures. Most books depict Blacks in a variety of everyday roles such as walking the dog, playing, or camping. However, the most common single role in which Blacks appear, with the exception of student, is that of athlete. Drawings of males playing basketball, football, or baseball usually include Blacks. Several texts include a few famous people, usually mathematicians; the only famous Blacks shown are not mathematicians but rather athletes such as Jackie Robinson.[112] Blacks occasionally appear in nonstereotypic occupations, such as cameraman and supervisor, but Blacks appear more frequently in lower-status occupations such as truck driver or tollbooth attendant. Only two books show Blacks in science professions: physicist, chemist, and astronaut.[113] Texts vary in the extent to which they depict Black children as serious students; while some show Blacks working calculators or computers, others such as the computer textbook[114] do so little or not at all. Most Blacks are portrayed as middle-class; however, in one book Blacks are the main people buying on credit or at a discount.[115]

Identifiable Hispanic Americans comprise between 1%[116] and 9%[117] of the pictures; most commonly, about 3% of the people pictured are identifiably Hispanic. Only one book contains equal numbers of each sex[118]; the rest show either mainly Hispanic females or Hispanic males. As many as 12% of the names in story problems are Hispanic.[119] Hispanics, like Blacks, appear mainly in everyday roles such as playing, eating, buying something, or doing class-work. No single role predominates for this group, as sports does for Blacks, although the main occupation in which Hispanics appear is that of teacher. Several are shown in nonstereotypic sex roles such as a male sewing[120] and a female working on a bike.[121] Only one book depicts Hispanics in upper-middle-class occupations: scientist and store owner.[122] Hispanics tend not to be shown as mathematicians; for example, in the computer book most Hispanics are not shown using computers.[123] Hispanics generally appear middle-class, although in one book a Hispanic male is borrowing money to buy a guitar.[124]

Native Americans are not identifiable in any form in six books.[125] They do not appear in pictures in two additional books, although each of these books has a Native American male in a story problem.[126] The remaining two books each depict one Native American of each sex. Roles in which Native Americans appear are extremely limited, as so few appear. Two male roles are telephone technician and owner of a bike shop; other roles simply illustrate story problems, such as a female weighing thumbtacks. Other people in the books could be Native American, but we could not tell.

White Americans, on the other hand, appear in large numbers in all nine books. Between 48%[127] and 80%[128] of the people in pictures are White; most commonly, Whites are about two-thirds of the people pictured. Four books show about equal numbers of each sex,[129] four show more males, and one shows more females. As with Blacks, images of Whites emanate mainly from pictures, as most names in story problems could fit anyone. The main famous people in the math texts have contributed to the history of mathematics; mainly White males appear, although a few White females also appear. In pictures, Whites appear in a wide variety of everyday roles. Some books clearly feature Whites in the most desirable or prestigious roles. For example, in one book the only people portrayed reading are White males, and the majority of people holding calculators are White.[130] In another book, White males are shown as initiators of progress and designers of time-saving formulas other people use.[131] Even books that do not have such obvious biases, however, tend to give Whites roles other groups do not occupy, if for no other reason than by virtue of their numbers. For example, Whites appear as cheerleaders, traders on the New York Stock Exchange, an oncologist, sunbathers at the beach, a veterinarian, an environmental engineer, and someone making pizza. Whites appear neither as obviously rich nor as needing to borrow money. The main impression the books give about Whites is that they are numerous and everywhere.

Gender

Equal proportions of males and females appear in pictures in three texts[132]; the rest show more males than females. The percentage of females in pictures ranges from 33% to 50%, and in story problems from 25% to 50%. Most books portray both sexes in fairly equal proportions in a variety of interchangeable roles, such as shopping, buying things, collecting things, doing math problems, feeding the dog, driving, running, and playing baseball. In fact, females appear as athletes as often, or almost as often, as males; both sexes appear in almost the same sports, although females rarely appear playing football. Females appear both in stereotypic roles such as ballet dancer, queen, sewing, and talking on the telephone, and in nonstereotypic roles such as letter carrier, lawn mower, construction worker, and engineer; texts vary considerably in their emphasis of one or the other. Males appear in a few texts in sex stereotypic roles only, such as astronaut, scientist, car sales rep, scout leader, and auto mechanic. Males are by far the main famous people (e.g., Pythagoras, Ben Franklin, Ty Cobb), and greatly outnumber females as store- or land-owners. However, most texts also feature at least a few males in nonstereotypic roles such as cook or babysitter. One can find additional subtle forms of sexism in some books, such as referring to unnamed people as "he" or consistently putting a male in the driver's seat when both sexes are in a car.[133]

Disability

People with identifiable disabilities do not appear at all in four texts.[134] People with disabilities comprise 1% to 5% of the pictures in the other five texts. Most of these are White people in wheelchairs; some sit and do nothing, others do things such as work problems with a calculator or pot plants. The computer text, which has the largest representation of people with disabilities, shows a greater variation of people with productive roles than the other texts; in addition to depicting people in wheelchairs, it also depicts a blind man programming a computer with the aid of Braille, and a person with no arms using a computer with a mouth utensil.[135]

Social Class

All nine texts attempt to avoid the issue of social class by portraying virtually everyone as middle-class. People are usually dressed simply, and there is usually little or no background setting. The few people who appear to be from a lower class are usually of color, such as the Hispanic male borrowing money to buy a guitar. The few people who appear financially well-off are White, Black, or Asian. To varying degrees, however, the texts also assume and encourage material consumption. Story problems frequently involve spending money to buy things, making money, or taking trips that cost money. Most financial transactions would fit an average budget, although a few involve spending relative large sums of money to buy fairly expensive things such as a microwave, a deluxe lawn mower, or a computer.

Discussion

As noted at the beginning of this chapter, students are presented in classrooms with usually only one version of reality. That version embodies certain interests, reifies certain interpretations and value judgments, and gives prominence to some pieces of knowledge while rendering others invisible. Many students may internalize what they are taught through textbooks, although others may marginalize it within their own thinking or reject it outright. But even if students forget, ignore, or reject what they encounter in textbooks, textbook content is still important because it withholds, obscures, and renders unimportant many ideas and areas of knowledge.

Looking across these four subjects areas clearly shows the extent to which the experiences, concerns, accomplishments, and issues of different groups appear on the curricular agenda. Whites consistently dominate textbooks, although their margin of dominance varies widely. Whites receive the most attention, are shown in the widest variety of roles, and dominate the story line and lists of accomplishments. Blacks are the next most included racial group. However, the books show Blacks in a more limited range of roles than Whites and give only a sketchy account of Black history and little sense of contemporary Black Life. Asian Americans and Hispanic Americans appear mainly as figures on the landscape with virtually no history or contemporary ethnic experience, and no sense of the ethnic diversity within each group is presented. Native Americans appear mainly as historical figures, although there are a few contemporary stories in reading books. Furthermore, very little interaction among different groups of color is shown. For example, Black cowboys were in the West with Native Americans, Mexican Americans were in Texas with Native Americans, and Mexican Americans, Chinese Americans, Japanese Americans, and Filipino Americans were all in California. These groups are only shown interacting with Whites. In addition, the books contain very little about contemporary race relations or issues for which these groups are currently struggling. They convey an image of harmonious blending of different colors of people, dominated by White people, and suggest that everyone is happy with current arrangements.

The books have successfully addressed gender issues mainly by eliminating most sexist language. Males predominate in most books; but even in books in which females have a major presence, females of color are shown fairly little. One gains little sense of the history or culture of women, and learns very little about sexism or current issues involving gender. Females are shown in many more nontraditional roles than males, suggesting that it is not important for males to broaden their roles. The books convey the image that there are no real issues involving sexism today, that any battles for equality have been won. Women of color are rarely shown as active agents in political, social, and economic struggle for equality. Harriet Tubman and Sojourner Truth are often given attention in their fight against slavery, but students could easily come to believe that these were the only two women of color who were active in the struggle for civil rights. The recent publication of *The Schomburg Library of Nineteen-Century Black Women Writers*[136] points out that many Black women were active fighters for social change, and that historians have neglected to report their story. For example, a Black woman, Maria W. Stewart, is recorded as being the first American-born women to speak before a male and female audience in defense of women's rights. Interactions among or differences between women of different racial groups are not shown; students could easily believe that women of all racial groups worked together for suffrage, or that Hispanic women experience gender just as White women do.

Social class is not treated in the books much at all. The great majority of people and situations presented are middle-class or involve at least a modest level of financial status. The image that books in all subject areas convey is that the United States is not stratified on the basis of social class, that almost everyone is middle-class, that there is no poverty and no great wealth. This not only leaves students blind to the social-class structure, it avoids helping students learn why people are poor, what poverty is like, or how people have struggled over how wealth should be distributed. Social class and poverty simply do not appear on the curricular agenda.

Disability is ignored as well. Of the forty-seven texts we analyzed, no people with disabilities appear in eighteen, and the rest give people with disabilities or issues involving disability only token recognition. Students reading these textbooks would gain virtually no understanding of the current issues that people with disabilities face, nor of the struggles for rights that people have waged. An image of invisibility or of passivity on the part of those with disabilities predominates.

Let us return to the concerns expressed in the opening of this chapter. Bloom is concerned about the American mind becoming closed, and Hirsch is concerned about the extent to which schools are promoting cultural literacy.[137] So are we. Our analysis of current textbooks clearly shows the extent to which the curriculum focuses on the White male and downplays or simply ignores the accomplishments and concerns of Americans who are of color, female, poor, and/or disabled.

In a time of changing racial and ethnic demographics and changing roles of women, textbooks today help provide a framework for interpreting diversity. That framework, however, is a fairly conservative one that helps maintain existing relations between groups. It acknowledges racial and gender diversity, but provides only minimal understanding of it. Earlier in this chapter we noted that symbolic representations in texts are important vehicles of social control insofar as they legitimate the status of dominant groups, render socially constructed relations among groups as natural, and "select in" some ideas and domains of knowledge while "selecting out" others.

Our analysis shows that textbooks continue to legitimate the status of White males, despite the inclusion of other groups. Some educators have claimed that increased focus on people of color and White women had diverted attention from White males.[138] This claim does not hold up in the books we examined; White males continue to occupy more space and attention in textbooks than any other group; White females come in second, and racial minority groups trail.

Educators also have claimed that attention to White women, Blacks, Native Americans, and other groups is superficial, forced,and occasionally ridiculous.[139] This is sometimes true, because content about these other groups is simply added into existing frameworks for organizing content. There is a danger here in the way most books treat diversity. For example, the math book that depicted a female Native American weighing thumbtacks was clearly oriented around a mainstream "middle America" conception of society in which people of color participate as visibly different individuals rather than as members of oppressed and culturally rich groups. Banks has argued that "the infusion of bits and pieces of ethnic minority groups into the curriculum not only reinforces the idea that ethnic minority groups are not integral parts of U.S. society, it also results in the trivialization of ethnic cultures."[140] Furthermore, it erroneously suggests that diversity is being reinforced and studied when it really is not.

Textbooks participate in social control when they render socially constructed relations among groups as natural. The vision of social relations that the textbooks we analyzed for the most part project is one of harmony and equal opportunity—anyone can do or become whatever he or she wants; problems among people are mainly individual in nature and in the end are resolved. The reading books treat individual problems exclusively, and most problems are resolved by the end of the story. The math and science books simply sprinkle people throughout, in roles selected almost at random. As math and science are often perceived as ideologically neutral subject areas, the fact that they are projecting an ideological image—that society as it currently exists is harmonious and equal—would probably not be questioned by most people.

Textbooks further participate in social control when they "select in" some ideas and domains of knowledge and "select out" others. Physical, visible differences have been "selected in," very clearly. This corresponds with a portion of the reality Americans experience when they see each other. Cultural differences are included only now and then, and sometimes portrayed as a problem, although in some of the readers problems brought about by cultural differences are resolved by individuals. Culture is shown to be a problem when, for example, a Hispanic family is misunderstood by Anglo-Americans or a Native American must resolve his or her identity conflict. White culture is not shown to be a problem. The differential distribution of power and wealth is an idea that is not present at all.

Textbooks also reinforce the notion of individuality. The idea that people are members of collectives appears only very selectively. For example, in history passages on the suffrage and civil rights movements, or in reading stories about Native Americans on reservations, the idea of collectivity appears. Otherwise, it simply does not. Students do not get information on groups dominating groups, nor are they given the vocabulary and concepts that would help them see themselves as members of social groups that relate in unequal ways with others. (Several of our students who have analyzed textbooks have expressed concern over stories that feature only members of a non-White racial group, commenting that such stories should be more integrated.)

It appears publishers roughly follow representation in the U.S. population to decide how much attention to give different racial groups, giving Whites the most space but less than their 83%, and groups of color a little more than their proportion of the general population. Women constitute slightly more than half of the population, but receive less than half of the attention; people with disabilities are estimated to constitute 12% of the school population and receive considerably less than 12% of the attention; and lower-class people clearly do not show up in any proportional way at all. But the issue of representation is an important one. Our analysis shows that any group that receives scant attention, regardless of their representation in the population, tends to be treated superficially and piecemeal. We would suggest giving enough attention to America's various groups so that students can gain a sense of each group's history, complexity, and achievements. This may involve reducing attention to White males further; however, it could also involve orienting more of the curriculum around real human experiences and less of it around bland, fictitious stories, skills taught out of the context of human experience (such as decoding or arithmetic skills), or content involving meaningless activities (such as story problems about drinking glasses of juice). Curriculum design might begin by selecting concepts, experiences, images, and contributions that should be taught about each racial, gender, social class, and disability group, then weaving this throughout the curriculum. Repetition, such as excessive numbers of adventure stories about White males, could be eliminated, and skill drills, such as multiplication story problems, could be contextualized within meaningful content.

Conclusion

Treatment of diversity in textbooks has not improved much over the past fifteen years or so, generally, although a few textbooks have improved in specific, limited ways. There was a flurry of activity to "multiculturalize" textbooks during the late 1960s and early 1970s, although that activity never did address social class in textbooks. That activity may have stopped, and we may be entering an era of backsliding, a return to more White- and male-dominated curricula. This would be quite dangerous, producing citizens with a shallow social consciousness and narrow sense of history and culture, and alienating from school lower-class children and children of color. Textbooks need to be scrutinized carefully, and those that fail to educate children meaningfully about America's diversity and its history of oppression should not be bought and used.

Appendix
Reading Textbooks

Allington, R. L., R. L. Cramer, P. M. Cunningham, G. Y. Perez, C. F. Robinson, and R. I. Tierney (1985). *Rough and Ready.* (Glenview, Ill.: Scott, Foresman & Co.).

Beech, L. W., R. Cramer, C. W., Feder, T. McCarthy, N. C. Najimy, D. Priplett (1984). *Language: Skills and Use,* 2d ed. (Glenview, Ill.: Scott, Foresman & Co.).

Chaparro, J. L., and M. A. Trost (1985). *Reading Literature.* (Evanston, Ill.: McDougal, Littell & Co.).

Clymer, T., R. Indrisano, D. D. Johnson, P. D. Pearson, and R. L. Venezky (1985). *Across the Fence.* (Needham Heights, Mass.: Ginn & Co.).

Clymer, T., R. Indrisano, D. D. Johnson, P. D. Pearson, and R. L. Venezky (1985). *Ten Times Round.* (Needham Heights, Mass.: Ginn & Co.).

Durr, W. K., J. M. LePere, M. L. Alsin, R. P. Bunyan, and S. Shaw (1983). *Honeycomb.* (Boston: Houghton Mifflin).

Durr, W. K., and J. Pikulski (1986). *Explorations.* (Boston: Houghton Mifflin).

Littell, J., ed. (1984). *Building English Skills.* (Evanston, Ill.: McDougal, Littell & Co.).

Littell, J., ed. (1985). *Basic Skills in English.* (Exanston, Ill.: McDougal, Littel & Co.).

Maccarone, S., ed. (1983). *Crossing Boundaries.* (Lexington, Mass.: D. C. Heath & Co.).

Matteoni, L., W. Lane, F. Sucher, and V. Burns (1980). *A Painted Ocean.* (New York: The Economy Company).

Matteoni, L., and F. Sucher (1986). *Can It Be?* (New York: The Economy Company).

Paden, F., S. Schaffrath, and S. Wittenbrink (1984). *Building English Skills.* (Evanston, Ill.: McDougal, Littell & Co.).

Rowland, P. T. (1982). *The Nitty Gritty Rather Pretty City.* (Reading, Mass.: Addison-Wesley Pub.).

Weiss, B. J., P. S. Rosenbaum, A. M. Shaw, and M. J. Tolbert (1986). *To See Ourselves.* (Fort Worth, Tex.: Holt, Rinehart & Winston.).

Mathematics Textbooks

Bolster, L. C., W. Crown, R. Hamada, V. Hansen, M. M. Lindquist, C. McNerney, W. Nibbelink, G. Prigge, C. Rahilfs, D. Robitaille, J. Schultz, S. Sharron, J. Swafford, I. Vance, D. E. Williams, J. Wilson, and R. Wisner (1987). *Invitation to Mathematics.* (Glenview, Ill.: Scott, Foresman & Co.).

Bolster, L. C., W. Crown, M. M. Lindquist, C. McNerney, W. Nabbelink, P. Glenn, C. Rahlfs, D. Robitaille, J. Schultz, J. Swafford, I. Vance, J. Wilson, and R. Wisher (1985). *Invitation to Mathematics.* (Glenview, Ill.: Scott, Foresman & Co.).

Carey, L., H. Bolster, and D. Woodburn (1982). *Mathematics in Life,* 2d ed. (Glenview, Ill.: Scott, Foresman & Co.).

Duncan, E. R., W. G. Quast, M. A. Haubner, W. L. Cole, L. M. Gemmill, C. E. Allen, A. M. Cooper, and L. R. Capps (1983). *Mathematics.* (Boston: Houghton Mifflin).

Eicholz, R. E., P. G. O'Daffer, C. R. Fleenor, R. I. Charles, S. Young, and C. S. Barnett (1987). *Addison-Wesley Mathematics.* (Reading, Mass.: Addison-Wesley Pub. Co.).

Golden, N. (1986). *Computer Literacy with an Introduction to BASIC Programming.* (Orlando, Fla.: Harcourt Brace Jovanovich).

Rucker, W. E., and C. A. Dilley (1982). *Heath Mathematics.* (Lexington, Mass.: D. C. Heath & Co.).

Thoburn, T., J. E. Forbes, and R. D. Bechtel (1982a). *Macmillan Mathematics.* New York: Macmillan Pub. Co.).

Thoburn, T., J. E. Forbes, and R. D. Bechtel (1982b). *Mathematics.* (New York: Macmillan Pub. Co.).

Social Studies Textbooks

Armbruster, B. B., C. L. Mitsakos, and V. R. Rogers (1986). *America's Regions and Regions of the World.* (Needham Heights, Mass.: Ginn and Company).

Arnsdorf, V. E., T. M. Helmus, N.J.G. Pounds, and E. A. Toppin (1982a). *The World and Its People: The United States and Its Neighbors.* (Needham Heights, Mass.: Silver Burdett Company).

Buggey, J. (1983). *Our Communities.* (Chicago: Follett Publishing Company).

Buggey, J., and M. E. Swartz (1983). *Home and School.* (Chicago: Follett Publishing Company).

Buggey, J. (1983). *Our United States.* (Chicago: Follett Publishing Company).

Buggey, J., G. Danzer, C. Mitsakos, and C. Risinger (1982). *America! America!* (Glenview, Ill.: Scott, Foresman and Company).

Cangemi, J., (1983). *Our History.* (Fort Worth, Tex.: Holt, Rinehart and Winston Publishers).

Clark, M. K. (1982). *The Earth and Its People.* (New York: Macmillan Pub. Co., Inc.).

Gross, H. H., D. W. Follett, R. E. Gabler, W. L. Burton, and W. D. Nielson (1980). *Exploring Our World: Regions.* (Chicago: Follett Publishing Company).

Harthern, A. T. (1982). *The World and Its People: Families and Neighbors.* (Needham Heights, Mass.: Silver Burdett Company).

Hyder, B. P., and C. S. Brown (1982). *The World and Its People: Neighborhoods and Communities.* (Needham Heights, Mass.: Silver Burdett Company).

King, D. C., and C. C. Anderson (1980). *America: Past and Present.* (Boston: Houghton Mifflin Company).

Schwartz, M., and J. R. O'Connor (1981). *The New Exploring American History.* (New York: Globe Book Company, Inc.).

Social Science Staff of the Educational Research Council of America (1982). *The Making of Our America.* (Needham Heights, Mass.: Allyn and Bacon, Inc.).

Science Textbooks

Abruscato, J., J. Fossaceca, J. Hassarc, and D. Peck (1984). *Holt Science.* (Fort Worth, Tex.: Holt, Rinehart and Winston Publishers).

Adams, D., J. Hackett, and R. Sund (1980). *Accent on Science.* (Columbus, Ohio: Charles Merrill Publishing Co.).

Alexander, P., Fiegel, M., Foehr, S. K., Harris, A. F., Krajkovich, J. G., May, K. W., Tzimo-poulos, N. and Voltmer, R. K. (1987). *Physical Science* (Needham Heights, Mass.: Silver Burdett Company).

Alexander, P., et al. (1987). *Earth Science.* (Needham Heights, Mass.: Silver Burdett Co.).

Appenbrink, D., S. Halpernslot, P. Hownshell, and O. Smith (1981). *Physical Science.* (Englewood Cliffs, New Jer.: Prentice Hall Publishing Co.).

Brandwein, P. E., B. Cross, and S. S. Neivert (1985). *Science and Technology: Changes We Make.* (Lawrence, Kans.: Coronado Publishers, Inc.).

Heimler, C. H., and C. D. Neal (1983). *Principles of Science, Book 1.* (Columbus, Ohio: Merrill Publishing Company).

Heimler, C. H., and C. D. Neal (1983). *Principles of Science, Book. 2* (Columbus, Ohio: Merrill Publishing Company).

Heimler, C. H., and J. Price (1987). *Focus on Physical Science.* (Columbus, Ohio: Merrill Publishing Company).

Mallinson, G. G., J. B. Mallinson, W. L. Smallwood, and C. Valentino (1985). *Science.* (Needham Heights, Mass.: Silver Burdett Company).

Notes

1. National Commission on Excellence in Education, *A Nation at Risk* (Washington, D.C.: U.S. Government Printing Office, 1983).

2. See, for example, Mortimer J. Adler, *The Paideia Proposal* (New York: Macmillan, 1982); Ernest L. Boyer, *High School* (New York: Harper and Row, 1983); John I. Goodlad, *A Place Called School* (New York: McGraw-Hill, 1984); National Science Board Commission on Precollege Education in Mathematics, Science and Technology, *Educating Americans for the 21st Century* (Washington, D.C.: National Science Foundation, 1983); Theodore R. Sizer, *Horace's Compromise* (New York: Houghton Mifflin, 1984); Task Force on Education for Economic Growth, *Action for Excellence* (Denver, Colo.: Education Commission of the States,

1983); The College Board, *Academic Preparation for College* (New York: The College Board, 1983); and Twentieth Century Fund, *Making the Grade* (New York: Twentieth Century Fund, 1983).

3. Carl A. Grant and Christine E. Sleeter, "Equality, Equity and Excellence: A Critique," in *Excellence in Education,* ed. Phil Altbach, Gail P. Kelly, and Lois Weis (Buffalo, N.Y.: Prometheus, 1985), pp. 139–60.

4. A. Bloom, *The Closing of the American Mind* (New York: Simon & Schuster, 1987), p. 381.

5. E. D. Hirsch, Jr., *Cultural Literacy: What Every American Needs to Know* (New York: Vintage Books, Random House, Inc., 1988), p. 4.

6. William J. Bennett, *Our Children and Our Country* (New York: Simon & Schuster, 1988).

7. Bloom, *The Closing of the American Mind,* p. 22.

8. J. Dewart, *The State of Black America 1988* (New York: National Urban League, 1988); and National Center for Education Statistics, *The Condition of Education* (Washington, D.C.: U.S. Government Printing Office, 1988).

9. Pierre Bourdieu, "Cultural Reproduction and Social Reproduction", in *Power and Ideology in Education,* ed. Jerome Karabel and A. H. Halsey (New York: Oxford University Press, 1977), pp. 487–510; Geoff Whitty, "Teachers and Examiners," in Geoff Whitty and Michael Young, eds., *Explorations in the Politics of School Knowledge* (Driffield, Eng.: Nafferton Books, 1976).

10. Bill Nichols, *Ideology and the Image* (Bloomington, Ind.: Indiana University Press, 1981), p. 290.

11. Cleo Cherryholmes, *Power and Criticism* (New York: Teachers College Press, 1988), p. 55.

12. Jean Anyon, "Workers, Labor and Economic History, and Textbook Content," in *Ideololgy and Practice in Schooling,* ed. Michael W. Apple and Lois Weis (Philadelphia: Temple University Press, 1983), p. 51.

13. Cherryholmes, *Power and Criticism,* p. 52.

14. Anyon, "Workers," p. 51.

15. L. J. Cronbach, "Introduction," in *Text Materials in Modern Education,* ed. L. J. Cronbach, F. Bienstedt, F. McMurray, W. Schramm, and W. B. Spalding (Urbana, Ill.: University of Illinois Press, 1955), p. 3.

16. M. W. Apple, *Teachers and Texts: A Political Economy of Class and Gender Relations in Education.* (Boston: Routledge, 1988), p. 81.

17. L. J. Cronbach and F. McMurray, "The Controversial Past and Present of the Text," in *Text Materials in Modern Education,* ed. L. J. Cronbach, R. Bierstedt, F. McMurray, W. Schramm, and W. B. Spalding (Urbana, Ill.: University of Illinois Press, 1955), p. 12.

18. James A. Banks, *Multiethnic Education: Theory and Practice,* 2d ed. (Boston: Allyn & Bacon, 1981) pp. 229–31 and 257–80.

19. See, for example, Robin A. Butterfield, Elena Demos, Gloria W. Grant, Peter S. Moy, and Anna L. Perez, "A Multicultural Analysis of a Popular Basal Reading Series in the International Year of the Child, *Journal of Negro Education* 57 (1979): 382–89; R. Costo and J. Henry, *Textbooks and the American Indian* (San Francisco, Calif.: *American Indian Historical Society,* Indian Historical Press, Inc., 1970); M. Dunfee, *Eliminating Ethnic Bias* (Washington, D.C.: ASCD, 1974); M. B Kane, *Minorities in Textbooks: A Study of their Treatment in Social Studies* (Chicago: Quadrangle Books, 1970); and Michigan Department of Education, *A Second Report on the Treatment of Minorities in American History Textbooks* (Lansing, Mich., April 1971).

20. G. Britton, M. Lumpkin, and E. Britton, "The battle to Imprint Citizens for the 21st Century," *Reading Teacher* 37 (1984): 724–33; Carl A. Grant and Gloria W. Grant, "The Multicultural Analysis of Some Second and Third Grade Textbook Readers—A Survey Analysis," *Journal of Negro Education* 50 (1981): 63–74; J. Reyhner, "Native Americans in Basal Reading Textbooks: Are There Enough?" *Journal of American Indian Education* 26 (October 1986): 14–21.

21. Ruth Charnes, "U.S. History Textbooks: Help or Hindrance to Social Justice?" *Interracial Books for Children Bulletin* 15 (1984): 3–8; Jesus Garcia and D. C. Tanner, "The Portrayal of Black Americans in U.S. History Textbooks," *Social Studies* 76 (September 1985): 200–204; Nathan Glazer and R. Ueda, *Ethnic Groups in History Textbooks* (Washington, D. C.: Ethics and Public Policy Center, 1983); C. L Hahn and G. Blankenship, "Women and Economics Textbooks," *Theory and Research in Education* 2 (1983): 67–76; and G. O. O'Neill, "The North American Indian in Contemporary History and Social Studies Textbooks," *Journal of American Indian Studies* 27 (May 1987): 22–28.

22. R. R. Powell and J. Garcia, "What Research Says . . . About Stereotypes," *Science and Children* 25 (1988): 21–23.

23. Glazer and Ueda, *Ethnic Groups in History Textbooks*, p. 59.

24. Britton, Lumpkin, and Britton, "The Battle to Imprint Citizens"; Kathryn P. Scott, "Whatever Happened to Jane and Dick? Sexism in Texts Reexamined," *Peabody Journal of Education* 58 (1981): 135–42.

25. Hahn and Blankenship, "Women and Economics Textbooks"; B. E. Selke, "U.S. History Textbooks: Portraits of Men and Women?" *Southwestern Journal of Social Education* (1983): 13–20; Mary Kay Thompson Tetreault, "Integrating Women's History: The Case of United States History High School Textbooks," *History Teacher* 19 (1986): 211–62; and Mary Kay Tetreault, "Notable American Women: The Case of United States History Textbooks" *Social Education* 48 (1984): 546–50.

26. Powell and Garcia, "What Research Says . . . About Sterotypes."

27. Britton, Lumpkin, and Britton, "The Battle to Imprint Citizens."

28. Hahn and Blankenship, "Women and Economics Textbooks"; Scott, "Whatever Happened to Jane and Dick?"

29. Butterfield et al., "A Multicultural Analysis of a Popular Basil Reading Series."

30. Britton, Lumpkin, and Britton, "The Battle to Imprint Citizens"; Butterfield et al., "A Multicultural Analysis of a Popular Basal Reading Series."

31. See Carl A. Grant and Christine E. Sleeter, *Turning on Learning* (Columbus, Ohio: Merrill, 1989), pp. 104–9.

32. B. B. Armbruster, C. L. Mitsakos, and V. R. Rogers, *America's Regions and Regions of the World* (Needham Heights, Mass.: Ginn and Company, 1986); V. E. Arnsdorf, T. M. Helmus, N.J.G. Pounds, and E. A. Toppin, *The World and Its People: The United States and Its Neighbors* (Needham Heights, Mass.: Silver Burdett Company, 1982); J. Buggey, *Our Communities* (Chicago, Ill.: Follett Publishing Company, 1983); J. Buggey and M. E. Swartz, *Home and School* (Chicago, Ill.: Follett Publishing Company, 1983); J. Buggey, *Our United States* (Chicago, Ill: Follett Publishing Company, 1983); J. Buggey, G. Danzer, C. Mitsakos, and C. Risinger, *America! America!* (Glenview, Ill.: Scott Foresman and Company, 1982); J. Cangemi, ed. *Our History* (Fort Worth, Tex.: Holt, Rinehart and Winston, 1983); M. K. Clark, *The Earth and Its People* (New York: MacMillan Publishing Company, 1982); H. H. Gross, D. W. Follett, R. E. Gabler, W. L. Burton, and W. D. Nielson, *Exploring Our World: Regions* (Chicago, Ill.: Follett Publishing Company, 1980); A. T. Harthern, *The World and Its People: Families and Neighbors* (Needham Heights, Mass.: Silver Burdett Company,

1982); B. P. Hyder and C. S. Brown, *The World and Its People: Neighbors and Communities* (Needham Heights, Mass.: Silver Burdett Company, 1982); D. C. King and C. C. Anderson, *America: Past and Present* (Boston, Mass.: Houghton Mifflin Company, 1980); M. Schwartz and J. R. O'Connor, *The New Exploring American History* (New York: Globe Book Company, 1981); Social Science Staff of the Educational Research Council of America, *The Making of Our America* (Needham Heights, Mass.: Allyn and Bacon, 1982).

33. The four are Gross et al., *Exploring our World: Regions;* Buggey and Swartz, *Home and School;* Buggey, *Our United States;* and Hyder and Brown, *The World and its People.*

34. Buggey, *Our United States.*

35. King and Anderson, *America: Past and Present.*

36. Ibid., p. 354.

37. The three are Buggey, *Our United States;* Schwartz and O'Connor, *The New Exploring American History;* and Hyder and Brown, *The World and its People.*

38. For example, Gross et al., *Exploring our World: Regions,* and Buggey et al., *America! America!*

39. Hyder and Brown, *The World and its People,* p. 167.

40. King and Anderson, *America: Past and Present,* p. 433.

41. Ibid., p. 434.

42. Gross et al., *Exploring our World: Regions.*

43. Social Science Staff, *The Making of Our America;* Buggey and Swartz, *Home and School;* Clark, *The Earth and its People;* and Harthern, *The World and its People.*

44. Gross et al., *Exploring our World: Regions.*

45. Buggey, *Our United States;* Harthern, *The World and its People;* and Hyder and Brown, *The World and its People.*

46. Buggey and Swartz, *Home and School,* and Gross et al., *Exploring our World: Regions.*

47. Armbruster et al., *America's Regions and Regions of the World,* p. 135.

48. Armbruster et al., *America's Regions and Regions of the World;* Buggey and Swartz, *Home and School;* Hyder and Brown, *The World and its People;* and King and Anderson, *America's Past and Present.*

49. Buggey, *Our United States,* and Gross et al., *Exploring our World: Regions.*

50. Buggey, *Our Communities,* p. 208.

51. Gross et al., *Exploring Our World: Regions,* p. 304

52. Buggey et al., *America! America!*

53. Cargeri, *Our History,* p. 89, our emphasis.

54. Buggey, *Our Communities;* Cargemi, *Our History;* Clark, *The Earth and Its People;* Gross et al., *Exploring Our World: Regions.*

55. Schwartz and O'Connor, *The New Exploring American History,* and Social Science Staff, *The Making of Our America.*

56. Buggey and Swartz, *Home and School.*

57. King and Anderson, *America: Past and Present.*

58. Ibid., p. 46.

59. R. L. Allington, R. L. Cramer, P. M. Cunningham, G. Y. Robinson, and R. I. Tierney, *Rough and Ready* (Glenview, Ill.: Scott Foresman and Company, 1985); J. L. Chaparro, and

M. A. Trost, *Reading Literature* (Evanston, Ill.: McDougal, Littell & Co., 1985); T. Clymer, R. Indrisano, D. D. Johnson, P. D. Pearson, and R. L. Venezky, *Across the Fence* (Needham Heights, Mass.: Ginn and Company, 1985); T. Clymer, R. Indrisano, D. D. Johnson, P. D. Pearson, and R. L. Venezky, *Ten Times Round* (Needham Heights, Mass.: Ginn and Company, 1985); W. K. Durr, J. M. LePere, M. L. Alsin, R. P. Bunyan, and S. Shaw, *Honeycomb* (Boston, Mass.: Houghton Mifflin Company, 1983); W. K. Durr and J. Pikulski, *Explorations* (Boston, Mass.: Houghton Mifflin Company, 1986); S. Maccarone, ed., *Crossing Boundaries* (Lexington, Mass.: D. C. Heath & Co., 1983); L. Matteoni, W. Lane, F. Sucher, and V. Burns, *A Painted Ocean* (New York: The Economy Company, 1980); L. Mateoni and F. Sucher, *Can It Be?* (New York: The Economy Company, 1986); P. T. Rowland, *The Nitty Gritty Rather Pretty City* (Reading, Mass.: Addison-Wesley, 1982); B. J. Weiss, P. S. Rosenbaum, A. M. Shaw, and M. J. Tolbert, *To See Ourselves* (Fort Worth, Tex.: Holt, Rinehart and Winston, 1986).

60. L. W. Beech, R. Cramer, C. W. Feder, T. McCarthy, N. C. Najimy, and D. Priplett, *Language: Skills and Use,* 2nd ed. (Glenview, Ill.: Scott Foresman and Company, 1984); J. Littell, ed., *Building English Skills* (Evanston, Ill.: McDougal, Littell & Co., 1984); J. Littel, ed., *Building English Skills* (Evanston, Ill.: McDougal, Littel and Co., 1985); and F. Pader, S. Schaffrath, and S. Wittenbrink, *Building English Skills* (Evanston, Ill.: McDougal, Littell & Co., 1984).

61. Clymer et al., *Across the Fence,* and Maccarone, *Crossing Boundaries.*

62. Littell, *Building English Skills,* and Paden et al., *Building English Skills.*

63. Beech et al., *Language: Skills and Use.*

64. Matteoni et al., *A Painted Ocean.*

65. For example, Dunn et al., *Honeycomb.*

66. Littell, *Basic Skills in English.*

67. Littell, *Building English Skills.*

68. Allington et al., *Rough and Ready,* and Matteoni et al., *A Painted Ocean.*

69. Dunn and Pikulski, *Explorations.*

70. Matteoni et al., *A Painted Ocean.*

71. Clymer et al., *Across the Fence;* Durr et al., *Honeycomb;* Littell, *Basic Skills in English;* Matteoni and Sucher, *Can it Be?;* and Rowland, *The Nitty Gritty Rather Pretty City.*

72. Dunn and Pikulski, *Explorations;* and Matteoni et al., *A Painted Ocean.*

73. Dunn and Pikulski, *Explorations;* Littell, *Building English Skills;* and Paden et al., *Building English Skills.*

74. Clymer et al., *Across the Fence,* and Dunn et al., *Honeycomb.*

75. Beech et al., *Language: Skills and Use;* Littell, *Basic Skills in English;* and Matteoni and Sucher, *Can It Be?*

76. Chaparro and Trost, *Reading Literature;* Clymer et al., *Across the Fence;* Clymer et al., *Ten Times Round;* and Maccarone, *Crossing Boundaries.*

77. Allington et al., *Rough and Ready;* Littell, *Basic Skills in English;* Beech et al., *Language: Skills and Use;* and Weiss et al., *To See Ourselves.*

78. Littell, *Building English Skills.*

79. Matteoni and Sucher, *Can it Be?*

80. Allington et al., *Rough and Ready;* Beech et al., *Language: Skills and Use;* and Littell, *Basic Skills in English.*

81. Clymer et al., *Ten Times Round;* Dunn and Pikulski, *Explorations;* and Littell, *Building English Skills.*

82. Maccarone, *Crossing Boundaries.*

83. Allington et al., *Rough and Ready.*

84. Clymer et al., *Across the Fence;* Dunn and Pikulski, *Explorations;* Littell, *Building English Skills;* Littell, *Basic Skills in English;* Matteoni and Sucher, *Can it Be?;* Paden et al., *Building English Skills;* and Rowland, *The Nitty Gritty Rather Pretty City.*

85. Dunn et al., *Honeycomb.*

86. J. Abruscato, J. Fossaceca, J. Hassarc, and D. Peck, *Holt Science* (Fort Worth, Tex.: Holt, Rinehart and Winston, 1984); D. Adams, J. Hackett, and R. Sund, *Accent on Science* (Columbus, Ohio: Charles E. Merrill Publishing Co., 1980); P. Alexander, M. Fiegel, S. K. Foehr, A. F. Harris, J. G. Krajkovich, K. W. May, N. Tzimopoulous, and R. K. Voltmer, *Earth Science* (Needham, Mass.: Silver Burdett Company, 1987); D. Appenbrink, S. Halpernslot, P. Hownshell, and O. Smith, *Physical Science* (Englewood Cliffs, New Jer.: Prentice-Hall, 1987); P. F. Brandwein, B. Cross, and S. S. Neivert, *Science and Technology: Changes we Make* (Lawrence, Kans.: Coronado Publishers, Inc., 1985); C. H. Heimler and C. D. Neal *Principles of Science Book 1* (Columbus, Ohio: Charles E. Merrill Publishing Co., 1983); C. H. Heimler and J. Price *Focus on Physical Science* (Columbus, Ohio: Charles E. Merrill Publishing Co., 1987); and G. G. Mallinson, J. B. Mallison, W. L. Smallwood, and C. Valentino, *Science* (Needham Heights, Mass.: Silver Burdett Company, 1985).

87. Alexander et al., *Earth Science.*

88. Heimler and Neal, *Principles of Science.*

89. Alexander et al., *Earth Science.*

90. Abruscato, *Holt Science,* and Mallinson et al., *Science.*

91. Alexander et al., *physical science.*

92. Adams et al., *Accent on Science.*

93. Appenbrink et al., *Physical Science,* 1981.

94. Alexander et al., *Earth Science,* and Brandwein et al., *Science and Technology.*

95. Adams et al., *Accent on Science;* Heimler and Neal, *Principles of Science;* and Mallinson et al., *Science.*

96. Abruscato et al., *Holt Science;* and Alexander et al., *Earth Science.*

97. Alexander et al., *Earth Science.*

98. Heimler and Neal, *Principles of Science.*

99. Adams et al., *Accent on Science.*

100. Abruscato et al., *Holt Science.*

101. Adams et al., *Accent on Science,* and Abruscato, et al., *Holt Science.*

102. R. P. Brown and K. Haycock, *Excellence for Whom?* (Oakland, Calif.: The Achievement Council, 1984).

103. L. C. Bolster, W. Crown, R. Hamada, V. Hansen, M. M. Lindquist, C. McNerney, W. Nibbelink, G. Prigge, C. Rahilfs, D. Robitaille, J. Schultz, S. Sharron, I. Vance, D. E. Williams, J. Wilson, and R. Wisner, *Invitation to Mathematics* (Glenview: Ill.: Scott, Foresman & Co., 1987); L. C. Bolster, W. Crown, M. M. Lindquist, C. McNerney, W. Nibbellink, P. Glenn, C. Rahlfs, D. Robitaille, J. Schultz, J. Swafford, I. Vance, J. Wilson, and R. Wisner, *Invitation to Mathematics* (Glenview, Ill.: Scott, Foresman & Co., 1985); L. Carey, H. Bolster, and D. Woodburn, *Mathematics in Life,* 2nd ed. (Glenview: Ill.: Scott,

Foresman & Co., 1982); E. R. Duncan, W. G. Quast, M. A. Haubner, W. L. Cole, L. M. Gemmell, C. E. Allen, A. M. Copper, and L. R. Chapps, *Mathematics* (Boston, Mass.: Houghton Mifflin Company, (1983); R. E. Eicholz, P. G. O'Daffer, C. R. Gleenor, R. I. Charles, S. Young, and C. S. Barnett *Addison-Wesley Mathematics* (Reading, Mass.: Addison-Wesley Pub. Co., 1987); W. E. Rucker, and C. A. Dilley, *Heath Mathematics* (Lexington, Mass.: D. C. Heath & Co., 1982); T. Thoburn, J. E. Forbes, and R. D. Bechtel, *Macmillan Mathematics* (New York: Macmillan Publishing Company, 1982); and T. Thoburn, J. E. Forbes, and R. D. Bechtel, *Mathematics* (New York: Macmillan Pub. Co., 1982).

104. N. Golden, *Computer Literacy with an Introduction to BASIC Programming* (Harcourt Brace Jovanovich, 1986).

105. Thoburn et al., *Macmillan Mathematics.*

106. Bolster et al., *Invitation to Mathematics,* 1985 and 1987.

107. Carey et al., *Mathematics in Life.*

108. Bolster et al., *Invitation to Mathematics,* 1985.

109. Bolster et al., *Invitation to Mathematics,* 1987, and Golden, *Computer Literacy.*

110. Carey et al., *Mathematics in Life.*

111. Bolster et al., *Invitation to Mathematics,* 1987; Thoburn et al., *Macmillan Mathematics;* and Thoburn et al., *Mathematics.*

112. Bolster et al., *Invitation to Mathematics,* 1985, and Rucker and Dilley, *Heath Mathematics.*

113. Thoburn et al., *Macmillan Mathematics,* and Thoburn et al., *Mathematics.*

114. Golden, *Computer Literacy.*

115. Carey et al., *Mathematics in Life.*

116. Bolster et al., *Invitation to Mathematics,* 1987.

117. Eicholz et al., *Addison-Wesley Mathematics,* and Thoburn et al., *Mathematics.*

118. Rucker and Dilley, *Heath Mathematics.*

119. Carey et al., *Mathematics in Life.*

120. Ibid.

121. Bolster et al., *Invitation to Mathematics,* 1985.

122. Thoburn et al., *Mathematics.*

123. Golden, *Computer Literacy.*

124. Rucker and Dilley, *Heath Mathematics.*

125. Bolster et al., *Invitation to Mathematics,* 1987; Carey et al., *Mathematics in Life;* Eicholz et al., *Addison-Wesley Mathematics;* Golden, *Computer Literacy;* Thoburn et al., *Macmillan Mathematics,* and Thoburn et al., *Mathematics.*

126. Bolster et al., *Invitation to Mathematics,* 1985; and Thoburn et al., *Mathematics.*

127. Thoburn et al., *Mathematics.*

128. Bolster et al., *Invitation to Mathematics,* 1987.

129. Duncan et al., *Mathematics;* Eicholz et al., *Addison-Wesley Mathematics;* Thoburn et al., *Macmillan Mathematics;* and Thoburn et al., *Mathematics.*

130. Eicholz et al., *Addison-Wesley Mathematics.*

131. Carey et al., *Mathematics in Life.*

132. Eicholz et al., *Addison-Wesley Mathematics;* Thoburn et al., *Macmillan Mathematics;* and Thoburn et al., *Mathematics.*

133. Rucher and Dilley, *Heath Mathematics.*

134. Duncan et al., *Mathematics;* Rucker and Dilley, *Heath Mathematics;* Thoburn et al., *Macmillan Mathematics;* and Thoburn et al., *Mathematics.*

135. Golden, *Computer Literacy.*

136. H. L. Gates, ed., *The Schomburg Library of Nineteenth-Century Black Women Writers* (New York: Oxford Press, 1988).

137. Bloom, *The Closing of the American Mind;* and Hirsch, *Cultural Literacy.*

138. *The New York Times,* November 18, 1987, p. 6.

139. Ibid.

140. Banks, *Multiethnic Education,* p. 158.

6

Reclaiming the Voice of Resistance: The Fiction of Mildred Taylor

Joel Taxel

Background

In his critical review of research in the "sociology of school knowledge," Philip Wexler suggests that this scholarship has demonstrated that "social power is culturally represented, and that knowledge and culture are essential moments in the process of social domination." Wexler argues that by selectively transmitting "class culture as common culture," the present order is seen as "natural and eternal" and the cultures of oppressed groups are silenced.[1]

Research in the sociology of school knowledge documents the extent to which the world views and perspectives of women, people of color, and the working class either are excluded from textbooks and literature or subjected to misrepresentation or distortion.[2] This research also validates Raymond Williams's claim that the curriculum, and culture in general, is governed by a "selective tradition":[3]

> It is a characteristic of educational systems to claim that they are transmitting "knowledge" or "culture" in an absolute or universally derived sense, though it is obvious that different systems, at different times and in different countries, transmit radically different selective versions of both. Moreover, it is clear that there are fundamental and necessary relations between this selective version and the existing dominant social relations.[4]

Williams suggests that this designation of certain groups' knowledge as officially sanctioned "knowledge for all" is central to the process of social and cultural definition and provides historical and cultural legitimacy for the social order. Selective traditions also are conceived of as vital elements in the "hegemonic" culture, the "lived system of meanings and values" that pervades the whole process of living and constitutes, for most people, "reality."[5] Bourdieu,

My sincere thanks to Susan Taylor Cox for her insightful comments and suggestions on an early draft of this chapter.

Willis, and Eagleton also point to the role of culture and society's cultural institutions in legitimating a conception of reality that is made to appear natural, inevitable, and eternal.[6] Eagleton, for example, referring specifically to literature, suggests that "from the infant school to the university faculty, literature is a vital instrument for the insertion of individuals into the perceptual and symbolic forms of the ideological formation, able to accomplish this function with a "naturalness," spontaneity and immediacy of no other ideological practice."[7]

Wexler, along with Apple, Giroux, and others seek to move theory and research in the sociology of school knowledge beyond its initial, often simplistic focus on the reproductive aspects of curriculum and culture.[8] Among the most significant points in their critique is the propensity of researchers analyzing curricular materials and literature to focus on content—the historical viewpoints, interpretations and perspectives, the role of women and minorities, etc. In so doing, insufficient attention is given to the claims of literary critics such as Lukács that "the true bearers of ideology in art are the very forms, rather than the abstractable content of the work."[9] Critics also note that sociologists of school knowledge tend to ignore Williams's crucial reminder that selective traditions are always "a process," the product of resistance, struggle, and contestation.[10] For Williams, hegemony is

> a realized complex of experiences, relationships, and activities, with specific and changing pressures and limits. . . . Moreover . . . it does not passively exist as a form of dominance. It has continually to be renewed, recreated, defended, and mediated. It is also continually resisted, limited, altered, challenged by pressures not all its own.[11]

Early research in the sociology of school knowledge, thus, fails to attend in any systematic way to instances of opposition, and, in the case of literature, to the existence of "oppositional texts," texts that conflict with or oppose the dominant, selective tradition.[12] In this vein, Aronowitz and Giroux note that little time is spent discovering the internal contradictions within prevailing school knowledge and the wider culture that can provide the basis for an alternative educational or social movement, what Wood refers to as "an ideology and consciousness that would support its own hegemony"[13]

In this chapter, I discuss the work of one of the most significant oppositional voices of contemporary American children's literature, that of Mildred D. Taylor. My discussion will point to some of the ways her books about the African American experience in America during the era of the Great Depression constitute an attempt to forge an alternative vision of that experience, one that departs from the one that has long dominated children's literature in the United States. Taylor's work is especially worthy of attention because it dramatically demonstrates that it is possible for literary works to articulate a progressive politics and historical vision in a form that sacrifices neither historical accuracy nor aesthetic value. Before presenting this analysis, I explain further the importance of uncovering and reclaiming oppositional texts and provide additional detail on the characteristics of the selective tradition that has governed writing about the experience of African Americans. I conclude by noting some of the implications of the analysis for theory, research, and pedagogy.

The Selective Tradition
and the Voice of Opposition

Michael Apple has spoke of the need to develop an historically grounded "language of possibility," and has contended that in order to see the possibilities of the present, "we need to recapture our past"[14] A similar understanding animated the efforts of African American historians of the late 1960s and early 1970s to find a "usable black past" as well as McLaren's more recent call for the construction of " 'dangerous memories'—depictions of events of human suffering and courage—through excavating, rescuing, and affirming the voices of those who have been silenced and marginalized by the dominant culture"[15]

The significance of efforts to restore, and place at center stage, the history, literature, culture, and experiences of women, African Americans, Native Americans, and Hispanic Americans also is noted by Edith Mayo, curator of political history at the Smithsonian Institute: "Any time you change the position of what has been an 'out' group in history, it tends to empower that group. People who know their own past have a better position from which to act in their present".[16] Similar sentiments were echoed by Virginia Hamilton in the afterward to her moving biography of Anthony Burns, an escaped slave who was recaptured, reenslaved, and finally freed after a bitter and violent attempt to challenge the Fugitive Slave Law. Hamilton spoke of the "enormous sense of relief and satisfaction" she experienced "at having at last set free through the word one man's struggle for liberty . . . whose painstaking and burning desire to 'get gone' from crippling bondage was all but forgotten by history." By writing about Burns, Hamilton claimed he came alive not only for herself, but "for all of us.. In gaining a sense of who he was we learn about ourselves. As long as we know he is free, we too are liberated."[17]

Recognizing that the building of a progressive educational and political movement requires, in the words of Apple, that we "stand on the shoulders of our forebears,"[18] sociologists of school knowledge have begun to unearth and closely scrutinize the efforts of women, people of color, and laboring groups to make their own history and develop their own cultural institutions. Teitelbaum, for example, has uncovered evidence of the vibrant culture that sprung up around the socialist movement in Milwaukee and Chicago during the Progressive Era. A central component of this almost forgotten movement were the Sunday schools, whose curriculum explicitly sought to counteract the competitive, chauvinistic, individualistic, often racist tendencies of the curriculum that dominated the schools of this era.[19]

Harris's study of the lamentably short-lived magazine *The Brownie's Book* provided a dramatic illustration of an effort to counter the selective tradition that, as she and others have shown, either excluded African Americans, their history, and their culture from children's literature or presented them in a grotesque and pejorative fashion.[20] Saul argued that the remarkable and all-but-forgotten *The Middle Five* by Native American author and anthropologist Francis LeFlesch was a conscious attempt to counter the insidious images of Native Americans that pervaded children's literature and the culture at large.[21] Finally, my reexamination of my study of children's fiction about the American Revolution—a study that *did* analyze the form or narrative structure of the novels and their relation to the dominant ideologies of the times in which they were written—stemmed from the belief that an adequate understanding of the role of children's literature in the maintenance of hegemony must admit to far more complexity and contradiction than many, including myself, had allowed.[22] This scholarship either reflects or implies an understanding of a critical point made by Omi and Winant:

> Social movements create collective identity by offering their adherents a different view of themselves and their world; different, that is, from the world view and self-concepts offered by the established social order. They do this by the process of *rearticulation*, which produces new subjectivity by making use of information and knowledge already present in the subject's mind. They take elements and themes of his/her culture and traditions and infuse them with new meanings.[23]

As we shall see, the views of African Americans, and the meanings attributed to their culture and traditions by writers like Mildred Taylor, constitute a significant break from the views and meanings that historically dominated the selective tradition in the United States. The preponderant focus of my analysis is on the *content* of Taylor's books, particularly her articulation of a vision of African American history quite different from that found in most textbooks and novels for young people. Attention, however, also is given to the way in which a very particular definition of social experience is expressed by the "models of social action" embedded in the *form or narrative structure* of the novels.[24]

African Americans and the Selective Tradition

The place or status of women, African Americans, and other oppressed minorities within the selective tradition is constituted in two basic ways. The first is through exclusion. In the case of Afro-Americans, invisibility has been an overriding and undeniable reality. In the three-year period 1962–64, for example, African American characters were present in only 349 of the 5,206

(6.7%) of the books published. Although African Americans have been more successful recently in challenging what Larrick had aptly characterized as the "all-white world of children's books," Sims described the present period as "another lean period in the publication of books about Afro-Americans."[25]

When African Americans *were* found in books written for young people, they were presented in a distorted and offensively stereotyped fashion, the second dimension through which the selective tradition was constituted. Sadker and Sadker stated that, until the 1950s, African American were presented in American children's literature as "shuffling, lazy, shiftless, singing subhumans" who, "without mind, purpose, or aspiration . . . danced across the pages of children's books fostering prejudice and ignorance in the minds of countless young readers."[26]

These stereotypes and caricatures diminished in frequency as a result of the heightened consciousness and sensitivity engendered by the Civil Rights movement, although they have not disappeared entirely.[27] Sims notes, however, that they were superceded by newer stereotypes, such as the "Super Negro" and the "Black Matriarchal Family." The books often presented "paternalistic white children solving problems for docile, subservient Black children, or presented Black children as a burden for white children." Also criticized were the often inaccurate and unauthentic portraits of black lifestyles as well as the implication that "positive Black images had to be cast in a white middle-class mold."[28] Significantly, the overwhelming majority of the books discussed by Sims, even those written from the point-of-view of a African American character, were written by white authors. However, a growing number of Afro-American authors and illustrators, seeking to counter what they viewed as an appropriation of important aspects of their culture, began creating a new literature for children, one that gave voice to the very aspects of the culture and history that were excluded from the selective tradition.

Culturally Conscious Fiction:
The Image Makers

In *Shadow and Substance,* a review of 150 books of contemporary realistic fiction about African-Americans fiction, Sims (1982) suggest that the books fell into three broad categories. The first was labeled "social conscience" because "they seem intended to create a social conscience—mainly in non–Afro-Americans, to encourage them to develop empathy, sympathy, and tolerance for Afro-Americans and their problems." Sims criticized these books as a group, not only for their "literary mediocrity," but also because most were created from an "ethnocentric, non-African American perspective." In addition, the books contained stock characters and stereotypes that led her to voice concern that they would result in the perpetuation of "undesirable attitudes."[29]

The second category, termed "melting-pot" books, concentrates on the idea "that people are people are people." While recognizing that all good literature speaks to those things which are "universal in each of us," Sims criticizes the melting-pot books' tendency of "recognizing our universality" to the "point of ignoring our differences."[30] Indeed, in many of the melting-pot books the only way the reader has of identifying the characters as African American is through the illustrations.

The final group of books is termed "culturally conscious." This designation reflects its inclusion of many of "the social and cultural traditions associated with growing up Black in the United States." These books differ from the social conscience books in that their primary audience appears to be African American children. In contrast to the melting-pot books, the culturally conscious books recognize, and often celebrate, "the distinctiveness of the experience of growing up simultaneously Black and American." The overriding aim of this group of books, according to Sims, "is presumably to help Black children understand 'how we got over.' "[31]

Sims believes that the most successful of the books in her survey are the culturally conscious books, and she is particularly interested in those written by Afro-Americans themselves, those she labels the "image makers." The possibility of altering the way the dominant culture perceives the Afro-American experience is greatest when the writers are people "whose souls who have been witnesses" to that experience, those who have "dared to live it."[32] Sims's analysis of the fiction of image-makers Lucille Clifton, Eloise Greenfield, Virginia Hamilton, Sharon Bell Mathis, and Walter Dean Myers led her to conclude that they "danced to the rhythms of the same drums. Whether the drums laugh or cry, Sims suggested the following emphases in their work:

(1) Afro-American heritage and history; (2) pride in being Black; (3) a sense of community among Blacks; (4) the importance of warm and loving human relationships, particularly within families; (5) a sense of continuity; and, above all, (6) the will and strength and determination to cope and survive.[33]

Sims's delineation of the characteristics of culturally conscious fiction raises the question of whether such works are, by definition, oppositional in nature. I would suggest that culturally conscious fiction *is* oppositional simply by virtue of its extension and expansion of discourse about African Americans in children's literature. That is, by presenting stories and representations of African Americans historically excluded from the selective tradition, culturally conscious works constitute a form of opposition to it. Taylor's work also makes evident the need to conceptualize more precisely our understanding of the different forms oppositional literature can take.[34] Although most of the culturally conscious literature about the African American experience draws on the themes outlined by Sims, the literature is rich and diverse, and comes in a variety of genres and forms. Picture-storybooks such as *Amifika, She Come Bringing Me*

That Baby Girl, and *Grandpa's Face* provide brief, loving glimpses of the warmth and love found in African American families. *Mirandy and Brother Wind* celebrates an important African American cultural tradition, the "cake walk." Clifton's *The Lucky Stone* is a longer work that tells of a stone passed from generation to generation in an African American family; it incorporates the themes of black pride, African American history and heritage, and continuity between the generations. Lester's *Long Journey Home* (1972) and *This Strange New Feeling* (1982) are collections of short stories set during and in the aftermath of slavery, about the struggles of African Americans for freedom and dignity. Novels such as *A Teacup Full of Roses* (Mathis 1972), *Fast Sam, Cool Clyde, and Stuff* (Myers 1975), and *Hoops* (Myers 1981) are novels about the will and strength and determination of African American youths to cope and survive in environments that have destroyed countless forebears and contemporaries. Finally, recent collections of African American folk literature by Hamilton and Lester dramatically illustrate the richness of the African American cultural heritage and point to the need for it to be integrated within the selective tradition.[35]

Mildred Taylor's fiction is unusual and significant not only because of its incorporation of the themes Sims claims are characteristic of culturally conscious writers, but also because her books are explicitly concerned with resistance and those who resist. In addition, contained within novels such as *Roll Of Thunder, Hear My Cry* and *Let The Circle Be Unbroken* are scenes in which stories of past resistance are celebrated, thus maintaining what might be termed a "storied tradition of resistance.[36] As we shall see, Taylor's books also address issues and themes rarely treated in *any* books written for young people. In treating themes related to the intersection of race, class, and gender, Mildred Taylor touches on matters that until recently have been either marginalized within or excluded from not only discourse within and about literature, but education as well.

Mildred D. Taylor

From as far back as she can remember, Taylor recalls hearing stories. Whether told "by the fireside of her Ohio home, or in Mississippi where she was born and where her family had lived since the days of slavery, these stories contained a "different history from the one I learned in school." The past she heard about in these sessions "was a history of ordinary people, some brave, some not so brave, but basically a people who had done nothing more spectacular than survive in a society designed for their destruction." Some of the stories related incidents that Taylor's father himself had experienced. Others had become part of the oral tradition of her family and had been told to Taylor's father, who had learned them from "his parents and grandparents, as they had learned them from theirs.[37]"

In a speech given upon receiving the prestigious Newbery Medal for *Roll of Thunder, Hear My Cry,* Taylor discussed some of the people and factors that had awakened in her the desire to chronicle life in rural Mississippi in the 1930s. Her "driving compulsion to paint a truer picture of Black people" was based largely on the enormous gap between what she knew firsthand through experience and via the oral tradition of her family, and what she had read and been taught in school.[38] After a number of years of study, traveling, living in Africa, and working in the black student movement, Taylor returned to her dream of becoming a writer. In so doing, she found herself turning "again and again to the stories she had heard from her childhood,[39]" "stories about the small and often dangerous triumphs of Black people . . . stories about human pride and survival in a cruelly racist society [that] were like nothing I ever read in the history books or the books I devoured in the local library."[40]

In pointing to the "terrible contradiction" between what books said and the "storied tradition" of her family, Taylor provided a sense of the distance between the lived experience of a people and its distortion by the dominant culture:

> There were no Black heroes or heroines in those books; no beautiful Black ladies, no handsome Black men; no people filled with pride, strength, or endurance. There was, of course, always mention of Booker T. Washington and George Washington Carver; Marion Anderson and occasionally even Dr. Ralph Bunche. But that hardly compensated for the lackluster history of Black people painted by those books, a history of a docile, subservient people happy with their fate who did little or nothing to shatter the chain that bound them, both before and after slavery.[41]

Taylor's works include two novels, *Roll of Thunder, Hear My Cry* (1977) and *Let the Circle Be Unbroken* (1982), and three novellas, *Song of the Trees* (1975), *Friendship* (1987), and *The Gold Cadillac* (1987). A third novel is nearing completion.[42] Except for *The Gold Cadillac,* all of the books deal with the experiences of the Logan family, especially those of narrator Cassie Logan. When we first meet Cassie, in *Song of the Trees,* she is, in Taylor's words, "a spunky eight-year-old, innocent, untouched by discrimination, full of pride, and greatly loved."[43] The four books about the Logan family deal with their daily struggles to retain control of their land, their destinies, and their self-respect. Above all, they are about the gradual stripping away of the veil of innocence with which the elder Logans seek to protect their children from the vicious, unrelenting racism that confronted African Americans in Mississippi in the 1930s. In the remainder of this chapter, I point to the ways in which Taylor's work incorporates, at both the level of content and form, the themes of culturally conscious writers and also places accounts of resistance at critical junctures of her narrative. In so doing, I argue that Mildred Taylor helps us to understand better the different forms that oppositional literature can take.

The power and forthrightness of Taylor's discussions of the *Afro-American history and heritage* can only be fully grasped and appreciated if read next to the evasions, superficiality, and banality of, say, the typical history textbook for middle-grade students. References to the past generally are to the lived experiences of members of the Logan family and often are made in order to put some present-day concern into perspective. These looks to the past serve to provide the Logan children with *a sense of continuity* between their own struggles and those of their forebears. What is especially striking about these direct and indirect references to the past is the contrast they provide to the stories of "docile, subservient people happy with their fate" who as, Taylor described, filled the books she read as a child. Harper noted that by maintaining an ancestral presence, interweaving historical incidents, emphasizing strong family ties, and incorporating rituals of Black life "the timeless struggle of a people to survive emerges."[44] In *Roll of Thunder, Hear My Cry* a history lesson taught by Mary Logan is interrupted by Harlan Granger and other members of the all-white school board. Granger is a wealthy landowner who covets the Logan land and his visit to Mary's classroom is part of his constant harassment of the Logans:

> Mama was in the middle of history and I knew it was bad. I could tell Stacey knew it too; he sat tense near the back of the room, his lips very tight, his eyes on the men. But Mama did not flinch; she always started her history class the first thing in the morning when the students were alert, and I knew the hour was not up yet. To make matters worse her lesson for the day was slavery. She spoke on the cruelty of it; of the rich economic cycle it generated as slaves produced the raw materials for the factories in the North and Europe; how the country profited and grew from the free labor of a people still not yet free. . . . Granger turned the pages [of the textbook], stopped, and read something. "I don't see all them things you're teaching in here."
>
> "That's because they're not in there," Mama said.
>
> "Well if it ain't in there, then you got no right teaching it. This book's approved by the Board of Education and you're expected to teach what's in it."
>
> "I can't do that."
>
> "And why not?"
>
> Mama, her back straight and her eyes fixed on the men, answered, "Because all that's in the book isn't true."[45]

In seeking to counter the distortions and misconceptions contained in state-sponsored history books with material gained from other sources, Mary Logan attempts to expand the discourse on history well beyond the boundaries of the selective tradition of that era. In presenting an oppositional account of slavery that contradicts the one sanctioned by the state of Mississippi, Mary engages in an act of resistance that leads directly to the loss of her job.

Let the Circle be Unbroken presents glimpses of a history rarely seen in other fiction for children. As was true *Roll of Thunder, Hear My Cry, Let the*

Circle be Unbroken provides a realistic picture of the brutal reality of the
sharecropping system, a system that served essentially the same purpose as the
slave system it replaced: it provided a stable, cheap source of labor. The Turner
family is typical of African American families who were tied to the land for as
long as their landlord wanted them there:

> Mr. Montier provided everything for them—their land, their mule, their plow, their
> seed—in return for a portion of their cotton. When they needed food or other supplies,
> they bought on credit at the store approved by Mr. Montier where the high interest
> upped the price tremendously on everything they bought. At the year's end, when all
> the cotton had been sold and the accounts figured by Mr. Montier, the Turners were
> usually in more debt then they were at the beginning of the year. And as long as they
> were in debt, they could not just up and leave the land on their own, not unless they
> wanted the sheriff after them.[46]

State-sanctioned intimidation and terror also was brought to bear in order to
keep African Americans "in line." In *Roll of Thunder, Hear My Cry,* for
example, an African American sharecropper is tarred and feathered, with fatal
consequences, for raising questions about his account at the Wallace store. This
not uncommon act of brutality leads the Logans to organize a boycott of the
Wallace store. This act of resistance, a direct defiance of the established order,
demonstrates the lengths to which the Logans will go to maintain their dignity
and self-respect. The boycott also provides perhaps the most instructive instance
of the Logan's *strong sense of community,* one of the characteristic themes of
Sims's image-makers. The Logan's willingness to use their land as collateral
for a boycott that would benefit their neighbors more than themselves makes
clear their commitment to the well-being of the African American community.

Sociologists of school knowledge such as Anyon have noted the paucity of
discussion given in United States history textbooks to unions and to the violence
that attended American workers' attempts to unionize.[47] That is, these issues
have long been excluded from the selective tradition. Nevertheless, a fictional-
ized account of a failed attempt to form a Farm Workers' Union is found in
Let the Circle be Unbroken. As the depression tightens its grip on the community, Union organizers seek to organize the beleaguered sharecroppers and tenant-farmers. The farmers are informed that Agricultural Adjustment
Administration funds designed to provide relief for tenant-farmers and sharecroppers were "getting put in the pockets of plantation owners." Such unscru-
pulous actions lead union organizers "to do something," and they enlist the aid
of some of the Logans' neighbors and begin a Farm Workers."[48]

What is truly radical about these efforts is that the Union is for both
"colored and white" Morris Wheeler union organizer explains:

> "It's colored and white 'cause that's the only way this thing can work. If we go one

without the other, we just ain't going to be strong enough. Now I ain't saying I'm for social changes across the board—I'm just being honest with y'all now, telling y'all the same thing I'd tell a white farmer—but we gonna win this thing, we gonna have to do it together. There's just no way around it, and folks are just gonna have to make up their minds what's more important: their racial feelings or keeping a roof over their heads."[49]

Taylor's account of one of the little-known attempts to forge an interracial class alliance is similar to the one described by Howard Fast in his (adult) novel of the Reconstruction era, *Freedom Road*.[50] In both books it is clear that such an alliance is as incomprehensible for blacks as it is for whites. The scenes in which white tenants and sharecroppers try to convince David Logan to join the Union reveal the revulsion of whites at the slightest hint that African Americans are on an equal footing with them. For example, in a conversation with David Logan, Charlie Simms, a vicious racist who figures prominently in the traumatic events detailed in *Roll of Thunder, Hear My Cry,* says: "I never did like the idea of beggin' no nigger—." Likewise, for African Americans "there had been too many years of distrust, too many years of humiliations and beatings and lynchings and inequalities" to enter easily into an alliance with whites.[51]

This portrait of an attempt to forge an interracial union illuminates how race hatred and red-baiting were used by wealthy plantation-owners to forestall an alliance that would be detrimental to their interests. This is perhaps most evident when the recently evicted tenants and sharecroppers arrive in Strawberry with their meager possessions loaded on wagons and declare their intention to camp out on the town common until something is done to alleviate their plight. As the crowd becomes increasingly unruly, Harlan Granger, the leader of the landlords, addresses the crowd:

> "I take it . . . y'all's for a dollar-fifty cents a day and keeping your farms!"
> Another cheer rose to the heavens.
> "I take it . . . y'all's for schooling with nigras, socializing with nigras . . . marrying nigras . . .
> Harlan Granger knew where to strike and he struck very well. . . . [He] waited a moment, as if pleased at having flushed out his prey. "Y'all think I don't want y'all to have more money and a roof over your head for yourselves and your families." But I say you can get it without this here Communist union. This here Communist union that mixes the races, colored with white. Y'all mark my words, this here union mixing is only the beginning of what's to come! Of nigras totally misguided by white people like Morris Wheeler there! Of nigras who get to feeling like they done mixed with white folks a little bit, they got the right to take white folks' things—. . . ."[52]

Granger "looked over the faces of the poor white farmers staring up at him with little more to hold onto than the belief that they were better than black people, and continued to chisel." He had won![53] It is important again to bear in mind that these matters are rarely, if ever, discussed in either the textbooks or the fiction available to young people in the public schools.

Among the most dramatic instances of what McLaren referred to as a "dangerous memory" is the quixotic attempt of Miss Lee Annie Lee to register to vote.[54] A warm and wonderful woman, Miss Lee Annie Lee never forgot that her father had voted during Reconstruction. Her *pride in being black* is evident in all she says and does. When the idea of voting is first mentioned, she explains to Cassie how terror was used to put an end to African Americans' short-lived exercise of the franchise: "Then them night men took to the road. Tarring black folks goin' to vote, beatin' 'em up, lynchin' 'em. Beat Papa somethin' terrible . . . Well, wasn't no more votin' after that, from hardly nobody."[55]

Despite efforts to dissuade her, Miss Lee Annie Lee is determined to vote, and she enlists the aid of Cassie in the seemingly impossible task of committing the Mississippi constitution to memory. This "literacy requirement" was yet another roadblock constructed by the white supremacist state legislature to impede African American suffrage. When asked to explain her dogmatic and dangerous insistence on voting, Miss Lee states:

> "All my life whenever I wanted to do something and white folks didn't like it, I didn't do it. All my life, it been that way. But now I's sixty-four years old and I's figure I's deserving to do something *I* wants to do, white folks like it or not. And this old body wants to vote and like I done said, I gots my mind made up. I's gon' vote too."[56]

This courageous, nearly illiterate women succeeds in mastering the bewildering complexities of the Mississippi constitution, a remarkable accomplishment that does not save her from being humiliated by the registrar, who is incapable of comprehending Lee Annie's principled, if futile, gesture. "I swear to God," exclaimes registrar Samuel Boudein, "the older they get, the more childlike they become."[57]

Mildred Taylor's fiction is so very significant precisely because her sensitivity to sociocultural and historical concerns are reflected in exciting narratives populated by varied, well-rounded characters. Her themes emerge naturally through the skillful development of character and plot; she is never didactic or pedantic. Among the most readily apparent literary values of Taylor's writing is her skill at characterization. Contributing to her rich and varied array of characters is an uncanny ability to use a variety of dialects that reflect the racial and ethnic backgrounds of a variety of characters.[58] It is through her development of the loving, tightly knit, fiercely loyal, and independent-minded Logan family that Taylor is able to develop another of Sims's themes: *the importance of warm and loving relationships, particularly within families.*

The significance of this theme was alluded to by Taylor when she noted that in developing the Logans she drew freely on "the warmth of [her] youthful years" She also stated that the biographical flavor of her work is the result of her conscious effort to "distill the essence of Black life, so familiar to Black families," into the Logans. In seeking to make the Logans "an embodiment of that spiritual heritage," Taylor sought to counter the dominant media image of the African American family as "fatherless and disintegrating. Certainly my family was not."[59]

The Logans are among the most vibrant, splendidly characterized families in all of children's literature. Echoing a point made above, Holtz suggested that the Logans "are so carefully drawn that one might assume the book [*Roll of Thunder, Hear My Cry*] to be autobiographical, if the author were not so young."[60] Although the *Song of the Trees,* the first book in the series, contains but thirty pages of text, Taylor provides a revealing first glimpse of the cast of characters that readers quickly came to love and respect.[61] Big Ma, is the matriarch of the clan, who years before, with her late husband, had purchased the land the family now clings to so tenaciously. Her daughter-in-law Mary Logan, is a tower of strength; she teaches at the local elementary school and oversees the management of the family homestead even as she shoulders most of the burden of raising four children. Her granddaughter Cassie's brothers include Stacey, the thoughtful, first-born one, whose impetuousness often leads to trouble; the sensitive Christopher-John; and the prideful, manly, almost obsessively clean "Little Man." Finally, there is Cassie's father, David Logan, the "cement" of the family, to whom all look for strength and guidance. This is the case despite the fact that he is frequently away from home, working to earn the cash needed to pay the taxes on the land.

Through warm and loving—if at times stern—interactions with their children, we see how Mary and David Logan seek to instill in their children not only a sense of pride, history, and continuity between past and present, but, above all, the will and determination to cope and survive. Because the Logans own a four-hundred-acre tract of land, they are able to shelter Cassie and her brothers from many of the daily insults and brutalities of the racist caste system of 1930s Mississippi. However, a series of events relentlessly strips away Cassie's innocence. Through Mary and David Logan's efforts to explain the bitter realities of their world, we see the natural, effortless way Mildred Taylor blends the themes of culturally conscious writers with stories of overt resistance, all within the context of exciting, at times spellbinding, narratives.

Easily the most significant event in Cassie's painful initiation occurs when she accompanies her grandmother to the nearby town of Strawberry, where she is first humiliated by Lillian Jean Simms and then brutally pushed into the road by Lillian Jean's father, Charlie. As Cassie notes at the conclusion of this traumatic episode, "No day in all my life had ever been as cruel as this one."[62]

Mary Logan immediately perceives the traumatic impact of the day's events on her daughter. She bids Cassie to understand that in the world outside their house, "things are not as we would have them be." Despite all that has transpired, Cassie is unable to comprehend that her humiliation is a consequence of Charlie Simms's belief that his daughter is better that she simply because she is white. Mary responds to Cassie's protest that "white ain't notin'" by explaining the evolution of important aspects of the ideology of white supremacy. She notes that in order to justify slavery, "the people who needed slaves to work in the fields and the people who needed slaves to work in the fields and the people who were making money bringing slaves from Africa preached that black people weren't really people like white people, so slavery was all right."[63] Mary also explains the way that religion was used to justify slavery:

> "They said that slavery was good for us because it taught us to be good Christians— like the white people . . . But they didn't teach us Christianity to save our souls, but to teach us obedience. They were afraid of slave revolts and they wanted us to learn the Bible's teachings about slaves being loyal to their masters. But even teaching us Christianity didn't make us stop wanting to be free, and many slaves ran away—."[64]

This exchange between mother and child has several significant dimensions. First, there is the obvious effort of a loving mother to assuage the anguish and pain felt by a much-loved child. Mary Logan's appeal to history seeks also to provide Cassie with insight and understanding into her painful experiences. The child's immediate reference to Great-Grandpa Luke, a slave who repeatedly ran away, makes it clear that this is not the first excursion into the history of the family and the group.

Similar themes appear again in one of the more memorable gatherings of the family in *Roll of Thunder, Hear My Cry*. (Family gatherings recur throughout the books and are modeled after those Taylor experienced as a child.) The gathering in question occurs on a Christmas eve when fears of the dreaded "night men" weigh heavily on the African American community. Mr. Morrison, a quiet, gentle, mysterious man of enormous physical stature, describes the massacre of his family "when Reconstruction was just 'bout over," about how his parents "fought them demons out of hell like avenging angels of the Lord,"—and died fighting. Referring to those skeptical of his ability to remember events that occurred when he "warn't hardly six years old," Mr. Morrison emphatically insists that he "remembers all right. I makes myself remember,"[65]

These gatherings are critical moments of family unity and bonding; they are also the site where we see the blending of a number of the themes outlined by Sims.[66] Through this oral tradition, family and group history, and the "storied tradition of resistance" mentioned earlier, are passed on to the young. By viewing family history and the family tradition of resistance in relation to, and in the context of, that of the larger group, *a sense of continuity* between past and present struggles against oppression is fostered. This continuity provides the foundation upon which the Logan elders cultivate their children's strength, will, and determination to survive.

"The will, strength, and determination to cope and survive," the last of Sims's themes, is in a sense a by-product of the others. Repeated references to history, stories about and everyday examples of resistance, the Logans' at times dangerous actions to defend the integrity of their community, the depiction of warm and loving family ties, all provide concrete models of life and living for Cassie and her brothers. The specifics of the model of social action contained in these novels is best summarized in an exchange between David and Cassie that occurs in the aftermath of the Strawberry incident.

Upon returning from the railroad, where he works to raise cash to pay the taxes on the land, David and Cassie discuss the Strawberry affair in the midst of the remains of a stand of trees decimated years before by a white man named John Andersen, an incident detailed in *Song of the Trees*. Referring to the biblical injunction to "turn the other cheek," David tells Cassie:

> "But the way I see it, the bible didn't mean for you to be no fool. Now one day, maybe I can forgive John Andersen for what he done to them trees, but I ain't gonna forget it. I figure forgiving is not letting something nag at you—rotting you out. Now if I hadn't done what I done [to save the trees], then I couldn't't've forgiven myself, and that's the truth of it."[67]

David explains to Cassie that he resisted his desire to give Charlie Simms "a good thrashing" because of the need to weigh the consequences of such an action in relation to the hurt she had suffered. In view of the fact that "Lillian Jean probably won't be the last white person to treat you this way," he bids her to weigh carefully the consequences of her response to Lillian Jean. He does, however, make one thing very clear:

> "There are other things . . . that if I'd let be, they'd eat away and destroy me in the end. And it's the same with you, baby. There are things you can't back down on, things you gotta take a stand on. But it's up to you to decide what them things are. You have to demand respect in the world, ain't nobody just gonna hand it to you. How you carry yourself, what you stand for—That's how you gain respect, but . . . ain't nobody's respect worth more than your own."[68]

Cassie heeds her father well. While her self-respect demands that the strawberry encounter with Lillian-Jean Simms be neither forgiven nor forgotten, Cassie exacts her revenge in such a way that Lillian-Jean is powerless to retaliate or even complain to her friends and family. The model of social action that is both discussed and lived by the Logans is that racism be confronted with the cautious, yet insistent demand that *all* people are entitled to dignity and respect. This code of behavior is articulated eloquently by David Logan when he compares the family's predicament to that of a fig tree on their property. Surrounded by larger oak and walnuts that take up so much room and "give so much shade that they almost overshadow that little ole fig," David explains that

> "that fig tree's got roots that run deep, and it belongs in that yard as much as that oak and walnut. It keeps on blooming, bearing fruit year after year, knowing all the time it'll never get as big as them other trees. Just keeps on growing and doing what it gotta do. It don't give up. It give up, it'll die. There's a lesson to be learned from that little tree, Cassie girl, 'cause we're like it. We keep doing what we gotta, and we don't give up. We can't."[69]

After reading *Roll Of Thunder, Hear My Cry,* most of the hundreds of readers with whom I have discussed this book report feeling optimistic about Cassie's prospects for the future. This optimism is a function of the ways in which Taylor describes Cassie's growth and maturation. It also is a function of the students' sense that her family has nurtured within her the strength, will, and determination to maintain her dignity and self-respect in a environment that denies her and her people the most elemental human rights and considerations. Despite the optimism afforded by this knowledge, readers remain painfully cognizant that the irrational, deeply rooted bigotry confronted by the Logans and that its institutionalized forms (i.e., the "Jim Crow" laws) will remain in place for decades to come.

A final theme demanding attention is one not among those enumerated by Sims (1982), although it is related to the theme of maintaining the will, strength, and determination to cope and survive. This theme, sexuality, is one that has long stood outside of the selective tradition of mainstream literature for young people. In contrast to the increased willingness of authors during the 1960s and 1970s to address issues related to sexuality, the more conservative climate of more recent years and the "vigilance" of fundamentalist censors and "book-banners" has led to a more cautious approach by many, if not all, authors. What is particularly striking about Taylor's treatment of sexuality is that she directly addresses an issue that long has been either avoided altogether or else shrouded in misconception and racist mythology. I refer to the issue of the sexual relationships between African American men and white women and, even more important, those between white men and African American women.

In *Roll of Thunder, Hear My Cry,* this theme is touched on at least twice. The first mention, which occurs during Mr. Morrison's account of the massacre of his parents, introduces the fact that some antebellum plantations served as places where slaves were bred for sale. This shocking, sensitive, and highly controversial subject is absent from virtually all textbooks for middle- and even high-school students and is one of the more significant aspects of African American history to be excluded from the selective tradition governing the curriculum in American schools. In the course of his harrowing tale, Mr. Morrison, whose towering physical stature has already been noted, states that his parents "was both of them from breeded stock and they was strong like bulls." Referring to "breeded stock," Cassie inquires, "what's that?"

> "Well Cassie, during slavery there was some farms that mated folks like animals to produce more slaves. Breeding slaves brought a lot of money for them slave owners. . . . My folks was bred for strength like they folks and they grandfolks 'fore 'em. Didn't matter none what they thought 'bout the idea. Didn't nobody care."[70]

The other occasion occurs when we learn that Mr. John Henry Berry and his brother were doused with kerosene and set afire for allegedly making advances to a white woman.[71] Taylor does not directly address the pervasive acceptance by whites of this bulwark of racist ideology, the belief that African American men are obsessed with white women. However, her more fully developed treatment of sexual issues in *Let The Circle Be Unbroken* clearly implies that the belief that African American men relentlessly pursued sexual liaisons with white women is in fact an *inversion* of an undeniable fact of history: that white men used their enormous social power for the sexual use and abuse of African American women.

Sexuality becomes a significant theme in *Let the Circle Be Unbroken* because Cassie and Stacey are older and more mature. Cassie has begun to attract the attention of some of the local boys, both African American and white. Taylor also introduces Suzella, a mulatto cousin who, along with her father, provide Taylor with the vehicles with which to introduce and explore these explosive themes. Taylor's treatment of the historic abuse of African American women by white men is perhaps best symbolized by the "fall" of Jacie Peter. Jacie is a bright and attractive young woman with whom Stacey Logan is secretly in love. Jacie also has attracted the attention of the sons of several of the wealthy plantation owners, who stalk her in a predatory manner. In a dramatic scene where the boys' intentions are expressed unashamedly, Cassie and her Uncle Hammer come upon the group talking to Jacie. In response to Hammer's question of what business he has with Jacie, the brash Stuart Walker responds, "What other business we'd have with a nigger bi . . . "[72] (Taylor 1982, 146). Jacie becomes pregnant, and her disgrace is a bitter pill for Stacey. It is also a critical factor in his decision to leave home and seek employment in the Louisiana cane fields, an action around which the last third of this somber novel revolves.

When Mary Logan's cousin Bud and his daughter Suzella arrive at the Logan house, his news that he had married a white woman is received with stunned, silent, disbelief. "I knew," remarks Cassie, "that by his words he had separated himself from the rest of us." Bud's action had violated one of the most rigidly adhered to of all taboos governing interracial relationships:

> White people were a part of another world, distant strangers who ruled our lives and

were better left alone. When they entered our lives, they were to be treated courte-
ously, but with aloofness, and sent away as quickly as possible. Besides, for a black
man to even look at a white woman was dangerous. A year and a half ago Mr. John
Henry Berry had been burned to death, killed for supposedly flirting with a white
woman. . . . A white woman was foreign, dangerous, and here Cousin Bud had gone
off and married one.[73]

The most extended discussion of sexuality occurs after Uncle Hammer
discovers a photograph of Jeremy Simms, a white friend of the children. Despite
being the son of Charlie and sister of Lillian Jean Simms, Jeremy sincerely
seeks the friendship of the Logan children. Barely able to control his rage,
Hammer insists that Stacey "start learning right fast how white men think 'bout
black women. . . . A white man think he can have his way with colored women,
can have them for the taking."[74] Speaking with brutal frankness, he tells of the
African American men killed for trying to protect their women from whites:

"They [the white men] come riding through our neighborhoods in broad daylight
trying to pick up our womenfolk and don't care nothing about how they use them.
White men like that ain't nothing but dogs far as I'm concerned, and I'd rather see
Cassie dead than take up with one of 'em . . .
"They think every man in the world wants one of their women, and if a colored
man even looks sideways at one of 'em, they start talking about a lynching. . . . A
boy . . . lived over by Smellings Creek . . . was messin' with a white girl, and a
bunch of men came out to his place one night and cut off his privates."[75]

The code of behavior demanded by Hammer was simple: "Cassie, you gotta
always respect yourself and your family and your menfolk, and you boys, you
gotta always respect your women and take care of your sister."[76]

The Logan children are stunned by their uncle's outburst. A while later,
the more reserved and dispassionate David Logan clarifies some of the issues
raised by his quick-tempered brother. Again recalling family history, David
reminds Cassie that his father (Cassie's grandfather), who had been born a
slave, had left Georgia for Mississippi after his mother had died ("he didn't
want to stay there any more"). He then tells his daughter about her grandfather's
father. He was

"a white man that kept slaves . . . owned them like you own cows or a pig, and the
slave women had to do what they said . . . and that's how your grandpa came to be
born. Your great-grandmama didn't have no say 'bout it. White men been using
colored women for centuries—they still doing it—and believe me it's a might hurting
thing . . . mighty hurting. . . . Anytime I see a colored woman with a white man, a
colored woman who wants to be with a white man, it makes me want to cry, 'cause
that woman don't care nothin' 'bout herself or how that white man look down on her
and her folks. You understand that?"[77]

Conclusion

In this chapter, I have sought to situate the work of Mildred Taylor in the context of some the recent debates within the sociology of school knowledge. By raising themes and issues rarely addressed by writers for young people, by showing an African American family and an African American community engaged in acts of resistance to white oppression, and by articulating a storied tradition of resistance, I have suggested that Taylor should be considered a voice of opposition, one that has sought to provide young people with a glimpse of the long and often tortured struggle of African Americans for freedom and dignity in the United States. At a time when the gains of the civil rights and women's movements are under assault, and in some cases are being reversed, voices of this sort are more important than ever.

Taylor's account of the African American experience as related through works like *Roll Of Thunder, Hear My Cry* and *Let The Circle Be Unbroken* at times makes for painful reading. The latter novel is especially grim in places as the tenacity of the bigotry confronting Cassie and her family is spelled out with an explicitness not common in books for young people. In introducing the theme of the sexual exploitation of African American women, Taylor also provides a rare glimpse of how gender oppression was joined to racial oppression in ways that are staggering to contemplate.

Although the Logans emerge from the crises described in *Let The Circle Be Unbroken* with their dignity and land intact, it is clear that the distance to be traveled to the kind of society that accords respect to people regardless of race or gender remains enormous. Just how great this distance is is suggested in an exchange between Cassie and her father midway through *Let The Circle Be Unbroken*. After Cassie asks if white folks will change the way they treat African Americans, David Logan replies: "I sure hope so, Cassie, but white folks ain't just gonna change out of the goodness of their hearts. . . . It's gonna take a whole lot of doing on somebody's part." Cassie responds with suitably childlike innocence: "I wonder if they ever think what it'd be like if they was the ones getting treated like us. . . . "They ever do," continues David, "I imagine they don't think about it too long." The exchange concludes with Cassie inquiring if her father thinks "they'll be changing anyway soon?" His response includes the tempered hopefulness that is a characteristic of the series: "Don't know 'bout soon, Cassie girl, but I tell you one thing. I'm sure hoping that if I don't live to see the day, you will. I'm praying right hard on that."[78]

The books of Mildred Taylor, like those of Lucille Clifton, Tom Feelings, Eloise Greenfield, Virginia Hamilton, Julius Lester, Walter Dean Myers, and others, reflect a conscious effort on the part of African American writers and illustrators to provide young readers with a realistic sense of what the African American experience is today and has been in the past. As I have sought to make clear in this chapter, much of this often tragic and painful experience has been excluded from the canon of children's literature, from other curriculum materials, and from the culture at large.

It also is essential to keep in mind that there is no assurance that other readers will be as attentive to the themes and issues raised by Mildred Taylor as I have been in this chapter. Research in the area of reader response points to the highly idiosyncratic nature of the response process, and to the fact that literary works can yield a variety of different interpretations. The interpretations just offered must be seen, at least in part, as the product of the concerns and preoccupations that I brought to my reading of Taylor. In addition, Christian-Smith (1989) has suggested that as long as reading remains an essentially individual, private activity,[79] there is the strong possibility that individualistic modes of reception may diffuse a text's oppositional possibilities. Despite these caveats, my experiences reading Taylor's books along with university students[80] and those of former students working with younger children, indicate that open-ended discussion of her books have enormous potential to raise critical issues and themes.

Mildred Taylor has provided us with exciting, brilliantly characterized, eminently readable narratives containing voices of those too often silenced and ignored by our society's dominant modes of cultural expression. It is my firm conviction that among the important responsibilities of progressive educators is to insure that such voices are heard by *all* children.

Notes

1. Philip Wexler, "Structure, Text, and Subject: A Critical Sociology of School Knowledge," in Michael W. Apple. ed., *Cultural and Economic Reproduction in Education: Essays on Class Ideology and the State* (London: Routledge and Kegan Paul, 1982), p. 279.

2. E.g., Jean Anyon, "Ideology and United States History Textbooks," *Harvard Educational Review* 49 (1979), pp. 361–86; Landon Beyer, "Aesthetic Curriculum and Cultural Reproduction," in Michael W. Apple and Lois Weis, ed., *Ideology and School Practice* (Philadelphia: Temple University Press, 1983); Allan Luke, *Literacy, Textbooks and Ideology: Postwar Literacy Instruction and the Mythology of Dick and Jane* (New York: The Falmer Press, 1988); Linda Christian-Smith, "Gender, Popular Culture, and Curriculum: Adolescent Romance Novels as Gendered Text," *Curriculum Inquiry* 17, no. 4 (1987), pp. 365–406; Joel Taxel, "The Outsiders of the American Revolution: The Selective Tradition in Children's Fiction," *Interchange* 12, nos. 2–3 (1981), pp. 206–28; Joel Taxel, "The American Revolution in Children's Fiction: An Analysis of Historical Meaning and Narrative Structure," *Curriculum Inquiry* 14, no. 1 (1984), pp. 7–55.

3. Raymond Williams, *Marxism and Literature* (London: Oxford University Press, 1977); Raymond Williams, *The Sociology of Culture* (New York: Schocken Books, 1982).

4. Williams, *The Sociology of Culture,* p. 186.

5. Williams, *The Marxism and Literature,* p. 177.

6. Pierre Bourdieu, "The Thinkable and the Unthinkable," *Time Literary Supplement,* October 15, 1971, pp. 1255–56; Paul Willis, *Learning to Labor: How Working Class Kids Get Working*

Class Jobs (Lexington, Mass.: D.C. Heath, 1977); Terry Eagleton, *Marxism and Literary Criticism* (Berkeley: University of California Press, 1976).

7. Terry Eagleton, *Criticism and Ideology: A Study in Marxist Literary Theory* (London: New Left Books, 1976).

8. Apple, *Education and Power* (London: Routledge and Kegan Paul, 1982) and *Teachers and Texts: A Political Economy of Class and Gender Relations in Education* (London: Routledge and Kegan Paul, 1986); Henry Giroux, *Theory and Resistance in Education: A Pedagogy for the Opposition* (South Hadley, Mass.: Bergin and Garvey, 1983); Wexler, ''Structure, Text, and Subject.''

9. Quoted by Eagleton, *Marxism and Literary Criticism,* p. 24.

10. Discussions of resistance also focus on demonstrating that students in school do not passively internalize and accept the ideas, values and ideologies as is suggested by, for example, Samuel Bowles and Herbert Gintis in *Schooling in Capitalist America* (New York: Basic Books, 1976). See also the influential work of Anyon, ''Social Class and School Knowledge,'' *Curriculum Inquiry* 11 (1981), pp. 3–42, and Willis, *Learning to Labor.*

11. Williams, *Marxism and Literature,* p. 112.

12. Joel Taxel, ''Children's Literature: A Research Proposal from the Perspective of the Sociology of School Knowledge,'' in Suzanne de Castell, Allan Luke, and Carmen Luke, eds., *Language, Authority and Criticism: Readings in the School Textbook* (London and Philadelphia: The Falmer Press, 1989).

13. Stanley Aronowitz and Henry A. Giroux, ''Ideologies about Schooling: Rethinking the Nature of Educational Reform,'' *Journal of Curriculum Theorizing* 7, no. 1 (1987), pp. 7–38; George H. Wood, ''Beyond Radical Educational Cynicism,'' *Educational Theory* 32, no. 2 (1982), p. 67.

14. Apple, *Teachers and Texts,* p. 177.

15. J. W. Blassingame, ''The Afro-Americans: From Mythology to Reality,'' in William Cartwright and Richard Watson, eds., *The Reinterpretation of American History and Culture* (Washington, D.C.: N.C.S.S., 1973), p. 53; Peter McLaren, ''Culture or Canon? Critical Pedagogy and the Politics of Literacy,'' *Harvard Educational Review* 58, no. 2 (May 1988), pp. 213–34.

16. Quoted by P. Aufderheide in ''The Have-Nots of History Find a Place in Museums,'' *In These Times* 12, no. 32 (August 1988), p. 21.

17. Virginia Hamilton, *Anthony Burns; The Defeat and Triumph of a Fugitive Slave* (New York: Alfred A. Knopf, 1988), pp. 179–80.

18. Apple, *Teachers and Texts.*

19. Kenneth Teitelbaum ''The Construction of an Alternative School Text: Teaching the ABC's of Socialism to Children, 1900–1920,'' paper presented to the American Educational Research Association Convention, Washington, D.C.: 1987.

20. Violet Harris, *The Brownie's Alternative to the Selective Tradition in Children's Literature,* doctoral dissertation, the University of Georgia, 1986; D. Broderick, *Image of the Black in Children's Literature* (New York: Bowker, 1973).

21. Wendy Saul, ''Recouping the Losses: The Case of Francis LeFlesch and *The Middle Five,*'' paper presented to the American Educational Research Association Convention, New Orleans, 1988.

22. Taxel, ''Children's Literature: A Research Proposal,'' and ''The American Revolution in Children's Fiction.''

23. Quoted by Michael W. Apple in "Redefining Equality: Authoritarian Populism and the Conservative Restoration," *Teacher's College Record* 90, no. 2 (Winter, 1988), p. 179.

24. Taxel, "The American Revolution in Children's Fiction," and "The Black Experience in Children's Fiction: Controversies Surrounding Award-Winning Books." *Curriculum Inquiry* 16, no. 3 (1986), pp. 245–81. Christian-Smith's study of teen romance novels ("Gender, Popular Culture, and Curriculum") also scrutinized the relation between novel content and form. Luke's study of the "Dick and Jane" readers, *Literacy, Textbooks and Ideology,* p. 103, noted that the often repeated form of the relationships in these widely used basal readers, "tend to underscore the theme of harmonious adaption to existing social relations."

25. Rudine Sims, *Shadow and Substance; Afro-American Experience in Contemporary Children's Fiction* (Urbana: NCTE, 1982), p. 102.

26. Myra Sadker and David Sadker, *Now Upon a Time: A Contemporary View of Children's Literature* (New York: Harper & Row, 1977), p. 129.

27. See, for example, M. Calhoun, *Big Sixteen,* illustrated by Trina Schart Hyman (New York: William Morrow, 1983); Margot Zemnach, *Jake and Honeybunch Go to Heaven* (New York: Farrar, Strauss and Giroux, 1982).

28. Sims, *Shadow and Substance,* p. 5.

29. *Ibid.,* pp. 17, 18.

30. *Ibid.,* p. 33.

31. *Ibid.,* p. 49.

32. *Ibid.,* p. 79. Jo Anne Pagano made a similar point when she noted that "some of us have stories told about us and some of us tell our own stories." "Household Language and Feminist Pedagogy," paper presented to the Conference on Curriculum Theory and Practice, Dayton, Ohio, 1988.

33. Sims, *Shadow and Substance,* p. 96. Illustrator Tom Feelings stated "that to me, pain and joy are the two strongest opposing forces affecting the lives of Blacks living in America." "Illustration is My Form, the Black Experience My Story and My Content." The *Advocate* 4, no. 2 (1985), pp. 73–82.

34. I am indebted to Susan Taylor Cox for helping me to clarify these important points.

35. Lucille Clifton, *Amifika,* illustrated by Thomas DiGrazia (New York: E.P. Dutton, 1977), and *The Lucky Stone,* illustrated by Dale Payson (New York: Delacorte Press, 1979); Eloise Greenfield, *She Come Bringing Me That Baby Girl,* illustrated by J. Steptoe (New York: J. B. Lippincott, 1974), and *Grandpa's Face,* illustrated by F. Cooper (New York: Philomel Books, 1988); Patricia McKissack, *Mirandy and Brother Wind,* illustrated by Jerry Pinkney (New York: Alfred A. Knopf, 1988); Julius Lester, *Long Journey Home: Stories from Black History* (New York: Dial Press, 1972)., *This Strange New Feeling* (New York: Dial Press, 1982), and *The Tales of Uncle Remus: The Adventures of Brer Rabbit* (New York: Dial Press, 1987); Sharon Mathis, *A Teacup Full of Roses* (New York: Viking Press, 1972); Walter Dean Myers, *Fast Sam, Cool Clyde, and Stuff* (New York: Viking Press, 1975), and *Hoops* (New York: Delacorte Press, 1981); Virginia Hamilton. *The People Could Fly: American Black Folktales,* illustrated by Leo and Diane Dillon (New York: Alfred A. Knopf).

   Collections of "feminist" folktales by Alison Lurie and Ethel Phelps also demonstrate that the folk tradition offers representations of women other than those contained in well-known tales as "Cinderella," "Sleeping Beauty," and "Snow White," Lurie, *Clever Gretchen and Other Forgotten Folktales,* illustrated by Margot Tomes (New York: Thomas Y. Crowell, 1980): Phelps. The *Maid of the North: Feminist Folktales from around the World* illustrated by Lloyd Bloom (New York: Holt, Rinehart and Winston, 1981).

36. I am indebted to Susan Taylor Cox for suggesting this term.

37. Quoted by Anne Commire in *Something About the Author,* vol. 15 (Detroit: Gale Research, 1979), pp. 275, 277.

38. Mildred Taylor, Newbery Acceptance Speech, *The Horn Book* 53, no. 4 (August 1977), p. 405.

39. Quoted by Commire in *Something About the Author* p. 277.

40. Taylor, Newbery Acceptance Speech, pp. 404–6.

41. *Ibid.,* p. 404.

42. Mildred Taylor, *Roll of Thunder, Hear My Cry* (New York: Bantam, 1976): *Let the Circle be Unbroken* (New York: Dial Press, 1982); *Song of the Trees* (New York: Dial Press, 1975); *Friendship* (New York: Dial Press, 1987); *The Gold Cadillac* (New York: Dial Press, 1987).

43. Taylor, Newbery Acceptance Speech, p. 405.

44. Mary T. Harper, "Merger and Metamorphosis in the Fiction of Mildred D. Taylor," *Children's Literature Association Quarterly* 13, no. 1 (Summer 1988), p. 76.

45. Taylor, *Roll of Thunder, Hear My Cry,* pp. 139–40.

46. Taylor, *Let the Circle be Unbroken,* pp. 89–90.

47. Anyon, "Ideology and United States History Textbooks."

48. Taylor, *Let the Circle be Unbroken,* p. 132, 133.

49. *Ibid.,* p. 135.

50. Howard Fast, *Freedom Road* (New York: Bantam Books, 1979).

51. Taylor, *Let the Circle be Unbroken,* p. 339, 186.

52. *Ibid.,* pp. 370–71.

53. *Ibid.,* pp. 370–72.

54. McLaren, "Culture or Canon?" pp. 232–33.

55. Taylor, *Let the Circle be Unbroken,* pp. 114–15.

56. *Ibid.,* pp. 195–96.

57. *Ibid.,* pp. 361–62.

58. Taxel, "Black Experience," p. 260.

59. Taylor, Newbery Acceptance Speech, p. 403.

60. S. W. Holtz, "Review of *Roll of Thunder, Hear My Cry,*" *The Horn Book Magazine* 52, no. 6 (December 1976), p. 627.

61. In referring to the responses of "readers" throughout this chapter, I am referring not only to my own personal responses to these books, but also to the responses of hundreds of readers in dozens of classes with whom I have discussed *Roll of Thunder, Hear My Cry* over the last ten years in my children's literature classes at the University of Georgia. The almost uniformly positive response of these readers to this book is especially significant in light of the fact that the majority of my students are white and southern. Many admit, with considerable embarrassment and guilt, that they themselves were raised in families rife with the very sort of racism that was the bane of the Logan family's existence.

62. Taylor, *Roll of Thunder, Hear My Cry.* p. 87.

63. *Ibid.,* p. 96.

64. *Ibid.,* p. 96.

65. *Ibid.*, pp. 111–113.

66. Sims. *Shadow and Substance.*

67. Taylor, *Roll of Thunder, Hear My Cry*, p. 133.

68. *Ibid.*, pp. 133–34.

69. *Ibid.*, p. 156. See Taxel, "The Black Experience in Children's Fiction," for a comparison of the model of social action in *Roll of Thunder, Hear My Cry* to the dramatically different one found in Ouida Sebestyen's *Words By Heart* (New York: Bantam, 1979). It is significant that, unlike Taylor, Sebestyen is white.

70. Taylor, *Roll of Thunder, Hear My Cry*, p. 113.

71. *Ibid.*, p. 125.

72. Taylor, *Let the Circle be Unbroken*, p. 146.

73. *Ibid.*, p. 162.

74. *Ibid.*, pp. 174–75.

75. *Ibid.*, p. 175.

76. *Ibid.*, p. 176.

77. *Ibid.*, pp. 178–79.

78. *Ibid.*, p. 181.

79. Linda K. Christian-Smith. "Going Against the Grain Gender Ideology in Selected Children's Fiction," paper presented to the American Educational Research Association Convention. San Francisco. 1989. See also, Elyse Eidman-Aadahl's discussion of the "solitary" nature of reading. "The Solitary Reader: Exploring How Lonely Reading Has to Be," *The New Advocate* 1 (Summer, 1988) pp. 165–76.

80. Joel Taxel, "Teaching Children's Literature," Teaching Education 1 no. 1 (1986) pp. 12–15.

7

Critical Lessons from Our Past: Curricula of Socialist Sunday Schools in the United States

Kenneth Teitelbaum

One of the primary focuses of critical curriculum scholarship during the past decade has been the linkages between school instructional materials on the one hand and social and economic inequities and the prospects for social transformation on the other.[1] Examinations of language arts and social studies curricula, for example, have revealed three tendencies in particular. First, text and trade books reinforce a sense of tradition, culture, and history that favors the material interests and ideological perspectives of white middle-and upper-class males. Second, by overemphasizing an ethic of individualism and by "selecting out" interpretations of our past that stress the role that grass-roots collective action has played in the improvement of social life, school curricula have provided a narrow understanding of the distribution of power and the possibilities for social change. And, third, by minimizing the role of conflict and disagreement in the advance of the social and physical sciences, schools have presented an overly consensual view of the nature of academic knowledge.[2]

Recent research on the political economy of textbook publishing in the United States has further highlighted a trend toward increased homogenization and standardization of school textbook adoption.[3] This development, combined with the increasingly direct intrusion of corporate interests (e.g., Adopt-A-School programs) and state government directives (e.g., standardized syllabuses and student testing) into local curriculum making, can seriously limit the opportunities for emancipatory educational practice.[4] Progressive teachers face increasing difficulty in their attempts to include more critically oriented curricular content and more participatory pedagogical forms in their elementary and secondary classrooms. During the "conservative restoration"[5] of recent years, these trends have tended to reinforce the role that schooling plays in perpetuating rather than alleviating existing social inequities.

Teachers who seek to introduce elements of more critical instruction are

This chapter is a slightly revised version of the one that appeared under the same name in *Curriculum Inquiry* 20 (4) (Winter, 1990).

further hindered by how few appropriate curriculum material are published and disseminated. They face having to construct, in piecemeal fashion, their own alternative "texts," with few exemplars to guide them. Of course, the development of one's own curriculum materials is by no means in itself a negative aspect of teaching, nor is it an impossible task for many committed and creative teachers. Indeed, social groups espousing egalitarian principles in the public schools have always competed with those who promote corporate interests, and progressive "resistances" to dominant ideologies have always occurred within the classroom.[6] Educational materials informed by a critical perspective do get published, and educational organizations that promote a more critical and participatory perspective of democratic practice do exist.[7] Still, there exists a general lack of available resources to inform the everyday practice of critical educators. This can lead to three related negative effects: first, the feeling that an overwhelming and perhaps ultimately hopeless task lies ahead; second, and unfamiliarity with the important alternative insights and curriculum work of others, both in the past and in the present; and third, the waste of valuable time. As Joseph Featherstone has argued, "In the United States of Amnesia, we keep having to reinvent everything from scratch, and this is one reason why educational practice doesn't develop in a cumulative way."[8] While access to concrete alternative ideas and materials will certainly not remove the conditions of the classroom that discourage critical educational practice, it could in fact be a major factor in the initiation of progressive instructional change.

It seems probable that most classroom teachers have a very limited awareness both of past struggles to introduce more critical perspectives into school settings and of, more specifically, the instructional materials that were adopted for this purpose. This essay presents one small piece of this history. It examines a "lost" body of texts, used for explicitly counter-hegemonic purposes, in U.S. Socialist Sunday schools for children. This collection of school texts, published at the turn of the century, stood in essence "outside" what Raymond Williams has called the "selective tradition." Indeed, these curriculum materials were used to *challenge* the dominant, selective tradition of ideological values, beliefs, and meanings been promoted in our public schools and other social institutions, a "selective transmission of class culture as common culture" that at least partially "silences the cultures of the oppressed, and legitimates the present social order as natural and eternal."[9]

That most of these texts were never used in public school settings should not serve to deflect attention from the lessons socialist educators drew from them and the lessons they may still hold for those attempting to cut a similar path today. More specifically, school texts that embodied an ideological perspective explicitly opposing the dominant messages of capitalist culture may help to illuminate the fundamentally political nature of mainstream school curriculum-making. An examination of alternatives that actually existed, even ones that are in parts clearly outdated, can help to make the familiar strange, thus "heightening our critical sensibilities'' and helping us to "reformulate our problems in fresh and constructive ways."[10] It may provide the stark contrast often necessary to recognize more clearly that what is taught in the public school classroom is not "reality" but a *particular* version of it. Moreover, while historians of American schooling need to avoid the possible distortions of description and interpretation that can result from attempting to draw from the past some direct lessons for current thinking and practice,[11] it may be the case that in a more general way an examination of these curriculum materials can help teachers not only to better understand but also to transform traditional practice. It may contribute to the clarification and elaboration of the very nature of what has been referred to as critical, transformative, or emancipatory pedagogy. Here, for example, is a tradition of alternative education that attempted to merge radical political principles with aspects of progressive educational theory. What kinds of curriculum materials did the socialists work with and why? What specific conceptual themes did they emphasize? Are they ones that could help to inform critical educational practice today?

It is vitally important to keep constantly in mind the historical context in which these curriculum materials were produced—and, for example, not to exaggerate the theoretical sophistication and practical achievements of the socialist activists who typically engaged in educational work on a part-time basis, the numbers of children involved in their Sunday schools, and the importance of these alternative school settings even within the larger radical movement. And yet it is also important to note that, as E. P. Thompson has put it, "the past is not just dead, inert, confining; it carries the signs and evidences also of creative resources which can sustain the present and prefigures possibility."[12] It may in fact be the case that some of the best sources of counter-hegemonic practice are historical in nature, for example, in "the recovery of discarded areas, or the redress of selective and reductive interpretations."[13]

The Emergence of the Socialist Alternative

Although members and supporters of the Socialist Party of America during the period 1900–1920 were rarely from the professional education community, they did seek to influence the direction of American public schooling in a number of ways. Along with allied radical groups, they agitated for democratic school reforms that would directly serve the interests of children from working-class families, and that would further the political principles for which their movement stood. Several decades before the era of the social reconstructionists, they sought to use the process of schooling to help usher in "a new social order," although from a perspective that was more explicitly socialist and class-conscious.[14] Their efforts took place not only within the corridors of the public schools, where they often joined with liberal Progressives, but outside of them as well.[15]

Sunday schools for working-class children, where the school texts discussed in this article were used, were a part of the more general attempt by American socialists to forge a radical culture. Indeed, the period 1900–1920 was a "golden age" of sorts for American socialism, with several hundred newspapers and journals being published and thousands of candidates for political office being elected.[16] While most attention was given to the effects of capitalist economics and its system of "wage slavery" on working-class life, a number of Socialist Party activists realized that there were significant cultural factors undermining the radical cause, such as the mainstream press, religious organizations, mass entertainment, and public schooling. These aspects of the dominant culture successfully promoted the interests and values of the capitalist class and subverted the spread of socialist beliefs. Public school knowledge, for example, was viewed by prominent radical activists as neither neutral nor innocuous in potential influence, nor, perhaps more to the point, as functioning in the economic and social interests of most workers. They criticized in particular the increasing tendency on the part of the schools to glorify private property, the profit motive, intense competition and individualism, anti–working-class attitudes, and knee-jerk patriotism.[17]

Thus, while American socialists generally viewed recruitment and political and labor agitation to be of primary importance, Party activists also considered the organization of counter-hegemonic educational activities for workers and their children to be crucial in the struggle to offset what were sometimes referred to as the "pernicious" or "poisonous" influences of everyday (capitalist) life. This meant going beyond a narrow reliance on socialist rallies and newspapers as educational tools to more formal attempts to educate working-class adults and children about the nature of industrial capitalism, the class struggle, socialist economics and philosophy, and the practical benefits of a socialist reorganization of society. Numerous lecture forums, study classes, correspondence courses, adult schools and colleges, and children's clubs were organized.[18] In addition, while generally supporting the institution of public schooling as a real gain for the working class, radical youth activists sought to "demystify" ruling ideas by presenting to working-class children, more formally, a perspective of events, people, and ideas that challenged the dominant messages of capitalist culture. They adopted a familiar form of schooling for this purpose, the Sunday School. It was hoped that in this setting the children of workers could be given a systematic supplementary education consistent with socialist ideals.

Proponents of the Socialist Sunday schools made it clear that "if the Public School system were what it should be, there would be no need for Socialist Schools."[19] Such a perspective illustrates the dialectical relationship that exists between attempts at ideological hegemony and the forces of counter-hegemony. As Martin Carnoy suggests, Antonio Gramsci's notion of the "war of position" was based on the idea of "*surrounding* the State apparatus with a counter-hegemony, a hegemony created by mass organization of the working class and by developing working-class institutions and culture.'' The norms and values of a new, socialist society would be created. It would confront the bourgeois hegemony in a war of position, "of trenches moving back and forth in an ideological struggle over the consciousness of the working class.'' In fact, only when this counter-hegemony was set in motion, when the outline of a new society had been in essence created and controlled by the working class (with an important role to be played by its own "organic intellectuals"), would it make sense to take over State power.[20] Although American socialism was certainly not successful in this effort, the organization of Socialist Sunday schools can be viewed in the light of this political movement's general attempt to develop counter-hegemonic working-class institutions and culture (and a cadre of organic intellectuals) for its eventual "assault" on the sites of economic and cultural power. Ardent supporters of the weekend schools recognized that a successful revolution meant not only changes in the ownership and management of industry but changes in the minds and hearts of the people as well, in particular those of the next generation. That these radical educators, and the political movement from whence they came, were not successful in bringing about a socialist revolution, or even in leaving a lasting legacy of radical pedagogy in the United States, should not be cause for eliminating from our collective memory the dynamic quality of their struggles and the specific examples of critique and practice that they offered.

Alternative Schools to Teach
"Critical Lessons" to Children

Socialist youth activists at the turn of the century had great difficulty in initiating and keeping afloat the Sunday morning schools for children. While the form of schooling was certainly limited, it amounted to a prodigious effort for a movement that was constantly low on funds, staff, and instructional materials. Despite the problems that were encountered, including a lack of tangible support from national and state Party organizations, grass-roots radical educators organized about one hundred English-speaking Socialist Sunday schools in sixty-five cities and towns across the country between 1900 and 1920.[21] Attendance at these alternative weekend schools ranged from a dozen children or so in the smaller ones for example, in Newport, Kentucky to several hundred in the larger ones for example, in Rochester, Milwaukee, Manhattan, and Brooklyn. Some schools lasted for barely one school year; others remained in existence for a decade or more. Certain schools had the benefit of instructors who had college or public school teaching experience for example, Bertha Howell Mailly in Omaha, Boston, and Manhattan; Benjamin Glassberg and David Berenberg in Brooklyn; Kendrick Shedd in Rochester and Milwaukee; May Wood Simons in Chicago; and Carl Haessler in Milwaukee; others were staffed primarily by long-time radical activists with no prior formal teaching experience for example, Edmund Melms in Milwaukee; Frederick Krafft in Newark; Edward Perkins Clarke in Hartford; and Lucien Saniel in Manhattan) or by those barely in their teens and eager to do more for the socialist movement than just be members of the Young People's Socialist League (for example, Edna Peters in Milwaukee; Isadore Tischler in Rochester; and Gertrude Weil Klein in Brooklyn). Taken as a whole, the socialist schools clearly lacked uniformity. But there was complete agreement about the need to contest integral elements of the hegemonic culture and to promote a concern for the expansion of democratic rights and economic justice, especially as they pertained to the working classes. Advocates of the Socialist Sunday schools believed that the public school and other social institutions, in their rush to emphasize industrial productivity and social order, were seriously undermining the advance of democracy and justice.

Socialist educators used a variety of text materials to help convey such a perspective to children. These texts were basically of three kinds. First, in the best tradition of creative educators, they adapted mainstream writings that were not originally intended for use by the radical movement. Similarly, they made use of radical writings that were originally written for adult readers. And third, particularly active socialist youth activists were able to produce a limited number of texts specifically intended for use by the Sunday schools and radical youth clubs. School participants believed that to varying degrees each of these sources could help to teach "critical lessons" and, as Kendrick Shedd of Rochester and Milwaukee put it, to encourage the children (ages five to fourteen) to become " good rebels. " The following sections of this article will discuss examples of each of these kinds of texts.

Nonsocialist Sources: A Case of Appropriation

The nonsocialist texts most often cited by Socialist Sunday School participants were those authored by Katherine E. Dopp. The Dopp books were used either as references from which to draw for curriculum development or, more directly, as classroom reading material; thus they illustrate the appropriation of mainstream text materials by socialist educators. The socialist Sunday School activists had recourse to such materials often, out of necessity, for this radical educational movement (like most others in our history) was constantly low on the funds, staff expertise, and time necessary to develop a sufficient supply of its own materials. The Dopp books represent the most widespread example of "selective borrowing" from middle-class culture by these working-class schools.[22]

After graduating from the State Normal School in Oshkosh, Wisconsin, in 1888, Katherine Dopp worked as a principal and a *"normal school"* instructor. While her background certainly evidenced no socialist leanings, she did study with John Dewey at the University of Chicago, and received her Ph.D. there in 1902. She worked for the next ten years as an instructor of correspondence study in the University of Chicago's philosophy department and as a lecturer of education in the school's extension division. She was also a participant in chautauquas and the author of several professional papers and journal articles. Apparently, at least later in life, Dopp identified herself as a Republican.[23]

In a forty-year association with the Rand McNally publishing company, Dopp authored three series of books: the "Industrial and Social History" series (1903–29), the "Bobby and Betty" series (1917–30), and the "Happy Road to Reading" series (1935–43). The first three of the six volumes of the "Industrial and Social History" series were used in a number of the Socialist Sunday schools (e.g., in Manhattan, Brooklyn, Bronx, Rochester, Brockton, Baltimore, Cleveland, Pittsburgh, Detroit, and Milwaukee). These were *The Tree-Dwellers: The Age of Fear* (1903); *The Early Cave-Men: The Age of Combat* (1904); and *The Later Cave-Men: The Age of the Chase* (1906). Utilizing the research of geologists, anthropologists, and others, Dopp's books included relevant narratives, questions, suggestions for practical activities, and numerous vivid illustrations to trace "the life of the early Aryans [*sic*]." Dopp stressed that her series focused on "the most significant steps in the early development of our industrial and social institutions, [and] is not only so closely related to [the] child's experience as to be readily appreciated and controlled by him, but it is of profound significance as a means of interpreting the complex of the present." Expounding views similar to the recapitulation notion of culture epoch theory, she wrote: "Since the experience of the race in industrial and social processes embodies, better than any other experiences of mankind, those things which at the same time appeal to the whole nature of the child and furnish him the means of interpreting the complex processes about him, this experience has been made the groundwork of the present series." Clearly influenced by the work of Dewey, Dopp envisioned the series as part of the larger attempt by progressive educators "to introduce practical activity in such a way as to afford the child a sound development—physically, intellectually, and morally—and, at the same time, equip him for efficient social service."[24]

The first volume, *The Tree-Dwellers,* can serve as a representative example of the "Industrial and Social History" series. Intended for children six-and-a-half years old (each of the ensuing volumes is intended for the next age group), it contains a 120-page story, questions "to think about" and "things to do" after each chapter, and twenty-five pages of "Suggestions to Teachers" that include recommended reference materials for each section of the book. The narrative, divided into two- to six-page "lessons," reveals how the animals "knew how to do one thing" but that "people could do a great many things." Significantly, people "could remember, too, what happened before." Dopp sought to link animals to humans at the same time as stressing the superiority of human life in "the struggle for existence." In addition, humans are connected across generations. For example, the early people are portrayed as not so very unlike twentieth-century people in their need for food, clothing, shelter, and means of protection. Dopp also makes clear to the young reader that those who came after the Tree-dwellers learned (or "remembered") from their predecessors and thus represent the continuing progress of the human species. They "take advantage of what has been accomplished during many long ages." Our indebtedness to those who have come before us, as well as the value of studying about them, is expressed in the book's very first story:

> You will learn how they become brave and strong.
> You will learn how they used their bodies and minds.
> They began the work we are doing to-day.
> They took the first steps.
> People who lived after them were able to do a little more.
> The next people could do still more.
> Many people have lived and worked since then.
> The work they have done helps us to-day.
> We have something to do, too.
> We can do our part better if we know what others have done.
> That is why we have this little book.

The story in *The Tree-Dwellers* revolves around the adventures of Sharptooth and her family, who are portrayed as often swinging from branch to branch instead of always walking on the ground. The early family structure, the beginnings of a textile industry (i.e., weaving) and the dangers of living at the time (e.g., among wild animals) are discussed. The point is made that the early people learned a great deal from the animals while at the same time seeking to "conquer" them to better their own conditions in life. Different geographic areas in which Tree-dwellers lived are described, as are the early use of tools, the fear and eventual use of fire, and the need for constructive use of "leisure time" even among these Tree-dwellers. Questions and suggested activities accompany each of the chapters for the purpose of helping readers to explore their own understandings and "emotional reactions" to the developing story. Examples of "Things to Think About" include: "What do you need in order to live? What do you think that the Tree-dwellers needed?"; "Why did the Tree-dwellers not live in families as we do?"; and "What have you learned from animals?" Among the suggestions for "Things to Do" are: "Go out where everything is growing wild and find a place where the Tree-dwellers might have lived"; and "Find a picture of Sharptooth running away from a wild animal [and tell] a story about this picture."

The Dopp series was by no means the only example of how the appropriation of nonradical texts of necessity infused socialist teaching in weekend schools for children. For example, one teacher from New York City recommended a poem by Robert Louis Stevenson, entitled "Where Go the Boats":

Dark brown is the river,
Golden is the sand.
It flows along for ever,
With trees on either hand.

Green leaves afloating,
Castles in the foam,
Boats of mine aboating
Where will all come home?

On goes the river
And out past the mill,
Away down the valley,
Away down the hill.

Away down the river,
A hundred miles or more.
Other little children
Shall bring my boats ashore.[25]

Another nonsocialist text that adopted by some of the socialist schools, especially in classes for younger children (five- and six-year-olds) was Emilie Poulsson's generally popular *Finger Plays For Nursery and Kindergarten.*[26] We would be hard-pressed to extrapolate any socialist content from Poulsson's own verses (e.g., "The Hen and Chickens," "Making Bread," "The Caterpillar," and "The Little Men"). Of course, the socialist teachers may have revised some of the verses to convey a radical message. But even if they did not, the Poulsson text could still be used to help promote important goals of the Socialist Sunday School movement: to make the weekend educational experience an enjoyable one for the children so that they would keep coming back (after all, it was not a compulsory school setting), and so that the children would identify being part of the socialist community in a positive ("fun") light.

It was a different case for the Dopp texts and poems like Stevenson's, however. The socialists' adoption of these nonradical sources was based on particular themes that could be drawn from them and discussed with the children. In the case of the Stevenson poem (whether this was his intention or not), it was to reinforce a perspective of the interrelatedness of individuals in society. This was an important theme in the Socialist Sunday School curriculum as a whole. What happens "up the river" will have an effect on the children who play "away down the river, a hundred miles or more." The relatedness of the individual with countless others, especially workers, was a theme that was promoted in opposition to the dominant emphasis on what Michael Apple has recently characterized as "atomization or the creation of the abstract individual."[27] Such texts could help to transmit a sense of social interdependence and social concern, themes that the socialists felt were missing from the public school experience. As May Reinhardt Schocken, who taught in socialist children's schools in New York City and Yonkers, put it, the intent was to teach a habit of thought, to teach children "to think socially, instead of individually." The children needed to learn "to question whether that which is best for ourselves, is also best for the community."[28]

The Dopp books were used to convey other messages as well. Radicals at the time were generally optimistic that, as expressed in Marxist theory, "the struggle for existence" of necessity included the capitalist stage of development before its natural progression to socialism. A similar focus could be found in the Dopp texts, with the early people of necessity going through distinct stages (tree-dwelling, cave-dwelling, etc.), which they learned from and then transcended. As one prominent school participant suggested, the Dopp books could be used to show the children that "change and adaptation are ever universal, . . . [and] to foster the general principle to go from old to new, from simple to complex, from concrete to abstract," as well as "to appeal to the imagination."[29] Another message appropriated from these texts was the constructive role that could be played by cooperative and collectivist social relations in a social world that seemed overly competitive and privatized. The success of the early people in surmounting the obstacles in their way (e.g., wild animals and severe climate) was portrayed by Dopp as often depending on their ability to work together.

Some radical activists, especially those influenced by child-centered progressive educators, criticized the ways in which the Dopp books were actually being used in some of the Socialist Sunday schools. For example, while strongly recommending their continued adoption, William Kruse of the Party's Young People's Department argued that the Dopp texts were not always used to their best advantage. He issued a caution: "My experience with several well-meaning teachers who are making use of the Dopp books convinces me that they are missing their chief point of value when they consider the stories themselves as of greater importance than the method by which the stories are put across." He also claimed that too many teachers were going through the books too quickly in their classes, within a few months' time. Kruse advised that "if properly used, these books would be sufficient for years of S.S.S. [Socialist Sunday School] exercises."[30] By the time Kruse's comments were published in 1920, however, most of the schools had closed as a result of the devastating split in Party ranks in 1918–20. While the dearth of relevant source materials does not allow us to assess with certainty the validity of Kruse's claims, the use of the Dopp texts by a number of Socialist Sunday schools does illustrate how mainstream curricula can be and have been reinterpreted and reconstructed for alternative, more radical educational purposes. This is perhaps similar to the suggestion made by Stanley Aronowitz and Henry Giroux in discussing the development of a "language of possibility." Instead of simply debunking existing theory, materials, and practice, it may be useful to rework aspects of them, "contesting the terrains on which they develop, and appropriating from them whatever radical potentialities they might contain."[31]

Radical Texts Not Intended for Socialist
Sunday School Use: A Case of Adaptation

Socialist Sunday School directors and teachers also made extensive use of radical materials not originally written for use in the Sunday schools. Again, the use of such materials was made necessary by the difficulty that school participants faced in developing and disseminating their own materials. Most of these sources were in fact intended for an adult audience. In referring to one such text, Walter Thomas Mills's *The Struggle For Existence,* Kendrick Shedd suggested excitedly that enough material could be gleaned "for a hundred lessons." However, he added, "it will need somebody with discernment to cull out the material and put it into form suitable for the child's mind."[32] When not successfully adapted, such lessons could appear overly abstract, complicated, and doctrinaire to the students. Indeed, the Party's National Education Committee warned in 1913 of the propensity of some of the Sunday schools to teach "stilted economics and dogmatic exercises to children."[33] This no doubt occurred in schools that over-relied on texts originally written for adults, such as those by socialist theorists like John Spargo, Morris Hillquit, William English Walling, and John Stuart Mills. While the content of these texts may have been suitably socialistic, the form of their presentation (e.g., lecture and recitation) may have sometimes represented the kinds of educational experiences that the National Education Committee criticized.

Walter Thomas Mills's *The Struggle For Existence* served as a source of lessons for a number of the socialist children's schools. Mills was a popular socialist lecturer and educator, whose most noteworthy written contribution to the radical movement was this textbook. Published by the International School of Social Economy, an "agitational academy" that Mills had established in 1902 in Girard, Kansas, the book was reprinted many times and was widely used in socialist encampments for educational purposes, allegedly selling half a million copies. As historian James R. Green notes, Mills's textbook contains "an encyclopedic approach to the science of society, harkening back to the early Owenite belief that education was the main road to socialism—that the laboring classes would control the world as soon as they understood it." With a mixture of Spencerism, enlightened Christian idealism, and Marxism, the book encapsulated the varying strains within the American radical movement at the time, in particular its moralistic and materialistic approaches to industrial capitalism.[34]

Mills's textbook was used as a reference for the construction of Socialist Sunday School lessons in New York City, Rochester, Pittsburgh, Milwaukee, Los Angeles, and elsewhere. For example, in the final year of its existence, a

Milwaukee school developed a curriculum of twenty-one lessons for the older grades (ten- to fourteen-year-olds) that represented a straightforward adaptation of the first eight chapters of Mills's book. The first three lessons presented an introductory discussion of capitalism as a "way of life," although generally conceived of in rather narrow economistic terms, and socialism as a viable alternative one. The ownership of "the machines and the buildings" by a few individuals was contrasted to a situation in which "the many would not have to get the permission of the few to work for a living—to live." Socialism was portrayed as putting "an end to the relation of master and servant." It would insure "equal opportunity" for all men and women as well as, for the workers, "an equal voice in the management of the industries carried on for the use of everybody," with "the value of the product to go to the workers."[35] (These topics correspond to Mills's introductory chapter on "Capitalism and Socialism.")

Following Mills's text, lessons at the Milwaukee school then focused on the fact that "all forms of life struggle for existence—struggle to survive." The evolution of "Man" from savagery and barbarism to modernity was traced, concluding with a discussion of the last stage ("civilization") as a time of "the invention of the alphabet," "the institution of property," "wars of conquest," and so forth.[36] The beginning of modernity was discussed with reference to the changing nature of the city, the need for slaves, and the transition to serfdom. The final lessons of the Milwaukee course of study focused on the beginnings of the wage system, depicted as "merely the last step in the long class struggle[,] . . . the last and final form of master and servant."[37] It is probable that these Milwaukee teachers planned to continue with Mills's 635-page text beyond the two (of six) sections covered ("Clearing the Ground") and "The Evolution of Capitalism"). It is less clear how they planned to relate the other four parts ("The Evolution of Socialism," "Social and Economic Questions of Controversy Between Capitalists and Socialists," "Current Problems of Public Interest and Socialism," and "Political Organization and Propaganda") more closely to Shedd's concern, "the child mind."

Radical essays and poems that were not originally intended for use in the children's schools were also often adopted by the socialist teachers. One popular poem was Thomas Hood's "The Song of the Shirt." Seventy years after she attended the East Side Socialist Sunday School in Manhattan, a former student remembered learning and reciting this stirring poem at the school and was able to still recall its final verse:

> With fingers weary and worn,
> With eyelids heavy and red,
> A woman sat, in unwomanly rags,
> Plying her needle and thread.
> Stitch! stitch! stitch!

In poverty, hunger, and dirt;
And still, with a voice of colorous pitch,
Would that its tone could reach the rich!
She sang this 'Song of the Shirt!'[38]

Also frequently used in the socialist children's schools were adult song-books. In fact, the singing of labor and radical songs was a regular feature of assemblies at most schools. While there were also many songs penned by local youth activists specifically for use in the schools, the children were often taught to sing the same songs as their elders. This is in keeping with another goal of the Socialist Sunday School movement: to instill a sense of continuity between the generations of workers and a feeling of being part of the larger socialist community. Two generally popular songbooks that were used by the children's schools were Harvey P. Moyer's *Songs of Socialism,* which went through five editions by 1910, and Charles H. Kerr's *Socialist Songs With Music.*[39] "The Red Flag," "The Internationale," "The People's Hymn," "Humanity's Call," and "We're Comrades Ever" were songs that could be heard at Party local meetings and labor rallies, as well as at the neighborhood children's schools. The chorus of one of these songs, "The Marxian Call," can provide a sense of their general tenor: "O, lab'rers, 'wake! and break your chains!/You've naught to lose, you've all the world to gain!/Your children's cries, your broth-ers' woes/To duty call; O'haste the glorious Socialist reign!" While the content of such a song may seem inflammatory for use with children, it may not com-pare so unfavorably with more traditional patriotic songs (e.g., "The Star Span-gled Banner" and "The Caissons Go Rolling Along") that can be heard in schools throughout the United States.

The Sunday schools' adaptation of these adult textbooks, essays, poems, and songs reveals several other themes that were embodied in this radical curric-ulum. One is a strong sense of class consciousness; the dignity of labor (if not all laborers) and a feeling of solidarity with other workers (although not with "scabs") were stressed. Social problems were viewed primarily from the per-spective of their effects on workers, and class struggle rather than class compro-mise was generally suggested as the appropriate political strategy to follow. It was necessary "to break your chains," for there was a "world to gain." It was also hoped that the children would gain an introductory understanding of capitalism and, more concretely, the everyday conditions of working-class life in a capitalist society. Indeed, what differentiated the curriculum of the socialist children's schools from other "social problems" approaches was their constant and consistent emphasis on poverty, unemployment, unhealthy and unsafe work conditions, and so on being endemic to working-class life in capitalist America. To help promote this emphasis, the schools used text materials that revealed, for example, that working women "with fingers weary and worn" and "with eyelids heavy and red" were living in "poverty, hunger, and dirt," and that only with the end of the current ownership and management of the means of production and the introduction of a more advanced stage of civilization, socialism, could such human misery be eradicated. As Kendrick Shedd argued, it was not only important for children to be knowledgeable about the problems that workers faced but also to appreciate the need for "rebellion" and for embracing the "right working-class spirit." In addition, the children were also to be given an awareness of "the possible," that is, of the potential of the Cooperative Commonwealth to foster more ideal conditions of human life.[40]

The use of the Mills text and sources like it led some radicals to admonish the Sunday schools for in essence trying to recruit for the radical movement and for simply "imposing . . . our [adult] opinions, our dogmas, our sympathies, and our antipathies, doing violence and injustice to the young."[41] Jeanette D. Pearl of New York City replied for her fellow socialist teachers that most schools were not trying to simply make "party converts." Moreover, she reasoned, "make no mistake, children of 10 and over know much of the sadness and sorrow of life which this system of capitalist exploitation inflicts upon them. Our children are the workers' children; and they have imbibed the suffering and privations of the working class with their mothers' milk." She insisted that while the "desirability and grandeur of free self-expression" should be pointed out, it should not constitute the primary goal of the socialist schools. Rather, it should be how to best educate for "the overthrow of a rotten ripe industrial autocracy." In fact, the ideal educated person was virtually an impossibility in "this capitalist mire . . . where, in order to live at all, we must first sell ourselves into bondage-wage slavery." In response to charges that the schools were simply teaching "isms," Pearl wrote: "I confess to the guilt of holding up to the children a high ideal and often telling them that the acquisition of a job is not the ultimate aim of life. If drawing sketches of the dawn of a new era, where poverty and suffering will be no more, where dreams are to be realized and ambitions fulfilled, be classed as an ism, I stand condemned."[42]

The adult-oriented texts that the Socialist Sunday schools adapted for use were intended to get such messages across to a generation of working-class children exposed every day, perhaps like never before, to the influences of capitalist culture. While these texts were clearly not always suitably revised for "the child mind," they did provide the usually unpaid weekend instructors with materials that embodied the basic outlines of a socialist argument.

Alternative Texts for Socialist Children's Schools:
A Case of Direct Intention

Despite the problems noted earlier, particularly committed radical activists, usually working only part-time in education, did manage to produce school texts that were intended for use in the socialist children's schools. Of course, they were produced under circumstances vastly different from those under which most mainstream school textbooks were developed. For example, there were few professors of education or full-time classroom teachers to help in the development of educational materials for the socialist movement. And when the socialist texts were professionally published at all, it was usually by "arms" of the political movement, not by the larger, more prominent, and financially secure publishing houses.[43] Quality of work was not the primary issue here. Rather, it illustrates the difficulty that can exist for those who attempt to promote knowledge and identities that stand "outside" the selective tradition. It is not often a simple matter to gain entrance into the public sphere. Such a situation is, of course, both a *cause* and an *effect* of the lack of legitimacy that alternative ideologies enjoy within the hegemonic culture.

As with the other kinds of texts used in the children's schools, a few examples will serve to represent this body of work, particularly the lesson outlines of three socialist educators. The first was a multiple set of lesson outlines developed by Kendrick Shedd, director of the Rochester Socialist Sunday School from 1910 until 1915 and organizer of three Milwaukee schools from 1915 until 1917.[44] Shedd also wrote a popular songbook, *Some Songs for Socialist Singers,* and numerous articles for socialist newspapers, including a short-lived column in the prominent *New York Call* about socialist youth work.[45]

Shedd's lesson outlines appeared in pamphlet and card form and were advertised in socialist newspapers and journals as available at little cost to other schools. He included additional suggestions for other teachers so that the intended use of his lessons would be clear to those with whom he did not have regular and direct contact. (While Shedd himself had been a professor at the University of Rochester for twenty-two years before being forced to resign for off-campus radical activities, he realized that many Socialist Sunday School teachers had no educational training.) For example, in "A Note to Teacher," which accompanied his *Lesson Topics for January–March 1914,* Shedd made it clear that he did not expect teachers to follow his outlines verbatim: "In each of the following lessons there are many points or ideas suggested by the questions and statements. It is not intended that you should touch upon them all, for your time is too limited. Use what you need. Much is left to your own discretion." In the same note, he provided some valuable instructional advice:

> Let us set the children thinking. Let us encourage intelligent questions. We want the little ones to grow up with inquiring minds. Can you help them to do this? Let us try to help them to get the economic viewpoint, the viewpoint of the working class.
>
> Be simple and clear. The children are not as experienced as we. They do not know all the words that we understand so well. Let us make things plain. Use story and illustration, if you can.

Shedd often emphasized the need to encourage "intelligent questions." For instance, in his *Lesson Topics for September–October 1913* he wrote: "Let us open the eyes of the children. Let us get them to asking WHY.'' But he just as often stressed the need to foster an understanding of and appreciation for ''the economic viewpoint, the viewpoint of the working class.'' One of the overall aims of his *Lesson Topics for May 1913,* for example, was ''to study the principles and ethics of Socialism, . . . to correct . . . false ideals by a thorough analysis and study of the true International principles of Socialism; and to sow in the minds of the young the seeds of Truth and Justice which shall some day ripen into a rich harvest for humanity and civilization.'' One might view Shedd's contrasting emphases on the teaching of a particular viewpoint (''Truth'') and the encouragement of ''inquiring minds'' as a sign of ambivalence or an inconsistent educational philosophy. On the other hand, it may have represented a sincere attempt, over the course of a relatively short period of time, to integrate two different and yet, in Shedd's mind, related aims. The dilemma with which he and other socialist educators were wrestling is, of course, a common one in the difficult task of developing critical educational practice.

Shedd's lesson outlines often included particular concepts or themes, much like the ''expanding environments or horizons'' social studies curriculum of today (e.g., Self, Family, Neighborhood, etc.). However, these socialist materials differed quite markedly in the conceptual themes chosen for study as well as in the suggested pedagogical approach to be taken. The emphasis was on discussion questions that would focus attention on the relationship between the general theme and the social conditions of most workers, concluding with a succinct definitional question. Two brief examples (''Success'' and ''Justice'') can serve to illustrate this radical ''text'':

What is necessary for it [success]; are the following: Possession of Money? High Position? Power?
Was Abraham Lincoln Successful?
Compare the Work of Abraham Lincoln and Karl Marx.
Do successful persons always realize their success?
Name some who did not.
Can true success be gained at the expense of one's brothers [sic]?
What is success?

Is competition just?
Do the workers get justice?
Have we political justice?
Name some instance of political injustice.
Are these things just:
    Child wage workers?
    Mothers employed outside of their homes?
    Use of militia to settle strikes?
    War? Capitalist courts? Capitalist press?

Suppression of Free Speech and Assemblage?
What is justice?

The children were thus encouraged not to accept submissively the tradition-ally accepted definitions but instead to view seemingly commonsensical notions such as "success" and "justice" critically and then, in the light of the unsatis-factory character of prevailing "capitalist" views, to formulate alternative per-spectives of them. Also present here is the linkage of what might be considered as abstract philosophical constructs to the social context in which they are lived out. Success, for example, only has meaning in relation to who benefits when certain people are "successful."

Another series of lesson outlines that Shedd offered was entitled "Home Destroyers." Unlike the traditional topics that are found in public school text-books, with rather idealized middle-class versions of family and community life, these materials include lessons on such themes as "Unemployment, Poverty and Drink," "Slums, Sweatshops, Sickness and Disease," and "Why Johnny Loses His 'Home.' " The primary focus was on the economic pressures that make working-class life so difficult. For example, if we "remove 'drink' from the world but keep Capitalism: would all have real homes? Why not?" Shedd concluded this series with a reminder: "Can't buy all necessities and pay high rent, too. High cost of living and profit-system are enemies of the home." Thus, it was not socialism that would destroy the home, as its turn-of-the-century critics often contended. Rather, it was the capitalist system that *was* destroying home life, particularly for those of the working class.

Shedd prepared several other lesson series for use in the Socialist Sunday schools. The later ones tended to include an increase in the number and com-plexity of suggested questions and were intended for the older grades. For example, one series of lesson outlines focused on the necessities (e.g., food, clothing, and shelter) of everyday life and the lack of equity in their availability, management, and ownership in capitalist America. His first lessons examined "The World's Coal and Oil and Who Should Own Them." Shedd suggested that teachers begin discussing the basic nature of these resources, progress to a discussion of the actual ways in which we secure them, and then conclude with a consideration of their ownership and how a socialist reorganization of society would alter current practice. Guiding questions included the following:

What is coal? What is oil? (Petroleum means "rock oil.") Where do they come from? Do they grow? What is coal used for? What is oil used for? Are they necessary? Could we do without them? How much is there of them? Will the supply last long? What do you know about Coal Mines? Any near here? What do you know about Oil Wells? Any near here? Is it easy or hard to get coal and oil? Who does the work? Who makes the money? Who owns the coal mines and the oil wells? Who ought to own and control them? Give several reasons. Would they cost less or more under Socialism? Why?

Another alternative school text was developed by Bertha Fraser, a Party activist who organized and taught in several socialist schools in the metropolitan New York area. Her *Outlines of Lessons for Socialist Schools for Children* was published by the Children's Socialist Schools Committee of Brooklyn. It was recommended to radical teachers by the Woman's National Committee of the Socialist Party in their pamphlet *How to Organize Socialist Schools* and favorably reviewed in a prominent radical journal, the *International Socialist Review*.[46] In the preface of her book, Fraser explained that one of her primary aims was "to show that all things necessary for our support come from the earth." The earth, of course, belongs to all people; therefore, in an argument similar to Shedd's reasoning, no one should be deprived of any of the necessities of everyday living. Moreover, "although nature provides everything in abundance," we can have none of the things necessary to support and protect life "without the expenditure of labor." Our indebtedness to labor necessitates an understanding of "the unequal distribution of the products due to the exploitation of labor, and the consequent suffering of the working class." Fraser also suggested a brief consideration of "the remedy" (i.e., socialism) and "how it is to be applied."

Like Shedd, Fraser strongly encouraged teachers to enlarge upon her 300 + -word essays, for example, in the form of "questions which bear upon the lesson." Although her lesson outlines were "not intended to be used by scholars," teachers needed to become well-acquainted with the material in advance so that they could then devote time to devising creative educational activities that would make the content interesting to children. The lessons themselves included some of the principal themes of the Socialist Sunday School curriculum, in particular with regard to the minimum essentials that all people should have (e.g., food, clothing, and shelter) in "the struggle for existence," the interdependence of the social world, and the important role played by workers in everyday life. Socialist educators like Fraser obviously believed—and the recent analyses of Jean Anyon, Frances Fitzgerald, and others have supported their views—that none of these themes were being stressed in the public school classroom.[47]

Another alternative school text was David Greenberg's fifty-nine–page *Socialist Sunday School Curriculum.*[48] Greenberg was a teacher at the Brownsville Socialist Sunday School in Brooklyn and, at one time, a student at Teachers College of Columbia University. He also offered a teacher training class at the Women's Trade Union League headquarters in Manhattan, edited the educational department of a short-lived Brooklyn-based journal, *Unity of Labor,* and authored a six-part series on "School's Place in the Democracy" in the *New York Call.*[49] Greenberg's textbook, compiled at the request of the Socialist School Union of New York, outlined a differentiated curriculum for six grades: Primary; Elementary (A); Elementary (B); Intermediate (A); Intermediate (B); and Advanced. Each grade level was to focus on a combination of historical and economic themes, beginning with simple concepts and then progressing to more complex notions for the older children. Short talks on ethics, morals, and social hygiene, as well as the opportunity for students to engage in physical exercises, music, and poetry readings, were also suggested. The materials were intended to help guide at least thirty Sunday-morning sessions a year, with each school session expected to consist of thirty minutes for general assembly (for general ethical lessons, brief discussions on current events, and "the usual school singing and reciting") and three thirty-minute periods for actual lesson work. Like Shedd and Fraser, Greenberg clearly expected his brief outlines to be approached as general suggestions only.

The "Primary" class outline of this text can be taken as representative of its orientation. Similar to Katherine Dopp's adoption of recapitulation theory, Greenberg intended for the historical lessons for six- and seven-year-olds to concentrate on "lead[ing]the children back to the sources of our laws and institutions, by reading about and acting (dramatically) the lives of the primitive people." As younger children were involved, this was to be done "in a pleasant, simple manner." Formulas and definitions were to be avoided; "real, living stories, vivid pictures, and relics" were to be used instead. For later grades, Greenberg suggested giving primary attention to the lives of "the people" rather than to "the rulers," an idea similar to the later critique of traditional historiography, which recommended "history from the bottom up."[50] Economic lessons were intended to "get children to see that the source of all things is the earth which belongs to everybody, and that it is labor that takes everything from the earth and turns it 1) into machinery and 2) the things that labor makes with the machine." Food, clothing (e.g., silk, leather, wool, and cotton) and shelter (e.g., wood, metals, brick, stone, and concrete) were to be examined from such a perspective. In addition, particular ethics and morals, such as a "passionate love of truth and justice," were to be taught through "strong stories" and discussions, not by means of proverbs and pledges. While such traits as obedience, honesty, courage, loyalty, gratitude, comradeship, patriotism, and duty were to be critically examined on a level that six- and seven-years-olds could understand, Greenberg was more forthright in suggesting that special attention be given to the "wickedness and wastefulness" of war, in particular that "murder is murder no matter by whom it is committed, by the individual or by the nation." Finally, the children were to be shown that "good air and good food are necessary to life, and that everyone has the right to live." A strong collectivist sense was intended here; it was important for the individual to live a healthy life not just for the sake of oneself but also because the habits of the individual can have a direct effect on the health of the community as well.

It is clear that Greenberg included the inculcation of particular attitudes, understandings, and dispositions in his lesson outlines. But he also strongly recommended that "at all times, in some form, allow the pupil to express every impression made upon him." Oral expression and simple composition work were to aid in this regard. Greenberg made a point of stressing that students were "not to be expected to take anything for granted." A "scientific attitude" should prevail, in which pupils "question everything and answer with care." Like Shedd, then, Greenberg understood, to paraphrase Eugene Debs, that if "the people" were "led" *into* the promised land, then they could be "led" *out* of it as well. The attempts by these socialist educators to balance these two aims, of allowing their students a "voice" while guarding against the perpetuation of the understandings and values of the hegemonic culture, may not have achieved a satisfactory result. Indeed, Shedd and the others seem to have been only dimly aware of the contradictions inherent in their own practice. But they had a very limited time in which to develop their teaching and curriculum practices, and they worked at a time when progressive educational ideas were just beginning to gain widespread attention. It might also be reasonably claimed that, with regard to the inculcation-vs.-independent-thinking dilemma, their efforts do not compare unfavorably with the curriculum content and form of contemporary public schools.

Only brief mention can be made of three other kinds of text materials that played a prominent role in many of the socialist children's schools. One was the *Young Socialists' Magazine,* published each month from 1909 to 1920. It was intended specifically for use in radical Sunday schools and youth clubs, and included numerous essays, stories, poems, riddles, games, lesson outlines, and the like. Biographical sketches were common, for example about such heroes and heroines as Eugene Debs, Mother Jones, Karl Marx, and William Morris. Excerpts from the writings of Charles Dickens, Leo Tolstoy, Edward Bellamy, Upton Sinclair, Charlotte Perkins Gilman, Thomas Paine, and other radical or socially concerned authors were published. Sayings and quotations were also often included, such as the following[51]:

> Talk about equal opportunity! Capitalism ties a balloon to the shoulders of the rich child, a ball and chain to the foot of the poor child, and tells them that they have an equal opportunity to fly!

> The difference between the reformer and the Socialist is that the reformer wants to abolish graft and the Socialist wants to abolish the necessity of graft.

> It would be easy for the workingmen to support their wives and children but for the fact that they have also to support the wives and children of their employers.

There were also songbooks, not only the abovementioned ones intended for adults but also those compiled specifically for use in the children's Sunday schools and clubs. In fact, Kendrick Shedd argued that "You can't talk Marxian economics to a 'kid,' but you can make an excellent rebel out of him by the right use of song and story."[52] Shedd's songbook was originally written for the Rochester Socialist Sunday School; schools in Milwaukee, Buffalo, Brooklyn, and elsewhere published their own song booklets as well. Many of the songs adopted the music of popular traditional songs but substituted radical lyrics. One song was vividly remembered years later by the former choir director of Milwaukee's International Socialist Sunday School. Sung to the tune of "Auld Lang Syne," it was called "Hands Across the Sea." Its first verses go like this[53]:

We stretch our hands across the sea, to men of every clime;
While human hearts in harmony strike a universal chime.

Chorus:
Around the world we stretch the hand in solidarity,
With brothers stand in every land for human liberty.

We stretch our hands across the sea, for peace the world around;
That bloody wars may cease to be, and strife no more resound.

Other songs were more original in music and lyrics and, while perhaps still containing a serious message, more festive in nature. More than sixty years after her involvement in the same Milwaukee school, a former student remembered vividly the fun she had in singing and acting out one of Shedd's songs with her friends. Entitled "In Competition's Way," it promoted a problematic and indeed critical view of intense competition[54]:

The earth was made for brother men
To live in peace, they say;
But men have turned it into hell
In competition's way.

Chorus:
You hit, you hurt; you laugh, ha, ha
You shoot, ha ha, you do them dirt
In competition's way!
Tra la la, tra la la, tra la la, tra la la
Tra la la, tra la la, tra la la,
Slap bang! Hit them hard again!
Dig them in the chin, Rip them through the skin,
Slap bang! Do them if you kin
In competition's way!

For it is so fine to cuss and swear,
To rend, and tear, to pull the hair;
Oh, it is so sweet to threat and scare
In competition's way.
[Chorus]

'Do unto others as ye would—'
You know the rest, you say;
But wolfish men have altered that

In competition's way.
[Chorus.]

Another group of text materials were dramatic scripts that were used for school festivals and fund-raising entertainments and that became an integral part of the curriculum of many schools.[55] While some of the playlets performed were not originally intended for use by socialist children's schools (e.g., Upton Sinclair's "The Second Story Man" and Seymour A. Tribbels's "Up Caesar's Creek"), others were written by socialist educators. Some of these plays were based on original themes, such as "Mister Greed" by Kendrick Shedd, "The Strike of Santa Claus" (author unknown), "When The Cry Was Stilled" by Ethel Whitehead (of Pasadena and Los Angeles), "The Best Day of All Is The First Day of May" by Bertha Mailly (of Omaha, Boston, and New York City), and "Shambles" by Henry Schnittkind (of Boston). Others were obviously adapted from familiar story lines, sometimes even keeping the same titles, such as "The Leading of the Children" (inspired by "The Pied Piper of Hamelin"), "The Sleeping Beauty (The Triumph of Socialism)," "Cinderella," "Jack and the Beanstalk," and "Aladdin and the Wonderful Lamp." What the socialists did here was similar to what has occurred over several centuries to folk tales such as "Little Red Riding Hood."[56] Like social groups before and after them, they imbued traditional story lines with different ideological content. A listing of the character's names in "Cinderella" may provide a hint of how one teacher, Carl Haessler of Milwaukee, was able to appropriate a well-known story line for more radical purposes. The prince is Prince Brotherhood. The stepmother is Baroness Capitalisma and her two daughters are Lady Idylrich and Lady Profiteeria. The fairy is called Fairy Solidarity. Cinderella is Cinderella, except when she is transformed by the fairy—and when she is finally reunited with the prince at the end—at which time she is then known as Princess Commonwealth. As performed by the children of the International Socialist Sunday School of Milwaukee, with scenery and costumes and before a large audience of parents and community members, the play thus represented the joining together and triumph of Brotherhood, Solidarity, and Common Wealth (Public Ownership) over Capitalism, the Idol Rich (the Capitalist Class), and Profiteering. Not great art perhaps, but no doubt great fun for the children to perform, and it got the intended message across.

Conclusion

The curriculum materials discussed in this article are clearly problematic in nature and not ones that teachers attempting today to develop a critical pedagogy would seek to adopt without carefully considered changes. It would be ridiculous to expect otherwise, as they were produced over seventy years ago, when social conditions were far different than at present, the prospects of an

American socialist movement seemed much brighter, and progressive educational ideas were first widely discussed. Additionally, the schools in which they were used were severely limited with regard to meeting time (only two hours a week), availability of resources and staff, the nature of the student population (only children from working-class backgrounds), and so forth. Moreover, the character of these alternative texts are clearly deficient. For example, although the social vision embedded within the curriculum stresses critique and collectivism, there is insufficient integration of opportunities for children to engage in creative self-expression, collaboration, and self-criticism (i.e., of the socialist movement itself). There are examples of students engaging in their own writing of songs and plays and playing a minor role in school governance, but these are few and far between.

In addition, although these texts are to be praised for their emphasis on the significance of material relations in our everyday lives, they are too economically oriented. Indeed, they contain a serious devaluing of other social categories besides class, most notably those of gender and race. Given the Socialist Party's general adherence to "scientific socialism" during the first decades of this century, this is not entirely unexpected. Both theoretically and politically, ethnic, racial, and gender issues were viewed by most Party officials and members as epiphenomena of class concerns. Thus, although "feminist" socialists, during the middle years of 1900–1920, agitated for a more active role for women in political and labor matters and for more active party involvement in important "women's issues" (e.g., suffrage, birth control, and sexuality), gender issues never played a prominent role in Party affairs. Likewise, although women played a decisive role in the Socialist Sunday School movement, a role that many national and state Party leaders thought them particularly "suited" for, a concern for gender inequities is not evident in the Socialist Sunday School curriculum. Even when "gender consciousness" did appear in the curriculum, it was usually in patriarchal fashion, in the form of the coming socialist order that would "free" women to return to the home (e.g., whether it was "just" that mothers were employed outside of the home). Women were clearly of vital importance to the work of the socialist schools, with many of the schools in fact being initiated by local socialist women's clubs, and they no doubt left a special imprint on the organization and operation of the schools. But while there is no evidence to indicate that these women believed that their "best work" could take place in the home, it does appear that many of the women who stayed active in the Socialist Sunday School movement did share the prevailing view subordinating issues of gender equity to the preeminence of the class struggle. Some of those who did not share this view became more actively involved in women's (and other political) matters and left the Sunday schools, which had a deleterious effect on the schools' operations. Many others who did not share the Party's orthodox perspective, like Margaret Sanger, left the Party entirely.[57]

Despite these and other serious weaknesses in the curriculum of the Socialist Sunday schools, a critical examination of these alternative texts can perhaps assist us in two related ways. First, it may help to provide the stark contrast sometimes needed to clarify the fundamentally political nature of school curriculum-making. "Political nature" is meant here not in the important but more narrow sense of how specific participants in the local selection process have more power to decide matters than others (e.g., which programs to fund), but in the broader sense of how social institutions legitimate particular identities and knowledge, with clear implications for economic and cultural reproduction.[58] Indeed, if the messages of these "critical lessons" seem overly propagandistic or political in tone, perhaps it is primarily because they are not the usual ones we have come to expect from school curricula. While textbooks may no longer be "guardians of tradition" in quite the same way that they were in the nineteenth century,[59] they continue to convey sometimes subtle but still powerfully partisan messages. For example, a recent analysis of the very popular Curriculum Foundation Readers (more commonly known as the "Dick and Jane" readers), which were published by Scott Foresman from 1935 to 1965, has revealed that they embodied a vision of literacy that aimed for "more efficient adaptation to existing social knowledges and organization." Social adaptation to capitalist culture without "a parallel concern with social transformation" were the norms included in these widely used school texts.[60] Another examination of the ideological content of seventeen United States history textbooks found that by and large they promote the idea that there has been no working class in the United States. Twelve of the textbooks do not describe the Socialist Party of America or its platform, nor do they mention the existence of various other radical groups. Of the five books that do discuss the Socialist Party, all but one contain disparaging remarks about the socialists' intentions, and four of the five minimize the extent to which workers were attracted to radical ideas.[61] Not only, then, is it the *messages* contained within these alternative school texts that may seem "surprising" to an American audience, but *the very existence* of socialist curriculum materials as well.

Second, the socialist curricula perhaps offer a concrete model of "really [or critically] useful knowledge" for children from which to draw. This idea of "really useful knowledge" has a long history in radical circles, dating back to the efforts of working-class educational associations in early nineteenth-century England.[62] The alternative lessons discussed in this study can be briefly viewed as having addressed six related aspects of this conception of educational knowledge. First, as a body of work they encouraged the children to take pride in their working-class backgrounds. This was in direct contrast to the predominant division and hierarchy of mental and manual labor that tended to minimize the significant contributions of laborers to American progress.[63] A similar focus on the significant contributions of other oppressed groups would constitute an important aspect of a critical pedagogy today. Second, they posited the subordinate status of workers as shared and systematic, and encouraged a sense of solidarity with other oppressed groups. While gender and race issues were viewed at the time as secondary to class ones, changed perspective, one that considers and integrates these and other social categories, could be adopted to better advantage today.[64] Third, there exists in these materials a strong vision of social interdependence and collectivism: that we rely on countless others for many necessities in life, and that it is in our interests to be socially concerned with and responsible for each other. Indeed, it is not necessary to look only to other countries for examples of educational strategies that promote a more (although not exclusively) collectivist discourse. Doing so is perhaps an indication of a lack of familiarity with our own "rebel roots."[65]

Fourth, a focus on the everyday concerns of working-class life was used to highlight the relationship between current social problems and the general nature of dominant economic and political relations. While these radical educators may have been mistaken in seeing the evil hand of the corporate capitalist behind every social ill, at least they were free of the rather myopic vision of most other contemporary observers. They sought to critique the concrete lived experiences of workers' lives, which most of the children could personally relate to, not as isolated and individual social problems but rather as the products of an inherently uncaring and inequitable social order. They were able to do this because, although perhaps politically naive, reductionist, or "incorrect" by the standards of today's leftist culture, they nevertheless had a comprehensive social vision and commitment to guide them in making the linkages between everyday life and the political sphere. Fifth, there was an emphasis on the need for fundamental social change. Only large-scale cooperative (rather than short-term and individualistic) strategies could effectively overcome the hardships and sense of powerlessness that the working classes (and other subordinate groups) experienced. While they certainly did not eschew more immediate strategies (e.g., running for local political office), they generally did not allow the possibilities of short-run successes to blind them to the need for more comprehensive changes. This should not mean subscribing today to the often paralyzing notion that "changing the world" is worth pursuing only on a grand scale but rather that smaller-scale strategies must be viewed within the context of the larger movement for democratization of the public sphere. And, sixth, the socialist curricula adopted a generally critical view of the nature and consequences of contemporary arrangements of social and economic power (e.g., the ownership and management of our coal supply) and of the commonsensical understandings of everyday life (e.g., the nature of "success"). Critical thinking here meant not step-by-step procedures for solving problems but an informed and vigilant posture toward the complex and inequitable nature of the social world. While the socialist schools may have been inadequate in the extent to which they actively engaged children in problem-solving and decision-making activities and attended to the development of personal identities, they did not confuse the need for critical understandings with the mental gymnastics of solving "puzzles." The point here is that while the "critical lessons" discussed in this study are seriously outdated and even wrongheaded in some ways, they did attempt to instill an understanding and concern for more equitable social and economic relations, and they may help to inform similar educational efforts today.

It seems overly pessimistic to claim that "alternatives are as scarce as hen's teeth, and, for the moment at least, hope is at a low ebb."[66] But for those struggling to resist dominant ideologies in their classrooms, there is a critical need for concrete suggestions of alternative cultural symbols and meanings and educational activities. An alternative identity guided by "the common good" cannot be based on critique and rejection alone. But neither can effective social reconstruction be based just on utopian or abstract visions of hope. It requires specific programs that people can consider, argue about, revise, and perhaps attempt to implement.[67] Historical examples can play a role in their development. The point is not, as Howard Zinn has perceptively written, "to invent victories for people's movements." But history can "emphasize new possibilities by disclosing those hidden episodes of the past when, even if in brief flashes, people showed their ability to resist, to join together, occasionally to win."[68] The "critical lessons" of American socialists should perhaps be viewed from a similar vantage point, as hidden episodes of the past that may help to indicate possibilities for the future—possibilities of understandings, of activities, and, perhaps most important, of the human spirit.

Notes

1. See, for example, Michael W. Apple, *Ideology and Curriculum* (London: Routledge and Kegan Paul, 1979); Michael W. Apple and Lois Weis, eds., *Ideology and Practice in Schooling* (Philadelphia: Temple University Press, 1983); and Geoff Whitty, *Sociology and School Knowledge: Curriculum Theory, Research and Politics* (London: Methuen, 1985). See also Ariel Dorfman, *The Empire's Old Clothes: What the Lone Ranger, Babar, and Other Innocent Heroes Do To Our Minds* (New York: Pantheon, 1983).

2. See, for example, Jean Anyon, "Ideology and United History Textbooks," *Harvard Educational Review* 49, no. 3 (August 1979): 361–86; Frances Fitzgerald, *America Revised: History Schoolbooks in the Twentieth Century* (Boston: Little, Brown, 1979); Joel Taxel, "The Outsiders of the American Revolution: The Selective Tradition in Children's Fiction," *Interchange* 12, nos. 2–3 (1981): 206–28; Henry A. Giroux, *Ideology, Culture, and the Process of Schooling* (Philadelphia: Temple University Press, 1981); Michael W. Apple, *Education and Power* (Boston: Routledge and Kegan Paul, 1982); Raphaela Best, *We've All Got Scars Now: What Boys and Girls Learn in Elementary School* (Bloomington, Inc.: Indiana University Press, 1982); Myra Pollack Sadker and David Miller Sadker, *Sex Equity Handbook for Schools* (New York: Longman, 1982); E. Wendy Saul, "We Gather Together: Collectivism in Children's Books," *School Library Journal* 29, no. 8 (April 1983): 30–31; Allan Luke, "Making Dick and Jane: Historical Genesis of the Modern Basal Reader," *Teachers College Record* 89, no. 1 (Fall 1987): 91–116; and Apple, *Ideology and Curriculum*.

3. Michael W. Apple, *Teachers and Texts: A Political Economy of Class and Gender Relations*

in Education (New York: Routledge and Kegan Paul, 1986); and Joel Spring, *Conflict of Interests: The Politics of American Education* (New York: Longman, 1988).

4. See, for example, Sheila Harty, *Hucksters in the Classroom: A Review of Industry Propaganda in Schools* (Washington, D.C.: Center for the Study of Responsive Law, 1979); Jean Lind-Brenkman, "Seeing Beyond the Interests of Industry: Teaching Critical Thinking," *Journal of Education* 165, no. 3 (Summer 1983): 283–94; Michael W. Apple and Kenneth Teitelbaum, "Are Teachers Losing Control of Their Skills and Curriculum?" *Journal of Curriculum Studies* 18, no. 2 (April–June 1986): 177–84; and Kathryn M. Borman and Joel H. Spring, *Schools in Central Cities: Structure and Process* (New York: Longman, 1984), pp. 172–96.

5. Ira Shor, *Culture Wars: School and Society in the Conservative Restoration, 1969–1984* (Boston: Routledge and Kegan Paul, 1986). See also Michael W. Apple, "The Politics of Common Sense: Schooling, Populism, and the New Right," in *Critical Pedagogy, the State, and Cultural Struggle,* ed. Henry A. Giroux and Peter L. McLaren (Albany, N.Y.: State University of New York, 1989), pp. 32–49.

6. See, for example, Andrew Gitlin, "School Structure and Teachers' Work," in Apple and Weis, eds., *Ideology and Practice in Schooling,* pp. 193–212; Martin Carnoy and Henry M. Levin, *Schooling and Work in the Democratic State* (Stanford, Calif.: Stanford University Press, 1985); William J. Reese, *Power and the Promise of School Reform: Grass-Roots Movements During the Progressive Era* (Boston: Routledge and Kegan Paul, 1986); and Apple and Teitelbaum, "Are Teachers Losing Control of Their Skills and Curriculum?"

7. I have in mind here such materials as Pal Rydberg et al., *The History Book* (Culver City, Calif.: Peace Press, 1974); Miriam Wolf-Wasserman and Linda Hutchinson, eds., *Teaching Human Dignity: Social Change Lessons for Everyteacher* (Minneapolis, Minn.: Education Exploration Center, 1978); and Nancy Schniedewind and Ellen Davidson, *Open Minds to Equality: A Sourcebook of Learning Activities to Promote Race, Sex, Class, and Age Equity* (Englewood Cliffs, N.J.: Prentice-Hall, 1983). See also Theodore Mills Norton and Bertell Ollman, eds., *Studies in Socialist Pedagogy* (New York: Monthly Review Press, 1978); Ira Shor, *Critical Teaching and Everyday Life* (Boston: South End Press, 1980); Henry A. Giroux, *Theory and Resistance in Education: A Pedagogy for the Opposition* (South Hadley, Mass.: Bergin & Garvey, 1983); David W. Livingstone, ed., *Critical Pedagogy and Cultural Power* (South Hadley, Mass.: Bergin & Garvey, 1987); Henry A. Giroux, *Schooling and the Struggle for Public Life: Critical Pedagogy in the Modern Age* (Minneapolis, Minn.: University of Minnesota Press, 1988); and Giroux and McLaren, eds., *Critical Pedagogy, the State, and Cultural Struggle.* Organizations include the Institute for Democracy in Education (based in Athens, Ohio), the Public Education Information Network (St. Louis), and Rethinking Schools (Milwaukee).

8. Joseph Featherstone, "Foreword," in Herbert Kohl, *Growing Minds: On Becoming a Teacher* (New York: Harper and Row, 1984), p. xiii.

9. Philip Wexler, "Structure, Text, and Subject: A Critical Sociology of School Knowledge," in *Cultural and Economic Reproduction in Education: Essays on Class, Ideology and the State,* ed. Michael W. Apple (London: Routledge and Kegan Paul, 1982), p. 279. See also Raymond Williams, *The Long Revolution* (Harmondsworth, England: Penguin Press, 1961); idem, *Marxism and Literature* (Oxford: Oxford University Press, 1977); and Apple, *Ideology and Curriculum.*

10. Herbert R. Kliebard and Barry M. Franklin, "The Course of the Course of Study: History of Curriculum," in *Historical Inquiry in Education: A Research Agenda,* ed. John Hardin Best (Washington, D.C.: American Educational Research Association, 1983), p. 153. Also, in *The Management of Ignorance* (Oxford: Basil Blackwell, 1985), Fred Inglis suggests that "to become aware of the limits on your imagination is to move them" (p. 117).

11. Kliebard and Franklin, "The Course of the Course of Study," pp. 152–53.

12. E. P. Thompson, "The Politics of Theory," in *People's History and Socialist Theory,* ed. Raphael Samuel (London: Routledge and Kegan Paul, 1981), pp. 407–8.

13. Williams, *Marxism and Literature,* p. 116. See also Henry Abelove et al., eds., *Visions of History* (New York: Pantheon, 1984).

14. See, for example, George S. Counts, *Dare the Schools Build a New Social Order?* (Carbondale, Ill.: Southern Illinois University Press, 1978, [originally published in 1932]; C. A. Bowers, *The Progressive Educator and the Depression: The Radical Years* (New York: Random House, 1969); and William B. Stanley, "The Radical Reconstructionist Rationale for Social Education," *'Theory and Research in Social Education* 8, no. 4 (Winter 1981): 55–79. The social reconstructionists are discussed with reference to "reclaiming the historical legacy of a critical theory of citizenship" in Giroux, *Schooling and the Struggle for Public Life.*

15. Reese, *Power and the Promise of School Reform,* and Kenneth Teitelbaum, "Outside the Selective Tradition: Socialist Curriculum for Children in the United States, 1900–1920," in *The Formation of the School Subjects: The Struggle for Creating an American Institution,* ed. Thomas F. Popkewitz (New York: The Falmer Press, 1987), pp. 241–46.

16. See, for example, David A. Shannon, *The Socialist Party of America* (Chicago: Quadrangle, 1955); James Weinstein, *The Decline of Socialism in America, 1912–1925* (New York: Vintage, 1969); Mari Jo Buhle, *Women and American Socialism, 1870–1920* (Urbana, Ill., University of Illinois Press, 1981); and Paul Buhle, *Marxism in the United States: Remapping the History of the American Left* (London: Verso, 1987).

17. Joselyne Slade Tien, "The Educational Theories of American Socialists, 1900–1920" (unpublished doctoral dissertation, Michigan State University, 1972); and Kenneth Teitelbaum, "Contestation and Curriculum: The Efforts of American Socialists, 1900–1920," in *The Curriculum: Problems, Politics, and Possibilities,*ed. Landon E. Beyer and Michael W. Apple (Albany, N.Y.: State University of New York Press, 1988). Evidence that the socialists' criticisms were not groundless can be found, for example, in Edward W. Stevens, Jr., "The Political Education of Children in the Rochester Public Schools, 1899–1917: An Historical Perspective on Social Control in Public Education" (unpublished doctoral dissertation, University of Rochester, 1971), especially chap. 5.

18. The wide scope of socialist educational activities for adults and children is discussed in Kenneth Teitelbaum, "Schooling for 'Good Rebels': Socialist Education for Children in the United States, 1900–1920" (unpublished doctoral dissertation, University of Wisconsin-Madison, 1985), especially chaps. 2–4. See also Patti M. Peterson, "The Young Socialist Movement in America From 1905 to 1940: A Study of the Young People's Socialist League" (unpublished doctoral dissertation, University of Wisconsin-Madison, 1974); and W. Bruce Leslie, "Coming of Age in Urban America: The Socialist Alternative, 1901–1920," *Teachers College Record* 85, no. 3 (Spring 1984): 459–76.

19. *Young Socialists' Magazine* 6, no. 12 (December 1912): 12.

20. Martin Carnoy, "Education, Economy and the State," in Apple, ed., *Cultural and Economic Reproduction in Education,* p. 88. See also Antonio Gramsci, *Selections from the Prison Notebooks,* ed. and trans. Quintin Hoare and Geoffrey Nowell Smith (New York: International Publishers, 1971); Carl Boggs, *Gramsci's Marxism* (London: Pluto Press, 1976); and Chantal Mouffe, ed., *Gramsci and Marxist Theory* (Boston: Routledge and Kegan Paul, 1979).

21. For more on the institutional characteristics of the Socialist Sunday schools, including a list of where they were located, see Kenneth Teitelbaum and William J. Reese, "American Socialist

Pedagogy and Experimentation in the Progressive Era: The Socialist Sunday School,'' *History of Education Quarterly* 23, no. 4 (Winter 1983): 429–55.

22. For a discussion of a somewhat different kind of ''selective borrowing'' from middle-class culture by members of the working class, see Paul E. Willis, *Profane Culture* (London: Routledge and Kegan Paul, 1976).

23. *Who Was Who in America,* vol. 5 (Chicago: Marquis Who's Who, 1973), p. 191; *American Women,* vol. 3 (Los Angeles: American Publications, 1939), p. 240; and *New York Times,* May 15, 1944. See also ''Recent Makers of Chautauqua Literature,'' *The Chautauquan* 43 (July 1906): 443; Katherine E. Dopp, ''A New Factor in the Elementary Curriculum,'' *American Journal of Sociology* 8 (September 1902): 145–57; and idem, ''A Report of the First Annual Meeting of the National Society for the Promotion of Industrial Education,'' *The Elementary School Teacher* 8 (March 1908): 393–99.

24. Katherine E. Dopp, *The Tree-Dwellers: The Age of Fear* (Chicago: Rand McNally, 1903), pp. 8–10 and 159.

25. *Young Socialists' Magazine* 4, no. 10 (October 1911): 14.

26. Emilie Poulsson, *Finger Plays For Nursery and Kindergarten* (Boston: Lothrop Publishing, 1893). Poulsson's text was so popular that it went through numerous editions and was even re-copyrighted by the author in 1921. A new, unabridged edition of Poulsson's *Finger Plays* was published as recently as 1971 by Dover Publications.

27. Apple, *Education and Power*, p. 84. Elsewhere, Apple writes: ''It is the case that our sense of community is withered at its roots. We find ways of making the concrete individual into an abstraction and, at the same time, we divorce the individual from larger social movements which might give meaning to 'individual' wants, needs, and visions of justice.'' Apple, *Ideology and Curriculum*, p. 9.

28. *Young Socialists' Magazine* 11, no. 12 (December 1917): 3.

29. *New York Call,* March 21, 1913.

30. William F. Kruse, ''How to Teach,'' *Young Socialists' Magazine* 14, no. 1 (January 1920): 14.

31. Stanley Aronowitz and Henry A. Giroux, *Education Under Siege: The Conservative, Liberal and Radical Debate Over Schooling* (South Hadley, Mass.: Bergin & Garvey, 1985), p. 161.

32. Walter Thomas Mills, *The Struggle For Existence* (Chicago: International School of Social Economy, 1904); *Milwaukee Leader,* January 14, 1916; and *New York Call,* January 25, 1916.

33. *Party Builder,* July 26, 1913.

34. James R. Green, *Grass-Roots Socialism: Radical Movements in the Southwest, 1895–1943* (Baton Rouge, La.: Louisiana State University Press, 1978), pp. 41–42 and 49. One historian refers to Mills's book as ''the most important educational text supplied to English-language Socialists'' during the early years of the twentieth century. See Buhle, *Marxism in the United States.* p. 91.

35. *Milwaukee Leader,* October 26, 1922; November 2, 1922; and November 9, 1922.

36. *Milwaukee Leader,* November 23, 1922; and January 11, 1923.

37. *Milwaukee Leader,* May 3, 1923.

38. Interview with Jennie Yavner Goldman, Putnam Valley, New York, July 4, 1981. Hood's poem is contained in the excellent collection edited and published by Upton Sinclair, *The Cry for Justice* (New York, 1921).

39. Harvey P. Moyer, ed., *Songs of Socialism* (Chicago: The Cooperative Printing Company,

1905); and Charles H. Kerr, ed., *Socialist Songs with Music* (Chicago: Charles H. Kerr Publishing, 1908).

40. *American Socialist,* January 2, 1915.

41. *New York Call,* October 12, 1911.

42. *New York Call,* October 29, 1911, and December 16, 1911.

43. See, for example, Luke, "Making Dick and Jane"; and Apple, *Teachers and Texts,* especially chap. 4.

44. All of Kendrick Shedd's lesson outlines discussed in this article can be found (unpaginated) in various folders and scrapbooks of the *Kendrick Philander Shedd Papers,* located at the University of Rochester Rush Rhees Library, Rare Books Department (Special Collections), Rochester, New York.

45. Kendrick P. Shedd, ed., *Some Songs for Socialist Singers* (Rochester, N.Y.: Rochester Socialist Sunday School, 1912); and, for example, *New York Call,* May 23, 1915, in which Shedd criticized the Party's failure to provide tangible support for what he referred to as the "Schools of Inspiration."

46. Bertha Matthews Fraser, *Outlines of Lessons for Socialist Schools for Children* (New York: Children's Socialist Schools Committee of Local Kings County, Socialist Party, 1910); Woman's National Committee of the Socialist Party, *How to Organize Socialist Schools* (Chicago: Socialist Party's Woman's National Committee, 1912), located in the *Socialist Party of U.S.: Materials,* 1912 Folder, Tamiment Institute Library, New York University, New York, New York; and *International Socialist Review* 10, no. 4 (April 1910): 946.

47. Anyon, "Ideology and United States History Textbooks"; and Fitzgerald, *America Revised.* For a contrasting view, in which it is argued that economics education in the United States has been deficient in developing among students a strong attachment to the normative foundations of the "free enterprise" system, see James S. Leming, "On the Normative Foundations of Economics Education," *Theory and Research in Social Education* 15, no. 2 (Spring 1987): 63–76.

48. David S. Greenberg, *Socialist Sunday School Curriculum* (New York: The Socialist Schools Publishing Association, 1913).

49. *New York Call,* February 3, 1911; November 19, 1917; and November 24, 1917; and *Unity of Labor* 1, no. 1 (April 1911): 3.

50. Jesse Lemisch, "The American Revolution Seen From the Bottom Up," in *Towards a New Past: Dissenting Essays in American History,* ed. Barton J. Bernstein (New York: Pantheon, 1968), pp. 3–45. Lemisch's concluding comments are worth quoting: "The history of the powerless, the inarticulate, the poor has not yet begun to be written because they have been treated no more fairly by historians than they have been treated by their contemporaries" (p. 29). See also Howard Zinn, *A People's History of the United States* (New York: Harper and Row, 1980); and Samuel, ed., *People's History and Socialist Theory.*

51. *Young Socialists' Magazine* 6, no. 2 (February 1913): 8; 8, no. 2 (February 1915): 3; and 11, no. 5 (May 1917): 13.

52. Kendrick Shedd, "Foreward," *Some Songs for Socialist Singers,* p. 1.

53. Edward Friebert, *Autobiography* (1945), unpublished manuscript, p. 274 of handwritten copy; and *Wisconsin Comrade,* 2 (April 1915): 2.

54. Interview with Othelia Hampel Haberkorn, Milwaukee, Wisconsin, May 14, 1981.

55. Dramatic scripts have been located in a variety of sources, for example, in old socialist newspapers and journals, and in the *Shedd Papers.* One collection, the *International Socialist*

Sunday School Dramatic Scripts, was secured from the University of Wisconsin-Milwaukee's Golda Meir Library, Milwaukee, Wisconsin.

56. Jack Zipes, *The Trials and Trials and Tribulations of Little Red Riding Hood: Versions of the Tale in Sociocultural Context* (South Hadley, Mass.: Bergin & Garvey, 1983).

57. Buhle, *Women and American Socialism, 1870–1920.* In this context, one should note that Victor Berger, the powerful Socialist leader of Milwaukee who was elected to the United States Congress in 1910 and 1918, was clearly not alone in the Party's ranks in his belief that Blacks were genetically inferior and required watchful paternalism. See Buhle, *Marxism in the United States,* p. 95.

58. See, for example, Apple, ed., *Cultural and Economic Reproduction in Education;* and Michael W. Apple and Kenneth Teitelbaum, "Education and Inequality," in *Democracy Upside Down: Public Opinion and Cultural Hegemony in America,* ed. Calvin F. Exoo (New York: Praeger, 1987), pp. 141–65.

59. Ruth Miller Elson, *Guardians of Tradition: American Schoolbooks of the Nineteenth Century* (Lincoln, Nebr.: University of Nebraska Press, 1964).

60. Luke, "Making Dick and Jane," pp. 109 and 111.

61. Anyon, "Ideology and United States History Textbooks."

62. Richard Johnson, " 'Really Useful Knowledge': Radical Education and Working-Class Culture, 1790–1848," in *Working-Class Culture: Studies in History and Theory,* ed. John Clarke, Chas Critcher, and Richard Johnson (London: Hutchinson, 1979), pp. 75–102; and Aronowitz and Giroux, *Education Under Siege,* pp. 157–58.

63. Harry Braverman, *Labor and Monopoly Capital: The Degradation of Work in the Twentieth Century* (New York: Monthly Review Press, 1974).

64. See, for example, Michael W. Apple and Lois Weis, "Ideology and Practice in Schooling: A Political and Conceptual Introduction," in idem, eds., *Ideology and Practice in Schooling,* pp. 3–33; Carl A. Grant and Christine E. Sleeter, "Race, Class, and Gender in Education Research: An Argument for Integrative Analysis," *Review of Educational Research* 56, no. 2 (Summer 1986):195–211; and Apple, *Teachers and Texts,* especially chap. 8.

65. See also Elizabeth Cagan, "Individualism, Collectivism, and Radical Educational Reform," *Harvard Educational Review* 48, no. 2 (May 1978): 227–66; and Saul, "We Gather Together." The phrase "rebel roots" is borrowed from the excellent film, *Northern Lights.*

66. Featherstone, "Foreword," p. xvi.

67. Marcus G. Raskin, *The Common Good: Its Politics, Policies and Philosophy* (New York: Routledge and Kegan Paul, 1986), p. 6.

68. Zinn, *A People's History of the United States,* pp. 10–11.

8

The Secular Word:
Catholic Reconstructions of
Dick and Jane

Allan Luke

A generation of inter- and postwar American and Canadian children was introduced to literacy through the Dick and Jane readers, which have been among the most widely selling textbooks in the twentieth century. The series was a prototype of the industrial-era, secular textbook, portraying a generic, middle-class possible world to an increasingly diverse population of North American children. It was also an exemplar of the application of the tenets of modern reading psychology and curriculum design—in both "technical form" and literary content a model for the basal readers that to this day dominate beginning reading instruction.[1] With the granting of "Ecclesiastical Approval" for Catholic editions in the 1940s, Catholic school children in the United States, Canada, and the Phillipines were also given access to this Middletown version of secular life, albeit in a revised form. Under the editorship of Reverend John A. O'Brien, Scott Foresman published the Cathedral Readers, church-sanctioned revised editions of the beginning reading textbooks *Fun with Dick and Jane* and *Our New Friends*.[2]

This paper centers on a discourse analysis of selected narratives from the Catholic revisions of the Dick and Jane textbooks for first graders. In an effort to trace how textbook narratives construct fictional and audience subjectivities, the "reading" developed here draws from work in critical linguistics, semiotics, and communications theory. The analysis highlights the culturally incorporative power of the modern multinational reading series, i.e., the capacity of the secular discourse of modern American schooling to incorporate nonsecular discourses under the auspices of psychologically defined instruction.

American textbooks of the inter- and postwar eras marked the historically unprecedented collaboration between the corporate publishing sector, exponents of an ideologically "neutral" educational science, and regional and state educa-

I wish to thank Linda Christian-Smith for first calling my attention to Catholic versions of the Curriculum Foundation textbooks and for her help in initiating this study; Cushla Kapitzke and Gabriel Oriti for their comments on the relationship of literacy and religion; and Carmen Luke, Gunther Kress, Rob Gilbert, and Kieran Egan for critical responses to earlier drafts.

tional jurisdictions.[3] However, the immediate historical predecessors of modern basal reading textbooks were the Protestant readers of the nineteenth century.[4] The installation of explicitly religious content in revisions of the modern reading textbook by U.S. Catholic educators thus marked a reframing of the long-standing explicit relationship between religious practice and the teaching of reading. In order to establish a broader historical and cultural context for revisions of the Dick and Jane texts, I here begin with an exploration of the complex relationships between literacy, textbooks, and religiously based reading practices.

Controlling the Word: Religious Ideology and Reading Practices

In early modern Western culture, the first formal textbooks were compiled for identifiably ideological purposes, specifically those of church and polity. As part of their promotion of mass compulsory schooling in fifteenth-century Germany, Luther and fellow Wittenberg academic Phillip Melanchthon collected various texts for introducing school children to the culture of literacy. The textbooks that resulted included passages from scripture as well as excerpts from the secular texts of antiquity. Yet the intents and consequences of the mass provision of early literacy training for children were not restricted to spiritual salvation.[5] Rather, Luther and colleagues conceived of their task *inter alia* as the means for the control of childrearing practices: the burghers and princes of the German state who sanctioned the break from the Vatican indeed saw in mass education and literacy an opportunity for nation building. Hence, they set up a (textual) "bureaucratic discourse"[6] that facilitated the development of a centralized school inspection system replete with inspectorates, syllabi, teacher guidelines, and mandatory curricula. It was within this overall institutional gaze that standardized textbooks played a key role.[7]

The relationship between literacy, education, and religion is an historically long-standing one that predates the Reformation. In *The Logic of Writing and the Organization of Society,* Jack Goody argues that literacy enabled a move from "religions of the word" to "religions of the book."[8] Text preserves the "word" across time and space, thus potentially enhancing its apparent authority and authenticity through a divorce of the word and its readings from historical authors and editors.[9] The Bible, like other sacred books, appears "unchanging, eternal, inspired by the divine and not by man alone," and "while the liturgy of the Catholic Church may change over time . . . , while interpretations vary, the word itself remains as it always was."[10] For religions, textuality thus enables orthodoxy and centralization of control over a diversity of possible practices and rituals as Goody states,

a written religion . . . makes and preserves its status as a universalistic creed and prevents it from disintegrating, not just into breakaway sects but into numberless "local cults." For the Book persists . . . as a permanent reference point—communication preserved as a material object and hence relatively immune to the transmuting power of the oral tradition, held only in memory, transmitted only in face-to-face situations. . . . [T]he New Testament immortalizes Christ, or the myth of Christ, so that the sufferings and victories of the Prophet (and consequently the places where these events occurred) remain of continuing significance for their followers over time and over space.[11]

The permanent textual recording of sacred oaths, codes, spells, and incantations was common before the advent of Christianity.[12] Within religious states, this writing down of the texts of religion and polity marked a shift in the locus of social control from the spoken word of the oral poet, shaman, regent, or priest, to the class of literati—scribes, copyists, and their patrons and contractors—who had (physical and/or intellectual) access to texts. Nonetheless we might generalize that literacy, by virtue of the portability and permanence of text, potentially facilitated a widened access to texts of power, whether those texts pertained to spiritual, economic, or political domains.[13] As a result, control over what people were able to do with texts, control over and prescription of appropriate norms for "literacy events"[14]—instances of social and linguistic interaction around text—became focal for church and state agendas. If texts were tied to both secular and nonsecular power, then the retention of controls over who had access to the book, over rituals of veneration of the book as icon, and over how people "read" the word, whether that of god, mammon, or the state, was to become a central concern of church and state authorities. It is not coincidental, then, that, historically, "religious literacy"—that is, the use of text as a means for learning about and communicating with a divinity—has been "restricted. . . . both in terms of the proportion who could read and the uses to which writing was put."[15]

Throughout the history of literacy, unbridled access to the word by educated masses has been viewed as a potential threat to existing secular and nonsecular structures.[16] Generally speaking, this has characterized the historical position of the Catholic church. Consider, for example, this early sixteenth-century Franciscan reaction to women of letters in Catholic France who had taken to consulting vernacular devotional literature and the Bible independently of the clergy: "Why, they're half theologians . . . running around from one [female] literate house to another, seeking advice and making much ado about nothing."[17] But any blanket claim that Catholic authorities were opposed to mass literacy per se would be erroneous. Despite some evidence that Catholic states lagged behind in the educational extension of literate competence,[18] from the time of the Counter-Reformation on, Catholic education moved inexorably, if at times hesitantly, toward the educational sponsorship of a literate lay public. In fact, in some locales the Catholic church had been promoting literacy and education as early as the end of the sixteenth century.[19] And from the seventeenth century on, the guiding educational dictum of both Catholic and Protestant churches was not the denial of lay access to reading practice, but the controlling of it.

By the 1570s, a "Catholic revision of the Genevan Scripture" approved by the Theology Faculty of Louvain, was published in the vernacular, in an inexpensive format for Catholic lay persons.[20] Over the next hundred years, in a bid to "maintain . . . orthodoxy . . . [as] a mode of control more suited to printing than an archaic form of sacerdotal monopoly . . . or censorship," Franciscans and Jesuits set out to "fix the meaning of a devotional text by an accompanying standardized religious picture and emblem."[21] In this way the interpretive possibilities of lay Catholic reading could be set out in a manner "in which the eye was guided by exposition and illustration."[22] That is to say, the text's total semiotic system could be realized in the effort to proscribe interpretation: in this case, pictographic information was used to "punctuate" the actual words and sentences of the text, providing a running metatextual commentary on the scripture in question.

By contrast, the modern Protestant church, so closely allied to the foundations of the American state and school, has retained an orientation in articulated theology at least towards individual interpretation of nonsecular texts, toward what Horace Mann called the right and sanctity of private judgement."[23] To this stated intent, however, Natalie Davis adds a crucial historical caveat: speaking of sixteenth-century France, she argues that "the Protestant method for guaranteeing orthodoxy was in the last instance censorship and punishment; but in the first instance it was *the combination of reading with listening to a trained teacher.*"[24] In lieu of rigid control over access to text, then, prescription of the norms for literacy events would suffice.

In terms of the residual cultural tradition expressed in and through reading practices, it was indeed this Protestant approach to literacy that formed the basis of public schooling in the eighteenth- and nineteenth-century United States, a modern Protestant nation-state where both freedom of (textual) expression and freedom of religious practice were constitutionally enshrined. From the nineteenth century on, the "ideology of literacy,"[25] of compulsory literacy training in both the United States and Canada, was largely embedded in this tradition: early readers like the McGuffey series in the United States and the Ontario and British Columbia readers in Canada tended to express orientations toward work, family, and ethics, orientations that were identifiably Protestant. The prototypical *New England Primer* displayed a caricature of the Pope with the textual imperative: "Child, behold the Man of Sin, the Pope, worthy of thy utmost hatred."[26] In addition, a significant historical footnote is that many of the nineteenth-century school promoters in both the United States and Canada had a stated allegiance to Methodist, Presbyterian, Congregational, or other sectarian interests.[27]

During the nineteenth century the structure and consequences of mass, compulsory, state-sponsored literacy instruction for newly arrived migrants did not escape the scrutiny of Catholic officials, who deemed it "Protestant prose-lytizing."[28] In 1840 a spokesperson for New York Archbishop John Hughes— the founder of Catholic schools in New York—outlined the difference between the religious reading practices of the state schools and Catholic "reading":

> The Holy Scriptures are read every day, with the restriction that no specific tenets are to be inculcated. Here we find the great demarcating principle between the Catholic Church and the Sectaries introduced silently. The Catholic Church tells her children that they must be taught by *authority*. The Sectaries say, read the Bible, judge for yourselves. The Protestant principle is therefore acted upon, slyly inculcated, and the schools are Sectarian.[29]

These comments accurately describe the Catholic attitude toward nondenomina-tional state education, and the nineteenth-century growth and expansion of the Catholic education in the United States marked an unprecedented secession from the compulsory state system. Through the early and mid-twentieth century there remained both a skepticism among U.S. Catholic church leaders toward secular education, and a general reluctance among Catholic theologians to accept the liberal approaches to modern lay biblical study advocated by many Protestant churches.

The latter trend was altered by Pope Pius XII, who in 1948 issued an encyclical entitled "Divino Afflante Spirtu." This document, part of an effort to counter the rapidly spreading fundamentalist movement, reduced the official constraints on lay analysis of Biblical text.[30] For Catholics the long-standing view of the Bible as "the school text par excellance"[31] was retained, while the encyclical had opened the possibility for some variance in reading practices. Hence, shortly after the release of the revised Catholic Dick and Jane readers for use in U.S. parochial schools, the official Vatican attitude towards textual interpretation was undergoing a major shift.

What we can glean from this brief historical overview is that a key and often overlooked Western educational legacy of Christianity, a modern religion of the book, has been the emergence of differentiated textual practices. From the Reformation of to this day, sanctioned ways of reading and (hermeneutically and/or literally) interpreting the word as encoded in the book have marked out the boundaries of theological division.

This is amply illustrated in recent and current American religious con-texts.[32] Since the Millenarian movements of the mid to late nineteenth century in the United States,[33] various modes of fundamentalism have prescribed a rote, literal approach to textual analysis. In a recent case study of Sunday School in one U.S. church, Carolyn Zinnser[34] found that the fundamentalist teaching of literate practice is a paradigm case of the "strong framing" of curricular knowledge, within which Sunday School "teachers can neither select nor reorder their material" and "students are limited in their responses. . . . , curtailed in both classroom display and interpersonal language during pedagogical discourse."[35] The sum pedagogical effect on children's literate practices is to establish univocally the authority of the text via its divine source, effectively putting the text beyond criticism. Differentiated sectarian reading practices and pedagogical texts thus have direct implications for children and religious educators: for theological and sociocultural purposes, churches choose distinct ways to initiate children into textual competence.[36]

Educational Science and the Neutralization of Textbook Content

Textbooks and reading practices, then, have a long history in the church and in schooling. Yet, with the twentieth-century development of the modern North American state school, the religious content of textbooks became a recurring issue of contention. First Amendment rights and the separation of church and state have led to an ongoing series of court cases in which Catholic, Protestant, Jewish, fundamentalist, and other groups have argued that either the inclusion or exclusion of religious/moral content violated their constitutional rights.[37] The claim of fundamentalist objectors to textbook content has centered on the argument that modern textbooks express an identifiable ideology of "secular humanism." This is a case in point of what Goody calls the "twin [textual] bureaucracies"[38] of Church and State—enabled by and reliant on literacy for the assertion of centralized codes of rules—at odds over what will count as the authorized textual word and canon.

The possibility of state mollification of religious and political controversy over textbook content lay in the production of a modern "neutral" discourse of curriculum and instruction. For the move from Protestant textbooks, traditionalist morality, and 3-R's pedagogy into the modern age of educational science, heralded at the turn of the century by the rise of educational progressivism, provided the state system with a discursive strategy—both the "true" (foundational) discourse of educational science, and the "practical" discourse of the standardized documents and practices of state schooling—a strategy capable of rendering moot the contentious issues of which values should be transmitted.[39]

Technocratic approaches to curriculum are epitomized in the redefinition of reading and the reformation of reading textbooks undertaken by psychologists in the early part of the twentieth century. When Wundt's students and colleagues returned to the United States in the late nineteenth century to establish psychological studies in institutions of higher learning and to apply the "scientific" study of the mind to the public domains of education, industry, policy work, treatment, and social policy toward migrants and the poor,[40] they brought with them a European prototype for the study of reading as a psycho/physiologial phenomenon. Pioneering work by Cattell, Dearborn, Huey, and others on eye movements and "reading hygiene"[41] was followed by the research of E. L. Thorndike, Gray, Gates, and others, research that sampled children's psychological reactions to various kinds and formats of text.[42] While the former corpus stressed the physiology of reading, the work of Thorndike, Gray and colleagues had the most immediate influence on what would count as reading and the reading textbook in U.S. schools. Specifically, Thorndike's early twentieth-century research on "silent reading"[43]—a relatively late historical invention in the history of the technology of literacy—signaled that, under the auspices of a behaviorist model of textual stimulus/reader response, reading could be empirically tested *and* textbooks could be designed to introduce children systematically to the "skills" of reading with optimal efficiency (i.e., demonstrable outcomes on silent reading tests).[44]

With his graduate student Arthur Gates at Teachers College, Thorndike developed word lists for the design of reading textbooks. Their ideal was a self-contained, instructional text fine-tuned to transmit literacy scientifically:

> If, by a miracle of modern ingenuity, a book could be arranged that only to him who had done what was directed on page one would two become visible, and so on, . . . much that now requires personal instruction could be managed by print.[45]

The truly self-contained textbook was decades off, to be reframed theoretically in Skinner's *The Technology of Teaching*[46] and implemented in the *SRA Reading* series. But Thorndike, Gray, and other members of the interwar instructional and reading psychology community could settle for a close approximation. The Dick and Jane series—and its many competitors, which were also designed by university-based psychologists—could boast of having achieved the "total" instructional program with self-instructional workbooks (the *Think and Do Book*) and teachers' guides for organizing social and textual relations around the core student text. The textbook that the child read was deliberately sequenced—through controls on lexical density and sentence-level syntax, through stress on repeated "sight words," and through story structures that limited literary trope and complexity—to evoke particular behavioral "skill" acquisition. Similarly, the teacher's behavior was sequenced through detailed teacher guidebooks that pushed a standardized approach to instruction and interaction.[47]

Hence, the "true discourse" of educational psychology placed traditional pedagogical concerns of literary quality and moral content in a subordinate position: reading was redefined in terms of the textual stimulus/reader response configuration, and reading pedagogy was redefined in terms of the optimal transmission of measurable psychological skills. As for the practical discourse of the classroom, carefully standardized instruction would supplant the traditional, rote approaches to the teaching of McGuffey-style moral parables and literary excerpts. The modern reading textbook thus marked the convergence of various needs: the needs of the expanding state school system for a new generation of "mass" texts that would express nondenominational values: the needs of the modern corporation for a mass-marketable, generic product that would have as universal an appeal as, say, McGuffey's readers had had in the previous century: and the public and professional demand for the most "efficient" and generalizable way of transmitting the skills of reading. At once, pressing practical needs facing schools and teachers *and* economic and political interests were reconciled by the technological representation of reading as a measurable set of psychological skills.

Gray, who had studied with Thorndike before returning to the University of Chicago, undertook the first revisions of Elson's reading textbooks in the late 1920s. He had been brought into textbook development by Scott Foresman with the expressed intent of bringing its series into line with developments in educational psychology.[48] Yet, while both educational scientists and Deweyians were allied in their opposition to the traditional regime of physical, intellectual discipline and the rote study of literary texts, the matter of the ideological content of reading materials was not ignored. Progressive themes of "learning by doing," creative play, and peer friendship, wholesome social relationships within the nuclear family, civic life, and duty became focal in interwar basal readers. In Gray's Dick and Jane series, we follow our protagonists through an idealized (Midwestern?) small-town community, observing the gendered social relations within the family, forays to the countryside, to the town, visits to grandparents.[49] Unifying these narratives—"Father Helps the Family," "Sally Finds Friends," "The First Day at School," and so forth—is a focus on goal-seeking, problem-solving social behavior. Within the auspices of play, Dick, Jane, Sally, and friends engage in the solution of problems and anomalies that arise in their social and physical environment.[50] Surely, as many progressive-era educators envisioned them, these were the consensual aspirations, if not the realities, of American society, that all subcultural, sectarian groups would subscribe to.

How was this ideology achieved in the discourse of the children's text? In the textbook layout of *Fun with Dick and Jane* and *Our New Friends,* the language and pictures of each discrete narrative constitute semiotic frames, which construct a possible world of seemingly natural social relations, orientations to action, and linguistic and behavioral norms.[51] Within this format, each of the twenty to thirty short narratives in turn stands as a closed text, picking up the same human and animal characters but starting "in virtual beginning,"[52] as a self-contained episode that can be read and understood autonomously.[53] Although there are cohesive repetitions of key vocabulary for the teaching of "word meaning" and "recognition" (e.g., "said," "fun," "play," "go," "happy," and the proper names of protagonists),[54] and intertextual repetitions of syntaxes of goal-seeking action (e.g., female encounters problem   →

male provides solution $\longrightarrow$ adult character utters the "lesson" to be learned)—there is no explicit reference to what has come before or to what might occur later. Dick and Jane come to stand as mythic figures: unchanging, they represent a set of static characteristics that seem to defy the passage of time and any actual growth or development.

A grammar analysis of the story further reveals that the text operates through several rudimentary literary devices. Lexicon, sentence-level syntax, and macropropositional sequences (of events and social relations) are repeated both within and across narratives. This is achieved without the direct intervention of a third-person narrator: the possible world is created by juxtaposed (textually presented) utterances and (pictorially presented) social actions. Readers thus literally "hear" and "see" the unfolding of progressive childhood. Within this childhood children talk, act, and interact, observing the physical and social world, and unknotting the problems that arise in peer and sibling interaction—all under the watchful didactic presence of Father and, to a lesser extent, Mother. But what is striking about the fictions of Gray and Arbuthret is the absence of explicitly portrayed motivation, premeditation, or cognition, all of which would require either the presence of an omniscient narrator or subjects engaged in verbal self-reflection. The latter is not in evidence: a detailed analysis of the verbs indicates a dearth of mental predicate verbs—those speech acts that signal cognition (e.g., "think," "imagine," "agree," even "wonder")—and an exclusive stress on verbs that mark out the actions of "doing" and "saying." Consequently, while Dick, Jane, and their family are portrayed as social actors, they do not appear to be cognate fictional beings.

These naturalized versions of the family, of social relations, of childhood itself, all take place in a generic environment—and this indicates a key difference between these texts and their nineteenth-century predecessors, wherein scripture, traditional poetry and Anglo-Saxon fables, and national history were interwoven. The Dick and Jane texts confront the reader with an unidentifiable but situated locale, one that resembles Superboy's "Smallville" or Disneyland's "Mainstreet, U.S.A." This certainly reflects an early twentieth-century literary trend apparent in U.S. works of adult fiction—but while the contemporary settings of works by Wilder, Lewis, and others provided for satirical or incisive social commentary, Dick and Jane's possible world asks to be taken at face value, absolutely literally and seriously.

Thus the scientization of reading practices authorized by the school and the secularization of ideational content were reciprocal aspects of one and the same discursive move: a new technology of power was established. These inter- and postwar textbooks, and many of their modern counterparts, were reproductive constructions in several interlocking ways: in overt content, in the kinds of reading/writing practices and positions they prescribed, and in the textual construction of the child her- or himself. We could surmise that textbooks projected a role of the reader, both by reference to the kinds of "readings" they enabled and precluded, and to the discursive positioning of the subjectivity of the reader. At the micropropositional level of sentence and word, this latter process occurs through a range of linguistic/semiotic methods: for example, (gendered) lexical choice codes and prescribed family roles[55]; nominalizations and sentence-level transformations locate agency with male characters.[56] At the level of generic structure, their component macropropositions constitute story grammars, which amount to syntaxes of culture.[57] Hence, learning the social texts of the basal reading textbook, children then and now encounter both a "glossification"[58] of the social and a cultural logic of "typical" patterns of action and interaction.

In this way, the paradigm shift toward psychology as *the* "true" discourse of modern schooling—if not altogether sanctioned by Deweyianism—combined with the mass marketing, adoption, and requirement of basal readers that as modern commodities bore an uncanny resemblance to each other. In all, these were the conditions that permitted U.S. instructional and curricular psychologists of the twentieth century to attain over a mass audience a degree of control of both access to and uses of literacy that had been unattainable for their post-Reformation forebears. With this singular achievement of modern state schooling in mind, we can turn to the Catholic versions of the same textbooks, to see how what counted as reading and what counted as childhood were revised.

With Ecclesiastical Approval:
The Syntaxes of Catholic Life

In the era of instructional commoditization, the adoption of a reading series entails the implementation of a regime of instructional practice and the acceptance, however tacit, of a dual theorization of reading and of reading pedagogy. That is, since Gray's time, the practical discourse of classroom texts, workbooks, and textual guidelines for classroom instruction has justified itself by reference to a metanarrative on "reading," a putatively "true" discourse historically drawn from psychological, or, more recently, psycholinguistic, theory.[59]

By choosing to adopt and adapt the Dick and Jane textbooks, Rev. O'Brien and colleagues were indeed buying into a particular construction of secular reading practices—specifically, the stress on word recognition and incremental skill building. Of course, other approaches were available, including phonics-oriented texts. That the Catholic revised edition displays similar linguistic and literary design constraints (e.g., vocabulary and sentence-length controls, an emphasis on the representation of child speech), moreover, indicates the degree to which it embraces a particular approach to reading, one that stressed skill acquisition and precluded speculative or critical interpretation. It also suggests that regardless of the kinds of (moral and religious) adjustments undertaken at the level of propositional content, the (secular) reading practices prescribed would remain the same.

The addition of frames/narratives that would express an identifiably Catholic ethos required the editorial deletion of some of the stories from the secular version, and minor augmentation of others. In *Fun with Dick and Jane*, for instance, six stories were deleted and six Catholic-oriented stories were added. Most of the omissions appear to serve the need for text economy rather than the elimination of objectionable secular content. It is difficult to see what could have been perceived as morally or religiously objectionable about "Pretty, Pretty Puff," in which the family cat disappears for a time, or "Something for Sally," in which Father brings Sally a gift. In other instances, scenes were added to the secular narratives to provide a Catholic backdrop. In the story "A Ride with Mother," Sally and friends take the bus through town. The Catholic editors have replaced a page where the children observe the colors of cars on the streets with a scene where the same bus passes a statue of the "Blessed Mother" surrounded by flowers (of the same color as the cars). Yet apart from such minor revisions, dispersed into otherwise unmodified secular narratives, action sequences and lexicon remain intact.

The added narratives, several authored by O'Brien himself, not surprisingly establish a quite distinct, if in some ways complementary, version of childhood from the secular Dick and Jane texts. But how exactly were complementarities between the Catholic and non-Catholic Dick and Jane, between nonsecular and secular possible worlds, achieved?

In *Fun with Dick and Jane*, four subsections—"Family Fun," "Fun at the Farm," "Pets and Toys," "Fun with Our Friends"—were retained, augmented by a new subsection entitled "God in Our Home." In *Our New Friends*, the subsection "Our Friends and God" featured five added stories. What follows is a discourse analysis of selected narratives from the Catholic versions of the two primer-level textbooks. Its aim is to show how the subjectivity of the Catholic child and the ideal possible world of Catholic family life are constructed discursively, and how the text operates didactically to ensure the authority of these constructions. These critical "readings" of the text are undertaken with an eye to elucidating how textual construction occurs at multiple linguistic/semiotic levels.[60] I begin with a close inspection of a single narrative from the Catholic version of *Fun with Dick and Jane*, stressing lexical choice and sentence-level syntax and isolating distinct stylistic and content features of the genre. The analysis then turns to reconstruct the story grammar of a second narrative. There the concentration is on how the larger syntaxes of action are established in the texts. Finally, drawing from various other of the Catholic revised narratives, we step back from the texts to survey dominant themes and contexts.

Here, then, is the text of "God Made Me," the first story in the section "God in Our Home." The major macropropositions of the story grammar are noted in brackets:

"God Made Me"

Sally said, "Guess, Mother.
Guess what I have for you.
It is little and pretty.
It is yellow.
God made it." [problem]
"Is it Puff?" said Mother.
"God made Puff.
He made all the animals." [try 1]
Sally laughed.
"Oh, no," she said.
"It cannot say mew.
It is not Puff." [consequence 1]
"Is it a flower?" said Mother?
"God made the flowers." [try 2]
"Yes Mother," said Sally.
"It is a little yellow flower.
A little flower for you." [consequence 2]
"Thank you," said Mother.
"Thank you for the flower.
Is that all you have for me?
I see something I want.
It is a little girl.
God made all little girls.
But He made this little girl
for me." [didactic reiteration]
Sally said, "Oh Mother.
I am the little girl
that God made for you.
Here I am." [acknowledgment]

This is a variation of a semantic pattern that occurs in several earlier episodes in both secular and Catholic textbooks, the "guessing game" where adult or older siblings suspend their knowledge of the world in order to generate conditions for the younger child's development to occur. A sequence of macropropositions (try   consequence) are repeated both in the text and pictures: this permits the didactic repetition of a set of behaviors and social relations (i.e., Sally asks, Mother answers), and of particular phrases and lexicon. This use of repetition parallels that of the secular texts. Here, in a narrative of 131 words, "it" and "is" appear together 6 times: "said"—the primary device for fixing utterances to speakers throughout *Fun with Dick and Jane*—appears 7 times; key nouns are repeated ("Mother," 6: "Sally," 4: "flower," 4) as are key adjectives (e.g., "little," 7). Together this core is .305 of the total lexicon.

The repeating of key macropropositions also enables the reiteration of a particular message: the divine origin of all things, whether "flowers" or "little girls.'' As in other *Fun with Dick and Jane* narratives, the personal pronouns (e.g., ''you,'' ''I,'' ''she'') occur frequently. However, what is distinct here is the repeated location of agency not in the secular domain of social and civic relations but rather in the transcendent domain. The phrase ''God made'' is repeated 5 times (.153 of the total story), in 3 instances with ''little girl'' as the object of the action. Relatedly, the reference to God as ''he'' foregrounds the following structure of transactive agentiveness[61]:

God (male) $\longrightarrow$ made $\longrightarrow$ little girls $\longrightarrow$ for Mothers.

As in other domestic narratives where Mother is, for instance, the receiver of Father's help, of the children's jokes and expressions of clothing needs, here Mother stands as the recipient of the child. The preposition ''for'' marks her passivity in the entire chain of conception, distancing her from both the act of conception and the conceived. This syntactic positioning would seem to match her theological status as the recipient of divine gifts (i.e., Mary) with her secular status as passive addressee of actions of and support for the Other (i.e., men and children). Further emphasizing the point, this proposition becomes the narrative's ''didactic reiteration,'' the utterance foregrounded as the object-level message of the story.[62]

What is interesting here is Sally's transformation of the adult theological explanation in her acknowledgement move: '' . . . I am the little girl that God made for you. Here I am.'' Here the agentiveness of the sentence is syntactically transformed:[63]

Sally $\longrightarrow$ is $\longrightarrow$ little girl $\longrightarrow$ God $\longrightarrow$ made $\longrightarrow$ for Mother.

In this passive transformation—whereby the relationship of actor (God) and affected entity (Sally) is reversed—Sally thus has acknowledged the lesson/proposition but has bracketed it, altering the transitivity by making herself both subject and object, object of both herself and of God. The traits of Sally's secular persona I have elsewhere characterized as those of a ''progressive-era Noble Savage.''[64] These surface here: she is egocentric (''Here I am''), requiring domestication and socialization into the gendered selflessness characterized in maturity by Mother, and in development by older sister Jane, who literally forgets herself while engaging in domestic chores in the earlier narrative ''Jane Helps.''

The former relationship is exemplified in the adjacent narrative, ''Sally and the Angels,'' where Jane introduces Sally to the religious practice of praying. While Sally's undersocialization requires that she learn to participate in family outings, games, and social relations, her Catholic education demands that she learn the linguistic and ritual structure of prayer. In this episode Jane physically and verbally models a prayer (e.g., kneeling at the window: ''Please,

God. Bless our home. . . . Bless me and make me a good girl . . .'') and then asks Sally to do the same. Sally's imitation is both ''creative'' and idiosyncratic (she claims she sees angels in the clouds), in alignment with her responses to secular games and relations. Her prayer thus requires Jane's intervention, which is ultimately ignored.

Difference in the development of gendered subjectivities is here marked out through pronominalization and agency. Jane, as in the secular narratives, operates from a learned selflessness, only using the personal pronoun ''I'' on one occasion: her prayer itself indicates that she has internalized, better than Sally, her status as transitive ''object'' of god (''Bless me and make me a good girl''). Sally, by contrast, in three conversational turns, uses the pronoun ''I'' eight times, expressing her idiosyncratic notion of communication with divinity in a way that stresses her volition: ''I will talk to my angel. I will say good night to my angel. And he can say good night to God . . .'' Of course, the cohesive pronominalization of ''angels'' is male. Sally, then, is the focal point of these two narratives. As in the mainstream narratives, her undersocialization constitutes the ''problem'' of the story grammar, and her introduction to religious practice by the child-rearing females constitutes the ''try'' components. Yet these actions by the central female subjects, their social and discursive relations, are attributed to overarching (male) transcendental agents.

A contrasting image of male agency, action, and social relations emerges in narrative that follows, entitled ''A Boat for a Friend.'' Because I want here to stress larger structures of action, this narrative is paraphrased in a story grammar format;[65]

''A Boat for a Friend''

Dick suggests to his ''new friend'' Jack that they play in the bathtub with two boats Father made [setting/initiating event], later, Jack must go home but laments that he does ''not have a boat at home'' [problem]; Dick is unhappy [consequence] and asks God to get Jack a boat [try]; Dick decides to give Jack one of his boats because ''that is what God wants me to do'' [consequence/didactic reiteration].

Dick, as in the secular narratives, is the initiator of subsequent social relations and action. Throughout *Fun with Dick and Jane,* infants and males are primarily responsible for initiating events, from independent play to family activities. Where females are focal in the ''problem'' component of the grammar (e.g., Sally needs a toy repaired: Patty loses her rosary), the equilibrium of the narrative is restored, the problem solved, by male agency. Therefore, a code of gender is achieved not only through the classification as ''feminine'' of verbs and adjectives, but through the cultural logic, the commonsense, typified in the sequencing of macropropositions. Dick is decisively in control. But in contrast with Sally's assertion of self-identity through the use of ''I'' and Jane's lack of it. Dick pushes along the action using the collective ''we.''

The conclusion of the story further stresses Dick's newfound selflessness: "Jack likes my blue boat. I will run to Jack with it now. That is what God wants me to do." This is a different, more charitable Dick than the subject who appears in the secular narratives. There Dick is something of a gloating figure, who tends to mock female error in play and family relations. Here an ethos of friendship is extolled, and it is reinforced by the intervention of a third-person narrator, rare in the secular texts. Her or his role is simple description of action: "Away went Dick with the blue boat. Away he went to find Jack." That description is matched by a closing picture of Dick handing Jack the toy boat. The effect is to reiterate Dick's charitable action both in word and picture: as in religious texts, to fix the meaning through an accompanying emblem.

Apparently, then, a new wrinkle of the male child-subject is introduced in the Catholic narratives. He still remains the source of gendered action, dominating most of the narratives in which he appears by initiating and/or concluding actions and, hence, framing the subjectivities of other (primarily female) characters. But his "try" move here is an extension of god's word: an implied communication with god leads him toward more charitable action than that which appears in the secular narratives.

Thus, several intertextual contrasts and complementarities between the Catholic and secular narratives emerge. The familiar problem $\rightarrow$ try $\rightarrow$ resolution sequence, through which the Deweyian problem-solving approach to growth is reproduced, is presented as focal to this story. Dick encounters a problem with the equitable distribution of wealth: toys. However, in contrast with the non-Catholic narratives, the resolution does not result solely from male ingenuity or guile, but through a return to a universal first principal: the Word. Agency within the narrative thus shifts from Dick to god, or, rather, Dick's action is qualified by its divine source. Another variation of this occurs in *Our New Friends* added story "The Lost Rosary," where Dick-clone Jim retrieves sister Patty's rosary from a tree at her request. The discovery of the rosary as well has been attributed to divine action invoked by prayer, but again the redemption of the narrative requires female recourse to male action.

The themes of the Catholic possible world of Dick and Jane, then, are established largely through linguistic and semiotic devices that match those used in the secular narratives. In all, the Catholic narratives of *Fun with Dick and Jane* and *Our New Friends* didactically mark out three strands of Catholic life: participation in religious belief and ritual, charitable works, and reading practice itself. The former two are intricately interwoven into patterns of everyday secular life. As noted, the viewing of the "Blessed Mother" becomes a passing moment in the children's tour through the community; in "Sally and Baby Jesus," the identification of icons of "Blessed Mother," "Baby Jesus," "St. Joseph," and various angels is central to the family ritual of Christmas tree decoration. In "A Surprise," the progressive learning-through-creative-play theme is picked up with an added incentive: "Every time I paint a flower, I say a prayer for Father." The matter of charitable "worldly" works becomes another point of intersection of the religious and the public. It too stands within secular play and daily social relations: the children play "store" in front of their house with the aim of gathering "pennies for God." "Learning by doing" thus takes on a decidedly different character here. The effect of this integration of the religious within the secular is to routinize the former and to show how it can be found embedded within the latter.

If, indeed, the sanction and control of nonsecular reading practices is at the heart of religious literacy, then of focal interest is the representation of "reading" itself. In the secular versions of the two textbooks, reading is portrayed twice: in the story "Fun at School," children are portrayed reading in a group, with basal readers in hand: in the story "Patty Reads to Baby," written by series author May Arbuthnot, reading to younger children is authorized as a sibling responsibility. In the Catholic revisions, "The Night Baby Jesus Came" and "A New Home for Baby Jesus" depict family and bedtime stories, with Father reading from picture books. In the first, Father, dressed in tie and business suit, is reading "something new" for all three children on the couch: a picture book depicting the Nativity. Again, the textual production of gendered subjectivities takes center stage. Both Jane and Sally take turns interpreting the pictures, but Dick remains mute throughout (curiously, no boy character is "heard" reading in either secular or Catholic stories). The text's pictures depict a book framed within the book, so that readers can " see" what the children would be seeing, all the while "hearing" the children's content-level questions directed to father (e.g., "Where did St. Joseph and Blessed Mother go?"). Father in turn confirms when their "reading" is 'correct' (e.g., "Yes, Jane." . . . "They came to see the new Baby and to say that He is God"). In effect, the children play at constructing a verbal text while Father, the surrogate author and (clerical) mediator of religious texts, provides the authorized reading.

In "A New Home for Baby Jesus," Sally brings a book for father to read, one he has read for her before. Sally here models the "correct" attitude toward family reading of religious stories: "I want you to read it over and over again. I want you to read it every day. I just love this story." When Father begins to read, Sally interjects long passages, at times with Father's prompt: "You know the story. You know what the Angel said." He concludes by encouraging her reading-like behavior, "Oh Sally, you are a funny girl. . . . Did you want me to read to you? Or did you want to read to me? You know the story as well as I do." Here Sally has taken control of the "reading," providing an apparently near-verbatim reproduction of the text, and Father cheerfully sanctions this.

Unlike the other stories, these about reading are not as ostensibly driven by a problem-solving structure. However, they are didactic sanctions of positions and relations of reading practice. The representation of reading as social action works together with closed narrative structure to constitute gendered reading positions.[66] The portrayal of reading in the secular *Fun with Dick and Jane* anticipates and prescribes its own interpretive uptake: a round-robin elementary school reading group is pictured in martial array reading a basal reading series. In Catholic "reading," a different site and set of interpretive practices and relations are presented. Father becomes the mediator of the word, but the responses of Sally and Jane model the kind of nonspeculative, literal recall and oral reading practice encouraged as part of secular "reading." The pattern that emerges is one of acquiescient reading practices. Sally is allowed to "discover" beliefs, but indeed "reading" about belief is not a speculative act, meanings are nonnegotiable and ascertained by recourse to an authoritative—not incidentally, male—reader. Hence there is an explicit prefiguring of the home literacy event. Children are encouraged towards the same skills of school-based secular "reading" but in response to religious texts and in a different context of authority relations.

What can we surmise, then, of the textually established continuity of secular and Catholic life, childhood and "stories"? Throughout the mainstream narratives, subjects are constituted by the participation in social routine and ritual, free will is asserted through undersocialized behavior (e.g., Sally), and aspiring adults Dick and Jane are constituted as non-cognate participants in adult-like roles. These gendered subjectivities are sustained, albeit in modified and augmented form, across the secular and revised narratives. Yet, in the latter, a distinct—if in some ways complementary—pattern emerges: those ascribed entities and patterns in the world are attributed to a transcendental source.

While the interleaving of secular life and Catholic life requires subtle editorial transformations in the discursive construction of subjectivities and social relations, constants remain. Males retain authoritative positions and infants require socialization; play is the primary mode of learning. But these constants are "repunctuated" and reframed. Intersubjectivity is constrained within a system of a hierarchical levels of context: individual relations, familial relations, and civic relations each are attributed to divine agency expressed through a variety of sources (e.g., "God," "The Blessed Mother," "Jesus," "Angels").

Figure 8.1 represents the discursive and social relations in the universe of Dick and Jane as a hierarchy of contextual constraints.[67] Each "higher" level constrains and defines the other: for instance, Dick's individual relations with Jack are extensions of and prefigured by his learned relations with other males and females within the family. Moreover, following the cadences of Deweyian "learning by doing," the play patterns between children are a rehearsal for roles in adult life, both in the family and in civic arenas. Family and gender relations within the extended and nuclear families in turn correspond to a model of civic life; the goal of the harmonious family is to reflect and reproduce the democratic, yet gendered and hierarchical society at large. These secular, "worldly" relationships and actions of the interpersonal, familial, and community/civic level are not canceled by the presence of an overarching religious,

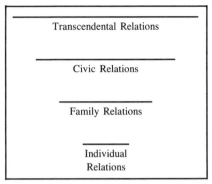

Figure 8.1. Levels of Discursive and Social
Relations in the Catholic Dick and Jane

"heavenly" context. Instead, they are intertextually informed and contextualized by the religious at another level of generality.

In this manner, the editorial inclusion of the Catholic narratives intertextually reconstructs all of the other narratives, without necessarily requiring their literal revision. Organism-environment relations are re-mediated by divine causality and arbitration, and, in several Catholic stories, secular "problems" are resolved through an actual *deus ex machina.* Even the structures of male agency—Father and Dick as the measure of all things—are re-framed and re-iterated by and through intertextual context. That is, the secular narratives, although literally the same, become different through their juxtaposition to the nonsecular Catholic narratives in the basal textbook. For agency lies not as in the secular world, with individuals (either undersocialized girls or well-socialized boys and men), but ultimately with "God." The patriarchal signifier becomes the first principle underlying all secular and nonsecular domains: the civic, the familial, and the interpersonal.[68] We might assume from this that "He" underlies the level of the Word of the textbook as well.[69]

The Incorporative Power of the Secular Textbook: The Word Re-Mediated

Texts reflect the ideological position and constraints of their genesis, and they constitute the subjectivity of their writers and readers. In related fashion, the kinds of reading that texts generate cannot be altogether attributed to the accidents and idiosyncracies of "individual" readership, for texts pragmatically prescribe the limits of their own interpretation and readership. As for the political and economic conditions of the generation of the Dick and Jane textbooks, it would appear that they represent a content-level ideology and "approach" to reading that publishers deemed to be marketable and adoptable in a broad range of national, regional, and local contexts. As for their reading(s), these texts can be seen to have produced both models of gendered subjectivity of and for the children in those locales, and models of secular and nonsecular reading practices for these same children.

Regarding the total selective tradition of literacy instruction, then, the modern basal readers developed by Gray and contemporaries consisted of the selection of ideational content, literary forms, and reading/writing practices. Inter- and postwar children were taught in early literacy training not just about the relative authority and power of particular values and genres, but about the authorized positions, practices, and sites for literacy events. The literacy taught by both the secular and Catholic texts of educational science thus was "controlled" in several senses. Scientifically designed curriculum explicitly set out to control both text content and reading practices. The total reading program— which dominates reading instruction to this day—both presented a univocal set of social messages (i.e., a version of interwar childhood in middle America) and fixed a set of practices (e.g., word recognition, recall, question-answering techniques), in effect precluding diversity of interpretation and response. Through the closure that characterized basal narratives, the possible world of Dick and Jane is placed beyond criticism, and acceptance of it becomes the inevitable result of the correct school reading.

Literacy instruction can thus be a form of ideological practice not just in terms of the overt values and surface-level messages about the world that curricular text conveys. It also dispenses a sensibility toward texts and textuality, a working knowledge of the norms governing literacy events, and the appropriate functions, uses, and sites of such events. It is curious that the secular, "scientific" skills of reading, bereft of a critical orientation toward texts and possible worlds, was seen to fit well with the reverent reading and values desired by Catholic educators. I began this discussion with an overview of the connection between reading practices, belief, and theological/state control. Although apparently different, the teacher-directed skills approach to the text extolled by educational psychologists and the acquiescent, acritical reading of scripture and Biblical study modeled by the Catholic narratives were similar in kind. Both stressed literal, object-level response, and neither placed the text's authority under critical scrutiny.

The fictions of the modern basal reader formed a unique and distinctive textual genre, a corporately generated fiction that "made" its audience as distinctively as the comic book or pulp romantic fiction. Yet the foregoing analysis of the Catholic revision of the Dick and Jane readers points to some larger textual and ideological characteristics of the modern reading textbook. Apparently, the basal reader laid out a generic shell, an ideological empty set. Just as this shell could be transformed with minor structural adjustment to accommodate other national contents,[70] it could as easily accommodate a decidedly non-secular, minority worldview. Congruent values could be added on accordingly; respect for the local policeman, the gender roles associated with auto mechanic and bus driver, and the orderliness of the suburban neighborhood went hand in glove with the rituals of praying, studying the Bible, or understanding immaculate conception.

This incorporative capacity of the texts of popular educational culture underlines the modern industrial state's ability to generate and to tolerate ideological diversity within capitalism. But the effect was to generate diversity within a sameness: in the Catholic revision, Baby Sally, Dick, and Jane retained their essential characteristics as progressive citizens, students, and children. There was also a sameness within the ostensible difference: a corporate and ultimately secular version of religious life was conveyed. As I have indicated here, the clause of divine agency intertextually re-mediated the secular text without, in fact, changing it. At the same time, the genre retained its "closed" syntactic and lexical structure and thereby asserted a comparable didactic effect on the subject/reader, regardless of surface variation in the ideational content per se. The reading practices and positions dispensed remained, regardless of clerical editorial additions and changes in the text content.

The incorporative power of the modern textbook is frequently overlooked precisely because of the public volatility of past and current disputes over textbook adoption and censorship. Overt textual content has been and continues to be a focal point for dissent, as Arons and others who have examined censorship and textbooks and First Amendment rights rightly point out.[71] But despite ongoing disputes over, for example, the selection of "controversial" literature in secondary literature curriculum, or Creationism in the science curriculum, it would be erroneous to see the contemporary textbook as constantly contested. For we hear little each year about the thousands of textbooks, produced by multinational publishers in English-speaking countries, that are adopted and taught without dispute. One reason, as we have seen here, is the capacity of the mass-produced version of secular school knowledge to incorporate difference, whether that difference is national—as in the case of "nationalized" multinational textbooks—ethnic, regional, or religious. As Gray and others in the reading research community would have assured us, from a psychological perspective "reading" is Reading—a stable, psychologically identifiable and explicable, universal, and teachable set of skills. Add to this insight the nostalgic acceptance of a version of American life unsullied by multiculturalism, bilingualism, homosexuality, and overt social conflict—and the content of the textbook is made nonproblematic.

Speaking of the capacity of narrative, through its universalization of problem-solving strategies, to normalize the social, Hodge and Kress explain that

> narrative is a culturally given way of organizing and presenting discourse . . . One effect of the use of . . . persuasive transparent signifiers is to naturalize the content of the narrative itself. By presenting various contingent cultural categories in a narrative frame, the categories themselves take on the appearance of naturalness, and come

to seem as inevitable as nature itself . . . . Narrative takes flux, incessant activity, insoluble problems, and turns them into stability, coherence, solution.[72]

In its Catholic incarnations the Dick and Jane readers provided seamless textual narratives, in which progressive childhood, the gendered division of labor and leisure in industrial democracy, the absence of social conflict, strife, or minorities were posed against the backdrop of religious orthodoxy. And the coherence of the construction of progressive childhood presented in the secular selections with the construction of Catholic childhood was naturalized: the human agency extolled by organism/environment theory was seen as having ultimate source in and reference to a deity.

Above all else, that the text should lend itself not only to adaptation by other nations but also by Catholic schools is a testament to the incorporative power of multinational textbook production. The educational propagation of a gendered American dream via mass-produced, mass-marketed corporate products apparently knew no boundaries, neither national, nor ethnic, nor religious.

Notes

1. On modern reading pedagogy, see Allan Luke, *Literacy, Textbooks and Ideology: Postwar Literacy Instruction and the Mythology of Dick and Jane* (London: Falmer Press, 1988), chap. 3; and Patrick Shannon, *Broken Promises: Reading Instruction in Twentieth Century America,* (South Hadley, Mass.: Bergin & Garvey, 1989). On "technical form" in curricular commodities, see Michael W. Apple, *Education and Power* (London: Routledge and Kegan Paul, 1983): Suzanne de Castell and Allan Luke, "Literacy Instruction: Technology and Technique," in Suzanne de Castell, Allan Luke, and Carmen Luke, eds., *Language, Authority and Criticism: Readings on the School Textbook* (London: Falmer Press, 1989), pp. 77–95.

2. For the secular versions, see William S. Gray and May Hill Arbuthnot *Fun with Dick and Jane* (Chicago: Scott Foresman, n.d.); *Our New Friends* (Chicago: Scott Foresman, n.d.); the same editions were published under license in Canada by W. J. Gage. The Catholic revisions were released as the "Cathedral Readers: Curriculum Foundation Series": see John A. O'Brien, *Fun with Dick and Jane* (Chicago: Scott Foresman, 1947), and *Our New Friends* (Chicago: Scott Foresman, 1942). All narratives cited here are drawn from these four editions.

3. Luke, *Literacy, Textbooks and Ideology;* de Castell and Luke, "Literacy Instruction"; cf. E. Wendy Saul and Jennifer Monaghan, "The Reader, The Scribe, The Thinker: A Critical Look at the History of American Reading and Writing Instruction," in Thomas S. Popkewitz, ed., *The Formation of School Subjects* (London: Falmer Press, 1987), pp. 85–122.

4. For a general review of the history of readers, see Richard L. Venezky, "A History of the American Reading Textbook," *Elementary School Journal* 87 (1987): 247–65; for specific critical analyses of nineteenth-century readers in North American schools, see Lee Soltow and Edward Stevens, *The Rise of Literacy and the Common School in the United States* (Chicago: University of Chicago Press, 1981), chap. 3; Harvey J. Graff, *The Literacy Myth: Literacy and Social Structure in the Nineteenth Century City* (New York: Academic Press, 1979); Ruth H. Elson, *Guardians of Tradition* (Lincoln, Nebr.: University of Nebraska Press, 1964).

5. Gerald Strauss, *Luther's House of Learning* (Baltimore, Md.: Johns Hopkins, 1978); Harvey J. Graff, *The Legacies of Literacy: Continuities and Contradictions in Western Culture and*

Society (Bloomington, Ind.: Indiana University Press, 1987), chap. 5; Carmen Luke, *Pedagogy, Printing, Protestantism: The Discourse on Childhood* (Albany, N.Y.: State University of New York Press, 1989).

6. Luke, *Pedagogy, Printing, Protestantism,* chap. 5.

7. On the "gaze," see Michel Foucault, *Discipline and Punish: The Birth of the Prison,* trans. Alan Sheridan (New York: Vintage, 1979).

8. Jack Goody, *The Logic of Writing and the Organization of Society* (Cambridge: Cambridge University Press, 1986), chap. 1.

9. Ibid. While the hypothesis of intrinsic cultural and cognitive effects of literacy does not hold up to cross-cultural evidence, it is indisputable that characteristics of literate technology historically have enabled sociocultural change. The argument for the "bias" of communications media can be traced to Harold A. Innis, *The Bias of Communication* (Toronto: University of Toronto Press, 1951), and Marshall McLuhan, *The Gutenberg Galaxy* (Toronto: University of Toronto Press, 1962).

10. Goody, *Logic of Writing,* pp. 6–7.

11. Jack Goody, *The Interface Between the Written and the Oral* (Cambridge: Cambridge University Press, 1987), p. 133.

12. See Goody, *Logic of Writing,* chap. 1: Graff, *Legacies of Literacy,* chap. 1.

13. See Goody, *Logic of Writing.*

14. Shirley B. Heath, "Protean Shapes in Literacy Events: Ever-Shifting Oral and Literate Traditions," in Deborah Tannen, ed., *Spoken and Written Language: Exploring Orality and Literacy* (Norwood, N.J.: Ablex, 1982), p. 93.

15. Goody, *Interface Between the Written and the Oral,* p. 139.

16. See Graff, *Legacies of Literacy.*

17. Cited in Natalie Zemon Davis, *Society and Culture in Early Modern France* (Cambridge, England: Polity, 1987), p. 76.

18. Ibid.: Graff, *Legacies of Literacy,* chap. 5.

19. For examples, see Francois Furet and Jacques Ozouf, *Reading and Writing: Literacy in France from Calvin to Jules Ferry* (Cambridge: Cambridge University Press, 1982); Rab Houston, "The Literacy Campaigns in Scotland, 1560–1803," in Robert F. Arnove and Harvey J. Graff, eds., *National Literacy Campaigns: Historical and Comparative Perspectives* (New York: Plenum, 1987), p. 53.

20. Davis, *Society and Culture,* p. 222.

21. Ibid.

22. Ibid.

23. Cited in Neil G. McClusky, *Catholic Viewpoint on Education* (New York: Doubleday, 1966), p. 9.

24. Davis, *Society and Culture,* p. 221.

25. Soltow and Stevens, *Rise of Literacy,* pp. 59–60.

26. Cited in McClusky, *Catholic Viewpoint,* p. 11.

27. See Soltow and Stevens, *Rise of Literacy,* and Graff, *Literacy Myth.*

28. McClusky, *Catholic Viewpoint,* p. 14; see also Andrew M. Greeley and Peter H. Rossi, *The Education of Catholic Americans* (Chicago: Aldine, 1966), chap. 1.

29. Cited in Edward M. Connors, *Church-State Relationships* (Washington, D. C.: Catholic University Press, 1951), p. 56.

30. I am endebted to Gabriel Oriti for this point; see J. Likoudis and D. K. Whitehead, *The Pope, the Council and the Mass* (Boston: Christopher Publishing, 1981), p. 23.

31. Beryl A. Smalley, *The Study of the Bible in the Middle Ages,* 3d ed. (Oxford: Blackwell, 1983), p. 99.

32. For a review, see Cushla Kapitzke, "Literacy as Ideological Practice: A Case Study of Literate Practices in a Community Church," doctoral dissertation (in preparation), James Cook University of North Queensland, chap. 1.

33. For a discussion of the cultural and economic bases of these movements, see Francis Fitzgerald, *Cities on a Hill* (New York: Simon and Schuster, 1986), chap. 3 and 6.

34. Caroline Zinsser, "For the Bible Tells Me So: Teaching Children in a Fundamentalist Church," in Bambi B. Schieffelin and Perry Gilmore, eds., *The Acquisition of Literacy: Ethnographic Perspectives* (Norwood, N.J.: Ablex, 1986), pp. 55–71.

35. Zinsser, "For the Bible Tells Me So," p. 68. For a contrasting description of how this textual "literalness" figures in a small fundamentalist secondary school, see Alan Peshkin, *God's Choice: The Total World of a Fundamentalist Christian School* (Chicago: University of Chicago Press, 1986). On the (textual) rituals and semiotic systems of modern Catholic schools, see Peter McLaren, *Schooling as Ritual Performance* (London: Routlege and Kegan Paul, 1986); Nancy Lesko, *Symbolizing Society: Stories, Rites and Structure in a Catholic High School* (London: Falmer Press, 1988).

36. These ritual ways with text may or may not be contiguous with the competence demanded in "mainstream" public schooling. Consequently, religious socialization into particular ways of using text may have larger implications for children's educational achievement: see Shirley B. Heath, *Ways with Words: Language, Life and Work in Classrooms and Communities* (Cambridge: Cambridge University Press, 1983), pp. 113–66; "What No Bedtime Story Means," *Language in Society* 11 (1982): 49–77. Heath describes Carolina white children who learn a community and family ethic of "saying it right": that is, their total linguistic socialization matches a particular (church-related) moral epistemology. Heath's analysis points to the ties between these children's learned ways with words, their literal approach to text, and the subsequent difficulty many experienced with interpretive, comprehension tasks in middle primary school.

37. Legal conflict over curricular content since the beginning of this century can be attributed in part to the ethnic and religious diversity of the U.S. population and to the enforcement and extension of compulsory schooling; the nineteenth-century United States was a de facto Protestant state. On the role of religious belief in controversies over textbook adoption and censorship, see Stephen Arons, "Lessons in Law and Conscience: Legal Aspects of Textbook Adoption and Censorship," in de Castell, Luke, and Luke, eds., *Language, Authority and Criticism,* pp. 203–19: the role of ideological, cultural, and religious diversity in the enactment of state law regarding curriculum and textbook adoption is taken up in David Tyack, Thomas James, and Aaron Benavot, *Law and the Shaping of Public Education, 1785–1954* (Madison, Wis.: University of Wisconsin Press, 1987).

38. Goody, *Logic of Writing,* p. 12.

39. On the distinction between "true" and "practical" discourses, see Michel Foucault, "Questions of Method," *Ideology and Consciousness* 8 (1981): 4–14.

40. Edward G. Boring, *A History of Experimental Psychology* (New York: Appleton-Century Crofts, 1950), chaps. 21 and 22.

41. See, for example, Edmund B. Huey, *The Psychology and Pedagogy of Reading* (New York: MacMillan, 1908).

42. Edward L. Thorndike, "Reading as Reasoning: A Study of Mistakes in Paragraph Reading," *Journal of Educational Psychology* 8 (1917): 323–32; "The Understanding of Sentences: A Study of Errors in Reading," *Elementary School Journal* 28 (1917): 98–114; William S. Gray, *Studies of Elementary School Reading through Standardized Tests* (Chicago: University of Chicago Press, 1917); Charles Judd and Guy Buswell, *Silent Reading: A Study of Various Types* (Chicago: University of Chicago Press, 1922).

43. Thorndike, "Reading as Reasoning" and "The Understanding of Sentences."

44. This practical calculus continues to guide approaches to reading pedagogy. On the problems with the testing of discursively constructed entities, see Cleo H. Cherryholmes, *Power and Criticism: Poststructural Investigations in Education* (New York: Teachers College Press, 1988), chap. 6; on the assignment of etiological metaphors to discursively constituted phenomena, see Alec W. McHoul, "Language and the Sociology of Mind: An Critical Introduction to the Work of Jeff Coulter," *Journal of Pragmatics* 12 (1988): 339–86.

45. Edward L. Thorndike and Arthur Gates, *Elementary Principles of Education* (New York: Macmillan, 1929), p. 242.

46. B. F. Skinner, *The Technology of Teaching* (New York: Appleton-Century Crofts, 1968).

47. Luke, *Literacy, Textbooks and Ideology,* chap. 6.

48. Nila B. Smith, *American Reading Instruction* (Newark, Del.: International Reading Association, 1965), p. 154.

49. The description of the secular Dick and Jane textbooks in this section is drawn from Luke, *Literacy, Textbooks and Ideology,* chap. 4.

50. This appears to be a textual and curricular interpolation of the Deweyian notion that growth proceeds through the experiential overcoming of obstacles that arise in the organism/environment relationship, described in Dewey's *Democracy in Education* (New York: Macmillan, 1916), pp. 74–81, and clearly articulated in his *Art as Experience* (New York: Putnam, 1958). However, Dewey's warning that schooling should not work toward the "conservative" end of "reproducing current habits" of a "static society" but rather endeavor to engage children in "continuous reconstruction" does not seem to have been heeded by the Dick and Jane authors.

51. On semiotic frames, see Robert Hodge and Gunther Kress, *Social Semiotics* (Cambridge, England: Polity Press, 1988), pp. 229–39.

52. Umberto Eco, *The Role of the Reader* (Bloomington, Ind.: Indiana University Press, 1979), pp. 117–18.

53. This intratextual autonomy of narratives within the modern basal textbook, of course, serves distinct pedagogical purposes: each narrative can be allocated to a limited and self-contained lesson.

54. The goal of vocabulary control was to build, incrementally, sight word recognition and knowledge. To this day most reading textbooks are assembled and edited according to core word lists of the type initially developed by Thorndike, Dolch, Gates, and others. *Fun with Dick and Jane* features ninety-nine new words; *Our New Friends* features 189.

55. On gendered verb assignments in current basal readers, see Carolyn D. Baker and Peter Freebody, *Children's First Schoolbooks: Introductions to the Culture of Literacy* (Oxford: Blackwell, 1989).

56. See Gunther Kress, "History and Language: Towards a Social Account of Linguistic

Change," *Journal of Pragmatics* 13, no. 3 (1989), in press: Gunther Kress and Robert Hodge, *Language as Ideology* (London: Routledge and Kegan Paul, 1979), chap. 4 and 6.

57. Allan Luke, "Open and Closed Texts: The Semantic/Ideological Analysis of Textbook Narratives," *Journal of Pragmatics* 13 (1989): 55–80.

58. Jacob L. Mey, "Gagner la parole sans perdre sa view ou somme zéro dans le jeu de langage," *Language et Société* 33 (1985): 33–42.

59. See Allan Luke and Carolyn D. Baker, eds., *Towards a Critical Sociology of Reading Pedagogy* (Amsterdam: John Benjamins, 1991); Allan Luke and Carmen Luke, "School Knowledge as Simulation: Curriculum in Postmodern Conditions," *Discourse* 10, no. 2 (1990).

60. Here I draw discourse analytic methods and perspectives from Luke, *Literacy, Textbooks and Ideology;* Baker and Freebody, *Children's First Schoolbooks;* Kress, "History and Language"; Kress and Hodge, *Language as Ideology;* Hodge and Kress, *Social Semiotics.*

61. On "agentiveness," see Kress, "History and Language"; Kress and Hodge, *Language as Ideology,* chap. 2.

62. On "didactic reiterations", see Luke, *Literacy, Textbooks and Ideology,* pp. 95–97.

63. Kress (personal communication, February 1, 1989) offers an alternative reading of Sally's move. He argues that that this is "not a transformation (i.e. the result of syntactic processes) but a reclassification . . . which represents the (gendered) differentiated selection from the set of transitivity forms available to a non-adult female." These different readings, as Kress rightly argues, mark out a "fundamental ideological dilemma" not only for critical linguistics, but also for a political sociology of the curriculum: the relative roles of agency and structure in the production of texts and utterances, both "real" and fictive. While Kress's reading "foregrounds *choice* from differentiated paradigms/discourses," emphasizing agency, the reading here "focuses on the act of transformation by subjects, from single a paradigm/ discourse," emphasizing structure.

64. Luke, *Literacy, Textbooks and Ideology,* p. 89.

65. For an explanation of the "story grammar" format used here, see ibid., pp. 31–39.

66. On gendered reading positions, see Mary Jacobus, *Reading Woman: Essays in Feminist Criticism* (New York: Columbia University Press, 1986), pp. 51–52.

67. This model of a "hierarchy of constraints" governing communication and exchange is drawn from Anthony Wilden, *System and Structure: Essays in Communication and Exchange,* 2d ed. (London: Tavistock, 1981): "Semiotics as Praxis: Strategy and Tactics," *Semiotic Inquiry* 1 (1981): 1–34; *The Rules Are No Game* (London: Routledge and Kegan Paul, 1987).

68. On gendered subjectivity in Catholic discourse, see Chris Weedon, *Feminist Practice and Poststructuralist Theory* (Oxford: Blackwell, 1987), pp. 96–97.

69. On woman's positioning as subject and entering into language via masculinist narrative, see Teresa de Lauretis, *Alice Doesn't: Feminism, Semiotics, Cinema* (Bloomington, Ind.: Indiana University Press, 1984).

70. On the "nationalization" of textbooks by editorial branch plants, see Rowland Lorimer, "The Business of Literacy: The Making of the Educational Textbook," in Suzanne de Castell, Allan Luke, and Kieran Egan, eds., *Literacy, Society and Schooling* (Cambridge: Cambridge University Press, 1986), pp. 132–44.

71. Arons, "Lessons in Law and Conscience."

72. Hodge and Kress, *Social Semiotics,* p. 230.

9

Readers, Texts, and Contexts:
Adolescent Romance Fiction in Schools

Linda K. Christian-Smith

An important theme in this volume is the central role played by written texts in ongoing ideological struggles for students' hearts and minds. School texts have often been a mode of social control through the "selective tradition" contained within their pages, which elevates the stories of powerful groups to the level of canon.[1] However, students are not some tabula rasa upon which the text inscribes their social identities. Rather, students approach texts from the position of their previously acquired gender, class, racial, ethnic, age, and sexual identities, which mesh with the words on the page. While texts may solidify students' social identities, there is also the potential for unsettling them through oppositional readings. The reading practices of actual students indicate that interpretation is characterized by variety and unpredictability rather than by certainty. Books are, as Foucault[2] observes, a mode of discourse whose authority and meaning is shaped and constrained within a field of use and negotiation. The knowledge and resistances that readers bring to reading also shape textual meaning, as Fetterly[3] and Morely[4] argue. Reading can become an act of opposition to dominant curriculum arrangements by students who feel oppressed and powerless. The text as a source of multiple, often contradictory meanings is especially apparent in today's popular teen romance novels, which exemplify how young women readers come to grips with the world and also refashion it.

In this chapter, I discuss how middle-and working-class young women, ages twelve through fifteen from diverse racial and ethnic backgrounds, construct their femininity while reading adolescent romance fiction in school. I analyze how the political climate of both the larger society and the classroom shape and constrain meaning production. I also consider the ways in which romance-novel reading relates to readers' future expectations as women. I begin by providing a context for romance fiction in schools by reference to recent events within American society and their relation to the romance publishing industry.

The Politics of the Romance

When young women read teen romance novels, they enter the world of a $500 million a year industry[5] whose stock in trade is not only fantasies of love and specialness but also politics. Teen romance fiction articulates the long-standing fears and resentments of segments of society regarding feminism and women's growing independence. Teen romance-fiction reading involves the shaping of consciousness as well as the occasion for young women to reflect on their fears, hopes, and dreams. The rise of teen romance novels to the third most widely read young adult book[6] in only ten years[7] parallels the shift in the political climate of the United States to the right-wing positions of Reaganism characterized by traditional perspectives on the family and gender relations.[8] For woven throughout teen romance fiction's saga of hearts and flowers is the discourse that a woman is incomplete without a man, that motherhood is women's destiny, and that women's rightful place is in the home. These themes are a part of the New Right's political, cultural, and economic agenda.[9] According-ing to Hall,[10] a key element here is winning the consent of the public by tapping into fears, needs, and dreams, and then using them to shape a new political consensus. Teen romance fiction represents the point of convergence of the struggle for gender hegemony, for the hearts and minds of young women. I am not implying an outright conspiracy against women. Rather, many segments of the culture industry, particularily publishing, are owned by multinational corporations[11]whose interests are politically conservative. These interests make their way into publishing through business practices and the content of books.

In early 1980 Ronald Reagan became president of the United States, and, in the same year, the first new teen romance series, "Wildfire," published by Scholastic Books, appeared in the bookstores. The concept of romance fiction written for teens dates back to the 1940s and 1950s, when Betty Cavanna, Maureen Daly, and Rosamond du Jardin wrote books focusing on young women's first love experience. The new romances have reappeared in the midst of several large-scale mergers within educational and trade publishing that have had the effect on endowing profit and loss sheets with a new importance.[12] Other changes are apparent. Editors in the old-fashioned sense are no longer key people. Rather, professional managers with business or legal backgrounds now occupy key decision-making positions. A consistent worry expressed by insiders in publishing[13] is that this business mentality may be narrowing the range of books published, making it difficult for initially unprofitable but im-portant books to be published. Teen romances are a response to dominant pub-lishing interests that center on profitability and instant appeal.[14]

One way in which publishers today increase their profit margins is to cultivate constantly new reader markets, and develop new books for existing ones.[15] Harty[16] notes that the schools have historically constituted a lucrative market for publishers. According to *Publishers Weekly,* in 1984 the schools spent $695.6 million on books, making the schools the third largest account— only surpassed by general retailers and college bookstores. Although textbooks comprise the bulk of these sales, the trade division is growing steadily as more schools use these general interest books for instruction along with or in place of textbooks.[17] Teenage romance fiction is a case of publishers developing new readers and books within a steady market. It is the product of school bookclub (TAB) market research conducted by Scholastic Inc., a leader in the el-hi (elementary and high school) market, regarding which books were most frequently ordered by young women readers.[18]

Teen romance novels also appear as components of a highly lucrative segment of educational publishing, the Hi-Low market, which is comprised of books with "interesting" content and limited difficulty of reading[19] aimed at "reluctant readers." Reluctant readers are often students who may be able to read, but refuse to do because they are disinterested in reading materials, or have some actual reading difficulties.[20] Aulls[21] suggests that reluctant readers can be best taught to read using Hi-Low materials. Series romance fiction shares all the characteristics of many Hi-Lows, especially the differentiation of content on the basis of gender. For example, Scholastic's *Action* books feature mystery and adventure for boys and romance, dating and problem novels for girls. The demand from teachers and librarians for reluctant-reader materials has increased in the wake of recent national debate[22] about both the imputed difficulty of many students in learning to read, and their boredom with standard reading texts such as basals.

However, the appearance of romance fiction has not been without controversy. Lanes[23] notes that in her interviews with educators, parents, and librarians general reactions ranged from annoyance to rage. Romance fiction has been criticized for its "limited roles for females" and their depiction of "a narrow, little world" in which virtue is rewarded with the right boy's love.[24] The most vocal critics, The Council on Interracial Books for Children, claims that the books teach young women to put boys' interests above their own, encourage young women to compete against each other for boys, and depict the life of suburban White middle-class nuclear families.[25] Others identify the new romance fiction with the political ideology of the New Right.[26] Still others have criticized the way in which romance fiction gets into the hands of young readers—primarily through school bookclubs.[27]

Despite these controversies and adults' misgivings, teen romance fiction remains a force to be reckoned with: it is immensely popular with young women readers, and plays a significant role in constructing their hopes and dreams for the future.

The Research Context

During an eight-month period in 1985–86, I studied teen romance-fiction readers in three schools in a large American midwestern city that I will call "Lakeview."[28] Once dominated by the automobile, farm-equipment, and alcoholic-beverage industries, the economic crisis of the late 1970s left its imprint of the city and surrounding communities. Plant closings have transformed Lakeview from a smokestack city to one of empty factories and glittering strip-malls. Most new businesses are in the service sector, such as fast-food and insurance companies, and employ the bulk of the working- and middle-class women and men in Lakeview.

Lakeview School District is a large district that draws students from the inner city and some of the outlying areas that were annexed to the city thirty years ago. My sites of research were Jefferson Middle School and Sherwood Park Middle School, two outlying 7-8 schools, and Kominsky Junior High School, an inner city 7-9 school. At the time of the study, Lakeview was in the process of converting the junior high schools into middle schools. Jefferson and Sherwood Park each had about three hundred students. Sherwood Park's student population was mostly White. Like Sherwood Park, Jefferson was predominately White, but had three Chinese students as well. Kominsky's 700+ student body was about one-half White, one-quarter each Black and Hispanic, with a small Vietnamese and Asian Indian population. Both Jefferson and Sherwood Park split their students into three tracks (low, medium, and high)[29] for reading instruction. Reading placements were based on the results of the following: district-wide and individual-school standardized reading test scores, teacher recommendation, and students' previous grades. Kominsky and Sherwood Park also had an additional reading support service through the federally funded Chapter I program, which enrolled one-half and one-quarter, respectively of their students.[30]

In order to study readers and their romance novels I used a variety of methods combining ethnography with survey research.[31] An initial sample of seventy-five young women from the three schools was assembled through interviews with teachers and librarians regarding who were heavy romance-fiction readers and by personal examination of school and classroom library checkout cards and bookclub order forms.[32] A reading survey[33] was given to all seventy-five young women. From this survey, I was able to identify the heaviest romance-fiction readers, some twenty-nine young women, whom I interviewed individually and in small group settings. These twenty-nine young women had five teachers for reading in the three schools. I observed these classes and interviewed these teachers. This chapter stems from the written reading survey of the seventy-five young women, and from observation of and interviews with the twenty-nine young women and their five teachers.

Romance Novels in Classrooms

Who reads teen romance fiction? My reading survey shows the that at Jefferson and Sherwood Park, the novels tended to be read by White middle-class young women ages twelve through fifteen, and to a lesser degree, by Black, Hispanic, and Asian young women at all three schools.[34] At Jefferson and Sherwood Park, romance novels accounted for thirty-six percent of all books checked out from school libraries and ordered through bookclubs as compared to twenty-five percent at Kominsky. This is in keeping with recent Book Industry surveys that have placed romance fiction within the top three kinds of books that adolescents read.[35] Another characteristic of readers concerns how readers were grouped for reading instruction. The twenty-nine young women were identified by school personnel as "reluctant" or "slow" readers and were tracked into remedial or low ability reading classes. This pattern was repeated in their math and English classes as well. These young women were also characterized by counselors and teachers as being more interested in boys than in academics, as young women who would have difficulty completing the remainder of their schooling and who would in all probability, marry early and be young mothers.

The twenty-nine young women's five reading teachers provided much insight into the complexity of teen romance fiction in schools. Three teachers were aware of the national controversy surrounding these books, and all felt some degree of apprehension regarding their use. The contradictory position of teachers is nicely illustrated by the observations of Mrs. M. (Kominsky) and Mrs. K. (Sherwood Park), both White middle-class teachers:[36]

> I feel guilty about letting the girls order these books through TAB [a school bookclub]. I read a couple of them once. They are so simple and the characters in the novels are stereotypes. You know, Mom at home in her apron, Dad reading the paper with his feet up. But the girls seem to like the books, and the classroom sure is quiet when they're reading them.

> The girls just love them [romance novels]. I see them reading their books in study hall and even in lunch. Can you believe that! I'm just happy that they are reading, period.

The romance-novel reading in these teachers' classrooms was the outcome of factors that indicate the delicate interplay of readers, teachers, texts, and context. The teachers' overwhelming desire to see students reading and reasonably interested in books generated Mrs. K.'s idea that "any reading was better than no reading." Teachers were also under tremendous pressure from the administration to improve students' measured reading scores. In the case of the Chapter I teachers Mrs. K. and Mrs. M., those scores were key ingredients in retaining yearly federal funding of their programs, and by implication, their jobs. All five teachers conceded the difficulty of keeping order in classrooms where students resisted instruction. Securing students' consent to read voluntarily made teachers' lives in the classroom "tolerable."

Most romance-novel reading occurred during independent study, which was in great abundance as instruction was mostly organized around individual-learning models to provide for the specific needs and interests of each student. This was especially the case in Sherwood Park and Kominsky. During the usual classroom period in each school, students read or worked on skill sheets. Student and teacher interactions were mostly limited to correcting skill sheets, updating reading folders, giving directions, and answering procedural questions. Students mostly read privately and rarely shared their reading with their teachers or other students.

Although most books were student-selected, teachers attempted to influence book choice by categorizing books as "quality"[37] award-winning books[38] or "fluff" books, like romances. That students did not automatically accept teachers' authority regarding book choice is illustrated by Mrs. B., a White middle-class Kominsky Chapter I teacher, and five of her students. As a strong advocate of "quality" teen literature, Mrs. B.'s room was crammed with an array of "quality" paperbacks, magazines, and newspapers. No romance fiction was to be found in this classroom library. The young women brought romance fiction from home or libraries, and often bought them from mail-order book-clubs. Mrs. B. more or less tolerated the romances in her classroom. This tolerance was the outcome of both pressure from the administration to show reading gains and protest from five young women.

Of all the teachers, Mrs. B. felt most apprehensive about granting any legitimacy to romance fiction. She fit the romances into her "quality literature" perspective by striking a bargain with her students: for every romance novel read, a student must read another type of book. The reality was that Mrs. B. hoped to draw the interest of the young women away from the romance fiction so that they would expand their reading to "quality" books. This tension was revealed in Mrs. B.'s exhortation during weekly library visits to "choose something good, something you'll want to stick with." When students inquired into the reasons behind Mrs. B.'s. dislike of romances, she neither offered any explanation nor encouraged any critical dialogue with romance-fiction readers about their reading.

Five of Mrs. B.'s students took matters into their own hands by fiercely championing romance-novel reading. Tina, a White working-class student, quoted Mrs. B.'s words "Read something interesting," to defend her choices. Tomeika and Jan, Black and White students from middle-and working-class backgrounds, respectively, supported their reading tastes by citing their mothers' devotion to the books. White middle-class Carol saw romance fiction as something truly pleasurable to read, in contrast to her other schoolbooks. Finally, all five young women would languish over teacher-selected books, mutilating the pages and covers, and complaining how boring the books were. Or they would retire to the "book-nook" and covertly read their favorite romances, which they had stashed among the floor cushions.

This discussion displays how some young women reinterpreted school policy regarding as to which texts have legitimacy and authority in the classroom. A teacher's attempts to impose her authority to choose texts had the effect of hardening the resolve of these young women to continue their reading. By resisting this authority, the young women wrested some control over the reading curriculum away from the teacher. However, as I will show later, this practice contained certain contradictions when viewed in light of their school experiences and their definitions of femininity.

Readers and Romances

An amazing amount of romance-fiction reading was done by the twenty-nine young women. Allowing for the fact that some young women were more avid readers than others, the young women as a whole read an average of six romances a month at home and school.[39] However, these young women were not indiscriminate in their romance-fiction reading—that is, not just any romance novel would do.[40]

Most of the young women were loyal to certain individual authors such as Stella Pevsner, Ellen Conford, Norma Fox Mazer, and Francine Pascal. High on their lists were also romance-fiction lines such as Silhouette'a "First Love" and "Blossom Valley," Scholastic's "Wildfire" and Bantam's "Sweet Dreams" and "Sweet Valley High." These novels were favored because they provided an easy and cheap way of securing books, through a bookclub. More important for Silhouette readers was the fact that Silhouette publishes a newletter soliciting letters from readers. The young women viewed the newsletter as important because in the words of Val, a working-class Hispanic student at Kominsky, "They [Silhouette] care about what we want in books . . I wrote once about a book I hated. I even got a letter back from Mrs. Jackson [an editor]. Funny thing, nobody ever asks us our opinions about nothing." That these opinion polls are part of Silhouette's sophisticated marketing program does not detract from the positive impact they had on these young women. The overall effect was to provide them with the experience of having their voices heard.

Why Young Women Read Romance Novels

In many ways, young women's reasons for reading romances compare with those of adult romance-fiction readers in Radway's (1984) study. In both studies the reasons combined elements of fantasy, knowledge and pleasure.

The seventy-five young women felt that romance fiction offered the following things:

1. Escape, a way to get away from problems at home and school.
2. Better reading than dreary textbooks.
3. Enjoyment and pleasure.
4. A way to learn about romance and dating.

The theme of escape from problems emerged over and over again. Some young women recounted how romance novels provided them with glimpses of a world quite different from their own: no family problems and always a solution to any conflict. Mary Jo, a fourteen year-old White middle-class student at Sherwood Park, commented that the romance novels portrayed the world as ''I would like it to be.'' The happy resolution of family problems in the romances of Francine Pascal was especially appealing to twelve year-old Carrie, a Black middle-class student at Kominsky. Carrie said: ''In her books things get all mixed up like fights and other stuff, but basically people still love each other. I'd love to have a family like the Martin's [in *My First Love and Other Disasters*]. Sometimes when I read I kind of pretend that the family in the story is my family.''

Precisely why romance-novel reading was highly valued in school is evident from the words of Claire, a White working-class student at Sherwood Park: ''It's really a bore 'round here. Readin' Sweet Valley turns the worst day into something special.'' Furthermore, romance-novel reading provided the young women with the space to engage in something truly pleasurable and personal during the school day. The books left them with the same good feelings as meeting with their friends at lunch and in the halls. The companionship of other students and romance reading sustained them through an otherwise tedious school day.

There was yet another aspect of the pleasure of the text. This involved the positive feelings that came from identifying with romance-fiction heroines. Without exception, these heroines were smart, funny, and resourceful. Being recognized as someone special, with the qualities of niceness, intelligence, and humor, was important to these young women. They were all aware of the social and academic significance of their placement in low-ability reading classes, and many of them felt that their teachers did not see them as intelligent or nice people. This desire to identify with a smart heroine coincided with the young women's desire to have teachers and other adults regard them as nice and capable, despite their academic placement.

The romance novels also were connected with the pleasure young women derived from imagining themselves as the heroine of one of these novels. Through their reading, they lived out much of the specialness and excitement associated with being the object of a boy's affection. Much of this desire seemed to hinge on their perception of romantic relationships in fiction as eminently satisfying, with all minor misunderstandings eventually resolved. However, very few of the young women envisioned romance in everyday life as anything like romance fiction. Pam, a fifteen year-old White working-class student at Jefferson, sums up the feelings of several of the young women:

> Nobody has these neat boyfriends. I mean, most of the guys boss you around . . . and bash you if you look at somebody else. But it's fun to read the books and think that maybe someday you'll meet a really nice guy who'll be good to you.

The novels operated at a distance from young women's own lives and provided a comfort zone where there were no consequences for risking all for love.

This process of identification was also evident when there was a mismatch between the young women's own lived romances and those they encountered in fiction. Marge, a Black working-class student at Kominsky, claimed that most of the romances she read did not accurately portray romantic relationships as she encountered them in everyday life.[41] By the same token, Marge wished the boys she knew were more like the boys in the novels: "treatin' you good. Not bossin' you 'round and tryin' to hit on you all the time." Marge went on to note that young women would probably always have to "fight off" the unwanted attention of boys, but that it would be nice to dream it could be otherwise. The romance novels provided Marge and Pam with the dream of an ideal romance. Romance-fiction reading allowed both of these young women to transform present and future romantic relations in imagination, according to their aspirations.

The romances gave the young women who were not dating, and some of the more shy young women, the opportunity to take romantic risks without consequences. Trina, a thirteen-year-old Chinese middle-class student at Jefferson, noted that "sometimes the way guys are in the books helps us girls understand them a lot better." This primer quality of romance fiction found favor with thirteen-year-old Marita, a working-class Hispanic Kominsky student. Marita's reading provided a valuable source of information about romance. Marita's family strictly controlled her whereabouts. Neither she nor her sisters were permitted to date until they were seventeen and her older sisters were not open with her about their experiences. Marita related that several of her friends were in similar situations and depended on the romance novels for information.

The Book of Love

Readers had very definite ideas about what made up a good romance novel. These centered on characteristics of the heroine and hero. The good romance novel has the following characteristics:

1. It is easy to read.
2. It does not drag.
3. Its heroine and hero are cute, popular, and nice, and have money.
4. It has a happy ending.
5. In it young women are strong and get the best of boys.

The appeal of many of the series romances is that they contain about 150 to 175 action-packed pages of easy reading. The young women placed a premium on these structural characteristics and on their ease in relating the books to their lives. Pat, a White middle-class student at Jefferson, explained that the novels "Are sure easy to read. I know all the words and don't have to skip any of 'em."

However, this preference for easy reading had unexpected consequences for the young women. Mrs. T., a White middle-class reading teacher at Jefferson saw a reciprocal, reinforcing relationship between the romances and the young women's status in the schools:

Some of the girls show great impatience at reading books that are long or contain a great deal of exposition. That's why they like romance novels. Sure, they like to read about boys—that's all they have on their minds. But they do like anything that's easy and doesn't make them think. The romances are mindless drivel.

Other teachers commented that the young women "only do what they have to do get by." In the eyes of teachers and school officials, romance fiction became emblematic of the young women's identities as reluctant readers. Stated another way, the young women's preference for easy reading "fixed" their identities in teachers' minds as pupils who seek "the easy route" in school and in life.

Young women also had definite ideas about what constituted an ideal heroine and hero. The former should be "pretty, smart, and popular." The preference for a popular heroine was closely linked to these young women's personal desires to be liked by both sexes in their everyday lives. Another priority was to be cherished and treated well by a nice boy. Those characteristics that helped heroines attract boys were precisely the ones they wished for in their own lives. The ideal hero had some similarities to the heroine. He should be "cute," "funny," "strong," "nice," "have money," and "come from a good home." While cuteness was certainly important, niceness and strength were indispensable. "Strength" for these women, did not have to do with physical prowess, but rather stood for an array of attributes such as courage, initiative, and protectiveness. The young women were repelled by teenage versions of the "macho man" in books and everyday experience. As Karen, a White middle-class student at Sherwood Park explained, "When I read a book, the guy has to be nice, has to be, he has to treat his girlfriend and everybody with respect." This notion of respect had much to do with the hero's being attuned to the heroine's needs and feelings. In these young women's real lives, there was the occasional boy who reminded them of the romance-novel hero, but mostly the boys they knew did not measure up to this ideal.

According to several young women, romance fiction should end happily, that is, the heroine and hero should have ironed out their difficulties, and become once again a couple by the end of the story. The overwhelming preference for a happy ending closely relates to the romance novel's power to involve the young women vicariously in the developing romance. Several of the older readers, who were romantically involved themselves, looked to romance fiction to provide in fantasy the hoped-for outcome of their own romances. Patty, a fifteen-year-old White working-class student at Kominsky exemplifies this position: "It would be nice to think that Tommy and me would end up like Janine and Craig [the couple from the popular *Blossom Valley* series], you know, married with kids and having a nice home, car, and money." The saga of this fictional couple's romance, separation, and eventual marriage held out to this reader the possibility of living happily ever after.

The final quality of a good romance novel was that it had to have a heroine who is strong and assertive, especially toward boys. May, a Black working-class Kominsky student, strongly expressed this sentiment: "I've got no patience with girls who let boys walk all over them. Believe you me, no boy mess with me or he be sorry." Linked with this preference for assertive heroines was a distinct pleasure in reading about heroines who "got the best of boys." In this regard, Victoria Martin of *My First Love and Other Disasters* (by popular writer Francine Pascal) was mentioned by several young women as a heroine whose courage and forthrightness they admired. This notion of "besting boys," "keeping them in line," was most often applied to situations where the heroine knew best, when the hero was treading on "female things" or trying to compel the heroine to do things against her beliefs.

So far I have indicated the fluid and often contradictory quality of these readers' interactions with texts where story-world and lived experience meet. An underlying theme is how readers' gender subjectivity is shaped through their reading. I will now discuss the dynamics at work during reading that help create young women's femininity, but also provide them with the occasion for pondering that femininity as well.

Creating and Pondering Femininity

I want to return to my earlier observations on the role of the text in shaping gender meanings. Although readers' life experiences are important in constructing meaning when reading, the text still exerts a measure of control over those meanings. In this regard, Iser[42] claims that the text's control happens through "blanks" or gaps in the text. Many times the threads of the plot are suddenly broken off, as happens between chapters. Or they continue in unexpected directions. These textual features prompt readers to "read between the lines." The blanks call for combining what has been previously read with readers' own life experiences and expectations. Although teen romance novels are not characterized by many unexpected twists and turns, they nevertheless require a certain amount of constitutive activity on the part of readers. When female readers encounter blanks in romance texts that involve matters of femininity, two things occur. Readers are offered models of femininity, but are also given opportunities to think about femininity. I will exemplify this dynamic by recounting the readings by three young women of Marshall's *Against the Odds*[43]

Annie, Marcy and Nancy, three White middle-class eighth-grade students in at Sherwood Park, all in Mrs. J.'s reading class, had recently read *Against the Odds*. This novel describes the struggles of four young women, Trina, Laurie, Joyce, and Marsha, who are among a group of twenty-five young women registering as new students at the all-male Whitman High School. This school's ninety-year history as an elite all-male college preparatory institution is about to change under court mandated affirmative action, and the four young women have decided to attend Whitman because it has the strong math and computer-science curriculum their old school lacks. The young women are initially greeted with protest signs of "No Girls at Whitman High!," catcalling, and constant harrassment. The young women confront the troublemakers and establish themselves as serious students. Trina in particular wins the respect, admiration, and affection of the most hardboiled of all the boys, Chris Edwards. The novel ends with the vision of a romantically involved Trina and Chris, and with the promise of a more gentle "battle of the sexes."

All the young women agreed that heroine Trina Singleton caused them to think about themselves as young women. Nancy clearly expressed this in her comments on her favorite romance heroine: "That's gotta be Trina Singleton in *Against the Odds*. Trina is the kind of person I want to be 'cause she's not afraid to fight for her rights, while another girl might chicken out."

Against the Odds has certain blanks that invite completion as part of the developing story and characterization as they develop. At one point, Trina and her friends have a plan to revenge themselves for all they have endured and to put a stop to the harrassment once and for all. Readers are left to contemplate what this plan might be for several pages, and even then it is only gradually unfolded. Annie filled the blanks in this manner:

A: It was fun trying to figure out what Trina and the other girls would do to get back at those boys. I thought that they would sneak into the boys' locker room and do something to their sports equipment. Marsha had the guts to do something like that.

LKCS: Was that something you might have done?

A: Are you kidding? No way! I'd never have the guts. Well, you'd have to do something, that's for sure. Hmm, I'd probably start a rumor about the guys or every time me and my friends would see them we would make like we were talking about them. They can't stand that!

Marcy's responses to the same passage also set up a conflict between who she is and who she would like to be:

M: I figured Trina and Laurie would come up with something fantastic. I never thought in a million years that they would stuff confetti drenched in cheap perfume into the boys' lockers.

LKCS: Would you do that, get even in this way?

M: Well, I'd like to do something like that, to get even with some of the boys in my math class who are real pains. But I'd get chicken and probably just fume.

LKCS: Can you tell me more?

M: It's kinda difficult, I mean, well, I guess I don't want to be seen as a girl who's too pushy with boys. You have to be careful about that. But then you can't let the boys push you around. I don't know.

Annie's and Marcy's hypothesizing revealed several things about the reader-text-context relation. For both young women, the blanks allowed them to imagine a course of action that tred a path between what was possible given the story they had constructed and what they thought would be possible given their imagination and femininity. The way Annie filled in the unwritten portions of the text reveals that gender tensions exist and that young women are not passive victims. Her predicted plan and subsequent response show a femininity that allows for collective action against boys, but sets limits on how forceful that action may be. Marcy adopts a position in relation to the text that sharpens a tension within her femininity when she admires the characters' plan, but expresses doubt as to her own ability to act in a similar manner. Like Annie, she draws on her femininity and the previous portions of the text to use the blanks as an opportunity to imagine a more assertive femininity. For both young women, filling in the blanks has set in motion reflections on their femininity.

As the twenty-nine young women read their romance novels, they constructed a story that put on center stage their own hopes for and fears of romance. While reading the romance-fiction text, they bring to bear their past and present positions within the school in becoming the subject of the romance text. Their school identities as reluctant readers, and their desire to be seen as capable influence their reading of the romances. Equally important was each young woman's ability to become the heroine and experience being an assertive and cherished girl. These constitute the contradictory and at times fragmenting gender positions young women construct in the course of their reading.

The young women's romance-novel reading had strong oppositional over-tones. Their identification with the assertive heroines fueled attempts to continue their reading at all costs. The young women's vision of the romance novel as a vehicle for instilling a certain vitality into their reading classes was in one sense a bid to have some power and control over their schooling. They attempted to legitimize a text that operates on the fringes of accepted instructional materi-als. In view of the fact that written texts form the mainstay of instruction in America, the young women's actions carry much significance.

With romance-novel reading as a symbol of their femininity, the young women brought a certain pleasure in their femininity into the classroom. McRobbie[44] claims that young women's pleasure has always been problematic in schools, whether it takes the form of flirting, wearing sexy clothes, or openly primping in the classroom. In a manner similar to Radway's Smithton readers, [45] the young women took pleasure in their ability to make sense of the novels and to articulate what these stories were about. This feeling of competence was not one they usually experienced in school. The young women's reading of romance fiction refuted in their own minds the judgments made by school personnel about their competence. The act of making meaning allowed them to refuse, if only momentarily, their identities as reluctant readers.

The young women constantly used the romance novels to escape temporar-ily the problems and unhappiness associated with school and general life diffi-culties. On the whole, the young women were barely passing their courses. Many experienced the strain and uncertainty of the downward economic trend in Lakeview. Their glimpses of an economy in trouble did not prevent many of the young women from dreaming of a secure and comfortable future to be achieved through a good marriage combined with their own employment. Al-though many of the young women were aware of the disjuncture between that world and their own, the novels provided the space for them to dream and construct reality as they would like it to be. The novels therefore played upon many young women's desires and yearnings for a different present and future.

Romance-fiction reading situates young women within heterosexuality through their identification with heroines. That young women discursively be-come the heroine was clearly indicated by twelve-year-old Annie, a White middle-class student at Sherwood Park: "It's just when you're reading, you're in some other world, well, not really, physically, I mean but you imagine you are. Sometimes I feel like I am the person going on dates, having loads of fun." Jenny, a fourteen-year-old Black middle-class student at Jefferson, describes the impact that one novel, Quin-Harkin's *Princess Amy* [46] has had on her: "My favorite part is when the girl and the guy first kiss. That gives me a squishy feeling in my stomach, sorta like I'm actually there, being the girl that's gettin' kissed." The reader's endorsement of these relations between the sexes affirms traditional gender relations. The young women never disputed the desirability of heterosexual romance; they tried to capture it over and over in their reading of other romance fiction and wished for this specialness in their own lives. This was even the case when the young women's relationships with boys were fraught with conflicts to such a degree that the only satisfying romance they could imagine was one occurring in a novel.

How does this view fit with the strong assertive heroines the young women preferred to read about? In many ways, the young women's version of feminine assertiveness was a bounded one, one constrained within traditional views. These young women could certainly "best" boys in everyday life and in the world of romance fiction, but the bottom line was that one could not be "too pushy" because this could result in alienating boys and destroying any romantic prospects. The latter was clearly something the young women would not do, even when boys did not treat them well as was the case with Marge and Pam, or in the "get even" fantasy of Annie. Hence, the young women's conception of the proper relationship between the sexes featured some assertiveness, along with staying in the good graces of boys.

Young women's romance-fiction reading is characterized by this tug of war between conventional femininity and more assertive modes of action. This central tension was considerably sharpened when the young women conveyed their thoughts on their futures in the world of work and at home.

Material Girls

For these twenty-nine young women visions of the present and future were shaped through romance-fiction reading, which affected them in contradictory ways. Working for pay while in school was important for most of these young women, since it was the ticket to consuming, which in turn fed into romance. Marriage and children were on the distant horizon, along with jobs. The young women's reading tapped into their desires for material things, and centered the gender, class, and racial aspects of their identities around consumption.

Beautification with an eye to romance underlay the young women's wage work and consumption. The young women saw a direct relation between appearance, popularity, and romance. All the young women believed that "pretty girls get nice boyfriends." Although having a nice personality was equally important, attractiveness was "something that a girl could not do without." These beliefs were validated in their everyday lives: the prettiest, most popular young women at their schools also had their pick of the boys. These descriptions of feminine popularity in everyday life were reminiscent of romance-fiction heroines. The linking of beauty with romance not only motivated the young women's consumption, but also provided the reason for working for pay.

All the young women were involved in various kinds of casual work, like baby-sitting and performing odd jobs to augment allowances or earn any spending money at all. Their earnings were spent on movies, fast food, records, and videos, with the greater part going for clothes and beauty products. With larger allowances, the White, Black, and Chinese middle-class young women baby-sat to buy "little extras" or "something extravagant" that allowances would not cover. For the White, Black, and Hispanic working-class young women, consumption was on a more limited scale. Little or no spending money from parents required amazing entrepreneurship to earn pocket money. This not only involved the usual odd jobs, but also doing paid domestic work in homes where they baby-sat. The young women had plans to continue working in high school in retail sales, clerical work, or the fast-food industry to have more spending money. They saw having a job as making the difference between doing without and having money to spend. This reality collided with the universe of the romance novel.

Affluence and even luxury generally characterize the world of romance fiction. Although most of the heroines do casual work, their families are economically stable. This was a different world for the twenty-nine young women I spoke with. The working-class young women glimpsed this world as bystanders. The designer clothes, elaborate homes, and glamorous vacations were not for them. Several middle-class young women saw this world slipping away. During the recent recession in Lakeview, many of these women's relatives had lost good paying jobs and were unemployed or working for drastically reduced wages. Austerity hit the middle class as massive white-collar layoffs continued. These glimpses of an economy still in trouble did not prevent the young women from dreaming of a secure and comfortable future. The romances, with their economically secure world, allowed these young women to realize their dreams.

The young women's future plans included marriage, children, some further schooling, and work for pay.[47] Over half of the twenty-nine young women expected to marry before they were twenty and to work for a few years before having children. However, they rejected the dominant vision projected by romance novels that married women are full-time mothers and housewives. The working- and middle-class young women, coming from two-paycheck families, recognized that they would have to work for a while after marriage in order to help out. However, along with their rejection of this model was a strong longing for more conventional roles. This tension was an outcome of their dawning knowledge of the difficulty of juggling housework, children, and paid work. The young women's own considerable domestic responsibilities at home and their mothers' dawn-to-dusk work routine were sobering glimpses of what might be in store for them.

Textual, Sexual Politics

I have stated that there was a considerable amount of tension surrounding classroom use of romance fiction at Kominsky, Jefferson, and Sherwood Park. In the larger institutional context, teachers were under mandates of state testing and pressured into demonstrating student growth in reading. These were factors in their decision to allow popular materials into the classroom. The five teachers also acknowledged that intensification of their workload, increasing numbers of students, and the immense amount of paper work for Chapter I teachers made it difficult to select materials carefully. Consequently, they strongly relied on the reputation of publishers. The selective rendering of experience in tradebooks and textbooks[48] along with recent charges of censorship in school editions,[49] makes this reliance politically problematic. The "higher production quotas," increasing accountability, and intensification of teachers' work are expressions of capitalist practices and values within the schools.[50] Romance fiction represents another aspect of this mentality within the schools. The very act of buying and reading romance novels put the young women in the position of consumer. In one sense the novels can be viewed as a series of commercials for beauty products and clothes. This supports Gitlin's observation[51] that symbolic relations are becoming more and more linked to politics and economics, especially when it comes to popular fiction, gender, and schooling.

Popular romance-fiction reading encapsulates the tug of war involved in securing consent to the new conservative political consensus. Romance reading is evidence of readers' desires along with their fears and resentment of the power of men and the subordination of women. Readers' preference for strong heroines and impatience with passive ones represents their desire to transcend current gender stereotypes and imagine a more assertive femininity, which, however, stops short of confrontation with boys. Through romance reading, readers transform gender relations so that men cherish and nurture women rather the other way around. This, together with readers' collective rejection of a macho masculinity, represents their partial overturning of one aspect of current traditional gender sentiments. However, readers' final acceptance of romantic love and its power structure undercuts the political potential of these insights. Romance reading in no way altered the young women's present and future circumstances, but rather was deeply implicated in reconciling them to their place in the world.

Popular romance-fiction reading also involves political actions around authority relations in schools. As Tina, Tomeika, Jan, and Carol wrested some control over their reading from Mrs. B., they de-centered the teacher's traditional authority on the question of reading choice. Their actions contested the power of teachers to decide what is best for students. In many ways, their actions here exemplified the assertive femininity that the young women constructed as they read. They were able to substitute this mode of femininity for the compliant femininity expected in the classroom. The struggles between these young women and their teacher were ultimately over whose gender meanings had legitimacy. However, their actions were contradictory in that they hardened the young women's opposition to "legitimate" texts and the official school knowledge they contain. Although the romance novels generated a high engagement with reading and provided readers with "really useful" gender knowledge, this knowledge did not count toward achieving academic success. The twenty-nine young women remained categorized as reluctant readers despite the rich and complex interpretations they made of romance fiction. Teachers did not interpret their reading as competent because of the contradictory status of romance novels. They were not legitimate texts in teachers' eyes, despite student efforts to confer authority on them. Although teachers and students compromised (as in the case of Mrs. B.), teachers still dispensed the rewards upon which academic success rests. There are few such rewards for teen romance readers.

Teachers allowing readers to substitute romance novels for other instructional texts unwittingly contributed to the young women's opposition to the academic aspects of schooling. The absence of meaningful communication between students and teachers about their reading allowed many of the gender interpretations to remain in place. This practice militated against what is perhaps the most important aspect of learning from reading, that of making sense of books through discussion with others.[52] While the very championing of romance-novel reading momentarily empowered young women to assert a claim to a kind of schooling that would relate to their interests, it also had a dark side. Readers resistances to the "official" curriculum set in motion the possibility that these young women might graduate with skills that only qualify them for low-skill exploitative jobs or not graduate at all. In view of the movement of Lakeview toward a service economy featuring low-paying jobs, the limiting of these women to this kind of job seems likely. Keeran[53] claims that by 1990 service-sector industries will employ almost three-quarters of the workforce and that most of these workers will be women. Romance reading prepared these twenty-nine Lakeview students for entering this society as middle-and working-class women.

Conclusion

Popular romance-fiction reading exploits the many ideological strains that exist within society, and it represents the continuing struggle over women's place in the world. This fiction does not so much impose meanings on its readers, but rather constructs readers' gender, class, racial, ethnic, age, and sexual identities in complex ways. Volosinov[54] has observed that language involves a "struggle over meaning." As the study of teen romance-fiction demonstrates, this struggle is a political one that has long concerned feminists and other progressively minded individuals. Although space does not permit a detailed account of the ways in which a political practice can be forged around popular texts,[55] it is important that educators help students to locate the contradictions between popular fiction's version of social relations and their own lives as well as help them to develop the critical tools necessary to make deconstructive readings that unearth the political interests that shape the form and content of popular fiction.[56] This means moving from a definition of reading as an apolitical, internal, and individual activity to one of reading as a socially and historically situated political practice.[57] The theory and practice of feminist pedagogy and that of Freire's political literacy[58] approach represent points of departure for a ''politics of reading.''[59] Politicizing text use is vital since much of the hegemonic power of ruling elites in the United States is consolidated through written forms, as the present volume demonstrates. As the control of publishing is in the hands of large corporate interests, it is vital that political struggles continue to be directed toward the corporate sector, and that alternative presses be supported.

Although what I have briefly outlined above poses challenges for educators, it is the challenge that makes the struggle so crucial. For gender, class, race, ethnicity, age, and sexuality are not immutable categories in teen romance fiction or anywhere else, but cultural constructs. Teen romance-fiction reading occurs at a time when many young women begin to consider their place in the world. Through the romance text, readers come to grips with the world, but also attempt to refashion that world, as well as their place in it.

Notes

1. See Linda K. Christian-Smith, "Gender, Popular Culture and Curriculum," *Curriculum Inquiry* 17 (1987): 365–406; Wendy Saul, "Excluded Work from the Selective Tradition," paper presented at the American Educational Research Association's Annual Meeting, April 1988; and Joel Taxel, "Reclaiming the Voice of Resistance: The Fiction of Mildred Taylor," in this volume.

2. Michel Foucault, *The Archaeology of Knowledge* (New York: Pantheon Books, 1972).

3. Judith Fetterly, *The Resisting Reader* (Bloomington, Ind.: Indiana University Press, 1978).

4. Dave Morely, "Texts, Readers and Subjects," in Stuart Hall, Dorothy Hobson, Andrew Lowe, and Paul Willis, eds., *Culture, Media and Language* (London: Hutchinson, 1980), pp. 163–73.

5. Market Facts, *1983 Consumer Research Study on Reading and Book Purchasing: Focus on Juveniles* (New York: Book Industry Study Group, 1984).

6. Ibid.

7. Refer to Linda K. Christian-Smith, *Becoming a Woman Through Romance* (New York: Routledge, Chapman and Hall, 1990), for a more detailed history of teen romance fiction.

8. Allan Hunter, "Virtue With a Vengeance: The Pro-Family Politics of the New Right" (unpublished doctoral dissertation, Department of Sociology, Brandeis University, Waltham, Mass., 1984).

9. Allan Hunter, "Why Did Reagan Win? Ideology or Economics?" *Socialist Review* 79 (1985): 29–41.

10. Stuart Hall, "Authoritarian Populism: A Reply," *New Left Review* 151 (1985): 115–24.

11. This point is developed at greater length in Linda K. Christian-Smith, "The English Curriculum and Current Trends in Publishing," *English Journal* 75 (1986): 55–57.

12. Louis Coser, Charles Kadushin, and Walter Powell, *Books: The Culture and Commerce of*

Publishing (New York: Basic Books, 1982); and Thomas Whiteside, *The Blockbuster Complex* (Middletown, Conn.: Wesleyan University Press, 1981).

13. Joseph Turow, *Getting Books to Children* (Chicago: The American Library Association, 1978); and Whiteside, *The Blockbuster Complex.*

14. Christian-Smith, "Gender, Popular Culture and Curriculum."

15. Walter Retan, "The Changing Economics of Book Publishing," *Top of the News* 38 (1982): 233–35; and Leonard Shatzkin, *In Cold Type* (New York: Houghton and Mifflin, 1982).

16. Sheila Harty, *Hucksters in the Classroom* (New York: Center for Responsive Law, 1979).

17. The growing implementation of a literature-based curricula for reading instruction that features many trade books lends an added urgency to the critical examination of romance fiction and its use in schools.

18. Selma Lanes, "Here Comes the Blockbusters—Teen Books Go Big Time," *Interracial Books for Children Bulletin* 12 (1981): 5–7.

19. Readability, or the difficulty of reading writing, is most often estimated through sentence length and word length. A number of the Hi-Low's that I have analyzed using readability measures are written at the fourth- to fifth-grade level. Publishers routinely estimate readability and print it in terms of grade level on the copyright page of their books.

20. Wayne Otto, Charles W. Peters, and Nathanial Peters, *Reading Problems: A Multidisciplinary Perspective* (Reading, Mass.: Addison-Wesley, 1977), p. 313.

21. Mark Aulls, *Developmental and Remedial Reading in the Middle Grades* (Boston: Allyn and Bacon, 1978).

22. Roger Farr, "Is Johnny's/Mary's Reading Getting Worse?" *Educational Leadership* (April 1977): 521–27; Rudolph Flesch, *Why Johnny Still Can't Read* (New York: Harper and Row, 1981); National Assessment of Educational Progress, *Reading in America: A Perspective on Two Assessments* (Denver, Colo.: Reading Report No. 06-R-01, October 1976); and The National Commission on Excellence in Education, *A Nation at Risk* (Washington, D.C.: U.S. Government Printing Office, 1983).

23. Lanes, "Here Come the Blockbusters."

24. Ibid.

25. Christine T. Madsen, "Teen Novels: What Kind of Values Do They Promote? *The Christian Science Monitor* 18 (1981): B14–B17.

26. A more thorough discussion is contained in Christian-Smith, *Becoming a Woman Through Romance.*

27. Pamela Pollack, "The Business of Popularity," *School Library Journal* 28 (1981): 25–28.

28. All names are fictitious.

29. The outlying schools tracked students in math, science, and language arts as well. Most of the girls in my sample were tracked together so they interacted with one another across a range of subject areas.

30. In 1965 Congress passed the Elementary and Secondary Education Act known as Title I (now Chapter I) as a part of its "War on Poverty." Chapter I's focus was improving the reading and mathematics knowledge of the poor and educationally disadvantaged. Although Chapter I funding has been severely curtailed of late, it still remains the major form of compensatory education within many urban school districts.

31. For a detailed discussion of the methodology and issues surrounding interpretive research, see Christian-Smith, *Becoming a Woman Through Romance.*

32. I focus exclusively on school because access to homes was difficult.

33. Refer to Christian-Smith, *Becoming a Woman Through Romance,* for the reading survey and a discussion of survey research.

34. There are very few romance novels in which characters are not White. Tracy West's *Promises* (New York: Silhouette, 1986) features Black main characters. However, the novel has no specifically Black cultural dimensions.

35. Market Facts, *1983 Consumer Research Study.*

36. All pauses and hesitations have been omitted.

37. Mrs. B. characterized "quality literature" as a superbly told story, rich characters, and a concise "literary" style. She did not view book quality as connected to the way women were represented.

38. The major adolescent book awards in the United States are the American Library Association's Notable Books, the Laura Ingalls Wilder Award, the Newbery Award, and The National Book Award.

39. The findings of the 1983 Consumer Research Study on Reading and Book Purchasing by the Book Study Group found that the average reader read 24.9 books for leisure or work over a six-month period.

40. A close textual analysis of a sample of teen romance fiction, including several of the titles favored by the twenty-nine readers, is contained in Christian-Smith, "Gender, Popular Culture and Curriculum" and *Becoming a Woman Through Romance.*

41. The young women of color were resigned to the lack of models of black femininity in teen romance fiction. In their estimation, the books merely reflected the way blacks are treated in the media in general.

42. Wolfgang Iser, *The Implied Readers: Patterns of Communication in Prose Fiction From Bunyan to Beckett* (Baltimore, Md.: The Johns Hopkins University Press, 1974); and Wolfgang Iser, "Interaction between Text and Reader" in Susan R. Suleiman and Inge Crosman, eds., *The Reader in the Text* (Princeton, N. J.: Princeton University Press, 1980), pp. 106–19.

43. Andrea Marshall, *Against the Odds* (New York: Silhouette, 1985).

44. Angela McRobbie, *Jackie: An Ideology of Adolescent Femininity.* (Stencilled Occasional Paper Birmingham, England: The Centre for Contemporary Cultural Studies, 1978).

45. Janice Radway, *Reading the Romance* (Chapel Hill, N.C.: The University of North Carolina Press, 1984).

46. Janet Quin-Harkin, *Princess Amy* (New York: Bantam Books, 1981).

47. Their plans beyond high school included technical college, beauty school, and training in computers.

48. Christian-Smith, "Gender, Popular Culture and Curriculum," and Taxel, "The American Revolution in Children's Fiction."

49. Anne Bridgman, "A.L.A. Study of Book-Club Alterations Prompts Shifts in Policy," *Education Week,* September 12, 1982, pp. 6–7.

50. Michael W. Apple, *Ideology and Curriculum* (Boston: Routledge and Kegan Paul, 1979).

51. Todd Gitlin, "Television's Screens: Hegemony in Transition," in Michael W. Apple, ed., *Cultural and Economic Reproduction in Education* (Boston: Routledge and Kegan Paul, 1982), pp. 202–46.

52. Unlike Radway's readers in *Reading the Romance,* the twenty-nine girls did not exchange books or share their reading. They read mostly as isolated individuals.

53. Roger Keeran, "AFL-CIO Report: Service Sector," *Economic Notes* 53 (October 1985): 4.

54. Vladimir N. Volosinov, *Marxism and the Philosophy of Language* (New York: Seminar Press, 1973).

55. Christian-Smith, *Becoming a Woman Through Romance,* provides a detailed discussion of this topic.

56. Specific strategies are discussed in Christian-Smith, *Becoming a Woman Through Romance.*

57. On a critical model of reading, see Allan Luke and Carolyn D. Baker, *Towards a Critical Sociology of Reading Pedagogy* (Amsterdam: John Benjamins, 1991).

58. Nancy Schniedwind, "Teaching Feminist Process," *Women's Studies Quarterly* 15 (1987): 15–31; Carolyn M. Shrewsbury, "What is Feminist Pedagogy?" *Women's Studies Quarterly* 15: 6–14; and Paolo Freire and Donaldo Macedo, *Literacy: Reading the Word and the World* (Granby, Mass.: Bergin & Garvey, 1987).

59. In calling for a combining of the two approaches I acknowledge the different traditions represented by feminist pedagogy and Freire's political literacy.

Most Popular Books Read by the Seventy-Five Girls
(in order of popularity)

1. Pascal, Francine. *Perfect Summer,* Bantam's Sweet Valley High.
2. Harper, Elaine. *Love at First Sight,* Silhouette's Blossom Valley.
3. Harper, Elaine. *Turkey Trot,* Silhouette's Blossom Valley.
4. Conklin, Barbara. *P. S. I Love You,* Bantam's Sweet Dreams.
5. Pascal, Francine. *My First Love and Other Disasters,* Viking.
6. Tyler, Toby. *A Passing Game,* Silhouette's First Love.
7. Quin-Harkin, Janet. *California Girl,* Bantam's Sweet Dreams.
8. Marshall, Andrea. *Against the Odds,* Silhouette's First Love.
9. Conford, Ellen. *Seven Days to a Brand-New Me,* Atlantic.
10. Pevsner, Stella. *Cute Is a Four-Letter Word,* Archway.

10

Textual Authority, Culture, and the Politics of Literacy

Stanley Aronowitz and Henry A. Giroux

Since the second term of the Reagan administration, the debate on education has taken a new turn. Now, as before, the tone is principally set by the Right, but its position has been radically altered. The importance of linking educational reform to the needs of big business has continued to influence the debate, while the demands for schools to provide the skills necessary for domestic production and expanding capital abroad have slowly given way to an overriding emphasis on schools as sites of cultural production. The emphasis on cultural production can be seen in current attempts to address the issue of cultural literacy, in the development of national curriculum boards, and in reform initiatives bent on providing students with the language, knowledge, and values necessary to preserve the essential traditions of Western civilization.[1] The Right's position on cultural production in the schools arose from a consensus that the problems faced by the United States could no longer be reduced to those of educating students in the skills they will need to occupy jobs in more advanced and middle-range occupational levels in such areas as computer programming, financial analysis, and electronic machine repair.[2] Instead, the emphasis must be switched to the current cultural crisis, which can be traced to the broader ideological tenets of the progressive education movement that dominated the curriculum after World War II. These include the pernicious doctrine of cultural relativism, according to which canonical texts of the Western intellectual tradition may not be held to be superior to others, student experience should qualify as a viable form of knowledge, and ethnic, racial, gender, and other relations play a significant role in the development and influence of mainstream intellectual culture. On this account, the 1960s proved disastrous to the preservation of the inherited virtues of Western culture. Relativism systematically downgraded the value of key literary and philosophical traditions, giving equal weight to the dominant knowledge of the "Great Books" and to an emergent potpourri of "degraded" cultural attitudes. Allegedly, the last twenty years have witnessed the virtual loss of those revered traditions that constitute the core of the Western heritage. The unfortunate legacy that has emerged during the recent past has resulted in a generation of cultural illiterates. In this view, it is not only the American economy that is at risk, but civilization itself.

Allan Bloom and E. D. Hirsch represent different versions of the latest and most popular conservative thrust for educational reform.[3] Each, in his own way, represents a frontal attack aimed at providing a programmatic language with which to defend schools as cultural sites—that is, as institutions responsible for reproducing the knowledge and values necessary to advance the historical virtues of Western culture. Hirsch presents his view of cultural restoration through a concept of literacy that focuses on the basic structures of language, and applies this version of cultural literacy to the broader consideration of the needs of the business community, as well as to the maintenance of American institutions. His view of literacy represents an attack on educational theories that validate student experience as a key component of educational formation and curriculum development. For Hirsch, the new service economy requires employees who can write a memo, read within a specific cultural context, and communicate through a national language composed of the key words of Western culture. In the same spirit, Bloom offers a much broader critique of education. Advancing a position that claims that schools have contributed to the instrumentalization of knowledge and that the population has fallen victim to widespread relativism and rampant anti-intellectualism, Bloom proposes a series of educational reforms that privileges a fixed idea of Western culture organized around a core curriculum based on the old Great Books. He writes:

> Of course, the only serious solution [for reform in higher education] is almost universally rejected: the good old Great Books approach, in which a liberal education means reading certain generally recognized classical texts, just reading them, letting them dictate what the questions are and the method of approaching them—not forcing them into categories we make up, not treating them as historical products, but trying to read them as their authors wished them to be read. . . . But one thing is certain: wherever the great Books make up a central part of the curriculum, the students are excited and satisfied, feel they are doing something that is independent and fulfilling, getting something from the university they cannot get elsewhere. The very fact of this special experience, which leads nowhere beyond itself, provides them with a new alternative and a respect for study itself.[4]

This propensity for making sweeping claims without even a shred of evidence raises serious questions about the nature of Bloom's position as well as the quality of his scholarship. Moreover, Bloom's position is hardly novel. It has been with us since the Enlightenment and has long been invoked as an argument for the reproduction of elites. It advocates a social system in which a select cadre of intellectuals, economically privileged groups, and their professional servants are the only individuals deemed fit to possess the culture's sacred canon of knowledge, which assures their supremacy.

Both of these books represent the logic of a new cultural offensive, one of the most elaborate conservative educational manifestos to appear in decades. But it is important to recognize that the contemporary cultural offensive represents a form of textual authority that not only legitimates a particular version of Western civilization as well as an elitist notion of the canon, but also serves to exclude all those other discourses, whether from the new social movements or from other sources of opposition, which attempt to establish different grounds for the production and organization of knowledge. In effect, the new cultural offensive is not to be understood simply as a right-wing argument for a particular version of Western civilization or as a defense for what constitutes a legitimate academic canon; instead, both of these concerns have to be seen as part of a broader struggle over textual authority. In this case, the notion of textual authority is about the right-wing shift from the discourse of class to the broader relationship between knowledge and power, and about the struggle to control the very grounds on which knowledge is produced and legitimated. What is at issue here is not simply how different discourses function to reference particular forms of intellectual, ethical, and social relations but how power works as both a medium and an outcome of what we might call a form of textual politics. Textual authority is both pedagogical and political. As a social and historical construction, textual authority offers readers particular subject positions, ideological references that provide but do not rigidly determine particular views of the world. As a pedagogical practice, the text has to be read not simply as a study in the production of ideology but as part of a wider circuit of power that calls into play broader institutional practices and social structures. In effect, textual authority represents the medium and outcome of a pedagogical struggle over the relationship between knowledge and power as well as a struggle over the construction and the development of the political subject. Needless to say, Bloom and Hirsch represent forms of textual authority linked to a cultural practice, forms that have broad implications for educational reform and for the wider crisis in democracy. We intend to analyze the ideological and pedagogical content of these books in the context of the current debates, beginning with an analysis of Bloom's *The Closing of the American Mind.*

Bloom's critique of American education does not address the indifference of schools to the realities of the international marketplace, as in the old technicist discourse that reduces schooling to job training. Instead, Bloom attacks modernity, especially what he considers the rampant relativism that marks the last hundred years of Western history. Like José Ortega y Gasset, his illustrious predecessor, Bloom seeks to restore the dominance of Platonism—that is, the belief in the transhistorical permanence of forms of truth—to education. Where President Reagan's secretary of education, William Bennett, and the older elitists reiterated the call for "excellence," but never succeeded in articulating its substance, Bloom presents his proposals in more concrete terms.

Bloom's attack on liberal educational practice and the philosophy that underlies it is a sobering reminder that political and social analyses, which have identified themselves with modernity as a critique of advanced industrial societies, constitute powerful weapons in the hands of both the Right and the Left. Here we have all the elements of an elitist sensibility: abhorrence of mass culture, a rejection of experience as the arbiter of taste and pedagogy, and a sweeping attack on what is called "cultural relativism," especially on those who want to place popular culture, ethnic and racially based cultures, and cultures grounded in sexual communities (either feminist or gay and lesbian) on a par with classical Western traditions. For conservatives, each of these elements represents a form of anti-intellectualism that threatens the moral authority of the state. Consequently, much more than economic survival is at state: at issue is the survival of Western civilization as it represents itself through 2,500 years of philosophy, historiography, and literature.

Bloom's sweeping agenda intends to eliminate culture as a serious object of knowledge. According to Bloom, the culturalist perspective is what Plato means by the allegory of the cave. Thus, we are prevented from seeing the sunlight by culture, which is the enemy of what Bloom calls "openness." Although vaguely apologetic on the subject, Bloom ends up arguing that Western tradition is superior to non-Western cultures precisely because its referent is not "cultural" but rather the universal and context-free love of wisdom; the underlying ethnic of Western civilization, according to Bloom, is its capacity to transcend the immediate circumstances of daily life in order to reach the good life. Lower cultures are inevitably tied to "local knowledge"—to family and community values and beliefs, which are overwhelmingly context-specific. As it so happened in the course of history, the Greeks managed to teach some thinkers—Bloom being one—the way to universal truth.

For Bloom, the teachings of Plato and Socrates provide the critical referents with which to excoriate contemporary culture. Bloom systematically devaluates the music, sexuality, and pride of youth, and traces what he envisions as the gross excesses of the 1960s (the real object of his attack) to the pernicious influence of German philosophy from Nietzsche to Heidegger as refracted through the mindless relativism of modernizers. Feminism is equated with "libertinism," or making sex easy; "affirmative action now institutionalizes the worst aspects of separatism"; and rock music "has the beat of sexual intercourse" and cannot qualify, according to Bloom's Socratic standard, as a genuinely harmonic reconciliation of the soul with the passions of the body. Instead, rhythm and melody are viewed as a form of barbarism when they take on the explicit sexual coloration of modern rock 'n' roll music. For Bloom, popular culture, especially rock 'n' roll, represents a new form of barbarism, whose horror he conjures up in the image of a thirteen-year-old boy watching MTV while listening to a Walkman radio:

He enjoys the liberties hard won over centuries by the alliance of philosophic genius and political heroism, consecrated by the blood of martyrs; he is provided with comfort and leisure by the most productive economy ever known to mankind [*sic*]; science has penetrated the secrets of nature in order to provide him with the marvelous, lifelike electronic sound and image reproduction he is enjoying. And in what does progress culminate? A pubescent child whose body throbs with orgasmic rhythms; whose feelings are made articulate in hymns to the joys of onanism or the killing of parents; whose ambition is to win fame and wealth in imitating the drag-queen who makes the music. In short, life is made into a nonstop, commercially prepackaged masturbational fantasy.[5]

Bloom's sentiments, in this case, have been shaped by what he perceives as indications of a serious moral and intellectual decline among American youth: a challenge to authority formed by the student movements of the 1960s and the leveling ideology of democratic reform characteristic of radical intellectuals.[6]

These judgments merely provide a prologue to a much more forceful and unsparing attack on nihilism, which, according to Bloom and his political and intellectual peerage, consistently devalues scholarship, or, in its more universal aspect, the life of the mind. Nihilism in Bloom's philosophy is a code word for the glorification of action and power and represents the real threat to contemporary civilization. Nihilism has a number of historical roots: the modernism of the good life that stresses pluralism and diversity; the vacillations of democracy that permit the ignorant a degree of freedom that, in four undergraduate years, students are not prepared to use; a fragmentation born out of the uncertainties of a moral order that cannot present to the young either a unified worldview or goals to overcome the greed of modern life; and, in a more politically charged context, the decade of the 1960s, which was marked by a flagrant disrespect for authority, especially the authority of the intellect. Here we have more than the usual tepid porridge of conservative discourse. Bloom invokes images of "chaos and decay" in the moral fabric of our society. However, the sources of decay are rarely seen to be economic and political. Indeed, there is not a whisper of criticism of capitalism. In fact, capitalism appears only as a side issue in Bloom's rather indirect discussion of Marxism.

This brief description does not exhaust the breadth of Bloom's hyperbolic tirade. Our concern is, of course, focused on Bloom's vision of the crucial role schools can perform in correcting the current state of academic and public national culture he so roundly despises. Naturally, Bloom does not expect all schools to participate in reversing our country's spiritual malaise. The task falls to the literally twenty or thirty first-rate colleges and universities that are blessed with the best students but are regrettably frittering away their mission to restore to the West the mantle of greatness.

Commanding his minions to do a radical revision of the curriculum, to purge it of allusions to student experience (which, in any case, is mired in ignorance), Bloom seeks to rid the classroom of cultural relativism and of all those areas of study that do not venerate the traditions of the past. Bloom's call for curriculum reform is clear: End the sham of the sexual, racial, and cultural revolution that animated the generation that confronted the White men at the Pentagon and at other institutions of economic, political, and cultural power twenty years ago. Reinstate Latin as the lingua franca of learning, and transmit Western civilization through the one hundred greatest books that embody its system of values.

Of course, the state universities and colleges are now populated by the casualties of contemporary culture: large numbers of children of divorced parents, who are portrayed by Bloom as unfortunate—even tragic—products of current conditions; Blacks and other minorities, whose university experience is "different from that of other students" because of their history of "disadvantage," and whose dedication is, except in rare instances, not to learning but to practical advantage; and dispirited faculty members whose dreams of living in a community of scholars have been destroyed by the "interruptions" of modern social problems. For Bloom, these conditions disqualify the state universities and colleges as appropriate sites for professors and students to experience the awe and wonder of confronting the "Great Minds" of the ages.

It would be too easy to dismiss this frankly aristocratic vision of education as simply an effort to establish a new status quo conforming to Clark Kerr's model: a three-tier postsecondary education system in which theoretical knowledge is confined to the Ivy League institutions and major state universities—principally, the University of California and some of the Big Ten—and private institutions such as Chicago, Duke, and Emory. But this would not do justice to the political intention in the neoconservatives' attack on higher education, or comprehend the danger and novelty of their argument.

For, unlike Irving Kristol's rantings against the New Left of the 1960s (which was trying to create an "adversary culture" in opposition to the supremely democratic and capitalist society that had become America), Bloom joins Hilton Kramer and the professors of the Cold War intelligentsia of the 1950s in advocating a return to the age of the medieval Schoolmen, or at least to the high European culture of the nineteenth century. Rather than praising democracy, he yearns for the return of a more rigidly stratified civilization in which the crowd is contained within the land of the marketplace and its pleasures are confined to the rituals of the carnival. What he wants to exclude from the precincts of reason is the majority of the population. At the same time, he would drive the vox populi from the genuine academy—where the Absolute Spirit should find a home, but does not, because of the confusion that reigns amidst the dangerous and flabby influence of the discourse of social commitment, politics, and equality. Bloom identifies the impulse to egalitarianism as the chief culprit in the decay of higher learning as well as the worst impasse of democracy. But university administrators bear equal responsibility for pandering to these base motives. Instead of feeling bound by tradition to transmit the higher learning that, after all, is the repository of what is valuable in schooling, they gave away the store. Universities lost their way in the scandal that is culture.

Pluralists and democrats might dismiss these elitist ruminations without grasping the valid elements of the complaint. For there can be no doubt that the reception that Bloom's book has enjoyed signifies that he has hit the elitists' collective nerve. Intellectuals are uneasy about their role as teachers because their own experiences, interests, and values seem profoundly at odds with the several generations they have taught since the 1960s. But even more searing is their growing feeling of irrelevance, not only with respect to the process of education, but also with respect to their role within public life.

In Bloom's exegesis, the past must play a crucial role in formulating the future. Intellectuals are to join in a classical evocation of a mythically integrated civilization that becomes the vantage point from which to criticize the current situation. In all of its versions, the integrated past is marked by the existence of a community of the spirit; it was a time when at least a minority was able to search for the Good and the True, unhampered by temporal considerations such as making a living. For the idyllic past is always constructed in the images of leisure, or, to be more fair, in an environment where society provides a sufficient social surplus to support a priest class, or their secular equivalents. In contrast, the contemporary construction of the intellectual is on the model of technical rather than pure reason. The intellectual transmits algorithms rather than ideas, and orients students to careers rather than criticizes the social structure.

Bloom's attack on higher education conveniently excludes the degree to which the existing arrangements of social and economic power have contributed to the shaping of the intellectual life that he so stridently laments. What Bloom fails to mention in his attack on the servants of higher education is that the disappearance of political intellectuals corresponds to the passing of politics from "public" life. Educational institutions, once charged with the task of providing a little learning to ruling elites and providing them with a mandarin class, have assumed a crucial place in the economic and cultural order. Their task is no longer to preserve civilization as it has been defined by the Greek and Roman aristocracies; these institutions are now filled with knowledge-producers, who, in advanced capitalist societies, have become part of the process of material and social reproduction. The idea of the intellectual as adversary of the dominant culture is utterly foreign to current arrangements (for example, the president of Barnard College, a former corporate lawyer, appears on television commenting as an insider on the stock market crash and barely refers to her role as educator except to observe that students are calling home nervously asking their parents, "How are we doing?").

In his last chapter Bloom alludes to business civilization and describes negatively the way economics has overwhelmed the social sciences in "serious" universities (taking the place once held by sociology in the days when students desired to "help" people rather than just look out for themselves). Sounding like the Frankfurt school of critical theory, he even manages to criticize the belief, common among natural scientists, that their disciplines yield the only "real" knowledge. Characteristically, Bloom appeals to the elite schools to introduce philosophy as a key component of liberal education in order to counter the threat to higher education that is posed by the rigid empiricisms of economics and natural science.

The tension between tradition and innovation plagues all who are seriously concerned with education. But Bloom refuses to go beyond scapegoating and ask how classical texts have failed to address the generations that came into postsecondary education after World War II: why Latin and Greek were no longer deemed essential for even the elite university curricula; why students, administrators, and the overwhelming majority of faculty came to view universities as degree mills at worst, or, at best, places where the enterprising student could be expected to receive a good reading list. These questions cannot be addressed, much less answered, by invective.

The conservative appeal to the past takes on the character of an ideological flag against the future. It is not that the relativists, of both left and liberal persuasion, want to destroy the spirit and form of Western cultural heritage. Rather, they seek to reveal how such a heritage has often been employed as a weapon against those who would democratize institutions, who would change relations of power. Every achievement of civilization—the pyramids, great works of Greek philosophy and science, the wonderful representations of the human body and the soul that emerged during the Renaissance—has been built on the backs of slaves, on a faraway peasantry; in short, on a material foundation that undermines the notion of an uncomplicated marriage between high culture and humanism. Ignoring this fact, as Walter Benjamin reminds us, helps to sustain the culture and civilization in general.[7] For this reason, the rebellion against privilege is frequently accompanied by an attack against the intellectuals. What oppressed people understand better than most is that intellectuals are typically servants of the mighty ; they often provide the legitimacy for deeds of state, private violence, and exploitation. This, of course, is the meaning of the argument that every achievement of high culture is preceded by the blood of those who make it possible.

When Bloom calls for reviving Latin as a requirement for educated youth, he opposes one of the crucial reforms of the eighteenth- and nineteenth-century democratic revolutions, which established the vernacular as the language not only of commerce and manufacture but also of public life, literature, and philosophy. His fealty to classical texts excludes the pre-Socratics and Aristotle and focuses instead on Socrates and his disciple Plato precisely because of their attempt to separate truth from knowledge. Truth in Plato's *Symposium* requires no external object for its justification but refers instead to itself, particularly to the purity of form. Knowledge is always onesided, referring to an external object. It constitutes a representation of things and not, in Plato's terms, the things themselves. This distinction was challenged during the Enlightenment. Increasingly, truth and knowledge have the same external referent; subjectivity is removed from the realm of science and occupies, as ethics, psychology, and philosophy, a quasi-religious margin.

The virtue of Bloom's tirade, despite its reactionary content, is to remind us of what has been lost in the drive for rationalization, for the supremacy of science over philosophy, history over eternal essences. That is, the twentieth-century obsession with defining and celebrating history as an evolutionary mode of ideological and material progress, produced through the marriage of science and technology, has resulted in a refusal to give primacy to the important and problematic relationship between truth, power, and knowledge. From the point of view of a conservative for whom the past is all that is worth preserving, the consequence of Enlightenment ideology finds its apogee in the brutality of the cultural revolutions of 1789 and 1968, but, of course, Bloom forgets to mention the response of traditional Schoolmen to Galileo's discoveries. The intellect, in this case, defends itself by threatening to obliterate its adversaries.

In effect, the historical legacy of technicization has been to turn universities into training institutions, an act that creates few spaces for intellectuals. Within the ranks of the democratic professoriate, a debate often rages between those who spurn the elitism that emanates from the new conservative attack on affirmative action, open admissions, and student-centered learning and others who would try to extract some self-serving half-truths from Bloom's critique of contemporary postsecondary education (for example, open admissions is detrimental to quality education, affirmative action is unfairly discriminatory, and so forth).

What must be accepted in Bloom's discourse is that anti-intellectualism in American education is rampant, influencing even those whose intentions are actually opposed to closing the doors to genuine learning. We know that the environment in most universities is inimical to broadly based, philosophically informed scholarship and dialogue concerning burning questions of politics and culture. In a few places, liberal and radical intellectuals are building micro-institutions (centers, institutes, programs) within the universities as outposts that attempt to resist the larger trends toward instrumentalized curricula. These programs wisely accept that they are engaged in an intellectual as well as a political project; but, for the most part, their influence is confined to the already initiated.

On the front lines, some teachers, buffeted and bewildered, continue to maintain a fresh creative and critical approach to their tasks. In doing so, they receive little or no sustenance from the intellectuals. The challenge, in our view, is to combine the intellectual work of cultural reclamation with the work of pedagogy. This would entail a deliberate effort to avoid the tendency toward exclusivity on the part of intellectuals; to refuse the temptation to reproduce the "community of scholars" that is the heart of Bloom's program, even if the scholars are democratic intellectuals. The intellectuals who boldly announce that the search for truth and the good life is not the exclusive property of the Right and, in fact, is largely opposed to the conservative sensibility, would be required to engage with students—to start, not from the new great texts, much less the old great texts, but from the texts of the vernacular experience; from popular culture, not only in its written forms but in its visual artifacts as well. As Bertolt Brecht quipped, "Let's start not from the good old things but from the bad new things."

This need not imply leaving aside consideration of the tradition. But the task of reworking it might be explicitly combined with current concerns. For if tradition is to become part of a popular canon, it would have to justify itself either by its claim to pertinence or as a sociological and historical trace of the culture against which the present contends. In this connection, it is instructive to follow the fate of scientific texts. Except for historians, practicing physicists and their students rarely, if ever, read the works of Newton, Galileo, Kepler, and Copernicus. Similarly, Darwin is left to the scholars. Surely, one would not want to construct a curriculum in which this rich past was left to gather cobwebs. Science has no need for a literary canon, because it has long since abandoned the search for truth, and is intent on discovery. In other words, science is interested only in the knowledge that can be derived from mathematics and experiment. Consequently, with few exceptions, it discourages the focus on meaning that still dominates the humanities. Like the social sciences, the natural sciences are content with explanation, and have forgotten that any object of knowledge is grasped not only quantitatively or by perception, but also historically.

The relationship between literary tradition and history is the most important one. For, unless we are to take the position made popular by Henry Ford that "history is bunk," we are obliged to take a historical perspective on the present and the future. That is to say, what we know is conditioned by historical precedents, and our natural and social world is constituted rather than merely given. For this reason, both knowledge and the truth of subjects themselves presuppose the elements of their formation. The danger lies in a position of sheer determination of the present by the past, in which case nothing really ever happens; events are reworkings of their antecedents. Instead, we propose that both disruption and continuity are characteristic of the nature of things. Disruption is a name for the proposition that things are constituted by interactions; in the first place, by intersubjective relations, but also by relations between what humans produce in the present and the past that appear as a part of the natural order. To critique the reification of the social as an unproblematic category does not dissolve everything into intersubjective relations including our own "nature," since our relation to what is taken as nature is part of human formation. This double relation has a history that is, to a great extent, embodied in literature and philosophy, and in folk narratives, which are incorporated into popular cultural forms.

While it is possible to make a strong case that reading classic texts is necessary even today because they continue to speak to our condition, we must take into account the massive shift that has occurred in the terms of the discourse: vernacular speech and popular language are now deeply embedded in the collective imagination. Thus, any effort to displace this language must be perceived as an imposition from on high, an effort by professional intellectuals to destroy or ignore what has happened in the last two hundred years. We do not want to argue that none of the privileged texts of Western culture should be incorporated into the curriculum. Nor are we defending anti-intellectualism, even as we explain some of its democratic impulses. But the responsibility of intellectuals for the current state of affairs must be acknowledged before the tension between tradition and modernity or postmodernity can be ameliorated. When intellectuals, whose alliance with the established order is their last best hope to save their status, make proclamations about educational reform, they must remain suspect. For what Bloom means by reform is nothing less than an effort to make explicit what women, minorities, and working-class students have always known: the precincts of higher learning are not for them, and the educational system is meant to train a new mandarin class. Their fate is tied to technical knowledge. This is Bloom's program. In part, this becomes clear not only in Bloom's complaint that "Harvard, Yale, and Princeton are not what they used to be—the last resorts of aristocratic sentiment within the democracy,"[8] but also in his attack on ethnicity and subordinate cultures. According to Bloom,

> when one hears men and women proclaiming that they must preserve their culture, one cannot help wondering whether this artificial notion can really take the place of the God and country for which they once would have been willing to die. The "new ethnicity" or "roots" is just another manifestation of the concern with particularity, evidence not only of the real problems of community in modern mass societies but also of the superficiality of the response to it, as well as the lack of awareness of the fundamental conflict between liberal society and culture. . . . The "ethnic" differences we see in the United States are but decaying reminiscences of old differences that caused our ancestors to kill one another.[9]

In commenting on the "sample" of students Bloom uses to construct his view of university life, Martha Nussbaum provides an illuminating insight into Bloom's treatment of students who do not inhabit the world of elite universities, particularly subordinate groups who make up the Black, ethnic, and White working class. She states that those students of Bloom who

> are materially well off and academically successful enough to go to a small number of elite universities and to pursue their studies there without the distraction of holding

a job are equated with those having "the greatest talents" and the "more complex" natures. They are said to be the people who are "most likely to take advantage of a liberal education," and to be the ones who "most need education." It would seem that the disadvantaged, as Bloom imagines them, also have comparatively smaller talents, simpler natures, and fewer needs. But Bloom never argues that they do. He simply has no interest in the students whom he does not regard as the elite—an elite defined, he makes plain, by wealth and good fortune as much as by qualities of the mind that have deeper value.[10]

For Bloom, philosophy after Hegel abandons the search for truth, becoming the servant of technical knowledge and thereby losing its claim to wisdom. But whereas Bloom wants to reconstruct the category of truth through an unproblematic, quasi-essentialist and elitist reading of history, we believe that recovering a notion of truth grounded in a critical reading of history that validates and reclaims democratic public life is fundamental to the project of educational reform. Consciousness must take itself as its object, recognize that the process of forging an identity should be tied not to representations of what should be the goals to which students should aspire, but to what students themselves want, what they think and feel, and—most important—what they already know. The assumption that students are a tabula rasa upon which the teacher, armed with the wisdom of ages, places an imprint is the basis of the widespread distrust of education among today's students. The elite professoriate is recruited from that tiny minority of every generation for whom the life of the mind represents the pinnacle of life. Such ideals are by no means shared by the preponderance of professors, much less by their students.

We are arguing for the parity of canonical text and popular text as forms of historical knowledge. In fact, what counts as high cultural text often originates as popular text (the work of Dickens, Dostoevsky, and Rabelais are just a few examples). Their narratives were inevitably drawn from the everyday lives of their readers as well as from those who had not (yet) gained their own voice, either in the public sphere or in literature. The novelist, argues Mikhail Bakhtin, creates a narration worthy of canonization when a multiplicity of voices, analogous to a polyphonic musical work, are placed in dialogic relation to one another.[11] Among these, one can discover the popular, if by that term we mean those excluded from literate culture, a basic feature of the early bourgeois epoch. In this example, we read literature as a social semiotic, as a string of signifiers that illuminates our past, that reveals our selves, that provides us with a heritage for our own times. But the rediscovery of the popular is not the only treasure that can be scrounged from the established canon. We may discover in Gustave Flaubert's *Madame Bovary,* in Mark Twain's *Huckleberry Finn,* and in Theodore Dreiser's *Chronicles of American Plunder* descriptions of the human sacrifices that were made for the sake of progress at the turn of the century. These are modern tragedies and comic narratives of the dark side of middle-class and native history or philosophy. In short, we may take literature as social knowledge, but the knowledge is not of an object, it is a part of the truth about ourselves.

We are sure that Bloom would find this program objectionable because it preserves what should be destroyed—historicity—placing our lives in relation to our times, seeing history as less than the unfolding of the Absolute Spirit, but instead, as the deconstruction of the myths of "civilization." The democratic use of literary canons must always remain critical. Above all, the canon must justify itself as representing the elements of our own heritage. In the final instance, it is to be appropriated rather than revered—and, with this appropriation, transformed. The canon is to be pressed, then, into the service of definite ends—freeing us from its yoke, which, even if unread, is acknowledged as the unquestioned embodiment of Truth.

At first glance, Hirsch's *Cultural Literacy* has little in common with Bloom's work. Bloom directs his attack against a number of institutions, social practices, and ideologies that challenge the dominant assumptions of contemporary social life. As we have mentioned, his targets include cultural relativism, higher education, popular culture, Nietzsche, the Left, feminism, rock music, and the social movements of the 1960s. Hirsch's focus is narrower; he argues for a view of cultural literacy that serves both as a critique of many existing theories of education and as a referent for a reconstructed vision of American public schooling. Whereas Bloom attacks the notion of culture as a referent for self- and social formation, Hirsch attempts to enlist the language of culture and the culture of literacy as a basis for rethinking the American past and reconstructing the discourse of public life. But the differences that characterize these two positions are minor compared with the ideological and political project that they have in common.[12] In a most general sense, Hirsch and Bloom represent different versions of the same ideology, one that is deeply committed to cleansing democracy of its critical and emancipatory possibilities.

At the same time, Hirsch and Bloom share a common concern for rewriting the past from the perspective of the privileged and the powerful. In this view, history becomes a vehicle for endorsing a form of textual and cultural authority that legitimates an unproblematic relationship between knowledge and truth. Both disdain the democratic implications of pluralism, and each argues for a form of cultural uniformity in which difference is consigned to the margins of both history and everyday life. From this perspective, culture, along with the authority it sanctions, is not a terrain of struggle: it is merely an artifact, a warehouse of goods, posited either as a canon of knowledge or a canon of information that has simply to be transmitted as a means for promoting social order and control. Learning, for both Hirsch and Bloom, has little to do with dialogue and struggle over the meanings and practices of a historical tradition. On the contrary, learning is defined primarily through a pedagogy of transmis-

sion, and knowledge is reduced to a culture of great books or unrelated cata-
logues of shared information. As we indicated earlier, both of their positions
are part of the most recent frontal attack by the aristocratic traditionalists to
restore knowledge as a particular form of social authority, pedagogy, and discipline in the classroom in order to replace democratic educational authority.
Each of their positions espouses a view of culture removed from the trappings
of power, conflict, and struggle, and, in doing so, each attempts to legitimate
a view of learning and literacy that not only marginalizes the voices, language,
and cultures of subordinate groups but also degrades teaching and learning to
the practice of implementation and mastery. Both of these discourses are profoundly anti-utopian and correspond to a more general vision of domination and
control as it has been developed during the Reagan era. Specifically, Bloom
and Hirsch represent the most popular expression of the resurgent attempt on
the part of right-wing intellectuals and ruling groups to undermine the basis of
democratic public life as we have known it over the last two decades. In what
follows, through an analysis of the major themes presented in Hirsch's version
of the conservative educational credo, we analyze in greater detail some of these
assumptions.

Hirsch has entered the debate on the nature and purpose of public schooling
by way of a discourse that has gained public attention within the last ten years.
In the manner of conservatives such as William Bennett, Diane Ravitch, Chester
Finn, and Nathan Glazer, Hirsch begins with the assumption that a state of
crisis exists in the United States, a state of crisis that reflects not only the demise
of public schooling but also the weakening of a wider civic and public culture.
Schools in this view are frontline institutions that have reneged on their public
responsibility to educate students into the dominant traditions of Western
culture.

Appropriating the radical educational position that schools are agencies of
social and cultural reproduction, conservatives such as Hirsch defend this position rather than criticize it, and make it a measure for defining both the quality
of school life and that of society at large. Implicit in this position is the notion
that schools represent a preparation for and legitimation of particular forms of
social life; they are cultural institutions that name experience and in doing so
presuppose a vision of the future. It is in these terms that Hirsch's book becomes
important. For Hirsch insists that schools be analyzed as sites of learning in
which knowledge, not merely skills, constitutes the most important consideration, if public schooling is to fulfill its imperative as a transmitter of civic and
public culture. To Hirsch's credit, he enters the debate regarding public schooling by arguing for a particular relation between culture and power on the one
hand and literacy and learning on the other. In doing, so, he not only provides
an important corrective to the view that the curriculum in general and learning
in particular should be organized around the developmental organization of
learning skills; he also argues for a definition of literacy that embraces a particu-

lar relationship between knowledge and power. Knowledge, in this case, is the basis not only for learning but also for entering the social and economic possibilities that exist in the wider society. These issues have been analyzed critically by a number of educational tradition as a key referent for challenging some of Hirsch's major assumptions. To pursue this analysis we will examine Hirsch's view of the crisis in education, his reading of history and tradition, his construction of the relationship between culture, language, and power and its contribution to a view of literacy, and, finally, the book's implications for teachers and classroom pedagogy.

Reiterating the arguments of Bennett, Ravitch, and Finn, Hirsch identifies the crisis in education through the general level of cultural ignorance exhibited in recent years by American students. In this view, students lack the knowledge necessary to "thrive in the modern world."[13] Relying heavily on the declining test scores of college-bound students, particularly those of the Scholastic Aptitude Test (SAT) and the National Assessment of Educational Progress, as well as on anecdotal evidence, Hirsch argues that there is indeed a literacy crisis in the United States. For Hirsch, the SAT is essentially a "test of advanced vocabulary," and as such is a "fairly sensitive instrument for measuring levels of literacy."[14] In these assertions, the relationship between ignorance and learning, between knowledge and ideology, first becomes evident in Hirsch's book. At issue is a definition of literacy that is organized within categories that favor knowledge as a shared body of information, and a definition of learning as the appropriation of this information. For Hirsch, the defining character of this knowledge is that it represents the unifying facts, values, and writings of Western culture. In this instance, the relationship between knowledge and power is legitimated through claims to a body of information that resides beyond the sphere of historical conflict and the shifting terrain of ideological struggle. Authority and meaning come together within a view of history that appears unproblematic and unchangeable in its determining influence on the present and the future. What you see is what you get.

More important, Hirsch's view of history is the narrative of the winners. It is the discourse of the elites in history, a discourse that constitutes the fund of cultural knowledge that defines literacy. Assured by his son, who taught high-school Latin, Hirsch recognizes that students do in fact know something. Ignorance, for Hirsch, is not merely the absence of information. At stake is *what* the students know. Literacy and illiteracy are defined by the information students possess regarding the canon of knowledge that constitutes, for Hirsch, the national culture. Hirsch characterizes the crisis in literacy by the lack of familiarity students have with Western culture's canon bequeathed by history as a series of facts—dates of battles, authors of books, figures from Greek mythology, and the names of past presidents of the United States. In effect, the crisis of literacy is defined primarily as an epistemological and political problem. In the first instance, students cannot read and write adequately unless they have the relevant background information, a particular body of shared information that expresses a privileged cultural currency with a high exchange value in the public sphere. In the second instance, students who lack the requisite historical and contemporary information that constitutes the canon of Western tradition will not be able to function adequately in society. In Hirsch's terms, the new illiteracy is embodied in those expanding ranks of students who are unable either to contextualize information or to communicate with each other within the parameters of a wider national culture.

Hirsch does more than rely on the logic of verification and personal anecdote to signal the new illiteracy. He also attempts to analyze the causes for its emergence in the last half of the twentieth century. Hirsch begins by arguing that schools are solely responsible for the current cultural blight that plagues contemporary youth. If students lack the requisite historical and literary knowledge, it is because both schools of education and the public schools have been excessively influenced by the theoretical legacies of the early progressive movement of the 1920s. Influenced by the theories of John Dewey and the liberal ideas embodied in the 1918 Cardinal Principles of Education, public schooling is alleged to have historically shifted its concern from a knowledge-based curriculum to one that has emphasized the practical application of knowledge. The result has been, according to Hirsch, the predominance in public schools of a curriculum dominated by a concern with developmental psychology, student experience, and the mastery of skills. Within this line of reasoning, progressive educational theory and practice have undermined the intellectual content of the curriculum and further contributed to forms of public schooling marked by an increasing loss of authority, cultural relativism, lack of discipline, poor academic performance, and a refusal to train students adequately to meet the demands of the changing industrial order.

Hirsch is not content merely with criticizing the public schools. He is also intent on developing a programmatic discourse for constructing curriculum reform. Hirsch's message is relatively simple. He believes that since literacy is in a decline caused by an overemphasis on process at the expense of content, schools should begin to subordinate the teaching of skills to what he calls common background knowledge. For Hirsch, this common background knowledge consists of information from mainstream culture represented in standard English. Its content is drawn from what Hirsch calls the common culture, which in his terms is marked by a history and contemporary usefulness that raises it above issues of power, class, and discrimination. In Hirsch's terms, this is "everybody's culture," and the only real issue, as he sees it, is that we outline its contents and begin to teach it in schools. For Hirsch, the national language, which is at the center of his notion of literacy, is rooted in a civic religion that forms the core of stability in the culture itself. "Culture" in these terms is used in the descriptive rather than anthropological and political sense; it is the medium of conservation and transmission. Its meaning is fixed in the past, and its essence is that it provides the public with a common referent for communication and exchange. It is the foundation upon which public life interacts with the past, sustains the present, and locates itself in the future. Psycholinguistic research and an unchallenged relationship among industrialization, nationalism, and historical progress provide the major referents that are mobilized in the name of cultural literacy. The logic underlying Hirsch's argument is that cultural literacy is the precondition for industrial growth, and that with industrial growth comes the standardization of language, culture, and learning. The equation is somewhat baffling in its simplicity, and Hirsch actually devotes whole chapters to developing this particular version of historical determinism. The outcome of his Hegelian rendering of history and literacy is a view of Western culture that is both egalitarian and homogeneous.[15] Hirsch dismisses the notion that culture has any determinate relation to the practices of power and politics or is largely defined as a part of an ongoing struggle to name history, experience, knowledge, and the meaning of everyday life in one's own terms. Culture for Hirsch is a network of information shrouded in innocence and goodwill. This is in part reflected in his reading of the relationship between culture and what he describes as nation building: "Nation builders use a patchwork of scholarly folk materials, old songs, obscure dances, and historical legends all apparently quaint and local, but in reality selected and reinterpreted by intellectuals to create a culture upon which the life of the nation can rest."[16]

There is a totalitarian unity in Hirsch's view of culture that is at odds with the concept of democratic pluralism and political difference. In fact, where difference is introduced by Hirsch, as in reference to multiculturalism or bilingualism, it appears to vacillate between the category of a disrupting discourse and of a threat to the vitality and strength of the Western cultural tradition. Hirsch's defense of a unified version of Western tradition ideologically marks his definition of cultural literacy as more than a simplistic call for a common language and canon of shared information. Hirsch's argument that to be culturally literate is "to possess the basic information needed to thrive in the modern world," or to enable us to master the standard literate language so that we can become "masters of communication, thereby enabling us to give and receive complex information orally and in writing over time,"[17] is not merely a prescription for a particular form of literacy and schooling. It is part of a hegemonic discourse that is symptomatic of the crisis in history currently facing this nation, and of a threat to democracy itself.

We will analyze some of the major arguments made by Hirsch in defense of his notion of cultural literacy. In doing so, we will not restrict our analysis to the defining ideas that Hirsch develops, but will also analyze the significant gaps in Hirsch's view of history, literacy, culture, and schooling. We hope to show that Hirsch's argument is more than a popular and politically innocent treatise on educational reform, but rather serves at best as a veiled apology for a highly dogmatic and reactionary view of literacy and schooling. At worst,

Hirsch's model of cultural literacy threatens the very democracy he claims to be preserving.

For Hirsch, the starting point for the crisis in literacy and education is the decline of student achievement as measured by the SAT and similar tests. Hirsch and other conservatives presume that the test scores accurately measure academic proficiency, and that the progress of educational reform can be accurately inferred from an upturn in SAT scores. In recent times this wisdom has been highly disputed. Not only is the validity of the SAT and other national measurement schemes being questioned, despite their alleged objectivity, but it is also being strongly argued that the reliance on test scores as a measure of school success contains in itself an ideology that is highly detrimental to improving the quality of school life and providing the basis for critical learning.[18]

We believe that Hirsch's reliance on such scores to analyze the nature of the problems public schools currently face in this country is theoretically impoverished and politically visionless. This position ignores the wider complex of social and political forces that deeply influence the way schools are structured to benefit some students at the expense of others. For instance, this position is silent regarding the ways that tracking, the hidden curriculum, the denial of student experience as a valid basis for knowledge, and school practices predicated on class, sexist, and racial interests discriminate against students. Nothing in Hirsch's position speaks to the 50- to 80-percent dropout rate of high school students in inner-city schools, or to the fact that in major urban cities like Chicago, schools with over a 50-percent Black and Hispanic enrollment manage to retain only 39 percent of the entering freshmen by their senior year.[19] These figures highlight a number of problems that cannot be accounted for or even understood through analysis of so-called aptitude tests. Hirsch's reliance on test scores also ignores the effect that the technical rationality of this position has had on the de-skilling of teachers, particular women, within the last decade.[20] State-mandated efforts to raise test scores, especially in the areas of reading and writing, have been part of a much broader educational reform movement tied to instrumentalizing teaching and learning around a variety of accountability schemes. As Linda Darling-Hammond reports, the results have had very little to do with genuine reform and a great deal to do with teacher disempowerment and despair:

> Viewing teachers as semiskilled, low-paid workers in the mass production of education, policymakers have sought to change education, to improve it, by "teacher-proofing" it. Over the past decade we have seen a proliferation of elaborate accountability schemes that go by acronyms like MBO (management by objectives), PBBS (performance-based budgeting systems), CBE (competency-based education) . . . and MCT (minimum competency testing). . . . [W]e learned from teachers that in response to policies that prescribe teaching practices and outcomes, they spend less time on untested subjects . . . they use less writing in the classrooms in order to gear

assignments to the format of standardized tests; they resort to lectures rather than classroom discussion in order to cover the prescribed behavioral objectives without getting "off the track"; they are precluded from using teaching materials that are not on prescribed textbook lists, even when they think these materials are essential to meet the needs of some of their students; and they feel constrained from following up on expressed student interests that lie outside the bounds of mandated curricula. . . . And 45 percent of the teachers in this study told us that the single thing that would make them leave teaching was the increased prescriptiveness of teaching content and methods—in short, the continuing deprofessionalization of teaching.[21]

Hirsch appears unaware that the politics of verification and empiricism that he supports frame his own agenda for reform in a way that is at odds with an ethical and substantive vision of what schools might be with respect to their potential for empowering both students and teachers as active and critical citizens. Hirsch's reliance on narrow models of psycholinguistic research forces him to use absolute categories; that is, categories that appear to transcend historical, cultural, and political contingencies. By ignoring a wide range of sociological, cultural, and historical research on schooling, Hirsch wrongly names the nature of the crisis he attempts to address. He completely ignores those theories of schooling that in recent years have illustrated how schools function as agencies of social and cultural reproduction.[22] He completely ignores existing critical research that points to how working-class and minority children are discriminated against through various approaches to reading[23]; he exhibits no theoretical awareness of how schools frequently silence or discriminate against students[24]; and he completely ignores the research that points out ways in which the state and other social, economic, and political interests bear down on and shape the daily practices of school organization and classroom life.[25] Consequently, Hirsch's analysis and prescriptions are both simplistic and incorrect. The crisis in education is not about the background information that young people allegedly lack, or the inability of students to communicate in order to adapt more readily to the dictates of the dominant culture. Rather, it is a crisis framed in the intersections of citizenship, historical consciousness, and inequality, one that speaks to a breakdown at the heart of democratic public life.

The limitations of Hirsch's view of the crisis are evident not only in the research that he selects to define the problem, but also in the factors he points to as causes of the crisis in literacy and schooling. Among the chief historical villains in Hirsch's script are the progressive principles embodied in the work of John Dewey. Hirsch holds Dewey responsible for promoting a formalism in which the issues of experience and process become a substitute for focusing on school knowledge in the school curriculum. Hirsch argues that Dewey is the major theoretical architect of a content-neutral curriculum (as if such a thing ever existed). Dewey's crime in this view is that he has influenced later generations of educators to take critical thinking seriously as opposed to learning the virtues of having students accumulate information for the purpose of shoring up the status quo.

Hirsch misinterprets Dewey's work. Even the most casual reading of Dewey's *The Child and the Curriculum* and *The School and Society* reveals a blatant refusal to accept any division between content and process or between knowledge and thinking. Rather than support this bifurcation, Dewey argued that information without the benefit of self-reflection and context generally resulted in methods of teaching in which knowledge was cut off from its organic connection to the student's experiences and the wider society. Dewey was not against facts, as Hirsch argues; he was against a mere collection of facts that is both uninformed by a working hypothesis and unenlightened by critical reflection. He was against the categorization of knowledge into sterile and so-called finished forms. We are certainly not suggesting that Hirsch's misreading of Dewey represents an act of intellectual dishonesty; more probably, since Dewey's views are so much at odds with Hirsch's theory of learning and schooling, it was easier for him to misread Dewey than to engage directly with his ideas on specific issues. For example, Hirsch's claim that memorization is a noble method of learning, his refusal to situate schooling in broader historical, social, and political contexts, and his belief that public culture is historically defined through the progressive accumulation of information represent major ideas that Dewey spent a lifetime refuting as educationally unsound and politically reactionary. But Hirsch refuses to argue with Dewey on these issues; instead, he cavalierly attributes to Dewey a series of one-dimensional ideas that Dewey never advocated. This is not merely a distortion of Dewey's work, it is also a view of history and causality that is, as we explain below, deeply flawed. Moreover, Hirsch reproduces in this view of educational history and practice a slightly different view of Bloom's profoundly anti-democratic tirade.

Underlying Hirsch's view of the major causes of the problem influencing American education is a notion of history that is reductionist and theoretically flawed. It is reductionist because it assumes that ideas are the determining factor in shaping history, somehow unfolding in linear fashion from one generation to the next. There is no sense of how these ideas are worked out and mediated through the ideological and material conditions of their times, or of how history is shaped through the changing patterns of communication, technology, language conflicts, struggles between different social groups, and the shifting parameters of state power. Hirsch's history lacks any concrete political and social referents, its causal relations are construed through a string of ideas, and it is presented without the benefit of substantive argument of historical context. While ideas are important in shaping history, they cannot be considered to be so powerful as to alter history beyond the density of its material and social contexts. Ideas are not so powerful that they exist, as Hirsch believes, in a real autonomy and independence from human activity.[26]

Hirsch practices historical inquiry not as a form of social memory but as a form of repression. It is history stripped of the discourse of power, injustice, and conflict. For instance, the struggle over curriculum in the United States emerged, in the first half of the twentieth century, amidst an intense war of ideological positions, each attempting to stamp its public philosophy and view of learning on the curriculum of the public schools. As Herbert Kliebard points out, curriculum represented a terrain of struggle among different groups over questions regarding the purpose of schooling, how children learn, whose knowledge was to be legitimated, and what social relations would prevail.[27] The contending groups included social efficiency advocates whose priorities were based on the interests of corporate ideology, humanists who were advocates of the revered traditions of Western cultural heritage, developmentalists who wanted to reform the curriculum around the scientific study of child development, and, finally, social meliorists who wanted to shape the curriculum in the interests of social reform. Kliebard not only provides a complex and dense history of the struggle for control of the curriculum in the public schools, he also argues that the most important force in shaping curriculum in the United States came not from the progressives but from the social efficiency movement. Given the history of public schooling since the rise of the Cold War and the launching of Sputnik, there can be little doubt that the efficiency and accountability models for curriculum have carried the day.

History for Hirsch is not a terrain of struggle[28]; it is a museum of information that merely legitimates a particular view of history as a set of sacred goods designed to be received rather than interrogated by students. We have stressed Hirsch's view of history because it influences every category he relies on to develop his major arguments. We began our criticism of his work by arguing that his discourse of crisis and cultural restoration missed the point. We want to return to this issue and argue that the real crisis in American schooling can be better understood through an analysis of the rise of scientism and technocratic rationality as major ideological forces in the 1920s; the increasing impingement of state policy on the shaping of school curricula; the anti-communism of the 1950s; the increasing influence of industrial psychology in defining the purpose of schooling; the rise of individualism and consumerism through the growth of culture industry in which the logic of standardization, repetition, and rationalization define and shape the culture of consumption; the gendered nature of teaching as manifested in the educational labor force and in the construction of school administration and curriculum; the racism, sexism, and class discrimination that have been reinforced through increasing forms of tracking and testing; and the failure of teachers to gain an adequate level of control over the conditions of their labor. While this is not the place to discuss these issues, they need to be included in any analysis of the problems that public schools are now facing. Moreover, these issues point to a much broader crisis in the schools and the wider society than Hirsch is willing to recognize.[29] It is a crisis that has given rise to cynicism about the promise of democracy, to a vast and unequal distribution of ideological and material resources both in the schools and in the wider society, and to the repression of those aspects of our history that carry the voices and social memories of groups that have been marginalized in the struggle for democratic life.

Central to Hirsch's concept of literacy is an understanding of the relationship between culture and literacy that also warrants close theoretical scrutiny. For Hirsch, culture, which is the central structuring category in his approach to literacy and learning, appears as a mythic category that exists beyond the realm of politics and struggle. It is systematically reduced to a canon of information that constitutes not only a fund of background knowledge but also a vehicle for social and economic mobility. Hirsch writes:

> Literate culture has become the common currency for social and economic exchange in our democracy, and the only available ticket to full citizenship. Getting one's membership card is not tied to class or race. Membership is automatic if one learns that background information and the linguistic conventions that are needed to read, write, and speak effectively.[30]

There is a false egalitarianism defining Hirsch's view of culture, one suggesting that while it is possible to distinguish between mainstream and what he calls ethnic culture, the concept of culture itself has nothing to do with struggle and power. Culture is seen as the totality of the language practices of a given nation, and merely "presents" itself for all to participate in its language and conventions. Hirsch refuses to acknowledge how deeply the struggle for moral and social regulation inscribes itself in the language of culture. He makes no attempt to interrogate culture as the shared and lived principles of life, characteristic of different groups and classes as these emerge within unequal relations of power and struggle. Not unlike Bloom's position, Hirsch's view of culture both expresses a single, durable history and vision, one at odds with the notion of difference, and maintains an ominous ideological silence—an ideological amnesia of sorts—regarding the validity and importance of the experiences of women, Blacks, and other groups excluded from the narrative of mainstream history and culture. Thus there emerges no sense of culture as a field of struggle or domain of competing interests in which dominant and subordinate groups live out and make sense of their given circumstances and conditions of life. This is an essentialist reading of culture. It deeply underestimates the most central feature of cultural relations in the twentieth century. That is, by failing to acknowledge the multilayered relations between culture and power, Hirsch ignores how the ideological and structural weight of different cultural practices operates as a form of cultural politics. In this case, he not only ignores how domination works in the cultural sphere, he also refuses to acknowledge the dialetic of cultural struggle between different groups over competing orders of meaning, experience, and history.

The failure of Hirsch's view of culture is most evident in his analysis of public schools. He provides little, if any, understanding of the kinds of struggle that take place in schools over different forms of knowledge and social relations. This is best exemplified in the research on culture and schooling that has emerged within the last twenty years both in the United States and abroad. Theorists such as Pierre Bourdieu, Basil Bernstein, Paulo Freire, Michael Apple, and others have investigated the relationship between power and culture, arguing that the culture transmitted by the school is related to the various cultures that make up the wider society, in that it confirms and sustains the culture of dominant groups while marginalizing and silencing the cultures of subordinate groups of students.[31] This is evident in the way in which different forms of linguistic and cultural competency, whether they are manifested in a specific way of talking, dressing, acting, thinking, or presenting oneself, are accorded a privileged status in schools. (For example, Ray Rist, Jean Anyon, and Hugh Mehan have demonstrated that White middle-class linguistic forms, modes of style, and values represent honored forms of cultural capital and are accorded a greater exchange rate in the circuits of power that define and legitimate the meaning of success in public schools.[32] Students who represent cultural forms that rely on restricted linguistic codes, working-class or oppositional modes of dress [long hair, earrings, bizarre patterns of clothing], who downplay the ethos of individualism [and who may actually share their work and time], who espouse a form of solidarity, or who reject forms of academic knowledge that embody versions of history, social science, and success that are at odds with their own cultural experiences and values, find themselves at a decided academic, social, and ideological disadvantage in most schools.)

A more critical understanding of the relationship between culture and schooling would start with a definition of culture as a set of activities by which different groups produce collective memories, knowledge, social relations, and values within historically constituted relations of power. Culture is about the production and legitimation of particular ways of life, and schools often transmit a culture that is specific to class, gender, and race. By depoliticizing the issue of culture, Hirsch is unable to develop a view either of literacy or of pedagogy that acknowledges the complex workings of power as they are both produced and mediated through the cultural processes that structure school life. Thus, Hirsch ends up with a view of literacy cleansed of its own complicity in furthering the cultural practices and ideologies that reproduce the worst dimensions of schooling.

Given Hirsch's view of culture, it is not surprising that he espouses a clothesline-of-information approach to literacy that ignores its function as a technology of social control, as a feature of cultural organization that reproduces rather than critically engages the dominant social order. When the power of literacy is framed around a unifying logic consistent with the imperatives of the dominant culture, the voices of those groups outside of the dominant tradition are often silenced because their voices and experiences are not recognized as legitimate. Hirsch's view of literacy decontextualizes learners both from the culture and mode of literacy that give their voices meaning and from that which is legitimated as knowledge in the name of the dominant version of literacy. Literacy for Hirsch is treated as a universal discourse, a process that exist outside "the social and political relations, ideological practices, and symbolic meaning structures in which it is embedded."[33] Not only is the notion of multiple literacies (the concept of cultural difference) ignored in this formulation, but those who are considered "illiterate" bear the burden of forms of moral and social regulation that often deny their histories, voices, and sufferings. To argue for a recognition of the dialectical quality of literacy, that is, its power either to limit or to enhance human capacities as well as the multiple forms of expression it takes, is a deeply political issue. It means recognizing that there are different voices, languages, histories, and ways of viewing and experiencing the world, and that the recognition and affirmation of these differences is a necessary and important precondition for extending the possibilities of democratic life. June Jordan has captured the importance of this issue in her comments regarding the problems in a democratic state:

> If we lived in a democratic state our language would have to hurtle, fly, curse, and sing, in all the common American names, all the undeniable and representative and participating voices of everybody here. We would not tolerate the language of the powerful and, thereby lose all respect for words, per se. We would make our language conform to the truth of our many selves and we would make our language lead us into the equality of power that a democratic state must represent.[34]

To acknowledge different forms of literacy is not to suggest that they should all be given equal weight. On the contrary, it is to argue that their differences are to be weighed against the capacity they have for enabling people to locate themselves in their own histories while simultaneously establishing the conditions for them to function as part of a wider democratic culture. This represents a form of literacy that is not merely epistemological but also deeply political and eminently pedagogical. It is political because literacy represents a set of practices that can provide the conditions through which people can be empowered or disempowered. It is pedagogical because literacy always involves social relations in which learning takes place; power legitimates a particular view of the world, and privilege legitimates a specific rendering of knowledge.[35]

This view of culture, knowledge, and literacy is far removed from the language and ideology of Hirsch and Bloom. The refusal to be literate in their terms means that one has refused to appropriate either the canon of the Great Books or the canon of information that characterizes the tradition of Western culture. In this view, refusal is not resistance or criticism; it is judged as ignorance or failure. This view of culture and literacy is also implicated in the theories of pedagogy put forth by Bloom and Hirsch. Both subscribe to a pedagogy that is profoundly reactionary and can be summed up in the terms "transmission" and "imposition." Both authors refuse to analyze how pedagogy, as a deliberate and critical attempt to influence the ways in which knowledge and identities are produced within and among particular sets of social relations, might address the reconstruction of social imagination in the service of human freedom. The categories of meaning that students bring to the classroom and that provide them with a basis for producing and interpreting knowledge are simply denied by Bloom and Hirsch as viable categories of learning. Pedagogy, for both Bloom and Hirsch, is an afterthought. It is something one does to implement a preconstituted body of knowledge. The notion that pedagogy represents a method or technique for transmitting information, as well as an essential dynamic in the production and exchange of knowledge, necessitates that educators attend to the categories of meaning that students bring to the classroom as well as to the fundamental question of why they should want to learn anything in the first place. This is an especially important consideration for those students in the public schools who know that the truth of their lives and experiences is omitted from the curriculum. A pedagogy that takes their lives seriously would have to begin with a question that June Jordan has suggested such students constantly pose to teachers through their absences and overt forms of school resistance: "If you don't know and don't care about who I am then why should I give a damn about what you say you do know about."[36] To legitimate or address a question of this sort would constitute for Bloom and Hirsch not merely bad teaching, but a dangerous social practice as well.

Read against the recent legacy of a critical educational tradition, the perspectives advanced by both Bloom and Hirsch reflect those of the critic who fears the indeterminacy of the future and who, in an attempt to escape the messy web of everyday life, purges the past of its contradictions, its paradoxes, and, ultimately, of its injustices. Hirsch and Bloom sidestep the disquieting, disrupting, interrupting problems of sexism, racism, class exploitation, and other social issues that bear down so heavily on the present. This is a form of textual authority and discourse produced by pedagogues who are afraid of the future, who are strangled by the past, and who refuse to address the complexity, terror, and possibilities of the present. Most important, it is a public philosophy informed by a crippling ethnocentrism[37] and a contempt for the language and social relations fundamental to the ideals of a democratic society. It is, in the end, a desperate move by thinkers who would rather cling to a tradition forged by myth than work toward a collective future built on democratic possibilities. There is no sense in Bloom and Hirsch of a notion of textual authority that recognizes the need to engage in a living dialogue with diverse traditions that because of their partiality and historical limits need to be reread and recreated as part of an ongoing struggle for democratic public life. In the end, Bloom and Hirsch cling to a notion of textual authority that neither produces critical citizens nor provides the foundation for a pedagogy in which the conditions of learning might become possible for the vast majority of diverse peoples who live in this society. What we are left with is the philosophy and pedagogy of hegemonic intellectuals cloaked in the mantle of academic enlightenment and literacy.

Notes

1. For an example of this position, see William Bennett, " 'To Reclaim a Legacy': Text of Report on Humanities in Higher Education," *Chronicle of Higher Education,* November 28, 1984, pp. 16–21; Diane Ravitch and Chester Finn, Jr., *What Do Our 17-Year-Olds Know?* (New York: Harper & Row, 1988); for an excellent critique of this position, see Robert Scholes, "Aiming a Canon at the Curriculum," *Salmagundi* 72 (Fall 1986): 101–17.

2. This issue is taken up in Martin Carnoy and Henry M. Levin, *Schooling and Work in the Democratic State* (Stanford, Calif.: Stanford University Press, 1985).

3. Allen Bloom, *The Closing of the American Mind* (New York: Simon & Schuster, 1987); and E. D. Hirsch, Jr., *Cultural Literacy: What Every American Needs to Know* (New York: Vintage Books, Inc., 1988).

4. Bloom, *The Closing of the American Mind,* p. 344.

5. Ibid., p. 75.

6. Given Bloom's tirade on popular culture and rock 'n' roll, it is both somewhat surprising and ironic that when a reporter asked him if he had anticipated the popular success of *The Closing of the American Mind,* he responded with "Sometimes I can't believe it. . . . It's like being declared Cary Grant, or a rock star. All this energy passing through you [my emphasis]." From James Atlas, "Chicago's Grumpy Guru: Best-Selling Professor Allan Bloom and the Chicago Intellectuals," *The New York Times Magazine,* January 3, 1988, p. 25. Maybe Bloom has missed the contradiction here, but it appears that his newfound energy undermines both his critique of the affective value of popular culture and his need to interrogate the underlying dichotomy he constructs between pleasure and learning. He may be surprised to find that the terrain of pleasure may be more complex and contradictory than he first imagined. See Henry A. Giroux and Roger I. Simon, "Popular Culture and Critical Pedagogy," *Cultural Studies* 2 (1988): 294–320.

7. See Walter Benjamin, "Theses on the Philosophy of History," in *Illuminations,* ed. Hannah Arendt (New York: Schocken Books, 1963), pp. 253–264.

8. Bloom, *The Closing of the American Mind,* p. 89.

9. Ibid., pp. 192–93.

10. In Martha Nussbaum, "Undemocratic Vistas," *The New York Review of Books,* November 5, 1987, p. 22.

11. Mikhail Bakhtin, *The Dialogic Imagination,* ed. Michael Holquist, trans. Caryl Emerson and Michael Holquist (Austin, Tex.: The University of Texas Press, 1981).

12. Robert Scholes provides an illuminating commentary on the conservative agenda underlying the differences and commonalities that characterize the Bloom and Hirsch books.

    Hirsch wants to save us through information. He thinks that knowing about things is more important than knowing things. Bloom, on the other hand, thinks that the only thing that can save us is a return to really knowing and experiencing the great books, especially the great works of political and social philosophy that follow in the train of Plato's *Republic.* Hirsch concerns himself with what every American student should know, whereas Bloom is concerned only about a tiny elite. Together, they set the conservative agenda for American education. Hirsch will make sure that everyone knows what the classics are and respects them, while Bloom will see to it that an elite can be defined by actually knowing these classics. In this way, the masses will be sufficiently educated to respect the superior knowledge of their betters, who have studied in a few major universities. Both Hirsch and Bloom emphasize certain kinds of traditional learning, but it is important to recognize that the attitude they take toward this learning is very different. For Bloom nothing less than a prolonged, serious engagement with the great books themselves can save the souls of our students. For Hirsch, just knowing the names of the great books and authors will suffice. Both Hirsch and Bloom share, however, a nostalgia for a not very closely examined past in which things were better. (Robert Scholes, "Three Views of Education: Nostalgia, History, and Voodoo," *College English,* 50 [1988]: 323–24).

13. Hirsch, *Cultural Literacy,* p. xiii.

14. Ibid., p. 4.

15. The simplicity, ignorance, and political interests that often form this particular view of Western culture are brilliantly analyzed and deconstructed in James Clifford, *The Predicament of Culture: Twentieth Century Ethnography* (Cambridge, Mass.: Harvard University Press, 1988).

16. Hirsch, *Cultural Literacy,* p. 83.

17. Ibid., p. 3.

18. For a criticism of this form of testing, see Allan Nairn and associates, *The Reign of ETS: The Corporation that Makes Up Minds* (Washington, D.C.: Ralph Nader, 1980); David Owen, *None of the Above: Behind the Myth of Scholastic Aptitude* (Boston: Houghton Mifflin, 1985); Peter Schrag, "Who Wants Good Teachers?" *The Nation,* October 11, 1986, pp. 332–45.

19. For both a statistical and a theoretical analysis of these problems, see National Coalition of Advocates for Students, *Barriers to Excellence: Our Children at Risk* (Boston: Author, 1985).

20. Michael W. Apple, *Teachers and Text: A Political Economy of Class and Gender Relations in Education* (London: Routledge and Kegan Paul, 1986).

21. Linda Darling-Hammond, "Valuing Teachers: The Making of a Profession," *Teachers College Record* 87 (1985): 210.

22. For a review of this literature, see Henry A. Giroux, *Theory and Resistance in Education* (South Hadley, Mass.: Bergin & Garvey, 1985).

23. See for example, Pat Shannon, "The Use of Commercial Reading Materials in American Elementary Schools," *Reading Research Quarterly* 19 (1983): 68–85; Patrick Shannon, "Reading Instruction and Social Class," *Language Arts* 63 (1985): 604–11; Kenneth S. Goodman, "Basal Readers: A Call for Action," *Language Arts* 63 (1986): 358–63.

24. See, for example, Michelle Fine, "Silencing in Public Schools," *Language Arts* 64 (1987): 157–74; Henry A. Giroux, *Schooling and the Struggle for Public Life* (Minneapolis, Minn.: University of Minnesota Press, 1988).

25. Martin Carnoy and Henry M. Levin, *Schooling and Work in the Democratic State* (Stanford, Calif.: Stanford University Press, 1985); Ira Katznelson and Margaret Weir, *Schooling for All: Class, Race, and the Decline of the Democratic Ideal* (New York: Basic Books, 1985); Stanley Aronowitz and Henry A. Giroux, *Education under Siege: The Conservative, Liberal and Radical Debate over Schooling* (South Hadley, Mass.: Bergin & Garvey, 1985).

26. Hirsch's view of history represents what Harvey J. Graff calls a radically idealist conception of historical causation, in which one speaks "in historical claims without studying or interpreting any range of historical evidence or [presumes] the universality and power of ideas without inquiring into them and their actual or alternative historical contexts or consequences." Harvey J. Graff, "A Review of: *The Closing of the American Mind: How Higher Education Has Failed Democracy and Impoverished the Souls of Today's Students,*" *Society* 25 (November/December, 1987):101.

27. Herbert M. Kliebard, *The struggle for the American Curriculum, 1893–1958* (New York: Routledge and Kegan Paul, 1986).

28. Hirsch's view of history is strikingly similar to that expressed by William J. Bennett in his "To Reclaim a Legacy." In this view, as Harvey J. Kaye has pointed out, history is not conveyed as a "sense of the conflicts between social and political groups over ideas, values, and social relations. Nor does it posit the necessity of examining the distance between 'ideal' and 'experience' in Western Civilization and world history." In Harvey J. Kaye, "The Use and Abuse of the Past: The New Right and the Crisis of History," in *Socialist Register 1987,* ed. Ralph Miliband, Leo Panitch, and John Saville (London: The Merlin Press, 1987), p. 354.

29. Hirsch argues for a notion of cultural literacy that suffers both from a misplaced faith in its social and economic possibilities and from a refusal to take seriously how a pedagogy consistent with the aims of this particular form of literacy might be constructed. In the first instance, Hirsch argues that literacy is an essential precondition for eliminating just about every social and economic evil that plagues contemporary industrial societies. In this view, literacy becomes an independent variable that operates as part of a simple cause-and-effect relationship to produce particular outcomes. The issue here is not simply that Hirsch claims more for literacy than it can actually do as an ideological and social practice; more important, Hirsch presents an argument for literacy that both ignores and mystifies the role that wider cultural, historical, and social forces play in defining both the different forms of literacy and in supporting particular political and economic inequities. Hirsch's view of literacy is one that is silent about the wider problems and inequities that plague American society, problems that are rooted in configurations of power and structural relations that call into question not simply the dominant forms of literacy but the political, economic, and social fabric of the society itself. This issue is discussed in Harvey Graff, *The Literacy Myth: Literacy and Social Structure in the Nineteenth-Century City* (New York: Academic Press, 1979); see also Colin Lankshear with Moira Lawler, *Literacy, Schooling and Revolution* (New York: Falmer Press, 1987). But Hirsch does more than mystify the nature and effects of literacy, he also completely ignores the issue of what makes students want to learn, to be interested, or to listen to pedagogues such as himself. As we point out in the latter section of this essay, pedagogy for Hirsch is an unproblematic and uncritical construct, a technique to be employed after one has decided on the content to be taught. Given the wide gap between what Hirsch expects from his view of literacy and the simplistic and reactionary view of pedagogy he employs, it is not surprising that he ends up with what Scholes has called "voodoo education." See Scholes, "Three Views of Education," p. 327.

30. Hirsch, *Cultural Literacy,* p. 24.

31. This literature is extensively reviewed in Giroux, *Theory and Resistance in Education.*

32. Ray Rist, "On Understanding the Process of Schooling: The Contribution of Labeling Theory," in *Power and Ideology,* ed. J. Karabel and A. H. Halsey (New York: Oxford University Press, 1977); Jean Anyon, "Social Class and the Hidden Curriculum of Work," in *Curriculum and Instruction,* ed. Henry A. Giroux, Anthony Penna, and William Pinar (Berkeley, Calif.: McCutchan Publishing, 1981); High Mehan, *Learning Lessons* (Cambridge, Mass.: Harvard University Press, 1979).

33. Kathleen Rockhill, "Gender, Language and the Politics of Literacy," *British Journal of Sociology of Education* 8 (1987): 158.

34. June Jordan, *On Call: Political Essays* (Boston: South End Press, 1987), p. 30.

35. The notion of literacy as a form of cultural politics that embodies a particular pedagogical practice is most evident in the works of Paulo Freire. See, for example, Paulo Freire, *Pedagogy of the Oppressed,* trans. Myra Bergman Ramos (New York: Seabury Press, 1968); Paulo Freire and Donaldo Macedo, *Literacy: Reading the Word and the World* (South Hadley, Mass.: Bergin & Garvey, 1987).

36. Jordan, *On Call,* p. 29.

37. Martha Nussbaum's comment on the narrowness of Bloom's reading of the fruits of Western civilization is worth repeating. She writes:

His special love for these books [the old Great Books of the ancient philosophers] has certainly prevented him from attending to works of literature and philosophy that lie outside the tradition they began. For he makes the remarkable claim that "only in the Western nations, i.e., those influenced by Greek philosophy, is there some willingness to doubt the identification of the good with one's own way." This statement shows a startling ignorance of the critical and rationalist tradition in classical Indian thought, of the arguments of classical Chinese thinkers, and beyond this, of countless examples of philosophical and nonphilosophical self-criticism from many parts of the world. (Nussbaum, "Undemocratic Vistas," p. 22)

11

Textbooks: The International Dimension

Philip G. Altbach

School textbooks are assumed to be a product of a particular nation to be used in its educational system. Textbooks, despite the recent criticism of them in the United States, are virtual icons of education. Textbooks also have an important and rapidly expanding international dimension. In some countries, mainly in the Third World, textbooks are frequently produced outside the country and often reflect foreign values.[1] In the United States and Western Europe, multinational publishers have entered the textbook business and their impact is just beginning to be felt. Two major multinational publishers, Britain's Pergamon and West Germany's Bertelsmann, are now among America's largest textbook publishers. American media giants, such as Gulf and Western, have also consolidated their role in the textbook field, buying up smaller firms and expanding their operations. In general, there has been a major centralization in textbook publishing in the United States. Foreign expertise helps to shape the nature of textbooks. Increasingly, textbooks are being printed in such major centers of low-cost printing as Singapore and Hong Kong.[2] The major industrialized nations—the United States and Britain in English, and France, West Germany, and the Soviet Union—play an increasingly important international role in the world of textbooks. The era of textbook multinationalism has arrived, and international influences will be increasingly felt worldwide.

The world of textbooks is an unequal world. The major metropolitan centers have the expertise, publishing infrastructures, access to paper, and capital to play a dominating role. They also use the major world languages (English, French, German, Russian, and Spanish). The major multinational publishers of textbooks—firms like Macmillan, Longmans, and Pergamon in Britain, Harper and Row, Gulf and Western, and Prentice Hall in the United States, Bertelsmann in West Germany, Hachette in France, and a few others—are all located in the metropolitan centers. Much of the rest of the world finds itself in a peripheral position, depending to varying degrees on the knowledge products of the centers. There are also some countries that have a good deal of autonomy within the system. Large Third World nations such as India and China have major domestic publishing industries and produce their own textbooks. Countries like Mexico and Egypt play a kind of mediating role, publishing their own textbooks, which are then exported to smaller Third World nations in their regions, but also working closely with firms in the industrialized countries, which often locate their branch offices in these countries.

Peripherality is not simply a matter of existing imbalances in wealth, the use of major metropolitan languages, and the like. There is also a direct political and economic dimension. Countries, and major publishers, that are at the center desire to retain their position. They often engage in policies that are aimed at maintaining the status quo. For example, the desire of major multinational publishers to export books to smaller markets rather than to build up an indigenous capacity that might, in the long run, provide competition has the result of retaining existing center-periphery relations. In many cases, the political and economic interests of the centers to maintain their dominant position work very much against the development of autonomy and independence at the periphery.

Publishing, especially, in the Third World, is also part of the tradition of colonial domination and neocolonial influence. Colonial powers such as Britain and France had policies with regard to book publishing and textbooks just as they did with regard to trade and commerce. Almost without exception, the colonial experience resulted in cementing inequalities within the intellectual system of a colony. As movements for independence emerged in the Third World, nationalist forces paid attention to cultural and educational policies. Efforts were made to build indigenous competence in publishing and in textbook development. However, the challenges have proved daunting, and few Third World countries have been able to build a fully independent indigenous publishing and textbook apparatus.

Peripheral nations are not necessarily all in the Third World. Canada, for example, has been concerned about its cultural autonomy and has worried about "Canadian content" in its textbooks.[3] Despite steps to protect its intellectual integrity, it is subject to major foreign influences from the United States and Britain and also from France with relation to French-speaking Quebec. The 1988 Canadian-American free trade treaty, similar to a much more far-reaching pact to be implemented in 1992 in Western Europe, will also have significant implications for Canada's intellectual marketplace.

In the industrialized countries, textbook multinationalism is largely hidden. It has more to do with the ownership of firms and the internationalization of expertise than with the import and export of books.[4] Textbooks are designed for national educational systems and are in the national language. Markets are large enough to sustain books specifically designed for the subjects, age levels, and orientations of educational systems. In the Third World, multinationalism is a much more direct and important factor. For smaller Third World nations, textbooks, even for the elementary levels, are sometimes imported from abroad. Even when they are "adapted" for local needs by multinational publishers, much of the content is unrelated to local circumstances and the books are often edited and printed abroad. Thus, internationalism in textbooks varies according to the specific circumstances of the country. It is, everywhere, a growing trend that needs to be considered in the increasingly complex world of textbooks.

Multinationalism in textbooks is not only a matter of ownership and markets. It is also has to do with conceptions of knowledge and of ideas about the nature of education and the role of textbooks in educational systems. As a worldwide textbook culture is created by the multinational firms, textbook ideas that dominate the Western countries come to predominate in the rest of the world. Since textbooks provide an intellectual "map" of the world and its knowledge for students, the ideas that shape textbook development have considerable importance not only for the books but also for the curriculum.

The International Knowledge System

Textbooks are part of an international system of knowledge that affects virtually all intellectual endeavors.[5] The fact is that a relatively small number of countries dominate the world's knowledge system, and this system has an impact on textbooks as well as on other knowledge products. The system is dominated by the major academic institutions, research laboratories, and publishers in the industrialized nations. Size is a key factor. Eighty percent of the world's R and D expenditures is spent in a handful of the major industrialized countries. This is as true for educational research and curriculum development as it is for applied microelectronics. The large academic institutions in the United States, Britain, and elsewhere contain the best libraries and the most advanced laboratories, and have the greatest commitment to research and the dissemination of knowledge. Wealth, of course, is also a factor. These key universities also have funds available for advanced scientific research and for maintaining the infrastructures of research. They stress graduate programs, which are research-oriented.[6] And they train large numbers of foreign students, many of whom return home to become key researchers and academic leaders there. The impact of their foreign training includes being socialized into the research norms and orientations of the "host" universities. Language is a factor. The major world languages, and particularly English, dominate science and scholarship. The major journals are published in these languages, and scholars, in order to have access to the most advanced work, must know them. Most of the advanced textbooks are published in the major metropolitan languages, and frequently these are the books that are either used or adapted in smaller countries.

There is a powerful "invisible college" of experts and scholars that plays a key role in the creation and dissemination of knowledge. These top experts almost invariably work in the major industrialized countries. They decide what knowledge is published in the major internationally circulated journals, and they are at the center of their research system. Their perspectives shape research agendas, and, ultimately, their perceptions of knowledge become what is accepted as legitimate. Key scholars also advise the large multinational publishers and interact with international agencies that work on curricular innovations and that have an impact on textbook development. The invisible colleges reflect the research concerns of the major industrialized countries.

Textbook development and production are affected by the international knowledge system in many ways. New technologies, such as computer-assisted instruction, generally emerge from the centers and, in part because they have the legitimacy of the key scholars and institutions, are disseminated widely. These technologies have an impact on thinking about textbooks and, ultimately, on the ways in which textbooks are used. New curricular ideas emerge from the centers, inevitably reflecting the conditions in the schools of the centers, and are gradually diffused to the peripheries. The very concept of the textbook is affected by international factors. The use of glossy paper, illustrations, and hard covers for most textbooks is related to the conditions in the schools of the affluent center countries. While poorer countries often produce less elaborate books, everyone is affected by what is considered the "gold standard" of textbooks. John Meyer and his colleagues are currently looking at international trends in the curriculum.[7] They have found a remarkable convergence, over time, of subjects and of the time spent on them in the classroom. While it is not clear what the mechanisms of this convergence are, it is very likely that curricular trends, and the textbooks that accompany the curriculum, go from the center to the peripheries.

The international knowledge system is a powerful combination of forces that dominates in many ways the development and dissemination of new ideas. The combination of resources, expertise, and size of academic systems and infrastructures means that ideas and knowledge products are to a significant degree centralized in a small number of countries and academic systems. This centralization helps to shape ideas about education as much as it shapes high energy physics. And ideas eventually shape educational practice and educational support systems—including textbooks.

The Infrastructure of Textbooks

The publishing of textbooks is a complex and little-understood process. It also has international dimensions that are growing in importance. The physical production of a textbook seems a simple enough matter. Yet it requires considerable coordination and is increasingly affected by international factors. The advent of computer-assisted design, high-speed printing equipment, and enhanced (and often considerably cheaper) graphic capability has affected textbook publishing. These new publishing technologies are international in the sense that they were developed and are largely produced in the United States, to some extent Western Europe, and, increasingly, Japan. These new technologies have given increased flexibility to textbook publishing and have in some areas reduced the cost of textbook development. These technologies will be of special relevance to the Third World. However, these new technologies must be purchased from the industrialized nations, and the investment is sometimes quite high. New expertise is required to use these innovations, and this fact requires further investment in personnel.

The infrastructures of many Third World nations are not geared to high-tech developments. For example, firms in India that use computer networks must have their own power supplies and often must rely on their own satellite-based communications systems to ensure success. Despite these logistical problems, however, the new technologies of publishing will have a continuing impact on textbook publishing in the Third World. New technologies are already widespread in the industrialized world and have major implications for the further internationalization of text publishing. Networks make it much easier to communicate across borders and to share data. The new technologies for design and printing will further link publishers to international software developers, to producers of sophisticated printing equipment, and, of course, to the supply and service facilities of these vendors. The implications for tying smaller publishing industries and publishers to the international marketplace may be significant.

Paper is, of course, a key ingredient in textbook publishing. Because of the large print-runs, paper is a major part of the cost of book production for a textbook series and an important concern of textbook publishers. Paper is also an international commodity, although it is not often considered in this context. Three nations dominate the international paper market—Canada, Sweden, and the United States.[8] The United States produces the bulk of its own supply of "book paper"—the high-quality paper used for book production as opposed to newsprint and paper use for packaging and other purposes. Thus the United States is not significantly dependent on overseas suppliers, although the price of paper in the United States is directly influenced by international trends. Most other countries must import significant quantities of paper for their textbooks, even when newsprint rather than "book paper" is used for texts. The international price of paper is determined by the process of supply and demand, and the major exporters have a significant influence on the price that is paid by the users. The importing nations of the Third World are very much at the mercy of variations in the export price of paper. Western European importers are also dependent on international paper prices but are better able to absorb variations. In recent years, paper prices have fluctuated significantly, and, overall, the price of "book paper" has increased, with shortages occurring from time to time. Efforts by some Third World nations to use nontraditional raw materials to manufacture paper, such as the leftovers from the production of sugar cane or rice materials, have met with some success, although the paper that is produced is not of the same quality.[9] Paper is part of the international infrastructure of text publishing, and there is need for further analysis of the politics and economics of paper.

Publishing is very much a matter of the coordination of skills and processes.[10] It requires both a very high level of expertise and the ability to bring together a large number of elements to produce a book. Publishers seldom own printing presses, for example, and find it much more economical to contract for printing services. They usually use typesetting firms to do the actual composing of books, although this is changing because of the advent of computer-assisted composing and design. Editing talent is also required in order to turn unpolished manuscripts into books. For textbooks, careful editing is particularly necessary because the style and presentation of material is important for pedagogical success. Publishing requires a significant amount of expertise within the firm. Publishers must also have access to additional, outside expertise and facilities. Without this expertise, a successful publishing industry cannot exist.

Expertise in publishing is increasingly becoming internationalized, in part as a result of the growing domination of the multinational publishers but also because of innovations in communications and technology. Books can be designed in one country, edited in another, and printed in a third. Computer networking, fax technology, and other communications technologies make decentralization practical.

The actual production of books is also increasingly international. While virtually all American school textbooks are still printed in the United States, it is likely that there will be more "offshore" printing in the future. Several factors come together to create this trend. The "manufacturing clause" that was part of U.S. copyright law until a few years ago meant that books with large print-runs had to be printed in the United States in order to qualify for copyright protection. This regulation is no longer in force, and publishers have been slowly moving to have more books printed abroad. The expanding role of multinational publishers with international experience will increase the use of overseas printing since these firms have international contacts. Finally, foreign printers and, to some extent, compositors have become more aggressive in the American market—and they have increased their sophistication. Printers in the newly industrialized Asian countries, especially in Hong Kong and Singapore, are already involved in the printing of scholarly books and some textbooks for European and Australian publishers; they also print many of the textbooks used in Africa. It is significant that several of the most important of these firms are owned by major Japanese printers and publishers.

There is an unmistakable trend toward the internationalization of the process of publishing. Publishers are moving to use the most efficient and least expensive expertise and processes wherever in the world they are found. The quest for ever cheaper labor and production costs must be emphasized. The process of textbook production is becoming comparable to what has happened in automobile manufacturing, with components being "outsourced" to countries with lower labor costs and the most efficient production techniques. The implications of this internationalization of the infrastructures of publishing are considerable, and they will inevitably make textbooks less of a "national" product than has, at least in the West, traditionally been the case.

Textbooks as an International Commodity

In the industrialized nations, textbooks at the elementary and secondary school levels are, on the surface, domestic products. They are prepared to meet the needs of domestic educational systems and are not published for export. International expertise increasingly affects how textbooks are developed, but the bulk of the professional knowledge—as well as the content that goes into the books—is domestic. For many countries in the Third World, the international ramifications are much greater. Textbooks are often imported from abroad or, although published by foreign multinational publishers to meet local or regional needs, are nonetheless printed abroad. In these instances, the countries involved have only a limited amount of control over the books used in their schools. Local ministries of education have specific goals and requirements, but in the end must select from products already in the marketplace.

It is clear that the basic concept of the textbook is a Western idea that has been revised in the industrialized nations and exported to the rest of the world. The textbook, of course, is directly related to the established curriculum. This, too, is a Western invention, one that has been developed over time and that shows a remarkable worldwide convergence. Various ideas about textbooks—that they should have illustrations, that they should be printed on glossy paper, that they should be "loaned" to students rather than given to them, and that they should be issued by private sector publishers—are all very much concepts of the capitalist West. Some Third World nations have diverged from the "gold standard" of textbook development, but only after careful consideration.[11] For example, there is a growing trend toward the use of newsprint and fewer graphics as a means of reducing the price of textbooks. China, for example, has produced inexpensive textbooks for a long period. The evolution of textbooks stems from a common Western tradition, however, and this has been a powerful influence on the development of textbooks worldwide.

Textbooks have become an international commodity to a considerable extent because the publishers that issue them tend more and more to be multinational firms. This has always been the case for Africa, for example, but it is a new phenomenon in the industrialized nations. The growing multinationalism of the publishers is a very new development; as a result of this, its full impact is not yet clear. As noted earlier, key European publishers are now a major influence in American publishing. It is likely that the trend toward multinational control of important European publishers will accelerate significantly in the period prior to 1992; and when the European Community drops all internal tariffs, Western Europe will become a virtually "open" market not only for trade but also for education and culture. European educators are concerned about the implications for education, including those implications posed by the increased concentration of the publishing industry. European multinational publishers are likely to want to design textbooks with an European market in mind and thereby reduce production costs. This may tend to homogenize the books and perhaps the curriculum in the European Community. It is possible to design a textbook with common graphics, examples, and pictures and then adapt the text according to language and specific national curricular guidelines. This is already done in Africa and by local publishers in India to produce books for diverse language markets. Publishers in Hong Kong, for example, produce secondary-school texts that are used not only in local schools but also in Southeast Asia and sometimes in other Third World regions. In Europe, this technique would be a significant change.

Internationalization of textbooks has gone farthest in Africa, where educators are faced with a proliferation of languages spoken by small populations, a lack of both the expertise and the funds to develop indigenous books, and an entrenched group of multinational publishers that have dominated the textbook market since the colonial period. Even in Nigeria, which has a very large internal market for textbooks, the multinational firms remain important. In Anglophone West Africa, the multinational firms, almost exclusively British, work with local education officials to adapt books for local curricular orientations.[12] The books are then prepared in Britain (or perhaps in a firm's regional offices in an African metropole like Lagos) based on a common book design and text, ones most likely originally developed for British schools and loosely adapted for the African context.

In some cases, the books are produced in English; in other instances, they are translated into the local language. They are then printed in Britain or, increasingly, in Hong Kong or Singapore, which offer low-cost printing. For Francophone Africa, the textbook scene is even more completely dominated by multinational publishers, in this case French firms. The French language is more widely used in Francophone West Africa than the English language is used in its former colonial sphere. Textbooks tend to be "Africanized" to suit the African environment and to meet the needs of local educational officials, but the books are printed in France and published by the French multinationals.

In Africa, much of the process of textbook writing, adaptation, and publishing is done by expatriates, frequently in the publisher's home office in Britain or France. It is often only the work of translation that remains in the hands of indigenous people. Local education authorities must, of course, approve the books, and in many cases they have significant input into the process of adaptation and publishing. The fact remains, however, that the books are basically foreign products produced for profit by multinational firms and sold in a marketplace that has few, if any, alternative sources of books. There are many reasons for this situation. At the time of independence, there was very little publishing capability in Africa. At the same time, the British firms were well-established and dominated the book trade. This situation not only satisfied local needs but also permitted newly independent countries to expand educational systems without worrying about the provision of textbooks. The domination of the colonial languages—English and French—which developed in the colonial era, was also due to the large number of locally—often tribally—based languages that, both for political and logistical reasons, could not be used as a national language. In many instances, these languages had no written tradition. Thus, the metropolitan languages retained their importance even where, as in Nigeria and Ghana, indigenous languages had also been introduced into the school.

Where the multinationals dominated, it has proved to be quite difficult to establish indigenous publishing firms. The initial cost of developing a publishing firm is high, both in fiscal terms and in expertise. Furthermore, in a marketplace that even in the best of circumstances does not yield very high profits, it is very difficult to compete with a well-established firm that has the ability to produce and sell books abroad. Indigenous markets in Africa are often very small and inherently unprofitable. Such markets can be served on a regional basis but only with considerable local subsidies. Local entrepreneurs have not been enthusiastic about entering publishing because so many risks are involved and profits are low at best. These are some of the reasons for the slow development of indigenous publishing in Africa and the continued domination of the multinationals. Despite these very significant problems, there have been some impressive developments.

In Nigeria, local firms have emerged, often with government assistance, to serve local publishing and textbook needs. There has been an impressive growth of text publishing in the larger Nigerian languages. Kenya, in East Africa, has also developed indigenous publishing capacity. In some instances, multinational firms have assisted local businesses or government agencies in developing publishing expertise. Zimbabwe as well has considerable success in developing indigenous publishing capacity and locally written and published textbooks. Nonprofit private publishers such as the Mambo Press have contributed significantly to local textbook development. But, even in Zimbabwe, the multinationals continue to be a major force in publishing, although increasingly they are producing locally written books for the educational market. In the decade of the 1980s, and to some extent even somewhat before, there was a dramatic expansion of government involvement in textbook publishing in Africa and in other Third World countries. In some cases, the government directly published books; in others, government ministries helped to set up of state-aided enterprises.

There has been more widespread development of indigenous textbook publishing in Asia, although the multinationals remain strong in some areas and new foreign firms have entered some markets, notably from the United States and Japan. The large majority of Indian schoolbooks in the nation's indigenous languages are now published either by government agencies or by indigenous private-sector publishers. Only schoolbooks for the small number of "elite" private schools that use English as the primary medium of instruction are published by expatriate firms, and, even in these cases the books are mostly written or adapted in India and also printed in India. In Southeast Asia, the picture is more mixed. Multinational publishers are entrenched in the marketplace, but they have been active in developing textbooks for local use in such countries as Malaysia. The *Dewan Bahasa dan Pustaka* in Malaysia has actively fostered locally produced textbooks. Some of these books have been written specifically for Malaysian schools; others have been adapted from Western sources and translated into Bahasa Malaysia (the national language).[13] There is some importing of schoolbooks from England or the United States as well. Most Asian countries use indigenous languages in the schools, and books must be published in these languages to suit local needs. In a few countries, such as Malaysia, Thailand, and Taiwan—which until recently have not been part of the international copyright network—there has been much adapting or sometimes translating from foreign (largely British or American) textbooks, without payment or attribution.[14] While this "piracy" has permitted local publishers to get a foothold in the local marketplace, it has to some extent inhibited the development of truly indigenous textbooks. As these countries have joined the international copyright community, and as their publishing industries and education agencies have become more sophisticated, there has been a rapid growth in indigenous textbook products.

Textbooks have, in the Third World, been international commodities for a long time. This is due both to the heritage of colonialism and to the problems of producing indigenous books. The multinationals have the expertise, the markets, and the capital to produce and distribute textbooks. In some countries they completely dominate the textbook scene. In others they remain a force, either directly or indirectly. Relatively few Third World nations are completely free of international influences on their textbooks. For the industrialized world, internationalization is a newer phenomenon, one that is only now emerging into full view. The ownership of firms is, of course, a key element in the equation, and it is not clear how the increasing concentration of ownership will affect textbook publishing in the United States and Western Europe. It is, however, clear that multinational publishers are becoming more and more important in textbook publishing worldwide.

Textbooks and International Expertise

Just as the infrastructures of textbook publishing have become more international, so too has the expertise that goes into textbooks. As noted earlier, the major academic systems of the large industrialized nations dominate research, including research on education and work on textbooks, reading, measurement, curriculum studies, and other fields relevant to the development of textbooks. The internationalization of expertise can be seen largely as a process by which research and expertise from the center are used by the peripheries.

Textbooks are increasingly developed by using research-based insights into what is most effective. International educational research thus has an expanding influence on textbook development worldwide. Traditionally, textbook publishers and authors paid attention mainly to the curricular guidelines set forth by government ministries and educational establishments. The system of textbook development has become more research-based in recent years, in part because there has been more research on various aspects of textbook effectiveness, design, and other factors. The largest proportion of this research has been done in the industrialized nations. It reflects the educational realities of these nations, especially those of the United States, which has pioneered research about the effectiveness of texts. The application of this research to other national contexts, and particularly to the very different cultural and educational circumstances of the Third World, is highly problematic because it is not at all clear that research results that are valid in industrialized contexts are useful in other contexts. But it seems that there is an increase in the use of U.S.-based research findings throughout the world. Again, the multinational publishers have played a role here as they operate on a worldwide basis and as their staffs can quickly obtain research results from around the world.

The internationalization of educational research has also been advanced by organizations such as UNESCO and the various philanthropic foundations involved in education worldwide. The World Bank, which has invested millions of dollars in textbook programs in several Third World nations, has also used international expertise. Experts from the industrialized nations have been directly involved in disseminating research results throughout the world, and this has played a role in conceptions of the textbook. Research has shed light on the effectiveness of texts and text programs (for example in basal reading), on "what works" in texts in terms of illustrations, on developing materials for teachers, and the like.

Many of those involved in the development of textbooks in ministries of education or other agencies throughout the world have been trained in the major metropolitan academic centers. Further, they remain in close communication with the centers through conferences, publications, and informal networks. The impact of overseas training is considerable in terms of instilling the norms and values of research and of approaches to knowledge. Research efforts such as the International Study of Educational Achievement (IEA) may also have had an impact on text development. IEA data rank educational systems according to student achievement on standardized tests, and these results become a kind of benchmark for achievement; efforts are frequently made to ensure that comparative scores are improved, and this often involves thinking about the curriculum and about textbooks.[15]

There is a growing international network of expertise in educational research in general, and this network plays a role in thinking about textbooks as well. Textbooks are increasingly written with attention to relevant research, and the research community is international. Agencies like the World Bank provide both concrete assistance through loans for textbook development and publication and also guidance concerning textbook development and policy. Their guidelines are generally based on research done in the major Western universities. Textbook knowledge is becoming more and more international in scope.

Textbooks in Higher Education: Variations on the Theme

It is often forgotten that postsecondary institutions require textbooks and that their provision is a significant element in the textbook business worldwide.[16] The international impact on university-level books is even greater than is the case for primary and secondary books. There are fewer controls on the provision of postsecondary texts, and there is more leeway for individual institutions and professors to adopt books without external interference. While primary and secondary textbook production in many countries is under government control and in the public sector, this is seldom the case for university-level books (except, of course, in the centrally planned economies). This relative freedom of production and assignment gives a wider scope for competing publishers and books in the international marketplace.

While there are no reliable statistics, it seems clear that postsecondary textbooks are more international than elementary and secondary school texts. Textbooks in many fields are used in many countries. University-level books are widely translated from one language to another.[17] Many of the major university-level textbook publishers are multinational firms. Considerable attention is given to the export of textbooks, and in some cases the export market is factored into the financial projections of texts. Books in some fields are more readily exported than in other disciplines. For example, books in the sciences can be easily exported because the knowledge in them is not so much affected by local conditions. Further, the cost of producing books in some scientific fields is high because of complex figures, illustrations, and the like; publishers in smaller markets cannot afford the high costs of publication of these books. In such circumstances it is more profitable to import the book or to arrange with an overseas publisher to translate the book into a local language. In some Third

World countries, until quite recently, college textbooks were pirated—reproduced without obtaining permission from the originating publisher. Books in history and in the social sciences are more difficult to use internationally because their content is tied to the country in which they are published. Nonetheless, there is a considerable degree of export activity for such books as well.

The bulk of the international trade in university-level textbooks is, not surprisingly, from the centers to the peripheries. Virtually all of the university texts used in the United States, for example, are published in the United States and written by American authors with the U.S. market in mind. This is true as well for Britain and for such large academic markets as France and West Germany. Smaller academic markets import a significant portion of their academic textbooks. Canada, for example, has long been concerned that many of the books used in its universities have little, if any, "Canadian content" and present material that is not relevant for Canadian readers. Even for a country as wealthy as Canada, with its substantial university system, there are problems with producing a sufficient number of textbooks for the undergraduate curriculum. For graduate studies, in Canada and in other small academic markets, the most of the textbooks are imported. Because it uses books in English and in French, Canada finds it easy to import books. Small academic markets that do not use "world languages" find the textbook situation even more difficult. For countries like the Netherlands, Finland, or Denmark, university students must read books in English although the universities use the local language for instruction. Greater stress is placed on knowledge of foreign languages in these countries. Textbooks are imported from the United States or Britain for use in local universities.

The situation in Third World countries is also quite difficult. For smaller Third World nations, virtually all postsecondary textbooks are imported from abroad, although, in a few cases, books from other Third World nations such as India are used as alternatives to Western books. Except for the largest Third World nations, such as India, Mexico, Argentina, and a few others, the production of postsecondary textbooks is an overwhelming task. In some cases, books are translated into local languages, but very often they are used in the original language, and this creates problems of comprehension for students who are insufficiently trained in Western languages.

There are several significant examples of Third World countries attempting to provide books relevant for their own students and at the same time building up an indigenous publishing infrastructure. Malaysia, with a relatively small population of fifteen million, has invested money and attention in ensuring that Malaysian students have books in the local language, *Bahasa Malaysia,* for undergraduate courses. The government-funded *Dewan Bahasa dan Pustaka,* sponsors new textbooks and translates books from foreign languages into the local medium. Progress has been slow, but there is a growing number of college textbooks in *Bahasa Malaysia.* However, the country still relies on books in English for graduate study.

India is another example of a country that has quite successfully created its own college textbook industry—an industry that has in fact helped to support other parts of the local publishing apparatus that earn lower profits. With three million students in its colleges and universities, India has a large internal market for its textbooks. There is also a large number of academics willing to write books aimed at this large local market, and there are publishers in the private sector able to publish college textbooks successfully. Indian publishers have had to compete, sometimes with difficult odds, against textbooks published in the West and sold in India at highly subsidized prices as part of foreign assistance efforts.[18] Such programs, which have been sponsored by the United States, Britain, and the Soviet Union, do provide books to Indian students. At the same time they make it more difficult to publish locally written and published books in a subsidized marketplace. India has been able to provide college texts in several of its indigenous languages as well, because local markets are large enough to sustain these attempts. There are successful university-level text publishers in such languages as Hindi, Marathi, Bengali, and Tamil. India has developed a significant export market for its English-language university textbooks in other Third World nations, which find Indian-produced books less expensive and sometimes more relevant than Western textbooks.

University-level textbook publishing is more international than other segments of text publishing. University-level books use the most current knowledge and rely on sophisticated research. They are less oriented to national conditions than are books at lower levels of the educational system. The multinational publishers are particularly active in the higher-education market and see this market as closely tied to their publishing programs in scholarly areas. Indeed, university text publishing is an important profit center for many publishers, including some of the nonprofit university presses.

The markets in individual countries for university-level books are often quite small, and local publishers cannot produce books for these markets. Thus, importing books is a necessity. While a number of countries have made progress in providing textbooks for local use, it is likely that there will continue to be a significant international market for such textbooks. As the university curriculum becomes more diverse and complex, the international market may in fact grow. Books may be translated, published under license, or even adapted to local needs, but there will still be an international presence in the market. For graduate study the international impact will be even greater. The Western-based multinational publishers will dominate, and books written in the major industrialized nations will be the most influential in the international marketplace.

The Future of Textbooks
in an Interdependent World

For many countries—those under colonial rule, many *Third World nations,* and countries with small populations—textbooks have always had significant international ramifications. Nations, and educational systems at the periphery, are always dependent to some extent on the centers. This is as true for textbooks and research expertise as it is for military equipment. The ramifications of peripherality include reliance on imported books, dependence on the multinational publishers, and the like.

Textbooks are without question an element in the struggle for cultural and educational independence for many countries, both in the Third World and in smaller industrialized nations. For the multinational publishers they are a commodity to be traded in an international marketplace. But for schools that must use books that do not reflect local circumstances or relevant pedagogical techniques, textbook development is a serious problem. For the poorest nations—for example, in most African countries today—there is a shortage of textbooks at all levels, and there are few signs of improvement. There are problems of development and a related problem of supply. The ramifications of issues of textbooks differ from country to country. Without question, however, textbooks are an element of controversy and struggle.

For the United States and other large industrialized nations, international influences on textbooks are newer and more subtle. The fact remains that the United States still influences the rest of the world much more than it is influenced by it, at least in terms of educational research and the production and distribution of textbooks. Education remains a growth industry in America, and it has a "positive balance of trade" because the U.S. exports a greater number of educational programs, expertise, and "knowledge products" than it imports.

Things are changing, and this will inevitably result in a more interdependent world and an increase in international influences on the United States. The recent growth of the multinational publishers and are penetration of the American publishing scene has significant ramifications. Key decisions concerning American publishing, including text publishing, are now being made in London and Frankfurt as well as in New York, Boston, and San Diego. So far, the foreign owners of key U.S. publishers have permitted considerable autonomy to their American branches and have limited themselves mainly to financial oversight. Whether this situation of benign supervision will continue is an open question. Foreign ownership may also bring with it a greater concern for foreign expertise.

Education has become more internationally oriented, and this too has an impact on textbooks. Educational policy-makers in the United States are increasingly concerned about how American students rank in comparison with their peers in other countries and what American students are learning in comparison with students abroad. The American economy is part of the international economy, and education inevitably plays a role: international competitiveness is a slogan in education as much as it is in computer software. As a part of this trend, the school curriculum and school textbooks will have to reflect trends in other countries and will have to reflect an awareness of what is being learned abroad in order to keep up with expanding economies in Japan and Western Europe.

The internationalization of school textbook development and publishing has implications not only for the publishing industry, but also for the knowledge imparted in these textbooks. There is evidence that with centralized production, textbooks are internationally homogenized. There is also evidence that curricular research, international tests of student achievement, and other international inputs are having an impact on what is taught in schools around the world. How far this homogenization will extend is not yet clear.

Technical innovations in publishing will also affect the internationalization of textbook development and production. The multinational publishers, faced with the very high cost of textbook development, may wish to try to spread this development over several different countries. This may be possible by planning common basic curricular materials, graphics, and illustrations for books that will then be adapted to different educational systems and languages. It is also possible that books will be composed and printed outside the country that will use them. These influences are already evident in nations as different as India and New Zealand.

It is clear that textbooks will remain a core element of the educational systems of every nation. It is also clear that there will be continuing pressure for texts to improve in quality. In the poorer nations, the problems in supplying an adequate number of textbooks to the schools will be an issue as well. Differing approaches to the development of text materials will continue to be debated. There are, of course, alternatives to the reliance on the multinational publishers. The Malaysian case, cited above, shows that a middle-sized Third World nation can create its own books, even at the postsecondary level. Many countries rely on government initiative to develop and publish textbooks; while there have been criticisms of the efficiency and cost of such programs, public-sector textbook publishing is a viable option.

Even in the United States, one of the world's major textbook markets, international considerations loom large. For much of the rest of the world, international factors are of crucial importance. Textbooks are one of the most important educational inputs: texts reflect basic ideas about a national culture, and, as noted, textbooks are often a flashpoint of cultural struggle and controversy.

Notes

1. For a broader consideration of textbooks in developing countries, see Philip G. Altbach and Gail P. Kelly, eds., *Textbooks in the Third World* (New York: Garland Publishing, 1988).

2. Stephen Heyneman and Joseph P. Farrell, eds., *Textbooks in the Developing World: Economic and Educational Choices* (Washington, D.C.: The World Bank, 1989).

3. S. J. Totton, "The Marketing of Educational Books in Canada," in *Royal Commission on*

Book Publishing: Background Papers (Toronto: Queen's Printer and Publisher, Province of Ontario, 1972), pp. 270–310.

4. Journals such as *Publishers Weekly* in the United States and *The Bookseller* in Britain are filled with news about corporate takeovers and restructuring in the industry. These developments have major implications for textbook publishing.

5. See Philip G. Altbach, *The Knowledge Context* (Albany, N.Y.: State University of New York Press, 1988).

6. Joseph Ben-David, *Fundamental Research and the Universities: Some Comments on International Differences* (Paris: OECD, 1968).

7. Professor John Meyer and his colleagues at Stanford University are currently engaged in research on the convergence of the curriculum in both historical and comparative contexts.

8. Jorg Becker, "The Geopolitics of Cultural Paper: International Dimensions of Paper Production, Consumption and Import-Export Structures," background study in preparation of the Unesco World Congress on Books (London: 1982).

9. On alternative approaches to textbooks, see Heyneman and Farrell, eds., *Textbooks in the Developing World.*

10. Datus Smith, Jr., *A Guide to Book Publishing* (New York: Bowker, 1966).

11. Krishna Kumar, "The Origins of India's Textbook Culture," in Altbach and Kelly, eds., *Textbooks in the Third World,* pp. 97–112.

12. Keith Smith, "Who Controls Book Publishing in Anglophone Middle Africa?" *Annals of the American Academy of Political and Social Science* 421 (September 1975): 140–50.

13. Datuk Hassan Ahmad, "The Role of the Dewan Bahasa dan Pustaka in the Advancement of Indigenous Academic Publishing in Malaysia," in *Academic Publishing in ASEAN,* ed. S. Gopinathan (Singapore, Malaysia: Festival of Books, 1986), pp. 150–56.

14. Philip G. Altbach, "Knowledge Enigma: The Context of Copyright in the Third World," in Altbach, *The Knowledge Context,* pp. 85–112.

15. See "Special Issue on the Second IEA Study," *Comparative Education Review* 31 (February 1987): 7–158.

16. Philip G. Altbach and S. Gopinathan, "Textbooks in Third World Higher Education," in Altbach and Kelly, eds., *Textbooks in the Third World,* pp. 45–64.

17. UNESCO statistics show clearly that the bulk of the world's translations are from the major Western languages into smaller languages, with relatively little "translation traffic" going the other direction.

18. See Philip G. Altbach, *Publishing in India: An Analysis* (New Delhi and New York: Oxford University Press, 1985).

12

Building Democracy: Content and Ideology in Grenadian Educational Texts, 1979–1983

Didacus Jules

In this beginning
we will rewrite
de history books
Put William (de Conqueror)
on de back page
Make Morgan (de pirate)
A footnote

We
Will recall with pride
Our own
Grannies to come
Will know
of de Arctic Ocean
But will know more
of the Caribbean sea
of the Atlantic Ocean
"The Lesson," Merle Collins*

It has been recognized for some time now that the curriculum is central to education and that the textbook is essentially the product of a political process of contestation over knowledge. The issue of *"whose knowledge, in what form, how it is selected and by whom, and to what ends"* has been at the heart of the ongoing work of critical educators like Michael Apple, Paulo Freire, Henry Giroux, Ira Shor, and others. The textbook, as an embodiment of what Apple calls "the legitimate knowledge of identifiable groups of people,"[1] becomes the site for intense ideological struggle in those historical moments at which the hegemony of the ruling classes comes into question. And that struggle over which forms and whose knowledge gets legitimated in the textbook involves not only the politics of cultural capital but also, and equally important, the politics of displacement: the debate over the ideology of textbook content prefig-

---

*Merle Collins is a Grenadian author and poet whose work utilizes Grenadian Creole to express folk and rural working class wisdom. Her publications include the anthology *Because the Dawn Breaks* (London: Karia Press 1985)—from which this poem is taken—and the novel "Angel" (London: Women's Press 1987).

ures the broader conflict over which class and gender perspectives are to gain ascendency and become the socially accepted purveyors of "commonsense."

This chapter examines these issues in the context of the evaluation and reconstruction of texts during a revolution. More specifically, it traces the curriculum development that was part of the transformation of education in the Grenada Revolution, and tries to explain, through an examination of the textbooks produced, how inherited knowledge was critically reworked. In doing so I draw on the work of critical educators, notably that of Apple and Giroux, and utilize three domains extrapolated by Luke from their work to explain the construction of revolutionary perspectives, the reconstruction of gender, and the reclaiming of language in these textbooks.

What is the justification for Grenada as a case study of the politics of the text? Examination of the Grenada texts provide us with a concrete historical experience through which to observe how the textbook "not only expresses ideology but is constitutive of it."[2]

Through the Grenada experience we can explore the text in its many politico-educational dimensions as:

- the expression of a process by which knowledge and values are reconstituted as men and women attempt to *reconstruct* (as distinct from *reproduce*) themselves and their relations in social context;
- an "argument" of particular ideological positions and elements in a political debate over socially "acceptable" knowledge (an outcome of the struggle of whose knowledge is selected by whom and by what means);
- the material expression of educational content and practice—embodying and constituting specific perceptions and forms of *knowledge interaction*.

What makes the Grenada texts theoretically interesting is not so much the historical record, but rather that experience's potential to elucidate how the text, in a particular historical time and place, becomes part of what Grey calls the hegemonic restructuring of knowledge and ideological consciousness. In examining how specific knowledge was incorporated in particular forms into the Grenadian texts, we shall confirm Carnoy's conclusion that "the struggle over the meaning of knowledge in fact reflects the struggle over the political definition of transition society, much more so than educational conflicts affect the definition of capitalist society."[3]

Luke's extrapolation of three domains from the work of Apple and Giroux on the curriculum is a useful analytic framework for an examination of the Grenada textbooks. These domains are:

1. An analysis of the form and content of prescribed curricula texts;
2. a detailing of the principles which governed and the economic [and, one might add, the cultural] forces which influenced the construction of these texts;

3. a reconstruction of the organization of daily classroom social relationships around the texts, as evidenced in the recoverable textual guidelines for teaching.[4]

The revolution of March 13, 1979 was the insurrectionary climax of a twenty-eight year struggle by the people of Grenada against the despotic and brutal rule of Eric Matthew Gairy. The popular armed uprising was initiated by the revolutionary party, the New Jewel Movement (NJM) which had unsuccessfully sought to defeat the regime by parliamentary means. The NJM was the central actor in an alliance of opposition forces and its leader, Maurice Bishop, was the official Leader of the Opposition. Deeply influenced by radical Caribbean nationalist thought and the revolutionary examples of Cuba and Tanzania, the NJM advocated the fundamental restructuring of Grenadian society in the interests of workers, farmers, women and other oppressed strata and called for the institution of a more participatory democratic system.

The conception of educational change within the Grenada revolution emphasized the function of education as a vehicle not simply for socialization and the acquisition of socially necessary skills but for the reconstruction of social mentalities as well. Transformation of education was part of the broader dynamic of sociopolitical change and economic transformation. In an address to teachers at the first National Consultation on Education, Prime Minister Maurice Bishop reflected on the function of education and its characteristics in revolutionary Grenada: "Whom should education serve? It should serve the broad masses of working people, the producers of wealth in society. What should education serve? It should serve the process of transformation from a colonial territory to a liberated self-reliant nation." He went on to state:

A revolutionary education system has at least four main elements:

a) Firstly, it attempts to teach people a greater critical appreciation of their own reality in order for them to understand how to change it;

b) Secondly, it attempts to develop the inate abilities of the masses of the people;

c) Thirdly, it should seek to develop the productive capacity of our society since it is only through an expansion in production that the standard of living including the educational system can be improved;

d) And fourthly, it tries to promote the democratization of our society—the process by which people are encouraged to take an active part in the educational system itself and in all major decisions that affect our lives.

The construction of a revolutionary educational system consistent with this philosophy required not only the transformation of the inherited system of formal education but also, and equally important, the systematic development of adult education to provide education at all levels for the working people. In Grenada, the development of a system of adult education proved far easier than the transformation of the inherited configuration of education. Building an adult education system meant both working with the emerging grass-roots structures to define a new network of social and political interaction and infusing these with an educational content drawn from practical and ideological need. Transforming a neocolonial educational system, on the other hand, involved a much more *contested process:* working at times with, at other times against, vested interests (like the Churches); struggling to institutionalize democratic forms of school administration (Student Councils, Community-School Councils); expanding educational opportunity while simultaneously attempting to improve quality; combating elitism while promoting excellence; and much more.

Thus, education developed within the revolution along two distinct "lines," lines that differed neither in their fundamental objectives nor in their philosophical orientation, but rather in the extent to which their organizational/ administrative forms and their curriculum embodied revolutionary perspectives.

1. The Curriculum Development Process

The Revolution of March 13, 1979, inherited an educational system marked by the absence of coordination (even within its subsectors), an ill-trained and fluid teaching force, unstandardized and poorly articulated curricula, and high dropout and repetition rates. Of the thirteen major causes of the high dropout rate that had been identified in 1974 by W. F. Fernando, a UNESCO consultant, seven had to do either with the curriculum or with the lack of professional preparation of the teacher. Curricula in the primary schools were unstandardized, yet all pupils had to take a "Common" Entrance Examination to qualify for entrance into secondary school. A UNESCO testing consultant who reported on these exams in 1975 noted poor performances in the sciences and social studies (particularly on questions related to the local environment), and concluded that in language arts, *"the results . . . reflected family background as much as what is learned in the schools. The more affluent families usually provide for greater opportunities for children to learn to use language well* [my emphasis]."[5]

Given these well-documented failures of the educational system (substantiated by "expert" pronouncements), there was broad social acknowledgement that a crisis existed in Grenadian education that required corrective action. Within educational circles, there was a consensus that the redefinition of the curriculum would be a necessary part of that action. Thus reworking of the curriculum, however, was not effected without considerable debate over what constituted acceptable" and " unacceptable" knowledge for the schools, some groups objected to what they claimed was the "lowering of educational standards and values" resulting from the inclusion of certain topics and perspectives in the curriculum.

M. K. Bacchus, in reflecting on the curriculum development approach used in the Caribbean, challenges the assumption "that what is actually taught in schools is the outcome of some rational curriculum planning process.'' He asserts that

> the curriculum content that was actually offered in the primary schools of these countries resulted from the conflicting interests of different groups in the society. Each group attempted to exert pressure on those engaged in delivering the educational services in order to ensure that the instructional programmes which the group offered were directed not only at teaching certain skills which they considered important, but also at inculcating a system of beliefs which would support the group's particular conception of what social reality was or ought to have been in these societies.[6]

The Grenada experience confirms these observations and demonstrates further the assertion by Apple that ''The curricula response fundamentally depends on the relative balance of power of contending groups both within the State and over the policies articulated by the State.''[7]

Curriculum development proceeded along the twin lines of educational development mentioned earlier. The articulation of curricula for adult education began in 1979 with the formation of the Center for Popular Education (CPE). A core of politically committed teachers—some of whom were associated with the Party, some of whom had prior experience in critical adult pedagogies, and some of whom were highly experienced but critical members of the "old school"—formed the National Technical Commission (NTC) and were given the responsibility of elaborating the curricula. The NTC's first task was the preparation of a literacy reader for use in the national literacy campaign. In the course of that campaign the NTC developed a network of parish and village technicians to assist in the training of volunteer teachers, to supervise the work of the Centers for Popular Education throughout the country, and to serve as a base of resource people for curriculum revision and the preparation of texts.

Within the general educational system, the immediate priority of the revolution was the establishment of a mass training program—the National In-Service Teacher Education Program (NISTEP)—aimed at professionalizing all untrained primary-school teachers within three years.[8] A National Education Consultation held in January 1980 not only called for such training but also contended that teachers, as the professionals most directly concerned with curriculum implementation, should play a central role in the articulation of the new curriculum. The Ministry of Education therefore designed NISTEP to fulfill the functions of teacher training and curriculum development: NISTEP subject panels were to be responsible for curriculum development in their respective subject areas, with the initial priorities being the language arts, mathematics, and general science curricula.

One year into the operation of NISTEP, the Ministry of Education noted that the initial conditions for the redefinition of the curriculum were being created:

Teachers are in a far better position to effectively participate in the development of a new curriculum for the schools. [They] have gained important insights into the history of education in the Caribbean; they understand better how children learn; they have upgraded their competence in the core areas of Language Arts and Mathematics; they have deepened their knowledge of the communities in which they live and work, by means of their research into the life of these communities. [T]he Community School Day Program has brought us closer to realizing two important goals of education identified and discussed by teachers: the integration of school and community, the integration of work and study.[9]

NISTEP used its extensive links with the schools through trainee teachers and the Teacher-Partners (their qualified peers who provided at-school assistance to trainees) to hold curriculum-development workshops for the preparation of texts, and to field-test the new texts. The successful innovations that teachers had developed in their schools were incorporated into the new curricula. It was through this process that the draft statement of the goals of primary education in Grenada was prepared and circulated throughout the system for discussion. The goals reflected the four main elements of a revolutionary system of education that had been defined by Maurice Bishop in his speech to the teachers one year earlier. The statement read: participate in the collective decision-making process.

Statement of the Goals of Primary Education (draft)

1. EDUCATION FOR NATIONAL DEVELOPMENT
    1.1 The development of national consciousness:
        a. To foster in the child a sense of self-worth, patriotism and pride in our identity as a Grenadian and Caribbean people.
        b. To develop in the child an understanding of Grenada's role in the regional and international community.
    1.2 The integration of school and community
        a. To develop in the child an awareness and understanding of the political, economic and social framework in which she/he lives, and a sense of his/her own role and responsibility within that framework.
        b. To foster the participation of pupils, teachers, parents and the community at large in the curriculum development process.
        c. To foster habits of co-operation with others for the building, strengthening, and protection of one's community.
    1.3 The integration of work and study
        a: To develop learning experiences which integrate practice and theory/ manual and intellectual activity.
        b. To train the child to be a productive member of society with posi-

tive work habits, through the involvement of the school in production.

2. EDUCATION FOR EQUALITY
  2.1 Equal Opportunity of Education
    a. To develop to the fullest the human potential of every child providing equal opportunity for the maximum physical, emotional, intellectual, creative, social and moral growth of every child.
  2.2 The spirit of equalitarianism
    a. To develop in the child a sense of equal dignity and worth of all human beings.

3. EDUCATION FOR DEMOCRACY
  3.1 The development of organizational skills
    a. To equip the child for participation in the democratic process through involvement in the running of the class school and school-based organizations.
  3.2 The development of critical sense
    a. To develop in the child the ability to analyze issues, and to form and articulate opinions in order to effectively participate in the collective decision-making process.

2. Overview of the new texts

During the four-and-a-half years of the Grenada revolution, twenty educational texts were produced, thirteen of which were published (the remainder were being field-tested in pilot classes). Seven texts were produced by the CPE for adult education; ten were language arts texts for primary schools (the series was named *Marryshow Readers* in honor of the great regional statesman and national hero, Theophilus Albert Marryshow); and three were general educational texts. Table 12.1 gives the titles of these texts.

2.1. The Adult Education Texts

The preparation of the CPE texts by the National Technical Commission involved three major activities:

1. a review of the content of the primary-school curriculum in order to obtain an overview of its knowledge base (a difficult undertaking given the absence of standardized curricula in the primary schools);
2. research into current issues at a national and local level (including an exhaustive review of back issues of all national newspapers), intensive discussions with leaders in different sectors on the development perspective and programs of the revolution, and consideration of the implications of these for adult education;

Table 12.1. Textbooks Produced during the Grenada Revolution

Text Title	Agency	Description
Let Us Learn Together	CPE	Literacy Reader
Forward Ever!		Literacy Teachers Guide
Let Us Continue Reading		Postliteracy Reader
Adult Education Book 1		Consolidated Basic Education Text
Adult Education Book 2		Consolidated Basic Education Text
Adult Education Book 3		Consolidated Basic Education Text
Adult Education Book 4		Consolidated Basic Education Text
MARRYSHOW READERS		
(published)		
All of Us	NISTEP	Infant 1A Reader
Step Forward		Infant 1B
We Work and Play Together		Infant 1C
MARRYSHOW READERS		
(unpublished)		
untitled		Infant 2A
untitled		Infant 2B
untitled		Infant 2C
untitled		Junior 1
untitled		Standard 2
Language Arts Programme		Term 1
English Grammar Drills		Infant 1 Term 2
FEDON BOOKS		
Revolutionary Voices	NISTEP	Anthology—children's poetry
Poems for Children—		
Renalph Gebbon	FEDON	Poetry
Grenada-Nicaragua: Being An		
Internationalist	NISTEP	Social Studies text

*The ideas for titles of these texts 6 were solicited from the schools engaged in testing them.

3. collection of material and review of available research on Grenadian history, geography, economy, and culture.

The first texts produced were the literacy reader *Let Us Learn Together* and a corresponding manual *Forward Ever!* Prepared within months of the triumph of the revolution, it contained fourteen reading themes aimed at reinforcing the dominant sentiment of that period. Many of the sentences used were those that people had spontaneously written up on walls in the communities, and these had been deliberately selected by the NTC because they represented the people's own linguistic universe. They expressed the lived experience and values of the people, and their inclusion in the literacy text simultaneously signaled the arrival and validity of popular experience as official (educational) knowledge and served to legitimize the text itself since it spoke in the language of the people.

Because the NTC considered the literacy campaign to be essentially a political task with pedagogical implications, the content of this reader embodied values of national unity, social commitment, and cooperation. As a first step in the appropriation of educational opportunity by the working people, the acquisition of literacy skills had to address the new historical reality by affirming the new values.

The generative themes emerged through an intense process of selection from a general range of themes prepared in a series of workshops by the NTC. The discussion involved debate, at times vehement, on technical issues in relation to or in opposition to political imperatives. For example, one member of the Commission objected to the inclusion of the word "revolution" in the text—on the technical grounds that the word was syllabically too complex and that only phonetically simple words should be used. This led to intense discussions of the political stances implicit in the technical rationality of different literacy methods and approaches, and to the clarification of the options available to the NTC. It became evident to the team that the fundamental issue in the preparation of the reader was not simply the selection of themes and words but the determination of the approach to literacy that would be used. The choice of literacy method had to be integrally related to the objectives of literacy in the revolution; it was a methodological reflection of our conception of illiterate people and their human potential. The method developed was therefore based on dialogue between learner and teacher on generative themes (which allowed for the incorporation and critical reflection on the discussants' worldview as well as the use of the learners' own sentences for literacy); it involved a mixture of whole-word recognition approaches and phonics. In such an approach "reading the world" was to be as important as "reading the word."

The generative themes finally selected for the reader were education (of adults and children); national developmental priorities of the revolution; and the values of the new political culture (popular participation, unity, and regional identity). The lessons and themes of the literacy reader *Let Us Learn Together* are given in Table 12.2.

The supplementary reader, *Let Us Continue Reading,* which was prepared for use in postliteracy, contained a collection of readings based on a much wider range of topics selected from a cross-sectional grouping of topics in which learners had shown interest.

After the literacy campaign, adult education was institutionalized in the form of basic education for adults. The program was geared to providing the equivalent of a comprehensive primary education to the neoliterate as well as to those who had not completed their primary schooling (the 1970 Population Census revealed that, of the 86% of the adult population who had attended primary school, 92% *had not passed any examination!*). The basic education program was divided into four levels over a two-year period and covered the following content:

Table 12.2. Contents of the Literacy Reader *Let Us Learn Together*

Lesson	Theme
1. Let us learn from each other	Learning as a cooperative activity
2. We build our communities	Working together to build Grenada
3. Grenada, Carriacou, and Petit Martinique	National pride and unity
4. The land must produce more	Agricultural self-reliance productivity
5. One Caribbean	Caribbean Unity, linguistic and ideological pluralism
6. Free milk for mothers and babies	Better nutrition; awareness of milk distribution program
7. The Revolution brings more doctors	Prioritization of health care by the revolution
8. Our International airport	The international airport as a national development priority
9. NCB—The bank of our people	Promotion of the National Commercial Bank/savings habits
10. Building a new Grenada	Need for unity, discipline and hard work for new society
11. Vigilance in our villages	Building the militia
12. Our history of struggle	History as collective struggle
13. Education is a must	Awareness of the importance of educating the youth
14. The Revolution had room for all of us	Promotion of popular participation; against sectarianism

Level 1—Language Arts; Mathematics; Natural Science;

Level 2—Language Arts; Mathematics; Natural Science; Geography

Level 3—Language Arts; Mathematics; Natural Science; Geography (including elements of the economy and the demography of Grenada);

Level 4—Language Arts; Mathematics; Natural Science; Grenadian History.

The National Technical Commission prepared a series of four consolidated adult education texts, *Adult Education Books 1–4,* as the core material for this program. The preparation process was preceded by the same research activities described earlier. The NTC divided itself into subject teams (supplemented by subject specialists from the formal system as well as technical personnel from various ministries or enterprises) to prepare the curricula and text content. Coordination meetings, systematic sharing, and collective critiquing of material as it was produced served to ensure integration and rationalization of knowledge across subject areas.

Integration and rationalization were important principles guiding the reproduction of the knowledge of the texts. They involved (1) the treatment of topics from the multiple perspectives of the different subject areas in a manner that was mutually reinforcing; (2) the location of the knowledge presented in a concrete historical context (in many cases that of Grenada itself); and (3) the attempt at application of the knowledge to improvement the condition of the learner and the community. All of this also implied new forms of social interaction around the knowledge of the text. Knowledge was no longer an abstraction of reality but something to be rediscovered and explored in a social process of remaking one's world; the texts invited inquiry into the community/nation and urged intervention by the learner. Knowing and changing were posited as two faces of the same dialectic.

Water, for example, was a topic of concern to many learners as well as an issue of importance to national development. The infrastructure inherited from the dictatorship was so dilapidated that most of the water mains in the capital needed replacement. Many rural communities were without pipe-borne water; rivers served as communal bath and laundry. *Water* was examined at all four levels and in all subject areas in the texts:

At level 1 (Book 1) there was a short reading passage. "Why drink water?" in the Language Arts section. In the Natural Science section, one of the two units featured *Water and Air* and focused on *The Distribution of Land and Water on Earth, Water in the Air,* and *The Water Cycle in Nature.*

At level 2 (Book 2) the Language Arts section contained a longer reading passage, "Save Water," which discussed water conservation in the context of improving the infrastructure (a supplementary guide to teachers suggests several practical community activities that could be undertaken by the class to help that effort). The Geography section took up the earlier topic *The Distribution of Land and Water on Earth* but concentrated now on the continents and oceans. In a unit on *The Physical Features and Climate of Grenada,* the island's rainfall patterns were described.

At level 3 (Book 3) a cultural feature article from the national newspaper on *River Washing—A Tradition* was reproduced as a reading passage. In a geography unit on *The Natural Resources of Grenada and Their Development,* Water as a natural resource and Grenada's resources of the sea were depicted.

A notable characteristic of the adult education texts is the multidisciplinary way in which language arts were used. Reading and comprehension passages covered a range of thematic topics from science to politics, from poetry to Caribbean dialect, from material written by neoliterates to selections from published Third World authors.

There were also several stories on the achievements of working people themselves, stories often deliberately selected in fields that, according to previous dominant conceptions, were either too humble to qualify as a field of human achievement (e.g., tree-climbing in *Silverspoon, the Island Climber*) or too scientifically esoteric for input by working-class intellect (native inventiveness in pest control in *Coonyar—The Inventor*). Through these stories, the message was transmitted that human invention and achievement were not the exclusive preserve of the educated classes, that they came out of pride in the social utility of one's labor and the power of critical observation and reflection.

The NTC maintained a critical posture in relation to the texts it produced, seeking and inviting critical feedback and recommendations from learners, teachers, and technicians in different fields. The educational text was seen as an incomplete expression of a knowledge base that was being appropriated and rewritten by the creative labor of the working people. As the people got more involved in the process of national development, new demands for other categories of knowledge would require the revision of the existing texts and the preparation of material addressing specific requirements.

By 1983 numerous requests for assistance with dissemination of public education materials were being made of the CPE by different agencies and ministries. It was decided that the conditions had been achieved to effect a rationalization of adult and popular education on a national scale and, at the same time, to revise the adult education texts (which had been in use a full year with significant useful feedback from teachers, learners, and technocrats). In March 1983, a workshop on Non-formal education in Grenada was held by the Ministry of Education under the sponsorship of UNESCO. Its objectives were:

1. To compare the curriculum and activities of the different agencies.
2. To assist agencies to understand each other's background and work.
3. To examine and analyze the curriculum of the Center for Popular Education and to make recommendations for improvements and integration.
4. To identify the material and human resources available among the agencies and to suggest areas of cooperation.
5. To foster better interrelationships among the workers of extension service agencies.[10]

The workshop was attended by virtually all public and private voluntary agencies that were either engaged in some form of public education or interested in having some input into the popular education process.

The workshop resulted in a detailed critique of the adult education texts and a plan for interagency collaboration in the preparation of printed and audio-visual materials for public education. The first-priority task agreed on was the revision of the texts, with various agencies assuming responsibility for provision of information for specific topics. The NTC also devised a plan for receiving submissions for the revisions (reading material, learners' writing, activity ideas, pedagogical recommendations) from the Centers for Popular Education throughout the country.

2.2 The Marryshow Readers

The preparation of the Marryshow readers followed the same principles that guided the adult education texts except that, unlike the adult education texts, the Marryshow readers were the outcome of a process of curriculum development linked to teacher training. The original plan of the Ministry of Education envisaged the simultaneous development of curricula in the core primary-education areas of language arts, mathematics, and general science. Unfortunately, by 1983 only the language arts panel (under the dynamic leadership of the noted Caribbean feminist author, Merle Hodge, and an English internationalist, Lisbeth deBlock) had actually reached the stage of producing textbooks.

A crucial difference between the process of articulation of the CPE texts and the Marryshow readers is that whereas the CPE texts—breaking untrodden ground—"prescribed" the knowledge base and practice of adult education in the country, the Marryshow readers came out of the dialectic of the new educational perspectives engendered by the revolution and the concrete experiences and practices of teachers. The curriculum was an expression of the process of professional formation as experienced by teachers. As part of their training, the teachers who were enrolled in NISTEP were actively involved in the process of developing and testing the new curriculum in their schools. They collected stories and material from their classes *and* communities; they worked with the Language Arts Panel to edit and incorporate this material into the curriculum; they pilot-tested drafts of the new texts with their classes, recommended alterations, and prepared supplementary teaching aids for use with the texts.

The Marryshow readers formed a language arts series that corresponded to the various grade levels of the Grenadian primary school system. Starting with the first year of the infant school, the reading scheme utilized the common structures of Grenadian and Standard English while gradually introducing Standard English structures hitherto unfamiliar to children. The scheme emerged from a careful analysis, using the insights into Caribbean Creoles resulting from the work of linguists at the University of the West Indies, of the language of Grenadian children. A basic aim of the scheme was to assist the Grenadian child in developing his or her language skills of listening, understanding, speaking, reading, and writing. It recognized the linguistic and cultural integrity of Grenadian English while providing the skills necessary to master the rules of shift from the vernacular to Standard English.

The first reader, *All of Us,* introduces an extended family using forms of introduction common to Grenadian and Standard English. Each reader thereafter uses short reading passages to explore themes of relevance to Grenadian children, themes stressing the values of family, cooperation, unity, equality, and pride in one's work. English structures that do not normally occur in the speech of Grenadian children are gradually introduced through these stories with an emphasis on oral preparation of the class by the teacher for mastery of these unfamiliar structures.

3. The Deconstruction of Neocolonial Ideology
and the Construction of Revolutionary Perspectives

A common feature of the curriculum in the educational systems that are inherited from the colonial state is its irrelevance to the social and economic reality of the nation. From its inception, the New Jewel Movement included the reform of the curriculum as an inseparable dimension of its sociopolitical and educational program. Speaking to an International Solidarity Conference in 1981, Minister of Education Jacqueline Creft, declared:

> We are determined to change a system which so powerfully excluded the interests of the mass of our people, and which also wove webs of fear, alienation and irrelevance around our children's minds. . . . The lucky few of us who went to secondary school learned about Cromwell's revolt but not about that of Fedon. . . . Right from the beginning of our struggle we called for an education system . . . [with] a curriculum which would eliminate absurdity from our classrooms and focus our children's minds upon their own island, their own wealth, soil and crops, their own solutions to the problems that surround us.[11]

The textbooks produced during the revolution challenged some of the old outlook (political sectarianism, competitive individualism, consumerism and the fetish of imported goods); reinforced some of the traditional values and institutions (cooperation, self-reliance, the extended family, hard work, etc.); and asserted new values consistent with the goals of education in the new society. One could identify four main principles through which neocolonial perspectives were challenged and revolutionary values emphasized:

1. the promotion of revolutionary nationalism and patriotism;
2. the advancement of Caribbean identity and internationalism;
3. the promotion of positive and indigenous cultural values;
4. the democratization of science and knowledge.

The promotion of revolutionary nationalism and patriotism was more overtly handled in the adult education texts than in the Marryshow readers. As Apple has pointed out, all curricula are the result of compromise between social groups in a particular historical context. The "hidden" curriculum accord in the Grenada context was the compromise in ideological content between the formal educational system and the adult education system. In the process of overt hegemonic restructuring that is part of a revolution, conservative elements are initially more likely to accept the articulation of revolutionary perspectives in adult texts than in those of children.

The literacy reader sought to promote revolutionary nationalism and patriotism by emphasizing a collective sense of belonging and of responsibility for the country. Themes such as *We Build Our Communities, Grenada, Carriacou, and Petit Martinique* stressed ownership of country; others encouraged pride in major national projects and institutions (*Our International Airport, NCB—The Bank of the People*). In the *Adult Education Books 1–4* revolutionary nationalism and patriotism were portrayed in different ways in the various subject areas. In language arts, it was communicated in reading passages on topics of Grenadian history (including memorable events in the revolution); Third World literature and poetry[12]; and explanations of policy and key legislation relating to women and workers, among others, and to the national economy. In mathematics, problems involved computation of costs and quantities associated with community work, national economic projects, and the budget—a mathematics of everyday life. The presentation of the geography of the country included issues of political economy—the identification of natural resources, and their use and conservation in the context of socialized ownership.

The representation of revolutionary nationalism and patriotism is far more delicately handled in the Marryshow readers than in the adult education texts. In fact, there is nothing explicitly revolutionary about the nationalism of these texts except the legitimation of working-class and peasant lifestyles, and the organic absorption of the texts' characters in the geography and circumstances of the children themselves. In the Infant 2C reader, some traditions are affirmed and others are discarded. The story "Today is Sunday" talks about the church bell ringing: "It is calling us to Church. All of us are going to Church." However after church, we see "Mammy *and Daddy* [my emphasis] cooking." And contrary to the colonial cultural norms that require that the best (read: "imported") food be cooked on a Sunday:

They are cooking fish and bananas.
The fish is from the sea.
The bananas are from the garden.

The religious observance of Sunday is reinforced, the belief that the best food is imported food is negated. Fish and bananas are the harvest of the family labor (Daddy is a fisherman) and, precisely for this reason, are fit for feasting.

In the Infant 2C reader, among the several local events that are excitedly seen through the eyes of a child is the March 13th Rally (anniversary celebration of the revolution):

We are going to the Park.
It is Revolution Day.
We are going to the rally.
The Park is in town and we are going on a bus.

The story proceeds to describe all the things that are striking to the child—

people singing on the crowded bus, the large number of people in the park, other children running about, the People's Revolutionary Army marching by:

> We hear the Pioneers singing.
> They sing *"We are the children of the Revolution."*
> My sister and I are Pioneers too.

The advancement of Caribbean identity and internationalism is the theme of the fifth lesson in the literacy reader used in the national literacy campaign. This lesson is entitled "One Caribbean" and summarizes the perspective of the revolution on Caribbean identity. It reads:

ONE CARIBBEAN

> I am from Grenada, Carriacou and Petit Martinique.
>
> You are from Martinique.
>
> He is from Cuba.
>
> She is from Aruba.
>
> We are from the Caribbean.
>
> We are one people.
>
> We are one Caribbean.

Each of the countries mentioned represents a different linguistic and political dimension of the Caribbean: Anglophone and revolutionary Grenada; Francophone (and still colonized) Martinique; Spanish-speaking and socialist Cuba; and Dutch Aruba. In this lesson, the technical requirements of literacy are interwoven with a vital political message rooted in the historical condition of the region. The message of unity across the linguistic barriers historically imposed by Western European colonialism and the contemporary imperative of cultural and political pluralism is expressed in a lesson structure meant to present the phonics of the "a" sound as it occurs most frequently in Grenadian English, and also meant to demonstrate the conjugation of the copula (the linking verb "to be," (a structure absent from Creoles but essential to Standard English). The political and the pedagogical reached their most organic fusion in such a lesson!

In the adult education texts, Caribbean identity and internationalism was handled in much the same manner as was revolutionary nationalism and patriotism. Reading lessons celebrated the Cuban Tamayo Mendez as the first Caribbean astronaut, spoke of the suffering and determination of El Salvador and South Africa, decried illiteracy in the Caribbean, described the village of Barrio Del Rio Maiz in the English-speaking Atlantic Coast of Nicaragua, and informed the reader of the global opposition to nuclear arms.

Caribbean identity and internationalism formed the very basis of the social studies text *"Grenada-Nicaragua: Being an Internationalist."* In 1980 two outstanding literacy workers from Grenada, Ceford Robertson and James Wilson, volunteered to work in the English literacy crusade on the Atlantic coast of Nicaragua. On their return, Wilson was interviewed at length by Chris Searle, a British educator and a leading proponent of internationalism in education. This interview was used by deBlock and Hodge to create a social studies text that exemplified the approach being developed by the Curriculum Development Commission, an approach that combined language arts teaching with social studies.

Through the eyes and experience of James Wilson, the past and contemporary history of Nicaragua was revealed, its geography was explored, the ancestry of the peoples of the Atlantic Coast was traced (and the ancestral migrations of Caribbean people probed). This knowledge in turn provided the opportunity for the development of specific skills like map reading, interviewing, and questioning skills.

In the Standard 2 reader, a class of Grenadian students, the protagonists of this reader, prepare for visitors from overseas. The teacher uses the announcement to quiz the class about history, geography, and politics. When asked from which country the visitors come, Teacher Carlton responds:

"I want you to guess. . . . Do you know where our great-great-great-grandparents came from?"

"Africa!" the whole class shouts.

"Very good," said Teacher Carlton. "Now, you know that Africa is a very, very big place. There are many countries in Africa, just as there are many parishes in Grenada. Now you have to guess which country in Africa our visitors come from. I will give you a clue: the leader of this country has visited Grenada."

"Kaunda!" shouted some children. Others shouted " Samora Machel!"

The promotion of positive and indigenous cultural values was also of importance here. As stated earlier, there were some inherited values that had to be explicitly challenged by the new texts. Given the fact that the political base of the Gairy dictatorship was comprised mainly of elderly agricultural workers, and given the political tribalism that characterized the multiparty Westminster system, political sectarianism had to be explicitly confronted. The leadership of the NJM was concerned that the triumph of the revolution not provide the opportunity to settle old scores. They themselves set the example by not prosecuting those members of the police force and the terror squad "Mangoose Gang" (terror squad) who had beaten the key leaders almost to death, in an incident known as Bloody Sunday, on November 18, 1973. The final lesson of the literacy reader was, to this end, entitled "The Revolution Has Room for All of Us."

In some of the reading units of the adult education texts, social values such as competitive individualism were challenged at the same time that other traditional values were affirmed. In units such as "Make a House a Home" and "Fight Vulgarity—Rise to New Heights" respect for others and the importance of setting the correct example are accentuated. In others, such as "The Habit of Drinking" and "Attitudes to Work," undesirable and anti-social traits are assailed.

The promotion of positive and indigenous cultural values provided a special challenge to the writers of the Marryshow readers. The series editor explained this challenge thus:

> The writer of children's books has always to keep a balance between . . . two elements—familiarity and value forming. This has to be carefully handled, as you can imagine, in a transitional era such as the one we are living in, when you want literature to be part of the process of changing society. The challenge is to reinforce what is good about the reality that we live in, and at the same time to inject new directions.
>
> Thus in the Marryshow Readers you will find families such as our children live in, where the concept and the sentiment of family extends beyond mother-father-child. You will find children and their elders engaged in agricultural work—children helping in the garden or on Cocoa day. You will find emphasized the value of cooperation which is a traditional feature of the society and which is being strengthened in the revolution. At every level there are stories based on the theme of working together. The word together *is introduced from the earliest level.* [13]

New perspectives are presented in relation to work and cooperation (as a collective approach to problem-solving). Individual dilemmas are resolved either by working together or through united action.

In the typically middle-class–oriented children's texts used in most Caribbean schools, children are invariably shown at play, and "work" is defined either as "school work" or minor household tasks allocated by gender. In the Marryshow readers, children participate in the real labor of the rural household; adult family members (grandmother, father, mother, uncle) work as farmers and fishermen alongside each other. Thus in the Infant 1B reader *"Step Forward,"* we read:

> Watch Patsy and Errol.
> They work in the garden with Mama and Uncle Andy.
> All of them work in the garden.
> They work together.
> All of them work together in the garden.

The middle-class children and their families represented in the modern Caribbean text are, as Merle Hodge points out, *consumers* rather than *producers*.

The main protagonist of the Marryshow readers was the average, (often rural), working-class, Grenadian family—the *producers* of the wealth of the country.

In the Infant 1C reader *"We Work and Play Together,"* we find a good example of how individual and collective progress can be achieved by working together on common problems. *"A Story about Some Fishermen"* presents several fishermen seated on the beach lamenting the condition of some essential part of their fishing gear. They discuss their problems and decide to work together to solve them. Their predicament and the "moral" of the story is expressed in a simple chant:

Fish in the sea
Fish in the sea
And fishermen sitting
on the beach
Watching the sea
Watching the sea
Fishermen sitting
on the beach.

I have no net
You have no boat
My net is not good

What can I do?
What can I do?
What can a fisherman do?

Come together
Help each other
Fishermen sitting
on the beach.

You help me and I help you
Help each other
Work together
Get up, fishermen,
Go to sea.

The democratization of science and knowledge was a fundamental objective of the new educational system. The democratization of knowledge and the acquisition of scientific knowledge was considered to be particularly important for the working people. Under the dictatorship, increasing attempts were made to manipulate the religious sensibilities of the people; prayers written by Gairy himself were circulated for recitation in the schools, superstition and occultism were promoted as part of the lore of the state, authoritarian leadership was equated with the divine right to rule, and a major foreign policy initiative of

Grenada in the United Nations was to champion the establishment of a U.N. agency for the investigation of extraterrestrial lifeforms.

All of this obscurantism could easily have been dismissed as the displaced imposition of an "extraterrestrial mind"; but the virtual absence of standardized curriculum in science in the primary schools meant that conditions existed for education to be infused with obscurantism. The comments of the UNESCO Education Advisor about the 1975 results in the Natural Science section of the Common Entrance exam, "indicat[ing] *considerable retardation* in Science," confirm this.

The development of an understanding and appreciation of science, particularly in relation to the natural and social environment, was an essential ideological and educational aim of the revolution. In a sense this objective emanated from what Young would call an understanding of the curriculum as practice—an attempt to help working people to master the "Science of Common Things."[14]

The adult education texts attempted to integrate scientific knowledge into the teaching of language (through reading and comprehension units) and mathematics (through the illustration of mathematical principles by everyday objects and processes). The natural science units in the texts combined geography, elements of basic physics, chemistry, and biology.

In the language arts in particular, the selection and preparation of science topics as reading passages deliberately emphasized the discovery of science in the everyday and the ordinary. A reading unit on *"Tools,"* for example, described the evolution of tools as part of human inventiveness in an effort to lighten labor, and pointed to simple tools in use in everyday life. Another reading unit, *"Coonyar's Invention,"* reported the invention of a simple Cocoa beetle trap using the gum of the African breadfruit by a humble agricultural worker in Grenada. The passage accented the fact that this invention was the result of astute observation of nature, that it was created by an "uneducated" worker (who, as a result, was selected as *"Worker of the Year 1980"*), and that this invention had the potential of saving cocoa producers thousands of dollars from reduced pesticide costs and higher yields.

Another objective was to present science topics containing knowledge that could be beneficially applied by the learners. For example, a reading passage entitled *"Why Drink Water?"* highlighted the importance of drinking adequate quantities of water for the maintenance of good health; another, *"Breast Is is Best,"* explained the political economy of baby food[15] and the medical benefits of breast feeding, and supported the World Health Organization's breast-feeding campaign.

4. The Reconstruction of Gender

In the Marryshow readers, the reconstruction of gender involved not only the confrontation of patriarchy but also the reconstituting of class. While the reconstituting of class values required the negation of patriarchal attitudes, the latter exceeded the boundaries of the former. In the construction of the texts it was recognized that to replace the upper-middle-class cosmos of the inherited texts with a working-class universe would result in the replacement of the expressions of patriarchy peculiar to one class with those of another. This was the subject of much discussion in the debate over the texts within the Curriculum Commission.

Thus the reconstruction of gender in the texts necessarily involved the redefinition of key constructs such as the family in class *as well as* in gender terms. Critiquing the modern Caribbean text, Merle Hodge contended that the children that were represented

> are all living in families . . . comprised of a Mummy, Daddy, and a child or two— not the extended family that most of our families live in, which might include a grandmother, an uncle or two, a cousin or two, an adopted child or two. The Daddies all work in offices, of course. They go off in their personal cars on mornings.[16]

In the Marryshow readers, traditional sex-role stereotyping was contested and supplanted with relations of gender equality. Throughout there are images and stories that depict girls *and boys* helping with cooking, washing, cleaning, and the care of babies. Girls and boys are seen working alongside adults on the land. In the reader *We Work and Play Together* (Infant 1C), boys and girls play football together in the schoolyard.

The new gender relations are symbolized within the family with men caring for and feeding babies, cooking with the women, and playing an equal role in the life of the household. In *All of Us* (Infant 1A), Daddy is first seen—in a family photo on the reader cover—seated on the steps of the home holding the baby. Inside, he is introduced mending his fishing net, then later seated on the steps feeding the baby:

Look at Daddy
and the baby
on the step.

Look at Daddy
on the step
with the baby.

He is joined over the remaining six pages with the other members of the (extended) family for the group "photo" on the steps.

Men and women are portrayed working together, without gender discrimination, as farmers, road workers, and teachers. However, in the story *"Under the Big Tree,"* we are reminded that gender unity requires opposition to patriarchy. In this story, girls collectively resist the macho attempt by the boys to scare them off from under the tree:

> The boys say to the girls:
> "Go away. We want to play here.
> You can't play here now.
> Girls can't play here.
> You have to go away
> and let us play under the tree."
>
> The girls say to them:
> "We are playing under the tree now.
> You can't make us go away.
> You can come and play with us.
> Let's play together.
>
> You can stay and play with us,
> or you can go away."
>
> The boys say: "Watch,
> we are not playing with girls.
> Go away or we are going to beat you up."
>
> All the girls get up.
> They stop playing and they get up.
> "WHAT?" they say.
> "YOU CAN BEAT US UP!
> Can you? Watch!
> We can beat you too.
> Come here. We want you to come here.
> Come under the tree."

In the face of this unexpected resistance to their domineering attitudes and their own refusal to play with the girls, the boys flee the scene. Later, however, in *"Let's Play Together"* (Infant 2A) the boys come to the realization that gender confrontation is unproductive. They first attempt to commandeer a ball from a girl, then resist including the girls in a game of cricket, and finally have no choice but to agree:

> The boys look at each other.
> They look at Dexter's bat.
> They look at Patsy's ball.
> Then they say: "Okay,
> Let's play together.
> All of us can play."
> All the boys and girls are glad.
> They are going to play a game together.

Patsy has the ball
and Dexter has the bat.

In the context of the revolutionary transformation of Grenadian society, the gender reconstruction in the educational texts affirmed the necessity for women's struggle and self-definition as equal but not separate partners. This was the message of the poem *"A Woman's Struggle"* written by Merle Clarke, which was included as a reading unit in the Adult Education Book 2:

Women, open your eyes wide enough to see
Inside the house is not the only place to be.
Take up your fork, your hammer, your spade,
Is not men alone dat could work trade . . .

Take up your guns, you are fit to fight,
All over the world, progressive women unite!

The reworking of gender in the textbooks was aimed essentially at confronting the everyday expressions of patriarchy and at unmasking the class inequities associated with it. The objective was to sensitize both men and women about these issues so that the struggle against gender inequality and patriarchy could become a common concern of equal but not separate sexes.

5. The Reclamation of Language

The outlook of the Grenada revolution on language was influenced by the work of those Caribbean linguists who saw the issue in a progressive but pragmatic perspective. One of the foremost of these Creole scholars, Lawrence Carrington, posited that language policy in the Caribbean ought to seek to develop

a comfortable relationship between the varieties [of language] that are available, and an awareness among the population that both of them [Standard English and the vernacular] have a function to perform, that neither is intended to eradicate the other, nor is any of them intended to be strictly prescribed in usage for particular situations.[17]

Writing on language and revolution in Grenada, the British internationalist educator Chris Searle maintained that

the Revolution was setting language free from all the complexes and mimicry of the past. There was the release of the subterranean, long-oppressed common language of the people. The dialect and Creole forms were given the freedom to speak to be legitimated through the network of democratic organs and forums set up by the revolution. . . . Yet simultaneously, and without competing against the Creole vernacular forms of language, Standard English began to be objectively seen for what it was, as an efficacious and powerful international tool to be used by the people to deepen scientific knowledge, communication and friendship with other peoples across the world, to wage diplomatic struggles and seek alliances in the cause of anti-imperialism.[18]

The language policy introduced by the revolution was unambiguously defined in a policy document of the Ministry of Education, *"Language Arts in the Primary School."* It asserted:

Language arts teaching no longer aims at erasing our first language and replacing it by the official language, but at adding another language to our repertoire, in our case International English. The educated West Indian is bi-lingual . . . [We] recognize that the vernacular is the language in which the child's development has taken place up to the time of his/her entry to the school, and that to suppress the use of this language before any other language has been learnt is to suppress the development of the child.[19]

The new language policy defended the indissoluble links between language, self-conception, and national culture. It stressed that "to scorn the child's language is to undermine the child's self-concept . . . [and to] build up in our pupils attitudes of passivity or resistance to the school, thereby defeating the aims of education." Recognizing that "Caribbean languages are an important expression of Caribbean culture," and that one of the universal functions of the school was "to deepen people's understanding of their culture," it proclaimed that "the best of Caribbean literature, drama, folklore and song, which makes artistic use of our language and which receives international recognition, has a place in the curriculum of our schools."[20]

In translating this policy into practice, the following principles were elaborated to guide the teaching of English in the new curriculum.[21]:

1. *Examine the Creole Language*—the need for teachers to understand the structure of Grenadian Creole in order to grasp its similarities with and differences from Standard English;
2. *A little English at a time*—the gradual introduction of Standard English grammatical features that are unfamiliar to speakers of the vernacular;
3. *A cumulative process*—reinforcement of grammatical and syntactical patterns by deliberately carrying forward those that have been taught into subsequent learning activities;
4. *Not rules but habits*—the teaching of English grammatical patterns "through lively habit-forming activities" and in a context familiar to the pupil, not as abstract technical rules;
5. *Speaking before reading and writing*—an emphasis on understanding and oral production rather than on mechanical reading and writing; the reproduction of speech patterns in their meaningful associative contexts;
6. *Reinforcement across the curriculum*—the reinforcement of language skills in the

teaching of other subject areas and, conversely, the incorporation of other subject knowledge in language teaching;

7. *Provision of supplementary materials*—preparation of class readers by teachers and students on topics of interest to students, exposure of students to a broad range of reading matter, reduced reliance on prescribed readers.

The Marryshow readers were more advanced in their treatment of language arts than the adult education texts, which, while moving from an acceptance of the vernacular, attempted to teach the rules of shift essentially as grammatical *rules*. The adult education texts were caught in the tension between intention and execution; while their content differed from that of the old textbooks, they were still circumscribed by the old pedagogical forms. In this respect the Marryshow readers represented a more sophisticated approach to language teaching and an advance in the pedagogical methods of the revolution.

The Marryshow readers used the language spoken by the child to help him or her to learn consciously the grammar of standard English by moving from the familiar to the unfamiliar. "Patterns that are unfamiliar are introduced systematically, little by little . . . and the child is taught a new pattern before it appears in the reading material."[22] The emphasis was on oral production and the acquisition of language as an *informed habit*. This emphasis derived from an understanding of language as a medium of cultural hegemony, from the understanding that, historically, language has been used as a tool for the affirmation of the forms of expression of the dominant classes and the (self) negation of those of the popular sectors. The teaching of language had therefore, as a political objective, the mastery of the rules of the shift to Standard English and an affirmation of the cultural integrity of the vernacular. "Good English" was no longer to be a psycholinguistic vehicle commanded by the few for the reinforcement of class privilege.

6. Conclusion

I have attempted an exposition of the issues of ideology and content involved in the production of Grenadian texts during the revolution. Two additional points need to be made:

1. a word about the political economy of publication of the texts;
2. a note (following the third domain extrapolated by Luke from Apple and Giroux) about the daily classroom social relationships around the text as contained in the textual guidelines for teaching.

As to the political economy of publication, the situation in many of the schools with respect to textbooks was dismal. In many classrooms around the country, as little as one-quarter of the class had textbooks. This was the result of the prohibitive cost of imported texts. It is important to acknowledge that given the underdeveloped state of the Grenadian economy, the prospects for local publication of textbooks were remote.

The publication of both the Marryshow readers and the adult-education texts were made possible through a publishing protocol in the collaboration agreements in Education and Culture between Cuba and Grenada. The Cuban publishing house Pueblo y Educación received the completed manuscripts with accompanying publication notes from Grenada; once the proofs had been prepared, Grenadian specialists worked with their Cuban counterparts and graphic artists to prepare the publication runs.

This collaboration made it possible for the Grenadian state to provide the adult education texts free of cost to almost five thousand adult learners and the Marryshow readers to all primary schools at the minimal cost of less than EC$1.00 per reader.

As to my second point, how did the CPE texts and the Marryshow readers affect or restructure the forms of daily classroom social relationships and interaction?

In both sets of texts dialogue was required as the central mode of interaction between teacher and learner. The texts legitimated the learner's knowledge through use of the learner's own experience and the acceptance of his or her language. The knowledge of the text was linked to (or, to be more precise, emerged from) the social reality, and mechanisms for the application of the knowledge of the text to the transformation of the learner's reality formed part of the organizational structure of the lesson.

The structuring of the classroom required by the new language arts curriculum (of which the Marryshow readers were the textual embodiment) involved different forms of interaction between teacher and student, and among students, than what had obtained under the old system. Rote learning was replaced by more interactive learning styles; authoritarian classroom relationships were to be supplanted by democratic forms of exchange of knowledge; and memorization was to be superseded by the cultivation of expression.

The preparation of teachers for these new roles was started shortly after the National Consultation held in January 1980. Over vacation periods, the ministry of Education held parish-level workshops with teachers and principals to discuss and formulate guidelines relating to policy implementation. A Ministry of Education circular sent to schools in preparation for a round of parish workshops included a policy paper on "Democratization and the Curriculum Development Process," which discussed democracy in the classroom, in curriculum development, and in school administration.

Another definitive document, the policy document on "Language Arts in the Primary School," provides, as an addition to the language policy quoted earlier, general guidelines for teaching in accordance with the principles of construction of the Marryshow readers. These included:

- Free discussions: fixing a regular time for children "to talk freely about current events that are interesting to them, not topics imposed by a syllabus"; maintaining a "Daily Happenings" section of the blackboard for highlighting these discussions (and the sentences were to be incorporated into the day's reading and writing activities);
- Assigning individual research to students; the organization of field trips;
- Question-and-answer sessions: taking children to interview people at their workplaces or inviting resource people to the classroom to answer children's questions;
- preparation of books by students using their own writings, drawings, clippings, etc.

In summary, what the Grenada experience demonstrates is that ideology is an inescapable dimension of text content and has a decisive hand in the molding of the forms not only of the text itself but also, and equally important, of the social and pedagogical interaction mediated by the text. In the case of Grenada, for historical reasons this process could not remain obscured as a dimension of the so-called hidden curriculum. The intense ideological contestation that happens in the political context of revolution ensured that the hidden was to be made explicit, if the hegemony of the former ruling classes was to be successfully contested.

What then are the essential lessons of the Grenada experience from a political and pedagogical point of view?

The struggles around the texts highlight the importance of the form and not just the content of the knowledge of the textbook. A progressive message can be contradicted or subverted by undemocratic *forms,* as form structures learning experiences (content provides substance). In transitional contexts, the politics of the text is conditioned by this dialectic. As Apple has asserted:

> We miss what is just as important if we neglect the form that the content takes—its organization of our meanings and actions, its temporal sequences and interpersonal implications, its integration with the processes of accumulation and legitimating ideologies.[23]

We also see how the text functions as a mediating factor in the social relations of learning, establishing what will be taught to whom and how. The text embodies specific forms of interaction in learning; it not only mediates the relations between learner and teacher but represents itself a mediation of social reality as well. To the extent that the textbook exposes gender, class, racial, and other injustice as social problems, it intervenes in social reality. Even where it apparently ignores these issues it is still committed to a particular political stance—educational texts speak politically as loudly by their silences as by their pronounced "truths." In the context of revolutionary transformation, the text assumes an additional dimension of *annunciation*: it either suggests the configuration of the emergent social reality or, in the particular manner through which it unmasks social relations, it problematizes and implies the reality that is to be created. The character of that annunciation is the stuff of curriculum accords: the extent to which and in what form the unmasking will occur; the strength of the annunciation (or the magnitude of the textual silences) is determined by the configuration of social forces and their balance of power at a given historical moment.

Selected Bibliography

Center for Popular Education texts

Adult Education Book 1. Havana: CPE/Editorial Pueblo y Educacion, 1982.
Adult Education Book 2. Havana: CPE/Editorial Pueblo y Educacion, 1982.
Adult Education Book 3. Havana: CPE/Editorial Pueblo y Educacion, 1982.
Adult Education Book 4. Havana: CPE/Editorial Pueblo y Educacion, 1982.
Let Us Learn Together. Havana: CPE/Editorial Pueblo y Educacion, 1980.
Let Us Continue Reading. St. Georges: CPE, 1981.

Marryshow Readers (published)

Gebbon, Renalph, *Poems for Children.* Barbados: Fedon Books, 1982.
Grenada-Nicaragua: Being an Internationalist. Havana: CPE/NISTEP, 1982.
Infant 1A: All of Us. Havana: CPE/NISTEP, 1982.
Infant 1B: Step Forward. Havana: CPE/NISTEP, 1982.
Infant 1C: We Work and Play Together. Havana: CPE/NISTEP, 1982.
Revolutionary Voices. St. Georges: Mined (mimeo), 1982.

Marryshow Readers (unpublished)

English Grammar Drills; Infant 1: Term 2. St. Georges: Mined (mimeo), 1983.
Infant 2A. St. Georges: Mined (mimeo), 1983.
Infant 2B. St. Georges: Mined (mimeo), 1983.
Infant 2C. St. Georges: Mined (mimeo), 1983.
Junior 1 (draft). St. Georges: Mined (mimeo), 1983.
Standard 2 (draft). St. Georges: Mined (mimeo), 1983.
Language Arts Programme (Term 1). St. Georges: Mined (mimeo), 1983.

Ministry of Education publications

Education Sector Survey. St. Georges: Ministry of Education, 1982.
Final Report on the Workshop on Non-Formal Education in Grenada. St. Georges: UNESCO/CPE/Ministry of Education, 1983.
Language Arts in the Primary School. St. Georges: Ministry of Education (mimeo), 1980.
Teachers Speak on Education For National Development. St. Georges: Ministry of Education, 1981.

Notes

1. Michael Apple, "Regulating the Text: The Socio-Historical Roots of State Control, *Educational Policy* 3, no 2. (1989):108

2. Michael Apple, "Reproduction and Contradiction in Education: An Introduction," in M. Apple, ed., *Cultural and Economic Reproduction in Education: Essays on Class, Ideology and the State*. (Boston: Routledge and Kegan Paul, 1982), p. 12.

3. M. Carnoy and J. Samoff, "Education, Social Transformation and the Transition State in the Third World," forthcoming, p. 60.

4. Allan Luke, *Literacy, Textbooks and Ideology*, (London: The Falmer Press, 1988), p. 26.

5. In "Education Sector Survey" (St. Georges: Ministry of Education 1982), p. 42.

6. M. K. Bacchus, *The Myth and Reality of Curriculum Planning: Insights from the Educational Development of the Caribbean*. (London: University of London Institute of Education, 1986), p. 8.

7. Michael Apple, "Social Crisis and Curriculum Accords," *Educational Theory* 38, no. 2 (Spring 1988): 198.

8. The Community School Day Program (CSDP) involved volunteer teachers from the community in teaching whatever skills they were proficient in at the primary schools on the days in which teachers were attending the NISTEP training; CSDP also provided for students to take work attachments in different economic enterprises.

9. "Teachers Speak on Education For National Development" (St. Georges: Ministry of Education, 1981), p. 2.

10. "Final Report on the Workshop on Non-Formal Education in Grenada" (St. Georges: UNESCO/CPE/Ministry of Education, 1983).

11. "The Building of Mass Education in Grenada," speech by Minister of Education Jacqueline Creft at the *First International Conference in Solidarity with Grenada*, November 1981.

12. Outstanding examples include poems by Marcelino Dos Santos *"We Must Plant"* and *"Here We were Born"*; extracts from *"Masters of the Dew"* by the Haitian Jacques Roumain and several works by Grenadian poets.

13. C. Searle, *Words Unchained: Language and Revolution in Grenada* (London: 2ed Books, 1984), p. 80.

14. Young (1975: 188) describes an early school movement founded by Richard Dawes called the "Science of Common Things" in which "people's experiences of the natural world, in their work, their houses, and their daily lives formed the basis of hte development of their enquiries in school science."

15. The scientific and economic history of this has been detailed for example in Apple, Rima *Mothers and Medicine: A Social History of Infant Feeding, 1890–1950"* (Madison: University of Wiscorisin Press, 1987).

16. Searle, *Words Unchained*, p. 79.

17. C. Searle, "Some Remarks on Language in Grenada and the Caribbean Region: Interview with Lawrence Carrington" (St. Georges: Ministry of Education [mimeo], 1980).

18. Searle, Chris *All Our Words* (London: Young World Books, 1986), p. 71.

19. "Language Arts in the Primary School" (St. Georges: Ministry of Education [mimeo], 1980), p. 2.

20. Ibid., p. 3.

21. These principles were outlined in a Ministry of Education policy paper, *"Language Arts in the Primary School"* published in September 1980.

22. Searle, *Words Unchained,* p. 82.

23. M. W. Apple, *Education and Power* (Boston: Ark Paperbacks, 1985).

Contributors

We are listing addresses, rather than the usual biographical statements, to make it easier for readers to write directly to the authors of individual chapters.

Philip G. Altbach, State University of New York at Buffalo, Faculty of Educational Studies, Christopher Baldy Hall, Buffalo, New York 14260.

Michael W. Apple, The University of Wisconsin, Department of Curriculum and Instruction, 225 N. Mills St., Madison, Wisconsin 53706.

*Stanley Aronowitz,*The Graduate School, City University of New York, Program in Sociology, 33 West 42nd Street, New York, New York 10036-8099.

Linda K. Christian-Smith, The University of Wisconsin, Department of Curriculum and Instruction, Oshkosh, Wisconsin 54901.

Henry Giroux, Miami University, School of Education and Allied Professions, Department of Educational Leadership, Oxford, Ohio 45056.

Carl A. Grant, The University of Wisconsin, Department of Curriculum and Instruction, 225 North Mills Street, Madison, Wisconsin 53706.

Didacus Jules, The University of Wisconsin, Department of Curriculum and Instruction, 225 North Mills Street, Madison, Wisconsin 53706.

Allan Luke, James Cook University, School of Education, Townsville, Queensland, Australia.

J. Dan Marshall, National College of Education, 2840 Sheridan Road, Evanston, Illinois 60201.

Christine E. Sleeter, The University of Wisconsin-Parkside, Division of Education, Kenosha, Wisconsin 53141-2000.

Joel Taxel, The University of Georgia, College of Education, Department of Language Education, Athens, Georgia 30607.

Kenneth Teitelbaum, State University of New York at Binghamton, School of Education, Binghamton, New York 13901.